Church
of
Churches

Church
of
Churches

The Ecclesiology of Communion

J.-M. R. Tillard, O.P.

Translated by
R. C. De Peaux, O. Praem.

A Michael Glazier Book
THE LITURGICAL PRESS
Collegeville, Minnesota

A Michael Glazier Book published by The Liturgical Press.

Church of Churches was originally published in French by Les Éditions du Cerf, Paris, France, in 1987 (copyright © 1987 by Les Éditions du Cerf) under the title *Église d'Églises*.

Cover design by Fred Petters.

1	2	3	4	5	6	7	8	9

Library of Congress Cataloging-in-Publication Data

Tillard, J.-M. R. (Jean-Marie Roger), 1927-
   [Eglise d'églises. English]
   Church of churches : the ecclesiology of communion / J.-M. R.
Tillard ; translated by R.C. De Peaux.
     p. cm.
   "A Michael Glazier book"
   Translation of: Eglise d'églises.
   Includes bibliographical references and index.
   ISBN 0-8146-5708-7
   1. Church. 2. Church—Unity. 3. Lord's Supper—Catholic Church.
4. Catholic Church—Doctrines. I. Title.
BX1746.T5313   1992
262—dc20
                                         91-36921
                                            CIP

To Julian Charley

Contents

Foreword

After rereading the principal documents of the Second Vatican Council, with a hindsight of more than twenty years, and drawing a parallel between them and the texts promulgated in 1870, as well as those which were in rough draft but never published, I was struck not only by the difference in language and tone but also by the climate in which they were written. And this is true despite the fact that Vatican II assumed—more profoundly than one would naturally think—the major declarations of Vatican I.

The difference comes from the fact that at Vatican II *communion*—however rarely mentioned—represents the horizontal line on which the major affirmations about the Church and its mission stand out clearly. Not very explicit, often intermingled with positions based on another ecclesiology and preserved at the request of a restless minority, this movement of Roman Catholic thought toward the old patristic vision—still manifest in the liturgy—is perceptible everywhere, except perhaps in the minor documents.

Therefore, it is surprising that, except for some excellent studies on the notion of *Koinonia,* so few works have been devoted to a revival of the entire vision of the Church around *communion.* What causes more astonishment is the fact that this notion, on the one hand, permits the understanding (beyond a purely institutional perspective) of the grace existence of the Church of God and, on the other hand, affords the ecumenical movement a providential means of resolving the visible unity. This work, the fruit of several years of research, teaching and ecumenical involvement, is intended to help overcome this lack. It is offered in all simplicity for discussion, knowing full well that it is not an exhaustive study and that it cites precise details. But since the time of our first book, *L'Eucharistie Pâque de l'Eglise,* published in January 1964 in the "Unam

Sanctam'' collection, we have held the conviction that the ecclesiology of Communion (or Eucharistic, in the broad sense of this term which does not correspond exactly to the one used by Afanassief) was the idea which conformed best to the biblical notion and to the intuitions of the great ecclesial traditions. Since that time we have never stopped examining this vision thoroughly, a vision which was hardly esteemed at that time. One of our professors at the Saulchoir found it "too sacramental." Circumstances have been such, because of a close link to ecumenical study, that we have discovered there a clear confirmation of the importance of this ecclesiology of *communion*. It alone, and we believe this more and more, permits the barrier of misunderstanding, suspicions, irascibilities, and claims in which the diverse ecclesial traditions are locked, to be broken down. This has been clear, especially for fifteen years for the orthodox and eastern Churches and it is becoming so, presently, for certain blocks born out of the Reformation. Moreover, it is no accident that the commission on Faith and Constitution of the ecumenical World Council of Churches has been led by the very logic of its research to a consideration of the nature of *communion*. That is why we believe it is urgent to present under the title *Church of Churches* the bases and the implications of this ecclesiology of *communion*.

We could not pretend to treat in depth a subject of such magnitude in such a brief study as this. So much the more because experience has taught us that ecclesiology remains, without a doubt, the most difficult question of the ecumenical debate. It was around this question that the Christian world was divided into two blocks, that of the old Churches, often called the "catholic" block and the one called "protestant." Our purpose, to be sure, is modest; to point out, in view of the latest discussions, the view which is found in the root of the article in the Nicean-Constantinople Creed: "We believe in one, holy, catholic and apostolic Church." This work has another limitation. Our research has indeed made this perception very evident: on this topic especially it is impossible to reflect while setting aside those things presupposed in one's own confessional tradition. We will not be above the rule, and it is clear that our reflection will be that of a Catholic theologian. We will try, however, by using our preferred method, to place ourself beyond polemics, in hope of providing the horizontal line for studies in ecclesiology, whose need is being felt in several ecumenical circles.

J.-M. R. Tillard, o.p.
facultes dominicaines
96 Empress, Ottawa.

Acknowledgments

N.B. Two short sections of this book have appeared in the *Nouvelle Revue Théologique* and in *Irenikon* (translated subsequently in *One in Christ*). But we have reviewed, corrected and completed them. We felt it was necessary to add more notes. But we have done so in such a way that the text can be read completely without them, so that they will not incovenience the reader who is not a specialist in this matter.

1

The Church of God in the Design of God

Whoever investigates very carefully the whole of the New Testament is surprised to discover in it diverse perceptions on points which deal with the nature of the Church and its mission. Diversity is not synonymous with contradiction. However, it is sometimes difficult to reconcile completely several of these visions. We will give no more than three examples. The way in which the relationship between Israel and the new community is understood is not the same in the letter to the Ephesians, Johannine literature, and the epistle to the Hebrews; the way in which the promulgation of the Good News is presented differs in the Gospel according to John, which insists on witness, and the Acts of the Apostles which seems to give preference to sign; the emphasis in the Johannine tradition on the immediate relationship between the believer, the Spirit and Christ contrasts with that in the pastoral letters where the emphasis is put on the make-up of ministries. But these are not secondary points in these texts.

It seems that the reader is faced with various visions of the Church, all founded (in faith) on common convictions concerning Jesus Christ and the finality of his work, but which nevertheless do not cloud one another over completely. If we set apart the particular case of the Johannine letters, nowhere is there perceived a condemnation of the others by the defenders of one of these visions. If different emphases coexist, the same basic certitude is understood in all of them: one belongs to the community of salvation, coming from God, joined to the Promise, born of faith, entrusted with faithfully protecting the contents of the Good News. However, the profile of the community established precisely from this basic certitude and from certain traits drawn from among the emphases of the

1

diverse visions, which lay out its essential characteristics doesn't seem to have emerged clearly at the outset. Such an emergence would have surely required the realization that the first discords would provoke confrontations with the Jews and persecutions. Isn't that the case with other essential articles of faith?

It is necessary to note further that as soon as it starts to assert itself, the identity of the Church is established more by its life than by any official texts. This is woven into the fabric of the Liturgies, the catecheses, the homilies of the Fathers, the acts of the martyrs; it penetrates the synodal debates; it manifests itself in the fact that all Churches recognize their faith in the Canon of the Scriptures. It has always been felt that it is an experiential fact whose theory is hardly sought to be elaborated on. The ecclesial being is what becomes real through acknowledgement of the same faith, celebration of the same sacraments, the same resistance to distortions in the teaching of the apostles, practice of the same charity, the same fruits of sanctity, with their rewards in martyrdom. Irenaeus, with his judgment on the link between today and the apostolic teaching, is perhaps the first real witness who made a significant effort at a more structured interpretation of this lived experience. Nevertheless, gradually a notion of the Church grew which, until the great disorder created by the Reformation, was not contested as to what the essential components were, with the formal quarrels arising over questions of jurisdiction, relationships between episcopal Sees, discipline, and interpretation of the faith. It is precisely this which will be the subject matter of our research.

I. The Church Revealed As Communion

A. Church of God and Gospel of God

1. The theologian who proposes to examine with some objectivity the certitude of faith which explains and underlines the article of the Creed "confessing," puts the Church in a difficult undertaking. He cannot be satisfied to choose, by listening to a specialist on the New Testament, one or the other line of thought which seems to him closer to the explicit teaching of Jesus, more coherent with his vision of Salvation. He must perceive the conduit which leads from the diversified experience of the communities to the main assertion which constitutes an official norm of faith. His task is, therefore, to capture the interpretation of the apostolic witness which, through the Holy Spirit, is gradually apparent to all of the Christian communities as the most coherent with their own nature. It is clear that this procedure makes sense only if it is based on the conviction that the Holy Spirit was part of the process of this realization or consciousness, of the clarification and the expressing of the notion of faith

which results in the Credo.[1] This process—which cannot be identified, without faint differences with the theory of the development of dogma—is inseparable from what the "old Churches" call tradition. It must be recognized that our groups of different doctrinal beliefs remain in disagreement on the importance, the nature, the role and the sense of this last point.[2] But, the unanimity of the first centuries in their perception of the profound Being of the Church—in spite of quite a broad diversity of points of view on what deals with ecclesial *praxis*—and the unquestionable intelligence of their vision (which we will try to clarify), are these not precisely elements which urge us to cast a new look at Tradition? This is what is at stake in our research, more extensive in its implications than the title given to these pages would suggest.

2. A first statement, filled with consequences, is imperative. The event of Pentecost dominates and conditions the vision of the Church which gradually becomes imbedded in the Christian consciousness. We do not think it is an exaggeration to assert that the coming of the Holy Spirit upon the apostles "about the fiftieth day" appears in that case, if not as the origin of the Church—which is often sought in the episode of the lance piercing Jesus' side and the flowing of water and blood or in the meeting of the Lord and his followers the evening of the Resurrection— at least the manifestation (*epiphaneia*) of its nature.[a]* This statement is surprising. In fact, except for Luke, the authors of the New Testament are discreet about the Christian Pentecost. Why is it in terms of this event—since the first centuries do not discuss the historical genuineness of it[3]—that the text of the Johannine tradition on the pouring out of the Spirit on Easter night (John 20:19-23) or chapters ten and eleven of the Acts of the Apostles concerning the gift of the Spirit to the pagans after Peter's vision at Jaffa are appreciated and in agreement[b]? Thus, the im-

---

[1]This is asserted in the report of the conference in Venice, June 1978, "Toward a confession of common faith," see *Faith and Constitution* 100, Geneva, 1980. See also our study J.-M. R. Tillard, "Towards a Common Profession of Faith," *Sharing in one Hope,* Coll. "Faith and Order Papers" 92, Geneva, 1978. The original French text is found in *DC* 75, 1978, 988–992.

[2]One can ask oneself whether the assertions of the World Conference on Faith and Constitution held in Montréal in 1963 truly determined the conscience of the Churches on this point.

[3]On the difficult problem of the historicity of Pentecost, see James D. G. Dunn, *Jesus and the spirits,* coll. "New Testament Library." London 1975, 136–156, which seems to us to be the most detailed study. The position of E. Haenchen, *The Acts of the Apostles,* London, 1971, 166–189 is well known. See also, M.-A. Chevalier, "Pentecôtes lucaniennes et Pentecôtes johanniques," *RSR* 69, 1961, 301–304; E. Trocme, *Le livre des Actes de l'histoire,* Paris, 1957, 301–224; J. Dupont, *Etude sur les Actes des Apôtres,* coll. "Lectio divina," 45, Paris, 1967, 481–502; Gerhard Schneider *Die Apostelgeschichte,* t. I, Fribourg, 1980, 239–295; J. Potin, *La fête juive de la Pentecôte,* coll. "Lectio divina," 65, Paris, 1971; P. H. Menoud, "La Pentecote lucanienne et l'histoire," *Jésus Christ et la foi,* Neuchatel-Paris, 1975, 118–164. But it must be remembered that the historical account did not have the same importance for the Fathers in the early centuries as it has for us.

*The letters a, b, c, d, e, refer to the *excursus* from pp. 74–82.

portance given to the event of Pentecost is, without any doubt, the result of a choice, based on a full understanding of the harmony of the mystery of Christ Jesus. In fact, two interpretations were possible. One was discarded, at least implicitly.

3. It is possible to look for the basic cell of the Church in the group, not yet organized, of men and women which the *acta et dicta* of Jesus had gathered around him, from the time of his baptism in the Jordan when God had "anointed him with the Holy Spirit and with power" (Acts 10:38). A community of recipients of the goodness of God, a community of disciples around the visible, audible and tangible Jesus, on the path towards the Death which will put the official seal on the mystery of his role as Savior, such would be the Church in its *initium*. It is known how, in certain periods of history, the temptation has been to resort to this vision.[4]

The small apostolic team is characterized in this entourage as the nucleus most intimately linked to Jesus and the most closely associated with his mission. But it does not seem to be an "organization" which makes up the majority of the disciples. Besides, the words which confer any authority upon it refer to the future (Matt 16:18; 19:28; Luke 22:28-30)[5] and sometimes seem to have merit for the community as it is at that moment (Matt 18:18). But, finding the basic cell of the Church in the crowd "around Jesus," presents the danger of running the risk of forgetting the change from top to bottom that the Resurrection of Jesus crucified was going to produce right in the apostolic nucleus, a change which, according to all evidence, would effect the expansion of the Gospel and the consciousness of the "ecclesial Being" in radical fashion. It is interesting to note that it then becomes difficult to give the full ecclesial meaning to the Last Supper of Jesus at which the apostles (Matt 16:20; Mark 14:17-30; Luke 22:30) are brought face to face prophetically with their eschatological role (Luke 22:14; cf. Matt 26:29; Mark 14:25).[6] In a somewhat exaggerated way it could be said that his vision considers the Church more as an adding up of disciples, joined by the relationship of each one to the person of Jesus, than as an experience of God's grace.

That there is a real link between those who were united to the person of Jesus as the first hearers of his words and the Church today there surely is no doubt. However, a certain statement is imperative. The New Testa-

[4]The ecclesial movements centered around charity and the show of mercy, have a tendency to grant special privilege to the relationship of the Church to the Jesus who passes by "doing good" more than to the Lord who gives the Spirit of the eschatological era. The spirituality of certain religious congregations proves this.

[5]John 20:20-23 takes place after the Resurrection.

[6]See E. Käsemann, *Essays on New Testament Themes,* coll. "Studies in Biblical Theology," 41, London, 1964, 108-135; H. Schürmann, *Comment Jesus a-t-il vécu sa mort?,* coll. "Lectio divina," 93, Paris, 1977, 83-116.

ment does not call *Ekklesia* the crowd of disciples called to witness before the death of Jesus on the cross. Neither does it make any exception for the nucleus of the apostles.[7] It only speaks of Church to designate the group of men and women who, after Easter, believe in the Resurrection. And this is so, even though the term was already used at the moment the synoptic traditions were put into writing. Luke's case is typical: despite the fact that the word *Ekklesia* appears nowhere in his first book, he uses it sixteen times in Acts.[8]

Is that entirely by chance? Reading and rereading the principal texts of the New Testament, considering all of the traditions which compose it, one becomes convinced that, for them, the reality of *Ekklesia* is radically inseparable from the event of the Death-Resurrection. This relationship is not derived solely from the fact that this Event signifies a continuity "beyond death" with the Jesus who "has died in doing good." It is derived principally from the fact that it also implies a change, and indeed a break. It is this change and break which are identified at the opening of the eschatological period. *Ekklesia* is understood entirely in this change. Also its link with the pre-Easter community depends on the link between the *acta et dicta* of Jesus and what happened to him by the Holy Spirit at his Resurrection. There is no reality which is precisely Christian outside of the tension between continuity and break which characterizes the event of the Death-Resurrection. Outside of the opening up of the eschatological period during the temporal age, there is no *Ekklesia*.

4. In that case, it is better understood why the first centuries see the revelation of the Church in the account of Pentecost as it is presented in Acts. Although in chapter two Luke does not use the word *Ekklesia,* there is no doubt whatsoever that the "event" which he reports concerns the group which, afterwards (from Acts 5:11) he will designate by this term.[9] Besides, what he describes as the immediate result of the gift of the Spirit is the community of the saved (2:38-40) united by the power of the Spirit and the acceptance of the apostolic witness, in a *communion* (of solidarity, of *koinonia,* of prayer, faith and sharing) which is very characteristic of the one brought out in the "summaries" in Acts (2:42-47; 4:32-35; 5:12-16). And these are much more than a casual description.

The situation that this account of Pentecost enhances is vastly different from the one of the crowd "around Jesus" which we brought out ear-

---

[7]Matt 16:18 deals with the future; Matt 18:17 could designate by *Ekklesia* a Syro-palestinian community of the 80's and would refer to an instruction concerning its disciplinary practices (cf. Pierre Bonnard, *L'Evangile selon saint Matthieu,* Neuchatel-Paris, 1963, 274). See Deut 19:15.

[8]See the illumating study by W. G. Kümmel, "Kirchenbegriff und Geschichtbewusstsein in der Urgemeinde und bei Jesus," *Symbolae Biblicae Upsalienses,* I, 1943.

[9]See James D. G. Dunn, *op. cit.,* 136.

lier.[10] If the principal actor in this scene is the Risen Lord pouring out the Spirit which he has received from the Father in his exalted state (2:33), the scene puts into the foreground the group composed of "Peter and the Eleven" (2:14, 37, 40) presented as witnesses of the Resurrection (2:32; cf. 5:32), and, that is so, whatever might be the identity of each one of them who are found at that time "All assembled together" (2:1).[11]

The "primitive" community described in Acts—which is formed by grace of acceptance of the spoken message (*kerygma*) and baptism "bestowed by the Holy Spirit" (2:38-41)—rightly has its origin in the Spirit and in the power of the Lord Jesus. But this power has brought together men and women only by the "testimony" and the action of the apostles (2:32, 37, 40-42). Moreover, it is by incorporating itself in the apostolic cell (2:41-47) that this community is formed. And if, motivated by the Spirit, the apostolic group then appears as the basic cell of the Church, it is because it alone is capable of bearing witness to the Death and Resurrection of the One whom "God has made Lord and Christ" (2:36), and, therefore, of testifying to the coming of the "last days" (2:17),[12] the opening up of the eschatological period—which belongs to the Spirit—during the temporal age. The marvels and wonders which reinforce his word (2:43; cf. 3:6, 16; 4:30; 5:15-16; 9:34) are the signs of this invasion, in the Resurrection of the Lord, of times to come. They must not be separated from the full sign of Pentecost.[13]

Based on this perspective that the early centuries adopt, the Church finds its initial form in a "communion" whose profound, invisible link is none other than the Spirit of the Lord, but it is the apostolic group in the act of witness which makes up the visible nucleus. The apostolic witness— words and "*semeia*"—centered entirely on the Risen Lord and associated with his Name (cf. 2:38; 3:6, 16; 4:7, 10, 12, 30; 5:41; 9:21; 16:18; 21:13; 22:16)[14] takes on the aspect of the experienced physical presence of the

[10]Concerning Pentecost, see, besides the authors cited above, note 3, the classic study by K. Lake, "The Gift of the Spirit on the Day of Pentecost," in K. Lake-J. J. Cadbury, *The Beginnings of Christianity, The Acts of the Apostles*, v. V, London, 1933 (Grand Rapids, 1966), 111-121. See also J. Munck, *The Acts of the Apostle*, coll. "The Anchor Bible," New York, 1967, 13-19 and 271-275 (note by C. S. Mann); J. Kremer, *Pfingstbericht und Pfingstgeschefen, eine exegtische Untersuchung zu Apg.* 2, 1-13, Stuttgart, 1973; D. Minguez, *Pentecotes*, ensayo de Semiotica narrativa in Hch 2, Rome, 1977. See A. Causse, "Le pèlerinage a Jérusalem et la premiere Pentecôte," *RHPR* 20, 1940, 120-141.

[11]On these *pantes*, see J. Munck, *op. cit.*, 14; E. Haenchen, *op. cit.*, 304-305; J. Dupont, *op. cit.*, 483-484, (a position to which we subscribe; it refers to the apostolic group such as the one described in the preceding chapter).

[12]On these "last days," see A. George, *Études sur l'œuvre de Luc*, Paris, 1978, 337-341.

[13]On this point, see the interesting analysis by James D.G. Dunn, *op. cit.*, 158-170 (on the connection between these signs and enthusiasm).

[14]For the importance of the Name in this context, its presence should be noted in all of the chapters from 3 to 12 (except chapter 7). See E. Haenchen, *op. cit.*, 200, 217-224.

One who prior to Easter was listened to or "followed" but whose saving work is proclaimed from this moment on. This apostolic *martyria* manifested and transfigured by the Spirit represents the "visible manifestation" of a God no longer limited to hanging over history but encompassing it, invading it. On the basis of what is accomplished in the Lord Jesus, there is a passionate invasion of human existence, of the personal destiny of every believer but also of Israel's fate as such and "of all those who are far away, all those whom the Lord our God will call to himself" (2:39).

To enter into "communion" is to have a share in this work of God, so as to belong to the mystery of the eschatological period, that which is to be found in the "future" of the human adventure. Perhaps it is not fruitless to recall that, upon rereading the *acta et dicta* of Jesus' ministry in the light of Easter, the genuine sense of it can be perceived. The age of the Spirit was manifested in it, sprouted forth in it. The Event which changes the earlier vision of the world's order was prepared in the qualitative change which Jesus brought about in the deepest recesses of the human consciousness and the heart of human relationships.[15]

5. It is very understandable that *communion*—presented in the "summaries" in Acts as something other than the result of simply adding generous people or a cluster of believers[16]—assumes its identity only if it is placed on the vast horizon of Hope. It exists, in fact, in the breach that the "last days" (2:17) open up before the whole assembly of the history of the world, upsetting the law of nature so that the "object of the Promise" (2:33, 39), might stand out. This Promise is like its formula. It is a Promise which expresses the destiny of man and his world.

Serious exegetes support the Fathers of the first centuries when they find a thin line between the account of Pentecost and the reverse side of it which is the drama of Babel.[17] Contrasted with the confusion of lan-

[15]See E. Käsemann, *Essais exégétiques,* Neuchâtel-Paris, 1972, 210–214.

[16]Later on we will return to the "summaries." Among the works that we will cite, see at this time J. Dupont, *op. cit.,* 503–520; Id., "L'union entre les premiers chrétiens dans les Actes des Apôtres," *NRT* 91, 1969, 897–915; H. Schürmann, "Gemeinde als Brunderschaft," *Ursprung und Gestalt,* Düsseldorf, 1970, 61–73. Notice that the word *koinonia* is used there with others which evoke also communion and not as the only synonym of it (on this point, see J. M. McDermott, "The Biblical Doctrine of Koinonia," *Biblische Zeitschrift* 19, 1975, 230; E. Haenchen, *op. cit.,* 190–191). The sense of the term is still not the one which the first Johannine letter will give it in a context which dominates the struggle against schismatic divisions (see Raymond E. Brown *The Epistles of John,* coll. "The Anchor Bible," 30, New York, 1982, 186–187).

[17]Thus J. G. Davies, "Pentecost and Glossolalie," *JTS,* n. s. 3, 1952, 228–231. See also the nuances by J. Dupont, *op. cit.,* 501, note 22, for whom "the parallel is suggestive and will be used extensively in Christian exegesis: the gift of the Spirit restores to men and to peoples the unity they had lost at Babel. The basis for this theme is found in the situations rather than in the texts; the narrative of Acts reveals no allusion which would permit one to think that Luke and the first Christians had already interpreted the mystery of Pentecost by contrasting it with the story of Babel. It is in relationship to the gift of the Law that the gift of the Spirit primarily

guages and the division of the human race that Babel symbolizes in chapter eleven of Genesis (Gen 11:1-9) is the reunification of humanity in the clear understanding of the apostolic witness and by it of the divine message. At Babel only one language, symbol of a vibrant unity, is shattered by a proud human intention. On the feast of Pentecost the diversity of languages, symbol of the barrier which has grown up among peoples, is unified in the common understanding of the apostolic Word. Such is the work of the Spirit of the "last days." The fire of this unique Spirit which took possession of each one of them (2:3)[18] embraces the multitude to mold them into one.

The pentecostal community—the basic cell of the Church—thus appears as the manifestation, the *epiphaneia,* of the opening up of the era of Salvation. This is so in the coming together, radically unbreakable, of three elements: the Spirit, the apostolic witness which centers on the Lord Jesus Christ, and the *communion* in which the human multitude and its diversity are contained within this unity and where the unity is expressed in the multitude and its diversity. These three elements belong to the very essence of the Church. It is certainly evident that for Luke "all the nations under heaven" (2:5)—and using a list that he inserts somewhat awkwardly into his text, he gives the names of them (2:9-11)—are the only ones represented on Pentecost as "the Jews and proselytes" (2:11) who come from these nations.[19] And so, "in a certain way, it is the entire universe which is present there, symbolically, to give witness to the coming of the Spirit and to hear the Word of God."[20] The time of the mission to the Gentiles has not yet dawned. It will arrive only after Peter's vision at Jaffa (10:9-48). Nevertheless, "all nations" are present on Pentecost

received its deep meaning." We are, however, struck by the parellel, even verbal, that J. G. Davies shows between the version in Gen 11:1-9 in the Septuagint and the text of Acts. See also E. Trocme, *op. cit.,* 206–209, and the long discussion by E. Haenchen, *op. cit.,* 173–175; C. Freeman Sleeper, "Pentecost and Resurrection," *JBL* 84, 1965, 389–399.

[18]See J. Dupont, *op. cit.,* 487–488, who points out that in the sentence the verb *echathisen* used in the singular has no subject. We concur with this suggestion: "The use of the singular can be due to the fact that the author is thinking less about 'tongues' than about the Holy Spirit manifested in these tongues": verse 4 continues the sentence saying: "and they were all filled with the Holy Spirit." We agree with him also on the sense of *echathisen:* "He rested" conveys imperfectly *echathisen,* which signifies more accurately: "he took up residence." At the time of the baptism of Jesus, the Synoptics state that the Spirit "descended on him" (Matt 3:16 par.); John states precisely: "descended and remained" (1:32-33). *Echathisen* implies a similar nuance: it is a question of taking possession; represented by the tongues, the Spirit installed himself in the disciples. On the sense of *eph'ena ekaston autōn,* we take the position of E. Haenchen, *op. cit.,* 168: "The Spirit is given to them in their individuality."

[19]"At Pentecost the time was not yet ripe for the 'ethne,' the Gentile peoples to be taken hold of by the Spirit. . . . God, at the proper moment, will direct the mission towards the Gentiles." (E. Haenchen, *op. cit.,* 174–175).

[20]J. Dupont, *op. cit.,* 500, cf. 407; see C. Freeman Sleeper, *op. cit.,* 391: James D. G. Dunn, *op. cit.,* 152.

in Jerusalem, at least by means of "believing" Jews who shared this event. Even more so, by the baptism—after the reception of *kerygma*—of men and women who belong to them, these nations of the entire universe known at that time enter *already* into the *initium* of the Church. It is not yet the mission, however, it is *already* the opening towards this universalism.[21] By the presence of the first baptized Jews descended from Babel, the Church comes into existence by inserting all of humanity into the breach opened up by the Resurrection. The Church is born inseparable from the human drama as such, but because humanity is so divided it is doomed to disaster and failure. From its initial cell it offers itself in the fervor of God's response to this universal situation. It is the manifestation and the "symbol" of it. Unity and catholicity are part and parcel of the very flesh of the Church. And these two factors denote its link with the human drama.[c]

6. Whatever connection there may be between Pentecost and Babel—which some exegetes consider alien to Luke—the extent of the links which the Church in its basic cell has with the tragedy of a humanity torn apart is also underlined by the context of the feast. Initially rural, from the second century before the Christian era, this feast had been associated with the renewal of the Covenant.[22] It was on that day at Qumran that the new members entered officially into the Covenant community. And everything points to the admission that well before the second century of our era—the first testimony being given at that time—the gift of the Law was com-

[21]This view is supported by several sentences from the address which follows and which are more typical of Luke than of Peter. When verse 17 ("I will pour out my Spirit on all flesh") is linked to verse 21 ("and whoever invokes the Name of the Lord will be saved") and to verse 39 ("because the promise is destined for you and for your children, and for all those who invoke the Name of the Lord our God"), it becomes clear that Luke is already thinking of the mission to the Gentiles even thoug'. he does not relate this stage until chapter 10 (C. Freeman Sleeper, *op. cit.,* 391; see *ibid.,* note 10a, the parallel with the way in which Luke presents the ministry of John the Baptist, by announcing already the moment when "all flesh will see the salvation of God"). See also J. Dupont, *op. cit.,* 500, who writes: "On the threshold of the Gospel, Luke has taken care to cite Isa 40:5: 'All mankind shall see the salvation of God' (Luke 3:6); Acts finishes with a declaration by Paul, who recalls the same oracle: 'Understand, then, that this salvation of God has been sent to the pagans' (Acts 28:28). Luke wished to conclude his gospel with a declaration by Jesus recalling that, according to the Scriptures, the message of forgiveness must be announced 'to all the nations, beginning with Jerusalem' (Luke 24:47); in the beginning of Acts, the last words of Jesus before his ascension state precisely: 'You will be my witnesses in Jerusalem, in all of Judea and Samaria, and indeed to the ends of the earth' (Acts 1:8). The conclusion of Saint Paul's inaugural address, which refers explicitly to the oracle in Isa 49:6, echoes this: 'I have made you a light for the nations, so that you may bring my salvation to the ends of the earth' (Acts 13:47)." See also *ibid.,* 393–419, concerning the salvation of the Gentiles (especially 404–409).

[22]See G. Kretschmar, "Himmelfahrt und Pfingsten," *Zeitschrift für Kirchengeschichte* 66, 1954–1955, 209–253.

memorated at the time of the theophany on Sinai.[23] First of all, it must be noted that when Deuteronomy evokes the assembly of the people of God on the day of the promulgation of the Law or of the renewal of the Covenant, it uses the word Qáhál (Deut 4:10; 9:10; 10:4; 18:16; 23:2-9). But this word, in the Septuagint, is translated by *Ekklesia*,[24] a term which incidentally has no other Hebrew equivalent and is ordinarily used to translate *Qáhál* only when it refers to an assembly brought together by a call from Yahweh. It seems that this term is avoided when the emphasis is put more on the socio-political aspect of the assembly than on its faith dimension.[25] When it says of the Pentecost "assembly"—"they were all united together, *epi to auto*" (2:1)—should it not, in the fire and sound of the Spirit, be understood, therefore, in the light of what the People of God affirmed about the assembly on Sinai, in the fire and thunder of the great theophany (Exod 19:1-25; Deut 9:6-15)? In this way Pentecost would become the theophany of the New Covenant. And *Ekklesia*—as the "assembly" of Christians will subsequently be called (Acts 5:11)— would be the "accomplishment" of the *Qáhál* united on Sinai on the feast of the Law. More precisely, it would be the "assembly" of the "last days." The entire context urges such a conclusion.[d]

Such an "assembly" is not neutral. In fact, Jewish tradition saw in the *Qáhál* of Sinai the event of the renewal of humanity as such, "a reorganization of its condition at the time of Adam before the fall,"[26] a sort of revival of Creation. Even more so, in some Jewish theological circles it was maintained that if in practice Israel alone had "received Divine Law, it was nevertheless destined for all peoples, whether God had gone among them to propose it to them,"[27] or rather whether he had spoken in seventy languages (the number of nations recorded in Genesis) so that all could understand it.[28] Alas, they refused it! The *Mekhilta* contains these lines:[29] "The Torah was given as common property (in other words, as something belonging to all peoples), publicly, at a place belonging to no one. Let each one, therefore, come and accept it! In that case, I could think

[23]E. Haenchen, *op. cit.*, 174. James D. G. Dunn, *op. cit.*, 140; Id., *Baptism in the Holy Spirit*, London, 1970, 48-49; J. Potin, *La Fête juive de la Pentecôte*, especially 117-142, 300-303.

[24]And not by synagogue as often happens. In 10:4 the translation overlooks the word.

[25]In the passages concerning the legislation for community life, for example, Qahal is translated by "synagogue." See L. Rost, *Die Vorstufen von Kirche und Synagoge im Alten Testament*, Leipzig, 1938, especially 127-130.

[26]J. Potin, *op. cit.*, 305. See *ibid.*, 248-259.

[27]*Ibid.*, 308-309, 254-257 (*Mekhilta*). See the important study by K. Hruby, "Le concept de révélation dans la théologie rabbinique," *Orient syrien* 11, 1966, 17-50, 169-198.

[28]J. Potin, *op. cit.*, 308.

[29]We quote them in the translation by K. Hruby, *op. cit.*, 46-49, repeated by J. Potin, *op. cit.*, 254-255. The *Mekhilta* is, as is well known, a relatively old cannaitique midrash.

that it was given during the night. That is why it is said (Exod 19:6): 'now on the day after tomorrow at daybreak.' I could as well think that the voices were not heard (in other words, the thunder). That is why it is said (20:18): 'all the people saw (= heard) the voices,' and it is likewise said (Ps 29:4-5): 'the voice of Yahweh in power, the voice of Yahweh in splendor; the voice of Yahweh shatters the cedars of Lebanon.' R. Yosse says: Here is what is written (Isa 45:19): 'I have not spoken in secret nor in some corner of a darkened land.' Why wasn't the Torah given in the land of Israel? So that the peoples of the world would have no pretext to have been able to say (at that time): it is because it was given in his land (the land of Israel) that we did not accept it! . . . That is why it was given in the desert as a common property, publicly, and in a place belonging to no one. The Torah was given in three things: in the desert, in fire and in water. Just as these three things are free for everyone, so is the Torah free for all the inhabitants of the world."

At the event of Pentecost, the one Spirit himself is given to the apostles.[30] It is they themselves, and no longer God in person, who express themselves in the languages of the nations. They are, in this way, wholly united to the theophany as witnesses of the Lord Christ Jesus. It is in their speaking about what they have witnessed, inspired by the Spirit, that the divine offer of Salvation passes in all its fullness to "all the nations which are under the heavens" (2:5). And as the "last days" come to pass, the Spirit of the Promise (and no longer only a Law given from outside) is henceforth freely offered to whoever welcomes their witness and is converted. The Church of Pentecost "fulfills" the vow of the theophany on Sinai because of the Lord Christ Jesus. But it can do so only in and by the apostolic witness. It does not suffice to say[31] that the apostolic group, therefore, receives a "prophetic investiture" which renders it herald of the Word. It must be asserted that it becomes an integral and essential part of the Church in its arrival on the scene. It is fundamentally in this sense that the Church is apostolic. Prolonging this relationship between Pentecost and Sinai,[32] it must be added that the Law whose promulgation is celebrated, contains a radical criticism of a world based on injustice, rivalries and covetousness (as in Deut 5:21). The Code of the Covenant changes the meaning of customary inter-human relationships. It also has a connection with social, economic, cultural and political contexts in which the destiny of a world cut off from God,[33] or blindly attached to doubt-

---

[30]According to the interpretation in Acts 2:1 that we follow, it is a question of the apostolic group "as such."

[31]As J. Potin, *op. cit.*, 312.

[32]Certified by serious exegesis.

[33]The work of René Girard wishes to illustrate it. See in particular *Des choses cachées depuis*

ful values, is played out. Philo, who seeks to discover why God chose the desert to reveal his Law, finds this reason: "They moved, first of all, to establish the norms of a political regime and to become proficient in its practices, thanks to which the peoples would be successfully governed. Then they would set themselves up in it to apply at the outset in the *koinonia,* the rules of law for which they would have made provision, containing a social sense and by rendering to each one his due."[34] The Rabbis, on their part, think that the Law must repair the "confusion" in the world, caused by the disobedience of Eve, then of Adam,[35] to bring the world back to its beginning.[36] What is remarkable is that Jewish tradition presents the characteristics of communion as an ideal for this return to the creative work of God: "Let all agree and be of one single mind," as the *Mekhilta* states, while other texts rejoice that the Israelites all come together on Sinai and all camp "as one, with a single heart."[37] Is it surprising then that the narrative of Pentecost ends up as a somewhat idyllic scene of the new community, centered precisely on the genuineness of realistic *communion,* going as far as a difficult community of goods (2:42-47)? Other "summaries" will specify this description but without adding anything essential to it (4:32-34; 5:12-16). The *Ekklesia* is born on Pentecost by the dynamism which recreates the flesh of the world. The Spirit of the Lord has the power to tear this flesh of the world loose from the network of injustice, rivalries and covetousness which is mortally wounding humanity because he knows how to break down the walls which imprison individuals and groups from each other in order to bind them together in *communion.* For humanity is truly itself only in *communion.* This is what saves it. The Church is, therefore, from its birth, involved in earnest in the world's problems.

7. The community which appears in full light on the day of Pentecost is the Church, but the Church of God, the *Ekklesia tou Theou.* Paul's speech to the elders of the city of Ephesus describes it this way (20:28),[38] reviving an expression which runs through the Pauline writings (1 Cor 1:2; 11:16, 22; 2 Cor 1:1; Gal 1:13; 1 Thess 2:14; 2 Thess 1:4). If, indeed, Paul

---

la fondation du monde, Paris, 1978 (especially 165-306); Id., *Le Bouc émissaire,* Paris, 1982 (especially 7-145).

[34]*De decalogo,* 14; trans. V. Nikiprowetzky, in *Les Oeuvres de Philon d'Alexandrie,* v. XXIII Paris, 1965, 45.

[35]See texts in J. Potin, *op. cit.,* 215-216.

[36]In a sort *anakephalaiôsis,* of summing up. The use that Irenaeus will make of this idea that he finds in the letter to the Ephesians is well known.

[37]Texts in J. Potin, *op. cit.,* 214-216.

[38]Well known is the exegetical problem posed by the variants of this verse, where, in order to avoid speaking of the "blood of God," a unique and bold metaphor, "Church of God" is changed to "Church of the Lord" or "of Christ."

does happen to speak of "the Church which is in God our Father and in the Lord Jesus Christ" (1 Thess 1:1; 2 Thess 1:1), he uses only once the expression "the Churches of Christ" (*Ekklesia tou Christou* Rom 16:16) and its parallel, the Churches "which are in Christ" (Gal 1:22). Everything tends to confirm that in the Acts of the Apostles, where the term *Ekklesia* is used alone, it refers to the "Church of God" (*tou Theou*). However, the choice of this genitive is not accidental and the preference for the theocentric expression does not stem from a vain scholasticism.

In fact, the relationships either with Babel or with the theophany of Sinai to which we have just referred show that what occurs on the day of Pentecost, in the radiance of the Death-Resurrection of the Lord Christ Jesus, is the accomplishment (the *teleisis*) of a drawn out design of God whose stages remain buried in the memory of the holy People.[39] Besides, the expression *Ekklesia tou Theou* (or *tou Kyriou*) comes from the Septuagint where it translates the words *Qáhál Yahweh* (as in Deut 23:2, 3, 4 where *Kyrios* is explicitly given as a synonym for Theos, cf. 23:6). Philo uses it to describe very precisely the ideal community which God called together in the desert.[40] The Pentecost community represents the emergence—at last!—of the "community of God" after the fall, because of what it has realized in and through Jesus the Nazorean. It is, therefore, the work of God's grace. And it is significant that Peter's speech is centered on what God, *Theos,* himself has done. God, and not Jesus, is the subject of the sentences in this Kerygma. Only one makes an exception, the one which explains that it is the one who has been raised *by God* who, having received *from God* the Spirit of the Promise, spreads it over the apostolic community.[41] Besides, the Church is radically unthinkable without the Spirit *of God.* In it results the relationship *of God* with the world, preceding and in a certain way transcending, since the Church puts at the service of the world the relationship of Jesus the Nazorean with humanity. But this Church of God is destined to be spread through the impetus of the Pentecost experience. It will spring up everywhere Babel will cease, everywhere human reconciliation will take shape because, in faith and in baptism, men and women will be placed under the mastery of the Spirit of the Lord. There will be communities and each one will be *Ekklesia tou Theou.* In this way the Church will multiply itself without being divided. In Acts (15:41; 16:5 and perhaps 9:31),[42] in Pauline

[39]See L. Cerfaux, *La Théologie de l'Église suivant saint Paul,* coll. "Unam sanctam," 10, 2nd ed., Paris, 1965, 69–88.

[40]Thus, *Leg. all.* III, 8, 81 (in *Les Oeuvres de Philon d'Alexandrie,* v. II, Paris, 1962, 173, 217). Perhaps one should see the repetition of it in Acts 7:38.

[41]The word *theos* appears in it eight times.

[42]According to excellent witnesses. See K. N. Giles, "Luke's Use of the Term *ekklesia* with Special Reference to Acts 20:28 and 9:31," *NTS* 31, 1985, 135–142.

literature (1 Cor 11:16; 14:33; 16:1, 19; 2 Cor 8:1, 18, 23, 24; 11:8, 28; 12:13; Gal 1:2; 1 Thess 2:14; 2 Thess 1:4), in Revelation (1:4, 11, 20; 2:1, 7, 12, 18, 23; 3:1, 7, 14; 22:16), indeed the Churches are spoken of as much as the Church—sometimes even of the *Churches of God,* as in 1 Cor 11:16; 1 Thess 2:14; 2 Thess 1:4—according to the context. Never, however, should it be understood that the Church which is at Ephesus (Acts 20:28) or "the Church of God which is at Corinth" (1 Cor 1:2) would only be a part of the Church, nor that the sum of the Churches of Syria and Cilicia (Acts 14:41) or of Macedonia (2 Cor 8:1) would have more ecclesial reality than the Church at Antioch (Acts 13:1). Whether it is a question of the gathering of believers in a given place (Rom 16:4), of the group that Christians establish in the heart of a city (Acts 13:1; 20:28), of the mass of communities in a region (Acts 9:31), in each of these local foundations, the full reality of the *Ekklesia tou Theou* is revealed and expressed concretely. Likewise, when we stated that in this *Ekklesia tou Theou* the multitude is enclosed by the Spirit in unity (*communion*), it must now be stated precisely that this authentic and perfect reality of the *Church of God* exists in every community welded together by the Spirit of the Lord Jesus Christ, thanks to the genuine reception of the apostolic witness and baptism. It is in this typical way, that it becomes present in the universe and so finds its universality. The whole of the Church is in Corinth, in Ephesus, in Rome. Its extension does not change its essence. Nevertheless, it becomes a reality in the design of God "all nations which are under the heavens," so that—according to the expression of James in the assembly in Jerusalem—God establishes for himself in all of them "a people for his name" (14:14). There exists throughout the universe one single *Ekklesia tou Theou* and, consequently, it is necessary to preserve the unity of it throughout the world and down through the ages. Besides, Paul himself comes to speak of the Church in a global way (Gal 1:13; 1 Cor 12:28; 15:9). Let us take note of the fact that Matthew—the only evangelist to use the word "Church"—will have Jesus speak of *his* Church as a sole and unique community (Matt 16:18).

The author of the letter to the Ephesians forces himself to go deeply into the nature of this *Ekklesia* which is established in all the communities. But this very nature wills that it be *communion,* and not simply an addition, of the *Ekklesiai tou Theou* scattered throughout the whole world and down through the ages, each one having its own characteristics, Church of Churches. On the one hand, it can only exist in them and through them, but on condition that each one already be an authentic *communion* established by the Spirit, in the local mold, based on the apostolic witness. On the other hand, it is singular, in that all of them must, nevertheless, be "recognized" in each other. At the outset, the local one—with what it contains culturally, "contextually," geographically, religiously, historically—belongs to the material from which the *Ekklesia tou Theou* springs forth in its fundamental truth. The inculturation or "contextualization" could not formulate itself *a posteriori*. It belongs to the very birth of the Church of God. It is woven into the catholicity.

8. The Church of God which is revealed as such in the event of Pentecost, as inseparably one and catholic, is in fact more than the accomplishment of the Promise, if it is considered in the strict sense which reserves it to Israel. It is the accomplishment of the Gospel of God. The presence of the nations on Pentecost, by the Jews born in them, makes them already part of the faith, enlarging the universalism of hope.[43] After the descent of the Spirit in Samaria (8:15-17), and especially his coming in power on the pagans (10:44-48), that becomes evident. The field of vision was enlarged and, henceforth, the Promise flows out to the Jews. James' speech attributes to Peter the announcement that "from the beginning God took care to take from among the pagan nations a people for his name" (15:14). So the assertion is made that God establishes a people for himself by drawing from among the nations, and no longer by being opposed to them as the sentence in Deuteronomy asserted (Deut 14:2) that Luke perhaps transposes here.[44] The Promise to the people is based on the *Euaggelion tou Theou*.

The Gospel of God is the Good News that, since the dawn of history, God has sought a humanity that would have a premonition of it, a humanity suffocating in its distress. Israel has been chosen with a view to the fulfillment of this project of God. And if the community confesses Christ Jesus as Savior, it is precisely because in him this Gospel of God is accomplished. His mystery is radically inseparable from it (Mark 1:14; Rom 1:1; 15:16, 19; 2 Cor 11:7; 1 Thess 2:2, 8, 9; 1 Tim 1:11; 1 Pet 4:17).

There is no better way to reveal the intuitive nature of this Gospel of God and to have its basic relationship to the Church of God perceived in the way that we present it, than to evoke in very broad strokes its presence in the web of biblical thought. It is discernible, as a fine thread, in the theology of the Yahwist. He speaks, indeed, of Israel, using for a background the work of God the Creator and the divine project of Salvation in regard to humanity as such,[45] ensnared in its misery. But what was said

---

[43]See P. Dion, *Dieu universel et Peuple élu*, coll. "Lectio divina" 83, Paris, 1975 which analyzes in great detail both the breakthroughs of the religion of Israel towards universalism and the tensions among the diverse perspectives. The opening towards universalism is undeniable, but it is marked with serious ambiguities. See in particular 29-36, 80-84, 135-154.

[44]"The people whom the Lord establishes is no longer only a people who will be his property in contrast to all other nations, but it is a people that is chosen from among the nations, that he forms from them," J. Dupont, "Laos ex Ethnôn," *NTS* 3, 1956-1957, 47-50 (49). Compare also with Exod 19:3, 8.

[45]"The Yahwist has understood well that everything did not begin with the origin of Israel:

to the serpent after the fall, the Protogospel (Gen 3:15), then the sign put on Cain after the murder of Abel (4:15) show how the Good News was inserted into the heart of the human drama. It envelops this human drama in a hope, an expectation. Subsequently, after the Flood, will come the utterances about repentance and the promise of Yahweh (8:20-22), then after the disastrous madness of Babel (11:1-9) the call of Abraham, understood as a new opportunity offered to all of humanity, to "all the families on the earth" (12:3) who have such a profound need to be blessed.[46] Is it not also surprising to see Abraham praying for Sodom and Gomorrah (18:17-33)? After the elite of the People have refined their soul in the wretchedness of mortification, sacerdotal Tradition will bring about a renewal, based on the idea of a divine benevolence extending to "all flesh which is on the earth" (Gen 9:8-17), a benevolence which will be valid forever. And it will link all flesh to the prohibition of all cruelty and every kind of murder (9:4-7). On his part, the author of the first two Songs of the Servant is thinking about the islands (Isa 42:4; 49:1) and about peoples in far distant lands (49:1). He is speaking of a "salvation" which must "reach to the ends of the earth" (49:6). The contents of this Salvation is the *mispát* in which it is probably necessary to view this as the new order which God is going to install and which concerns the entire earth.[47] Elsewhere, (Isa 25:6-8) the author speaks of the banquet prepared "for all peoples" on the mountain of Zion, at the moment when tears and death itself will disappear, and where "the covering that is cast over all peoples, the veil that is spread over all nations" will be destroyed. Here we have a distant disciple of Isaiah (19:16-25) thinking about a Yahweh calling Egypt "my people" and Assyria "the work of my hands," alongside of Israel called "my heritage" (19:25)! Jonas will go even further: Yahweh has a universal mercy for all his creatures. The author of Tobias dreams of a restoration which involves "all peoples of the whole earth" (Tob 14:6-7).

It is this presence, never perfectly clear, but, nevertheless, indisputable, of a Word of hope going beyond the destiny of Israel as such to include

since Yahweh had surely been active from the beginning of the world, he could not have been interested solely in the children of Abraham. The Yahwist, like the wise men of his time and of all times, asked questions besides about human life which did not concern the Israelite as such. . . . But the human condition surely did not begin with Israel—it goes back to the first works of Yahweh, to the first steps of this humanity which the Yahwist portrays spontaneously as one large family." (P. E. Dion, *op. cit.*, 30). See also the interesting study by G. A. Danell, "The Idea of God's People in the Bible," in Anton Fridrichsen, *The Root of the Vine,* London, 1953, 23–36.

[46]See especially H. W. Wolff, "Das Kerygma des Jahwisten," *Gesammelte Studien zum Alten Testament,* Munich, 1964, 345–373. See for the meaning of this blessing, P.E. Dion, *op. cit.,* 33–35. This last reference emphasizes, however, following P. Altmann, the limits in this regard for whomever does not belong to Israel (*ibid.,* 31–32).

[47]See J. Coppens, "La mission du Serviteur de Yahvé et son statut eschatologique," *ETL* 48, 1972, 343–371; P. E. Dion, *op. cit.,* 82–84.

it in a wider divine plan which we call the gospel of God. And this God, although linked to a particular People, is the universal God. The tension between particular and universal is already encountered on this level. The Church of God which springs forth on Pentecost has its roots there. It is formed, the Fathers will say, *jam ab Abel justo.*[48] Also it is Christ the Lord—whose role for all of creation is shown in the letters to the Colossians and the Hebrews—who gives it his Spirit. Paul's speech to the inhabitants of Lystra (Acts 14:15-18) and his address to the philosophers in Athens (Acts 17:22-31) will present at the outset Jesus in the light of belief in a Creator God. They bring about a brief reminder of the history of the Promise. And yet they are sprinkled throughout with biblical citations.

9. If we had to sum up in one word the real context of Salvation, as much individual as collective, announced in the Gospel of God, we would use, following many of the Fathers, *communion,* the word which sums up Acts. In biblical thought, as it is understood in the first centuries, Salvation is called *communion.* It is surely not by chance that down to the present time Jewish and Christian thought have conveyed a view of the "authentic man," underlining the fact that the human being finds his authenticity and affirms his full singularity only in communion.[49] According to this thinking, the drama of our history is precisely that man has become an isolated being, creating a broken world in which individuals live side by side without establishing authentic bonds of communion. In this way, humanity has condemned itself in reality to a state of nonexistence. It has reduced itself to becoming hardly more than a collage of individuals. The individual does not reach his fulfillment in this way, because "not being monopolized by oneself, always looking beyond oneself and ourselves, is the fundamental state necessary for an individual to be able to exist. Restricted by egocentrism, man is a being entirely deprived of personality. . . . The person, metaphysically, is a social being who needs to communicate with others. . . . The struggle for the individual is a struggle against 'egomania.'"[50] The quest for individuality is satisfied only in a solidarity that is sought after and welcomed. Martin Buber said that "all true life is a discovery of others," that the *I* exists only through the *you* and that "it is by becoming *I* that I say you."[51] He

[48]See Y. Congar, "Ecclesia ab Abel," *Festschrift Karl Adam,* Düsseldorf, 1952, 79–110.

[49]We refer to the fine book by Alain Finkielkraut, *La Sagesse de l'amour,* Paris, 1984, which very much influenced thought of Emmanuel Lévinas. See also the classic work by Martin Buber, *La Vie en dialogue,* Paris, 1959, and E. Lévinas, *De l'existence à l'existant,* Paris, 1947.

[50]Nicolas Berdiaeff, *Cinq méditations sur l'existence,* Paris, 1936, 173-175. The well known discussions by Christian philosophers on "the individual" and "the person" fall right into the heart of this vision.

[51]*Op. cit.,* 13.

gave credibility to the poet who describes the human being as "a dwelling place of brotherhoods, discernible or not, plural and yet singular."[52] But this communion causes a unique *I* to exist which will never be reproduced,[53] a "once-in-a-lifetime" equal to himself. Communion (which is not divided) and singularity (which is not absorbed) sketch together the nature of the created being "in the image of and resembling" a God whose trinitarian nature is proclaimed by Christian faith.

To state that the Salvation announced by the Gospel of God and manifested in the rise of the Church of God on Pentecost is communion, amounts to recognizing in the Church of God the place where the humanity-that-God-wills is recreated. The *communion* found in the summaries in Acts—using alongside other terms the word *koinonia* which we find mentioned, with varied meanings, in Paul's epistle to the Hebrews (13:16) and especially in the first Johannine letter (1 John 1:3, 6)—always implies the negation of isolation or of *egomania* in which, since the sin of Adam, humanity is suffocating. In several Pauline and Johannine passages, the word *koinonia* appears as the one which best expresses what establishes and expresses all communion. Then *koinonia* taken in this very rich sense which will assert itself gradually signifies nothing else than the restoring of the fundamental relationship between communion and singularity, making authentic human existence for each person individually, as for the collective destiny of humanity.[54] Never explicitly defined

[52]Pierre Emmanuel, *La Face humaine*, Paris, 1965, 246.

[53]See N. Berdiaeff, *op. cit.*, 177-199, 111-119; see also, in an entirely different context, Jean Hamburger, *L'Homme et les hommes*, Paris, 1976, 13-15.

[54]On the notion of *koinonia*, see the studies by F. Hauck, "Koinônos, etc.," *TWNT* 3, 1938, 798-910; P. Neuenzeit, "Koinônia," *LTK* 6, 1961, 368-369; a synthesis in H. J. Sieben, J. McDermott, H. Manzanera, H. Bacht, J.-M. R. Tillard, "Koinônia, communauté, communion," *Dictionnaire de spiritualité*, 1976 (with bibliography); H. Seesemann, *Der Begriff koinonia im Neuen Testament*, Giessen, 1936; P. Bori, *Koinonia, L'idea della communione nell'ecclesiologia recente e nel Nuovo Testamento*, Brescia, 1972. See also J. Y. Campbell, "Koinonia and its Cognates in the New Testament," *JBL* 51, 1932, 352-380; E. Groenewald, *Koinonia (Gemeenskap) bij Paulus*, Delft, 1932; G. Jourdan, "Koinonia in I Corinthians 10, 16," *JBL* 67, 1948, 111-124; S. Munoz Iglesias, "Concepto biblico de koinonia," *XIII Semana Biblica Española (1952)*, El Movimento Ecumenisto, Madred, 1953, 197-223; E. Dumont, "La koinonia en los primeros cinco capitulos de los Hechos de los Apostoles," *Revista Biblica* 24, 1962, 22-32; A. George, "La communion fraternelle des croyants dans les epîtres de saint Paul," *Lumière et vie* 16, 1967, 3-20; J. Dupont, *Études sur les Actes des Apôtres*, 503-519; Id., "L'union entre les premiers chrétiens dans les Actes des Apôtres," *NTR* 91, 1969, 897-915; H. J. Degenhardt, "Die Liebestätigkeit in den Gemeinden der apostolischen Zeit," *Volk Gottes, Festgabe für J. Hoefer*, Fribourg-en-Brisgau, 1967, 243-253; H. Schürmann, "Gemeinde als Bruderschaft," *Ursprung und Gestalt, Erörte-rungen und Besinnungen zum Neuen Testament*, Düsseldorf, 1970, 61-73; M.-E. Boismard, "The First Epistle of John and the Writings of Qumrân," in James H. Charlesworth, *John and Qumrân*, London, 1972. 152-165; J. M. McDermott, "The Biblical Doctrine of Koinonia," *Biblische Zeitschrift* 19, 1975, 64-77, 219-233; Schuyler Brown, "Koinonia as the Basis of New Testament Ecclesiology," *One in Christ* 12, 1976, 157-167; G. Panikulam, *Koinonia in the New Testament*, coll. "An. Biblica," 85, Rome, 1979; M. J. Suggs, "Koinonia in the New Testament," *Mid-Stream* 23, 1984, 351-362. The term *koinonia* appears in Acts 2:42; Rom 15:26; 1 Cor 1:9; 10:16; 2 Cor

as *koinonia,* the Church is perceived as the bearer of this concept in its full sense of uniting, and therefore, in its diverse forms, all those things which bring about Salvation. Briefly, *koinonia* in the New Testament context designates, in its most profound sense, the entrance of every baptized person and of each community of believers into the sphere of reconciliation opened up by Christ on the Cross and which the Spirit makes apparent through the break on Pentecost. And this sphere is found enclosed in the eternal mystery of communion which brings forth the existence of God himself. The first letter of John goes as far as saying: "Our communion is communion *with* the Father and *with* his Son Jesus Christ" (1 John 1:3). Christians are in this sense *sun-koinonoi* (cf. Phil 1:7; Rev 1:9). That is almost equivalent to their definition and affirmation of what Salvation is: "Because, in Christ on the cross, the constraint which kept men in a state of egoism was broken—what kept them in their own dimension. A new possibility of existence, a new vital sphere was opened up to them in the Body of Christ on the cross—in the love of Christ; in him they can open themselves up to God and, consequently, to one another. In this Body of Christ on the cross . . . the new humanity is established and made ready. It is borne and supported by God, reconciled among themselves; this is, therefore, a humanity of peace. In this Body of Christ crucified, 'reconciliation' is opened up to man as the only dimension. The new possibility of existence is opened up to men, not only through the Body of Christ on the cross, but, as a new state of existence. Humanity has been raised up in the Church by the resurrection of Christ incarnate and by his ascension through the power of the Holy Spirit. Strictly understood, this new possibility of existence through the cross of Christ is nothing else than the Church built by the power of the Holy Spirit through the resurrection and ascension of Christ. In a real sense, the Church is the new living sphere of all people opened up for them by Christ on the cross. It is nothing other than the concrete dimension of the opening that Christ obtained by bearing us with him on the cross."[55]

6:14; 8:4; 9:13; 13:13; Gal 2:9; Eph 3;9; Phil 1:5; 2:1; 3:10; Phil 1: 6; Heb 13:16; 1 John 1:3, 6, 7. In a general way the word *koinonia* has as its primary meaning "participation with *others* in a *similar* reality." Therefore, there is an objective level (the common reality) and a subjective level (the interpersonal bond which results from it). Sometimes the term does not have a formally religious meaning (as in Rom 15:26; 2 Cor 8:4); sometimes on the contrary it is a question of common participation in the Spirit, in Christ, in the sufferings of Christ, which establishes Christian brotherhood; the Johannine texts give a mystical dimension to brotherhood, rooting it in the relationship of the Father to the Son. But nowhere does it say *explicitly* that the Church is defined as *koinonia.* Concerning the thinking of the Fathers, see P. Lebeau, "Koinônia; la signification du salut selon saint Iréée," *Epektasis. Mélanges J. Daniélou,* Paris, 1972, 121-127; H. Bacht et H. J. Sieben, "Koinônia," *Dictionnaire de spiritualité* 1750-1758.

⁵⁵H. Schlier, *Le Temps de l'Église,* coll. "Cahiers de l'actualité religieuse," 14, Tournai, 1961, 292.

Perhaps exegetes do not sufficiently underline the theological intention of a characteristic that is testified to in Acts (11:27-30). The gesture of solidarity by the Church of the pagans towards the Church of Judea, a victim of want, shows the widening of the concrete *communion* that the summaries described as typical of the Church of Pentecost (2:44-45; 4:32-35). To the movement which brought the faith from Jerusalem to Antioch is a responding one which brings generosity from Antioch to Jerusalem. Luke persists in showing that, hardly had the Church of the pagans been given birth by the Spirit, than it also puts *communion* into action, but giving it a scope of universality which appeared totally clear as one of its essential components from the moment when the meeting between Peter and Cornelius took place.

B. Communion in the Body of Christ

1. The writers in the first centuries did not find it sufficient to view the Church as born in this way by the eschatological bursting forth of Pentecost. Nor were they content to perceive it as the beginning of a shaking up of the world in all its dimensions, or to declare that the gift of the Spirit of the Lord restores humanity by opening up communion to it, and thereby changing its destiny.[56] They persist also in affirming the specific relationship to Christ Jesus which supports the reality of the *Ekklesia tou Theou*. They find it in the idea of the Body of Christ.[57] It seems to us that their view is presented with depth and finesse in an Augustinian text, *Sermon* 341.[e]

> Indeed, the head and the members form only one Christ, not that Christ is not complete in himself, but because he has deigned to form one whole with us, even though he is complete without us, not only as Word, only Son equal to the Father, but also in this human nature with which he clothed himself and in which he is God and man wholly together. . . . We are, therefore, all members of the body of Christ, not only we who are here, but all Christians spread throughout the earth, not only those who exist at the present time, and what shall I say here?, but also all those who, from the time of the just man Abel, have existed and will exist until the end of the world, as many as men will beget and will be begotten; all the just who pass through this life, and all those who exist now, not in this place but in this life, and all those who are to be born in the future; all form the one body of Jesus Christ, and they are, each

---

[56]This aspect has been vigorously emphasized by Ernst Käsemann, especially in regard to Paul's thinking, but by basing it also on the opening of the mission to the pagans. See in particular, in *Essais exégétiques*, 217-220. On the background for Käsemann's vision, see Pierre Gisel, *Vérité et histoire*, coll. "Théologie historique," 41, Paris-Geneva, 1975, 293-310.

[57]The principal texts were presented and studied in the important work, which has become a classic, by E. Mersch, *Le Corps mystique de Christ, études de théologie historique*, Paris, 1951.

one of them, members of Jesus Christ. Therefore, all form his body and are, each one of them, his members. . . . And as it is said of him besides "that he is the head of every principality and power" (Cor 2:10), we unite this Church, a voyager at the present time on the earth, to this Church in the heavens, where we have the angels for fellow-citizens. . . . Christ is so revealed to us in the scriptures, sometimes as the Word, equal to the Father, sometimes as mediator, when the Word was made flesh and lived among us (John 1:14), sometimes, finally, as being at the same time head and members. . . . In the same way as a husband is joined to his wife, you should understand that there is only one Christ. That is why the same apostle, when he was still only Saul, heard Jesus saying to him: "Saul, Saul, why do you persecute me?" (Acts 9:4) because the head is joined closely to the body. And when Paul, who had become a preacher of Jesus Christ, was suffering from others, persecutions similar to those he had inflicted himself, said: "It is to complete in my flesh what is lacking in the suffering of Jesus Christ" (Col 1:24), showing in this way that his sufferings should be looked upon as the very sufferings of Christ: what cannot be understood of the head himself who in the heavens can suffer nothing similar; they must be understood, therefore, as being in his body, in other words, in the Church, because this body joined to its head makes only one Christ.[58]

From the time of Pentecost, according to this outlook, Christ the Lord is inseparable from the Church, although he transcends it and it owes to him what it is. Indeed, even the title of Christ—as that of Savior—implies this relationship. The power of the Holy Spirit makes the Crucified One the Christ only by joining him to the humanity over which he will reign. His singularity and his transcendental title exist only in a real harmony and to make it a reality with "all nations which are under the heavens." This explains why there is a powerful current among the early Fathers of the Church which makes Pentecost and the Resurrection one feast, the "historical" face of the mystery hidden in the exaltation of Jesus,[59] clarifying Easter Sunday in the feast of the Spirit. Besides, this made it possible to unite in complete accord the Johannine Pentecost and the one found in Acts.[b]

So it is in the mystery of the glorification of Jesus that the individual and the multitude have made the Lord Jesus Christ their point of soli-

---

[58]*Sermo* 341, 11–13 (*PL* 39, 1499–1500). Compare Sermo 455 (*PL* 38, 265); *"Quid est ipsa ecclesia? Corpus Christi. Adiunge illi caput et fit unus homo, caput et corpus, unus homo. Caput quis est? Hic qui natus est de virgine Maria"*; *Enarr. in ps.* 56, 1 (*CCL* 39, 694); *"Et quoniam totus Christus caput est et corpus . . . caput est ipse Saluator noster . . . corpus autem eius est ecclesia . . ."*; *Enarr. in ps.* 60, 2–3 (*CCL* 39, 766): *"in illo nos tentati sumus"*; *De unitate Ecclesiae* 4, 7 (*CSEL* 52, 238): *"Totus Christus caput et corpus est: caput Unigenitus Dei Filius et corpus eius ecclesia, sponsus et sponsa, duo in carne una."* See the excellent study by A. Piolanti, "Il mistero del 'Christo totale' in S. Agostino," *Augustinus Magister*, III.

[59]See J. Danielou, *Bible et liturgie*, coll. "Lex orandi," 11, Paris, 1951, 429–448.

darity. *Communion* finds its locus there. Such is the work of the eschatological Spirit. He anoints the *Christos* as a reality, and not as an empty
and honorary title, only by giving him a "community" defined in the first
letter of Peter as the chosen race, the royal priesthood, the consecrated
nation, the people set apart (1 Pet 2:9).[60] He establishes the Church of
God only by enclosing it in the reality of the *Christos* of God. There is
no Christ without Church, just as there is no Church without Christ.

Such a perception is based above all on the great theme of the Body
of Christ as it is explicitly stated in the writings of Paul, both the letters
to the Colossians and Ephesians.[61] It is intrinsically linked to the very
dynamic of the event of Pentecost:

> The believer, caught up into the destiny of Christ, is the representa-
> tive of a new world and member of a Church which is the new world
> of God. The theme of the Church as the Body of Christ, an idea which
> is perhaps already pre-Pauline, is justifiably for this reason an exact ex-
> pression of an ecclesiology adapted to the situation, because, better than
> any other concept about the Church, it shows the worldwide expansion
> of Christianity, manifesting itself in its mission among the pagans, and
> the universality of Salvation, which this mission already indicates.[62]

The theme of building is, truthfully, close to the same insight (1 Cor
3:9; 10:23; Eph 2:20-22), especially when it is closely associated with the
theme of Temple (1 Cor 3:9-17; 2 Cor 6:16; Eph 2:20-22). The letter to
the Ephesians also will go from the theme of Body to that of building

---

[60]For this text to which we will return, consult the article by P. Grelot, "Le sacerdoce commun
des fidèles dans le Nouveau Testament," *Esprit et vie* 94, 1984, 138–144, and especially J. H.
Elliott, *The Elect and the Holy; an Exegetical Examination of 1 Peter 2, 4–10 and the Phrase
basileion hierateuma,* Leyde, 1966.

[61]Let us go back once and for all to the following studies: for a global view read the very profound study by J. Armitage Robinson, *S. Paul's Epistle to the Ephesians,* London, 1909, and
the commentary by Markus Barth, *Ephesians 1-3.* coll. "The Anchor Bible," New York, 1980.
For the more formally ecclesiological analysis, see L. Cerfaux, *La Théologie de l'Église suivant
S. Paul,* 201–218, 243–259, 276–280; Id., *Le Christ dans la théologie de S. Paul,* Paris, 1954,
264–266, 320–322; P. Benoit, "Corps, tête et plérôme dans les épîtres de la captivité," *RB* 63,
1956, 5–44, reprinted in *Exégèse et théologie,* t. II, Paris, 1961, 153–197, analysis of the book
by J.A.T. Robinson, "The Body," *RB* 64, 1957, 581–585, taken up again in *Exégèse et théologie,*
t. II, Paris, 1961, 165–171, see also L. Malevez, "L'Église Corps du Christ, sens et provenance
de l'expression chez S. Paul," *RSR* 32, 1944, 27–94; H. Schlier, *Le Temps de l'Église,* 169–193,
291–309 (a revival of former articles); B. M. Ahern, "The Christian's Union with the Body of
Christ in Cor., Gal. and Rom." *CBQ* 23, 1961, 199–209. J. Havet, "La doctrine paulinienne
du corps du Christ," *Lit. et théol. paul.,* Louvain, 1960, 183–216; J. A. T. Robinson, *Le Corps,
étude sur la théologie de saint Paul,* Paris, 1966; K. Usami, *Somatic Comprehension of Unity,
the Church in Ephesus,* coll. "The Anchor Bible," 101, 1983; V. Gugnel, *Le Corps et le corps
du Christ dans la première épître aux Corinthiens,* coll. "Lectio divina," 114, Paris, 1983; George
S. Worgul, "People of God, Body of Christ : Pauline Ecclesiological Contrasts," *Biblical Theological Bulletin* 12, 1982, 24–28.

[62]E. Käsemann, *Essais exégétiques,* 217–218.

and of Temple (2:14-22).[63] This theme inspired the thinking of the early centuries. But its thorough investigation of the nature of the Church is especially connected to the idea of the Body of Christ.

This preference for the theme, Body of Christ, is understandable. Certainly, whether Paul was inspired or not by Aesop's fable which deals with the social life of Menenius Agrippa,[64] one point is evident: the letter to the Romans (Rom 12:3-6) and chapter twelve of the first letter to the Corinthians (1 Cor 12:4-27) use the theme of Body to underline the strict union and especially the solidarity of the members (1 Cor 12:26). Paul indicates in these texts that each person discovers his or her singularity in communion with the whole membership (1 Cor 12:21-27) and that this reality comes from the Spirit (1 Cor 12:13). But if it were a question of this dimension alone, the themes of building and of Temple would be, on the whole, as evocative and richer in biblical resonance. Paul's insight becomes clear only if the solidarity which these two texts speak about is linked closely to what he affirms—in the same letter to the Corinthians—about *communion* at the Eucharistic Table.

Why are Christians then a single Body of Christ? Why do they lack this solidarity, especially when it stretches all the way to the Table of the Lord? Is it a lack of discernment about the Body (1 Cor 11:17-34)? Because the bread which is broken is a "communion" with the Body of Christ (10:16-17). The internal unity of the community comes from the fact that all—each one with his or her uniqueness and singularity—are gathered into the one and indivisible Body of Christ the Lord. It is not, therefore, the fact of their addition which forms the Body. The Body of the Lord, on the contrary, assumes their multitude in him, the Spirit of his Lordship unifying this multitude in *koinonia*.[65] The coming together of singularity and communion, by which the members retain their singularity and yet, at the same time, are turned towards one another and bound to one another—which is the fact that saves them—is exercised in this embrace of the Body "of peace," "of unity," "of reconciliation," "of charity."

The letter to the Ephesians—written also, it seems, in a context of intra-ecclesial tensions—is the key document concerning this unitive function of the Body of Christ. It puts, in fact, at the heart of its thinking on the Church—whose Head is Christ, the Ruler of the entire universe (Eph

---

[63]See in another context John 2:21, and the article by C. F. Moule, "Sanctuary and Sacrifice in the Church of the New Testament," *JTS* n.s. 1, 1950, 29–41.

[64]See L. Cerfaux, *op. cit.,* 204.

[65]Commenting on 1 Cor 10:16, W. D. Davies, *Paul and Rabbinic Judaism,* Philadelphia, 1980, written as: "L'idée qui sous-tend ce passage est celle d'une participation commune au Sang du Christ et que cette participation constitue la communauté" (253).

1:20-23)—the assertion that hatred, division, separation, antipathy have been abolished, put to death, utterly destroyed by the blood of the Cross: "You who used to be so far apart have been brought very close by the blood of Christ. . . . What was divided he has united: in his flesh he has destroyed the wall of separation and hatred. . . . He wished to reconcile Jews and pagans into one single body by means of the Cross: on it he killed hatred" (2:13-16). The crucified Body of Jesus, his "body of flesh" (Col 1:26; cf. 2:11), perishable and mortal, is the place of reconciliation (Col 1:22) because forgiveness has been acquired in the bloody assassination on the cross (Eph 1:7). In this body, given up to death so that the benevolent plan of God might be accomplished (the "mystery"), aiming at binding together the entire universe (1:9-10), is engraved the salvation it has brought forth. Entrance into it is by baptism.

Also the personal Body of Christ, a Body in which is lived the drama of forgiveness and reconciliation, is, in truth, the "meeting ground" of the new humanity, the exact spot where *koinonia* (which Paul described as a body) is formed and present, already totally there in its very principle. According to the fine expression which will describe in a concrete way the "mystery," the blocks or factions of broken humanity are seen there "concorporated" (the *sunsoma* in Eph 3:6). The Resurrection of this Body of flesh into a Body of glory confirms through the power of the Spirit, the "summing up" or the "return to unity" of all humanity in Christ (1:10). The ecclesial Body rises up in and *with* the risen Body of the Lord (2:6) which is its Head in the twofold sense of source of life (according to the medical theory of Hippocrates) and as head (master). And so gathered into him, the ecclesial Body appears as the fullness of Christ (1:23), "without which Christ would not be completed but with which he is completed."[66] The Body as it is understood in Paul's letters to the Corinthians and to the Romans[67] exists only in the Body of the Crucified, glorified by the Spirit. They are inseparable. But including the ecclesial Body in the Body of the Risen Lord is only the other side of a basic dependence: the Spirit who causes it to be *koinonia* comes to it from the Body of the glorified Lord.

2. From this interpretation of the reality of the ecclesial Body to the assertion that the Church finds its full reality only in the Eucharistic mystery, and even that "the Eucharist makes the Church," is only one step. It will be quickly surpassed. Besides, we have seen that the Pauline notion itself requires an assertion:

---

[66] J. Armitage Robinson, *op. cit.,* 42–43.

[67] This Pauline sense is the one found in Col 2:19, Eph 4:15-16 but this time linked with the declaration of the transcendence of the Head, Christ.

The hellenistic comparison of the body and the members is applied to the Church, and it is moreover, in the realm of Christian things, a reality: not only *are we like* a body, but we belong in a real way to Christ, and since his life is ours, *we are* truly members and Christ is the principle of unity and of life among us as the body towards the members. Baptism has consecrated us into the body of Christ and the eucharist identifies us with this body of Christ to which it relates us, in such a way that Christ is really for all Christians, their body. Christians are a body, not by the simple reason of comparison, but in a sacramental and mystical realism.[68]

Cyril of Alexandria will state this conviction very explicitly in his commentary on John's Gospel:

We benefit from a bodily union with Christ, we who participate in his sacred flesh. Saint Paul testifies to this when he says in regard to the mystery of piety: God had not made this mystery known to men of past generations as he has now revealed it through the Spirit to his holy apostles and prophets. This mystery is the fact that the pagans are part of the same heritage, the same body, and share in the same promise in Christ.

If we all form among ourselves one and the same body in Christ, and not only among ourselves but with him, since evidently he is in us through his own flesh, how is it that our unity among ourselves and in Christ is not already visible? Because Christ is the bond of unity, being in himself both God and man.

As far as unity in the Spirit is concerned, we will follow the same path and we will state again that since we have all received one and the same Spirit, I mean the Holy Spirit, we are in some way intimately involved with one another and with God. In fact, although we are a multitude of individuals and Christ causes the Spirit of his Father and himself to dwell in each of us, there is, however, only one single indivisible Spirit, who gathers in himself the Spirits who are distinct from each other by

---

[68]L. Cerfaux, *Le Christ dans la théologie de saint Paul,* 265 (these lines have stamped catholic thought); see also P. Benoit, *Exégèse et théologie,* t. II, 117 ("by receiving in their body, through the sacramental rite, the Body of Christ, they *are* all together one single body, individual at first, but assuming in it all the bodies of those it joins together"). This is what shows the history of the expressions *corpus mysticum* and *corpus verum.* The expression *corpus mysticum* designated in the beginning the eucharistic body, a body given in mystical prayer, received at the mystical banquet, signifying and creating mystically the Church, made present in the liturgical mysteries, while the expression *corpus verum* designated the ecclesial body, a body in its fullness, its accomplishment, the realization of its finality. So, *corpus mysticum* (sacramental) and *corpus verum* (ecclesial) designated the two modes of the individual body of the Lord in his rapport with humanity willed by the Spirit, through him and in him, to constitute the Church of God: the *corpus mysticum* is the *sacramentum* both of the Lord and of the Church, the *corpus verum* is the union of the body of the Lord and the body of the faithful. Later, the formulas will be reversed, the emphasis being put on the sacramental body qualified from then on as *corpus verum.* Then the attention will be centered on the "real presence"; the rapport filling up the Church will be disregarded.

the fact of their individual existence, and makes them seem, so to speak, as if they all have one single existence in him.

Just as the strength of the sacred flesh makes one body of all those into whom it has come, in the same way, in my opinion, the Spirit of God, one and indivisible, which lives in us, leads us to spiritual unity. This is why Saint Paul exhorts us in this way: Bear with one another charitably; do all you can to preserve the unity of the Spirit by the peace that binds you together. There is one Body, one Spirit, just as you were called into one and the same hope when you were called. There is one Lord, one faith, one baptism, one God who is Father of all, who is over all, through all and within all. If the one Spirit lives in us, the one God, Father of all will be in all, and he will lead through his Son everyone who partakes of the Spirit to a mutual union and to union with him. . . .

We are all, therefore, one being in the Father, Son and Holy Spirit. One being, I declare, in an identical state. . . ., one being developing in a manner consistent with piety, by our communion in the sacred flesh of Christ, by our communion in the one Holy Spirit (11, 11, Pg 74, 559-562).

What must be underlined especially is a conviction of the early centuries, forgotten since then in the West. Because the Eucharistic Body is truly the Body of the Lord[69] assuming all believers unto himself, every Eucharistic celebration causes the entire Church to receive communion. The universal Church is immanent in the local church through communion in the Eucharistic Body. And correlatively, the local church, when it celebrates the Memorial of the Lord, is in a sacramental way communion of the Church in its totality, a totality which embrace all times "since the just man Abel," all places, all situations.[70] When Tradition asserts that the Church is Eucharistic it proclaims the profound sense of the unbreakable unity of the Church of God, inseparable from its catholicity, grounded in its Sanctity, in other words, in its insertion into Christ the Lord. Wherever there is a Eucharistic celebration, there is the Church of God as it is in all the Eucharistic communities where the Eucharist is celebrated, as it has been and as it will be.

---

[69]See J. A. T. Robinson, who writes (*op. cit.*, 85–86): "It is good to be very prudent when speaking of the "metaphor" of the body of Christ. Paul uses the analogy of the human body to explain that Christians form the body of Christ. But the analogy has value only because Christians *are*, literally, the raised up body of the person of Christ, in all its concrete reality. What is remarkable is that Paul identifies this personality with the Church. But to say that the Church is the body of Christ is no more a metaphor than to say that the flesh of Jesus incarnate or that the eucharistic bread are the body of Christ. None of these three realities, Church, flesh, bread, is *like* his body (Paul never says that): each one *is* the body of Christ, . . . all three of them are the expression of one and the same christology. It is almost impossible to exaggerate the realism and the raw force of the Pauline doctrine."

[70]That is why the liturgies mention the saints of past ages, as much as the needs of humanity today.

In addition, it is in the Eucharist "proclaiming the Death of the Lord until he comes" (1 Cor 11:26), in the midst of a world where the power of Pentecost wishes to be at work, that the local Church enters into communion with the supreme *martyria* of Christ Jesus, that of the Cross, of the earthly Body so that the plan of the Father might be accomplished. But this *martyria* of Christ is then enlarged by the ecclesial Body assumed into his Body as Lord. The "communion of saints" which designates both Eucharist and Church states something other than a mutual help through what has been earned and merited. It signifies, in particular, the depth of a *koinonia* contained in the *unique* witness given since Pentecost by all generations, to the Gospel of God triumphant in the Resurrection of the Crucified. At the Memorial of the Lord, the community is, therefore, in sacramental but true communion with the apostolic witness which it is to echo and which is now its own. By giving to the community the Body of Christ, the Father makes it an integral part of the singular missionary event which extends from the *martyria* of the Lord until the day when "he hands over the kingdom to God the Father, having done away with every sovereignty, authority and power" (1 Cor 15:24). The involvement of the community in the world for the sake of the kingdom is, therefore, joined to that of the entire Church, which is taken hold of by the Lord suspended between his paschal exaltation and his Parousia of the last day, the *already* and the *not yet*.[71]

3. The missionary task of the Church reveals its ultimate purpose and its authentic nature only if it is understood in light of this theology of the Body of Christ. Even if there is hesitation concerning the Eucharistic foundation of the whole ecclesiology, what must be recognized is that the insertion of the ecclesial Body into the personal Body of the Lord gives the mission its breadth and scope. In its essence the Church is missionary because of its Lord.

It is not a question, as already seen, simply of a profound anxiety or intensive zeal for the salvation of individuals. The aims within the dimen-

---

[71]In Cor 15:20-28, "the apostle proclaims . . . the certainty of our resurrection, but in a singular way, by inserting from the beginning the anthropological hope in a more extended context. In the resurrection, it is not a primary question of anthropology but of christology. It is the work of the second Adam, and its sense is not first and above all our resurrection, but the sovereignty of Christ. 'Because he must reign': There is the direct line of this development, and the foundation which gives us an assurance for our own destiny also. Yet Paul is not satisfied with that. Very strangely, to this declaration he immediately adds a second one: the sovereignty of Christ is limited and temporary, its sole purpose is to prepare the reign of God alone. Christ holds the place of God in a world which is not yet fully submitted to God, although its eschatological submission is on course since Easter and its end is in sight. No perspective can be more apocalyptic. It seems here with the greatest evidence that Paul cannot and absolutely will not speak of an end of history which has already arrived, but that he envisions very well that the end has begun." (E. Käsemann, *Essais exegetiques,* 222.)

sions of the Lordship of Christ in which the Church—with its being, its destiny, its fidelity—is inscribed. But, whether it is a question of strict Pauline thinking (1 Cor 15:20-28), assertions contained in the letters to the Colossians, Ephesians and Philippians (Col 1:16-20; Eph 1:10, 20-23; Phil 2:9-11), according to Scripture this Lordship must be exercised over the universe *as such* and in it over humanity *as such*. What must be changed is the allegiance of the world, replacing the authority of powers with the sovereignty of Christ and consequently, the Reign of God. Only then will the gospel of God be fully accomplished.

In the missionary activity of the Church, it is, therefore, the power of the Lord himself—that of the Spirit received at his Resurrection—which through the ecclesial Body which is his own penetrates the world. It is a question of the Lord of glory putting his power into practice through his Body. This notion permits the mission of the Church to transcend a descent into individualism. It aims at "con-corporation" in action, in the *Kyrios,* of everything which weaves human existence together, first of all, the small corner of the world implied in the life of each Christian community to the vast universe on which this little corner is interdependent. This is the action of the Lord in his Body.

According to this perspective, it becomes impossible to separate Body and mission, ecclesial *koinonia* and involvement "for the world." If there is no Church of God without its being missionary, there is no missionary Church unless it is welded into the unity of the Body of Christ. It is erroneous in the Church of God to separate its interior reality of grace from its role as an instrument of Salvation. There could not be one without the other.

4. The Church of God shows itself by the dimension of Salvation. Since the time of Pentecost, God brings about his reign by enclosing every community and (in this community) every believer within the unity which precedes them and brings them into existence, without, in any way, denying their singularity: the unity of the Body of reconciliation of all of humanity. The Church could not be identified simply as the community of men and women who "imitate" Christ. Nor is it first of all an ethical organism, as noble as its understanding of humanity and the world might be. It is not an adding together of moral consciences. It is, radically, the community *of* Christ, in other words, the group of men and women whom the Spirit brings into existence generation after generation "reconciled" and which has only one abode: the Body of the Lord with his dynamism who wishes to gather the whole world together. This is why wherever there is *true* Eucharist there is *truly* Church.

Church is, therefore, every local community gathered together by the Eucharist. Originally, it seems, because every town had only one Eucharist, those places where the Eucharistic assembly took place were counted and considered as Churches. The local Eucharistic community was the local Church. But with the expansion of the Church beyond the cities Eucharistic communities were found everywhere, at the same time as the Church felt the need to become organized and take on form and structure. Around the town, but in conjunction with those responsible for its Church—with a presider "authorized" by them, as stated later by Ignatius of Antioch—communities celebrated for themselves the Memorial of the Lord. Often the link with the Eucharist of the town, presided over at that time by one called the bishop, will be referred to as the rite of *fermentum*. The local Church becomes the totality of these Eucharistic communities in communion with this bishop, and also within the area of his See. The Church is itself, therefore, a *communion* of local communities. In today's terminology it is a diocese (entrusted to a bishop), made up of parishes, each one of these being a Eucharistic community. Henceforth, whenever, throughout this long work we speak of the local Church, what we mean by it is the diocese, not the parish. It is in this sense that we state that the Church of God is Church of Churches, a *communion* of local Churches, therefore, a *communion of communion*.[72]

C. The Church of God, a communion of communions

The nature of the Church, as early Tradition understands it, is, therefore, summed up in *communion, koinonia*. It is the *Church of Churches*. Understood in its full context, it is the *communion of communions*, appearing as a *communion* of local Churches, spread throughout the world, each one itself being a *communion* of the baptized, gathered together into communities by the Holy Spirit, on the basis of their baptism, for the Eucharistic celebration. This existence as *communion* constitutes its essence. And the relationship to *communion* with the Father, Son and Spirit shows its deep-rootedness even in the eternal reality of the mystery of God.

1. To speak in this way of the *communion of communions,* however, without perceiving all of the things that relate to it, would be tantamount to the use of a hollow formula. The things that are related to it must be mentioned since they are numerous. The major facets of the Christian-being present in every baptized person, all declare, in fact, that there is an essential rapport in some way with *communion*.

This rapport is evident as far as charity is concerned in its twofold reference to God and to one's "brothers," emphasized especially in Johan-

---

[72]When M. J. Sheridan, *The Theology of the Local Church in Vatican II,* Rome, 1980, speaks of circumincession between a particular Church and the universal Church (especially 6:85), he uses a traditional category which adapts itself badly to the plural, *some* local Churches. But the intuition seems to us to be correct.

nine tradition (John 13:34; 15:12, 17; 1 John 3:17). But it is also valid
as far as faith is concerned, since it is always communion with a Word
of God transmitted and received from the witness of a believing community or from one of its members as the intermediary (Rom 10:14-21). Because even if it should happen that God would touch the heart of a man
or woman without going through the action of a witness—as in the case
of Paul, it will always be necessary to have recourse to some Ananias so
that the authentic contents of the faith might be revealed. It is the very
same thing for hope, even personal, directed towards the full coming of
a Kingdom in which the sources of anguish and grief are abolished. The
list is well known: hatred, envy, continual searching for "scapegoats,"
egoistic exploitation of another person, racism, pride-filled domination,
casual inter-human relationships corrupted by the forces of sin.[73] The first
letter of Paul to the Corinthians takes a careful look at this definitive event
and the resurrection of those men and women who "belong to Christ"
(15:23), at the moment of his Parousia (15:52). This Parousia is a result
of *communion*.

More broadly still, the exegetical study of the Judgment scene in Matthew (Matt 25:31-46) shows that it is presented here as "the transition
from the Kingdom of God which is hidden and preached to the Kingdom
manifested at the end of time."[74] It is a question of an "ethical prophecy," teaching that the fidelity of the "disciples" has as its *sacramentum*
this difficult make-up, but essential for the Gospel, of the human condition which is, in reality, solidarity with those who are outcasts. It is on
this that the final judgment of everyone is established, based on one's refusal or acceptance of a communion with the misery abiding in humanity.

These few examples make it evident that *communion* defines and measures the Christian experience as such. Already the summaries in Acts have
suggested this with their description of a life centered around the hearing
of the Word in common, the sharing and breaking of bread,[75] and prayer.
However, there is something here that is more profound still. Visible unity
and solidarity with the human drama are the expression of an interior *communion,* manifested as such in the eyes of God alone, which the Spirit
creates in the heart of every believer and which makes him part of the
Body of Christ Jesus. It is a question of Christ who is in *communion* with
human misery and in whom God himself is in *communion* with human
misery, according to the fine definition which Irenaeus gives of the Incar-

[73]It is to René Girard's credit to have shown it. But his vision is disputed. The silence of
F. Varone, *Ce Dieu censé aimer la souffrance,* Paris, 1984, 21–22, should be noted. Are we reduced
to the sole salvific message of Jesus? We would give more subtle differences.

[74]P. Bonnard, *L'Évangile selon saint Matthieu,* 364.

[75]Whether it is a question or not of the Eucharistic in the strict sense (see J.-P. Audet, *La Didachè,*
coll. "Études bibliques," Paris, 1958, 403–424).

nation in Book IV of the *Adversus Haereses* (IV, 20, 4–5), "the joining together and communion of God and man." Thomas Aquinas stated, synthesizing Augustinian tradition: "Life belongs only to the members joined to their head, and that is why it is necessary in baptism for one to be incorporated into Christ, as his member."[76] Entrance into Christ in a state of *communion* with humanity and entrance into the ecclesial Body coincide.[77] But if, in his deepest recesses, the Christian being is this relationship with the Savior Christ, it is in so far as this Savior Christ possesses the power of the Spirit. The Spirit saves by reconciling the individual with what God ponders him to be: a being who discovers his fullness only by opening himself up to others and, in this way realizing his "image and likeness," *in communion* with him.

To assert that the Church is the *communion of communions* amounts certainly to a recognition that in the Church are assumed all the concrete spheres of solidarity by which the humanity-willed-by-God can be realized. We have encountered all of them during our reflection on this matter: the sphere known as the immediate human community in which diversity is recognized and promoted, without it resulting in division, even the sphere of the urban community which originally was the typical birthplace of ecclesial communion,[78] that sphere pertaining to the region, that also of *oikoumene,* historically a unity spanning centuries encompassing generations and which makes up the course of Tradition. But it is a recognition, besides, that the Church is not limited to these dimensions which are inherent in the social human condition. It is intrinsically created and maintained by *communion* with the divine realities which establish the relationship, based on the Trinity, which we have just evoked, and it is these divine realities which are the ultimate explanation of what Tradition calls the grace-filled being. We will uncover it better by examining carefully the notion of *mystery,* the mold which contains it. *Communion* has a flesh, the flesh of Salvation. Ecclesial *koinonia* ties together the *communions* which create the fabric of the Christian-being. The communion of communities implies these basic *communions* which are the new creation.

2. In line with the Fathers, the link between the sanctity of the Church—the extent of which will be examined later—and the Eucharist is readily understood. Because in this sacrament *communion is given* as the realization of the gift of Salvation present in the Body and Blood of the Lord. And this gift is the gift of sanctity.

[76]III, 69, 5, see also the *Sed contra* going back to Augustine.

[77]See *ibid.,* obj. 1 and ad 1 where *incorporation* is already used for union with Christ the Savior through faith, having access to the sacrament.

[78]The Church which is in Corinth, Rome, Antioch, Laodocia, etc. It was at the arrival of the fourth century that a change of place was made in the ecclesial life towards the countryside, which will bring about changes in structures for the communities which will be confided to presbyters.

This is why the Christian community is, in all reality, the holy Church of God in the Eucharistic celebration. It is there that the Spirit unites the personal Body of the Lord with the ecclesial Body and unites the members of it to one another. But the Spirit does this by enfolding them in the fire of forgiveness of the Cross: "This bread is the remission of sins," declares Ambrose of Milan.[79] There alone coincide the basic sanctity of belonging to God, in Christ, and the moral sanctity of the members. Once the Eucharistic celebration is finished, believers will be compelled, by the Spirit of the Risen Lord received in response to the epiclesis, to lay bare and confess their sin; at the Eucharistic Table they find themselves caught up in the holiness of Christ. It is also in an explicitly sacramental context, referring to baptism, that the letter to the Ephesians evokes the holiness of the Church, described as the Spouse of Christ, due to the fact that he loved her. He delivered himself up for her in order to sanctify her by purifying her in the baptismal waters. It is this sanctification that he is seeking, because he wishes "to present her to himself in full splendor, with no speck or wrinkle or anything like that, but holy and faultless" (Eph 5:26-27). The link with marriage, by which husband and wife become one flesh, a mystery which "applies to Christ and the Church" (5:31-32), clarifies the true nature of this holiness. It is that of Christ himself, imparted to his Spouse, who has become "his own flesh," "his own Body" (5:29-30). Paul's letters—in a different context, it is true,—have indicated that this belonging to the Body of Christ is linked to the bread and cup of the Lord's Supper. The holiness of the Church is its *communion* in the holiness of Christ. Outside of this *communion* it would only be a gathering of sinners.

The First Letter to the Corinthians depends also on this quality of being a member of the Body of Christ in order to condemn the serious faults of Christians (1 Cor 6:16-20). And Peter's letter which extolled the "holy nation" (1 Pet 2:9) remains, nevertheless, uneasy about the conduct of some members of the community, including its leaders (5:2-3). Therefore, it is not sufficient for the Church to be caught up in the holiness of Christ through Eucharistic *communion*. It is necessary that, day after day, its members "be what they have become," according to Augustine's remarkable intuition. They must become instruments of *communion* and by that fact instruments for the Salvation of humanity. Christian morality is not primarily a quest for personal fulfillment. It is transporting *communion* into Christ Jesus. This transporting into Christ Jesus has its demands (Gal 5:13-26).

Eternal life will be nothing more than the supreme development of this *communion*. Thomas Aquinas stated it in these very beautiful words:

---

[79]*De Patriarchis* VI, 39 (*PL* 14, 686). See B. Studer, "L'Eucaristia remissione dei peccati secondo Ambrogio di Milano," in S. Felici, *Catechesi battesimale e Reconciliazione nei Padri del IV secolo*, Rome, 1984, 65–79.

> In eternal life there is, first of all, union with God. . . . It consists
> of all the blessed in a jubilant society, and this society will be extremely
> delightful because everyone will possess all the benefits which all the
> blessed possess. Because everyone will love the other as himself and, con-
> sequently, will rejoice over the good of the other as over his own good.
> By this fact, the happiness and joy of the individual person will grow
> in proportion to its being also the joy of all.[80]

D. Communion: *always fragile, forever being put to the test*

Except perhaps for the texts linked to the tradition of Pentecost, it is
remarkable that the major documents in Scripture concerning ecclesial
koinonia (in the global sense of the word) are in one way or another conditioned by tense situations, perhaps even by conflicts which are able to
lead to splits or divisions. The clay vessels which contain the treasure are
not only individuals but also communities.

Besides, the history of the Church can be viewed, from a certain angle,
as marked by splits which can be sensed to be brewing, that can be fore-
seen and then healed, but which always leave their mark. We have examples dating from the frictions of the Greeks and the Hebrews, the
conflicts between disciples of James and Christians who had come over
from paganism, and the tensions between the Johannine communities and
others. *Communion* does not shine forth in all its splendor except on too
few occasions, even if the obstacles that are perceived in the New Testament do not necessarily indicate a break or separation. Rarely has communion been realized in its perfection on the universal plane. Here we
put our finger on the interplay between grace and freedom, likewise also
the presence—until the Day of the Son of man—of the powers of evil,
always at work, penetrating into the heart of the Christian community
as the Johannine writings which reflect what is said in Paul's letters point
out (1 John 2:18-22, 26; 4:1-5; 2 John 1:7-10; Rom 15:5; 1 Cor 1:11-12;
11:19; Gal 1:6-9; cf. Phil 2:1; 4:2). On this earth, as Augustine says, the
Church is a *corpus permixtum* and not a *corpus bipartitum*,[81] because the
limits of good and evil pass through the lives of Christians.

Today, after centuries of division, even though periodically measures
have been taken to reunite them, all Churches are not in *communion*. This
situation can no longer be explained by an enduring unwillingness to remain divided, which would be *hic et nunc* re-activated. It comes most often

---

[80]*Opusc. theol.* 2, ed. Marietti, Turin, 1954, 217.

[81]Augustine is opposed to the formula by Ticonius. See *De doctrina christiana* III, 32, 45, which
is the best known text. On the whole question of sinners in the Church, see especially F. Refoulé,
"Situation des pécheurs dans l'Église d'après saint Augustin," *Studia theologica* 8, 1954, 86–102.
But it is difficult to see clearly into Augustine's vision concerning the status of the evil which
faces the Church.

from the simple fact of prolonging or delaying decisions taken in the past which have not been abrogated by succeeding generations who sometimes are not even aware of the motives for these decisions. Besides, in the Protestant world, groups spring up without wishing to be separated from whatever is in existence, around the insight of an inspired religious individual. Furthermore, there must be a careful distinction made between communities and individuals who compose them. One is Lutheran, Anglican or Baptist because of circumstances which are often accidental and do not imply the least desire to create a schism. A person has been baptized in one particular confession and not another. And completely in good faith a person is ordinarily instinctively convinced that the truth is found in his confessional community. The communities as such, because of their history, remain canonically schismatic; their faithful are only indirectly so, by the very fact that they "belong" to them.

The state of *koinonia,* therefore, is not what it is called upon to be. Often, although it is not a question of the responsibility of Christians today, communities exist side by side, without being able and sometimes even without being willing to live an authentic *communion* among themselves. The Church is wounded by that. There is nothing which permits this wound to be considered a relative matter. In fact, even if the Church is never formally defined as *koinonia* in the New Testament, we have, nevertheless, ascertained that there is a perception of it there as the bearer and guarantor of it, and that *koinonia* belongs to its essence. There is no better way, therefore, to evaluate and gauge the state of the Church of God than to examine the state of *communion* today.

It is very obvious that ecclesial *communion* finds its profound quality in *communion* with the intimate life of God mentioned in Johannine literature and perhaps the Second Letter of Peter (2 Pet 1:4). It is a question of the sphere of grace, of what the scholastic calls *res tantum.* But this sphere is invisible, known by God alone. Augustine remarked, in an often quoted text, that many who seem to be outside of the ecclesial community are, nevertheless, on the inside, whereas many who seem to be on the inside of the ecclesial community do not really belong to it.[82] It is indeed unquestionable that, in its real depth, ecclesial *communion* goes beyond visible *koinonia.* If there are no anonymous Christians—because to be a Christian is to confess Jesus Christ as the source of Salvation—there exist those who are saved but ignorant of the fact that they are. And they belong to the *communion* of grace, which is for the Christian faith the

---

[82]*De baptismo,* V, 27, 38 (*CSEL* 51, 295): *"In illa ineffabili praescientia Dei multi qui foris videntur intus sunt et multi qui intus videntur foris sunt."* It is important to note that this sentence is drawn from a polemic treaty against the Donatists!

essential value, the great reality announced in the Gospel of God and which takes shape *jam ab Abel justo.*

In addition, because the Creator is none other than the triune God acting with "his two hands, the Word and the Spirit," according to the striking imagery of Irenaeus, and because by his Resurrection Jesus is made Lord of Creation, it would be difficult to say that, in itself, *communion* would be only for some. Every upright human being who has his conscience open to others, humbly admitting his weakness, is undoubtedly invited to it. And since there is only one God, everything urges us to believe that on a profound plane all those who adore God, faithful to their religion or to their faith are spiritually united. In the midst of a world that is more and more alien to the transcendental, there exists a solidarity among believers. This is perceived in the feeling that one experiences, for example, at the sight of a Muslim performing his prayer ritual under the sarcastic smiles of others who observe him: one feels oneself instinctively affected by this derision. On a profound plane this man at prayer and we become one.

2. But *communion* must also be visible. This visibility is necessary especially for two reasons. The first has to do with the human condition.

According to the great intuition which underlies Judeo-Christian anthropology, the individual is both turned towards his own center and oriented towards others. He achieves his identity only in what we have described as the coming together of his singularity and "others." But such an encounter wishes to become visible, perceptible, first of all, by the interested parties. Using Martin Buber's language, the *I* must perceive that the *you* is turned towards him and waits for his response. And this perception cannot be invisible. We should note that this applies even to one's relationship with God. Even if it remains invisible, we feel the need to express in an external form or ceremony, in prayer or in religious gestures our relationship with him. This is why Johannine literature suggests that the visibility of Jesus' humanity remedies this unattainable transcendence of God (John 1:18). Adding to this the particular intuition found in chapter twenty-five of Matthew (Matt 25:31-46), it makes the word "brother" the connecting link with this visibility of Jesus (1 John 4:12; 3:17).[83]

---

[83]"On this invisibility of God made "visible" in the Incarnation, see in particular Peter Chrysologus, *Homélie sur l'incarnation* I, 147 (*PL* 52, 594–595): "But because of all these facts which we have recalled, where the flame of divine love sets hearts on fire, where the rapture of God's love is poured out into all man's feelings, certain ones, their soul being wounded, wished to see God with their human eyes. How could the human gaze, as narrow as it is, understand God, whom the world cannot contain? But the code of love does not consider what love can be, what it must and can do. Love is unaware of judgment, it lacks reason, it is not conscious of limits. Love does not let itself be comforted by impossibility, it does not admit that difficulty is a remedy. Love, if it does not attain the object of its desires, destroys the one who loves, and that is why it goes wherever it is carried away, not where it should go. Love gives rise to desire, is inflamed with

There is another reason why the *communion* of Christians must necessarily become visible: the will of Christ, in the form in which it is expressed in John's Gospel (John 17:21-23). And this call for unity is echoed throughout all of the apostolic literature (cf. Rom 15:5; 1 Cor 1:10-16; 2 Cor 13:11; Phil 2:2; 4:2). It is very obvious that Christian witness as such (the *martyria*) is tied to the visible unity of the disciples of Christ. Because how can one announce *truly* and in a credible way the Gospel of reconciliation in Jesus Christ while presenting oneself to the world as disciples of Christ who are divided among themselves and who have put up new barriers? But what is at stake here is not limited to the missionary impact of the message. It is essentially a question of being what one has been called to be, of doing what is necessary so that the work of God has the quality that it should have, to glorify the Father by manifesting the authentic nature of his plan, of giving Salvation its full dimension.

We said earlier that Johannine literature,[84] the Epistle to the Ephesians,[85] and even other Pauline texts, are marked, even conditioned, by the existence of tensions which were apparent here and there, right from the beginning. The Acts of the Apostles shows how much this type of situation, in some way, was part of the evangelization process. Subsequently, the Johannine community will see some of its members leave its communion (cf. 1 John 2:18), and it even seems that the reactions caused by the "enthusiastic" groups soon caused some splits.[86] Nevertheless, the Gospel for-

---

fervor, its fervor takes it beyond what is granted to it. What good is it to insist? It is impossible not to see what it loves; that is why all the saints judged everything they had gotten as worthless, if they did not see the Lord."

On the visibility of God in fraternal love, see Augustine *Sur l'évangile de Jean* 17, 7-9 (*CCL* 36, 174-175): "Here is what you are told: Love God. If you say to me: Show me the one whom I must love, what will I answer, if not what Saint John says: Has no one ever seen God? But do not imagine that you are excluded from the life of God! Saint John tells us: God is love, and the one who lives in love lives in God. Therefore, love your neighbor, look inside yourself to see where this love of neighbor comes from; there you will see God, in the measure in which that it possible for you."

[84]See R. E. Brown, *The Community of the Beloved Disciple: the Life, Loves and Hates of an Individual Church in New Testament Times*, New York, 1980. See also Pheme Perkins, "Koinonia in 1 John 1:3-7, the Social Context of Division in the Johannine Letter," *CBQ* 45, 1983, 631-641.

[85]The position of H. K Weizsacker, *Das apostolische Zeitalter*, Tübingen, 1886, is well known (especially 560-565) which is thinking about a rivalry with the Johannine communities. See also H. Chadwick, "Das Absicht des Epheserbriefes," *ZNW* 51, 1960, 145-154.

[86]See Ernst Käsemann, *Essais exégétiques*, 174-198, 214-226. R. E. Brown, in *The Churches the Apostles Left behind*, New York, 1984, 146-148, presents a very detailed review of the ruptures brought about by doctrinal differences during the first decades of the history of the Church. He writes: "It cannot be proved that one of the Churches that I presented has broken *koinonia* or communion with another. Neither is it likely that the New Testament Churches of the sub-apostolic period had any sense of *koinonia* among Christians and had been conventicles closed in on themselves, each one going its own way. Paul is eloquent on the importance of *koinonia* and in the Pauline heritage concern for Christian unity is visible in Luke/Acts and in the letter to the Ephesians. Peter is a connecting figure in the New Testament and the concept of People

bids hiding behind these facts to justify the actual division which existed or to proclaim that ecclesial unity could only be eschatological. Fidelity to the Spirit of Pentecost demands that we not be content to "accommodate divisions," to "learn to live with them." It wishes that, while knowing that on this earth *koinonia* will always remain imperfect and fragile, Christians will do the impossible to bring about the visible unity of the Body of Christ.

3. Ecclesial *communion* is expressed both in a visible way and is built deeply in the Church's act, par excellence, which is the Eucharistic celebration. This special relationship between the Eucharist and visible *communion* holds up for several reasons that are useful to mention, even at the risk of repeating some things already said, but probing more deeply into them.

At the heart of Eucharistic *communion* is, evidently, the local community which celebrates the Memorial. It is there, in the sharing of the one bread and cup, that those who participate find themselves absorbed into the one and indivisible Body of the Lord which is *truly* given to them. No matter what age, social condition, sect, race or culture, men as well as women, repentant sinners as well as holy people, clerics as well as lay people, rivals as well as allies in civil life, they form *in truth* only one single Body, everyone enclosed in the power of reconciliation of the one whose Death on the Cross and Resurrection "they announce" (1 Cor 11:26). Their gathering together—the celebration—not only "around" Christ Jesus but "in him" is then the most profound expression possible of their *koinonia* both with the Lord and each other. It makes it, in the strictest sense possible, visible and tangible.

But, depending on its history and the fact that there is no canonical break with them, and on condition that they can recognize their own faith in what it does and proclaims at its Eucharistic celebration, this community signifies also its *communion* with other communities which, elsewhere in the world, celebrate the very same Eucharist. Besides, it makes men-

---

of God in Peter's first letter requires a collective understanding of Christianity. In spite of all its individualism the fourth gospel speaks of the other sheep which do not belong to this flock and of Jesus' desire that they all be one. Matthew has a vision of the Church and extends the horizon of Christianity to all nations. The greatest part of the New Testament was written before the great breaks in *koinonia,* revealed during the second century, and so the diversity attested to in the New Testament could not be used to justify Christian division" (147). It states precisely: "Certainly there was a time when Peter, Paul and James were not in agreement, but these differences as far as can be determined, did not cause a break in *koinonia.* Towards the end of the first century, however, Christian groups resisted vehemently developments which appeared in other groups and different points of view on important points became truly contradictory. In my opinion, it is in this way that the major breaks in *koinonia* appeared, for example in the Johannine community, as 1 John 2:19 certifies. The second century saw a struggle to determine which one of these contradictory visions preserved the apostolic understanding and which one distorts it in an important way" (*ibid.,* note 201).

tion of it, in a global way, in its Canon (Anaphora). This *communion* has a much greater visibility when the presider at the Eucharistic celebration invites the minister of another community, who is passing through, to concelebrate with him. This visible *communion* is also expressed on a daily basis, although not as readily perceived, when a Christian from one community participates in the celebration at another local Church without feeling that he or she is "another." At every Eucharist he or she is "at home."

This geographical *communion* itself is contained within a more unifying, more comprehensive *communion*. It is the one which spans history, from the first apostolic Eucharist to those which will be celebrated on the last days preceding the Parousia of the Son of Man. Because if the community which celebrates the Memorial is today, *hic et nunc,* in a communion of faith and structure with the apostolic Church, its Eucharist is none other than that of the Apostles, due to the fact that there is found in it—with the obvious difference of rites—what they said, did and wished to transmit. Mentioning Apostles, martyrs and saints in the Anaphora (Canon) makes this link explicit.

This explains the richness of the expression: "the Church is Eucharistic." It relates, in an inseparable way, to the profound being of the Church of God and the visible expression of ecclesial *koinonia*. The Fathers of the early centuries, still followed today by the Churches said to be in the "catholic tradition," refuse for this reason any Eucharistic celebration which would bring together members of Churches which are canonically or explicitly divided. There is a falsehood—which even affects the truthfulness of the sacrament of the Lord, often described as a "lack of recognition of the Body" (cf. 1 Cor 11:29) in expressing visibly a *communion* which does not exist. The Eucharistic expression, in a visible form of *koinonia* must, the early Fathers believe, take as its material the concrete situation of this *koinonia*. The sacrament of the Church is valid only if it is not cut off from the ecclesial reality.

Along this same line, it is illuminating to note how even the link with Israel that received the Covenant—which belongs to the ecclesial reality—is certified by the Eucharist. Something from the Jewish Memorial of the Passover is infused into the Memorial of the Lord: the intense straining towards the great Day of God, an historical term. The expectation of the People of God passes over to that of the Eucharistic community. It is not by chance that in several Anaphora (Canons) the patriarchs are named and the Old Testament is read in the Eucharistic celebration.[87] In this way

[87]This is a matter that we have often pointed out. See in particular J.-M. R. Tillard, "L'Eucharistie sacrement de l'Église communion," *Initiation à la pratique de la théologie,* t. III, Paris, 1983, 437–463 (442–443).

communion with Israel is expressed—in its full reality—a profound and fundamental but imperfect *communion.*[88]

In spite of the will to distinguish itself from the Jewish faith—evident in Johannine literature (John 6:4; 7:2; 15:25) and in the Letter to the Hebrews (8:5, 7, 13; 9:10; 10:1, 9), clarified perhaps in Revelation (2:9; 3:9), brought up at the end of Acts (28:28)—this *communion* with the old trunk and its roots has a very special character. Because it manifests the consciousness of a creative continuity in the plan of God. Sometimes there is a temptation to speak, analogically, of a "succession" in the Revelation to Israel, somewhat as we speak, in the theological sense, of a "succession" of Churches and of their ministers in apostolic teaching. When the Paul we find in Acts is explaining to governor Felix: "It is according to the Way which they [the accusing Jews] describe as a sect that I worship the God of my ancestors, retaining my belief in all that the Law contains and in what is written in the Prophets" (Acts 24:14), he expresses in an excellent way this profound quality found in *communion.* The fact of going beyond this, which Christ Jesus brings about, is not a break. It is a flourishing, a blossoming forth. The short sentence by Paul in Romans: "All Israel will be saved" (Rom 11:26), can express the thoroughness of this continuity. It is like a "succession" beginning with the appointment of the patriarchs (which implies all the rest of the holy ones who were appointed) to Christ Jesus and all of the real Israel. This Israel spoken of is not the sociological and political Israel (which includes the irreligious) but *all the remaining elect,* the one which is already in the Church (with the Judeo-Christians) and the one which has not yet permitted itself to be united by the Word of Christ Jesus, but will one day perhaps be submissive to the faith. This essential *communion* is the one which the Eucharist expresses.

The Eucharist signifies, therefore, the authentic catholicity of a *communion.* It shows the essential quality of it as well as the universality. In fact, it is not simply a question of a *communion* among all the nations called to enter into Salvation. Catholicity expresses the entrance of this totality of nations into the gift given to the Israel of the Covenant. It is *communion* of the pagans privileged to share in the suffering of the People of Abraham. The *Ekklesia* which celebrates the Eucharist is the commu-

---

[88]On this question concerning relations between the Church and Israel, J. A. Fitzmyer, *The Gospel according to Luke (I-IX),* New York, 1981, 9-10; Schuyler Brown, *A Historical Introduction to the New Testament,* Oxford, 1984 (especially chapter V); R. E. Brown, *The Churches the Apostles Left Behind,* 22-27, 115-116; P. Grelot, "Le cantique de Siméon," *RB* 93, 1986, 481-509. For the interpretation of Rom 11:25-32, see F. Refoulé, *Et ainsi tout Israël sera sauvé,* coll. "Lectio divina," 117, Paris, 1984 (to be compared with the very different views of Arthur Petrie, *The Regathering of Israel,* New York, 1967, a little book to popularize this, but which is an interesting witness of views shared by most Christians). Concerning the vision of the New Testament in regard to the cultural realities of Israel, see C. F. D. Moule, *op. cit.*

nity arisen from the fact that in Jesus Christ the pagans (outside the Promise) have been admitted to the *communion* of the People of Hope and of the Covenant.

4. There is, therefore, full and perfect visible *communion,* the kind that Christ wills, only where it is possible to assemble an authentic Eucharistic *congregation.* What we have stated about *communion* with Israel, even as far as the Eucharist is concerned, already shows that *communion* allows for degrees, and none of these could be eliminated. Together they make up the ecclesial universe. This universe—completely absorbed into God's fidelity—certainly has its center and fullness, made visible, in the Eucharistic *koinonia,* the place of the authentic manifestation of the divine plan. But it is not a question of "all or nothing." The Eucharist forms a *communion* already given but which has not yet been sealed. This center of fullness and truth is surrounded by zones of more or less majestic *communion.* What is important, especially today, is to give a visible expression to these zones, thereby showing how, although it is by their own errors that Christians have broken *communion,* nevertheless—by the grace of God—the basis on which they can always reestablish it remains present in each one of their divided communities. They are still brothers and sisters "in Christ." It even happens that what separates them is so tenuous that, as is the case with the Orthodox and Catholic Churches, each one "recognizes" in the other, to all intents and purposes, its own identity (faith, Eucharist, ministry, sacraments, and evangelical ethics).

All these zones of *communion,* more or less extensive or deep, are bound together by one baptism (celebrated according to apostolic tradition) which seals the acceptance of the one *kerygma.* Communities become separated when they stray from the explicit meaning of the doctrinal content of this *kerygma.* They do not have the same propositions about God and the absolutes of faith. However, they all are in agreement on the essential point that God offers Salvation in Jesus Christ, that he makes a proposition of grace to humanity, and that by accepting it in the "yes" of baptism, a new meaning is given to humanity, giving it an opening into the Kingdom. It is regrettable that this limited *communion,* but one that is fundamental and already sacramental, is made visible so seldom. The visible *communion* of the Eucharist is based on it, as Justin has already testified.[89]

Among the zones of *communion* thereby bound together, is one of great intensity, *communion* in the highest witness of martyrdom. We are speaking, of course, of those men and women who, in order to show an ex-

---

[89]"We call this Eucharistic food and no one can partake of it if he does not believe in the truth of our doctrine, if he he has not received the bath for the remission of sins and rebirth" (*Apologie* I, 66). Concerning the "yes" of faith see J.-M. R. Tillard, "Pluralisme théologique et mystère de l'Église," *Concilium* 191, 1984, 109–124 (119–123).

plicit fidelity to Christ, do not hesitate to submit to death. Today even, in prisons both in the East and in the West, in concentration camps, Christians of every denomination are suffering for having refused to sacrifice to false gods by playing tricks with the Gospel. They confess, in this way, that for them—and their communities—fidelity to Christ wins out over everything else, even over the most precious good of all, life itself. This visible *communion,* reaching the greatest intensity of existence is, outside of the Eucharistic celebration, the most authentic manifestation of the bond which, in spite of everything, continues to unite those who have been baptized. No community would dream of ex-communicating a martyr of another belief. The respect they had in the early centuries is well known—testified to in the writings of Cyprian and Hippolytus[90]—for "those who professed the faith" after returning from captivity. And if these Christians remain faithful to the point of martyrdom, it is not in spite of their community but thanks to it. It is in it that they have nourished their faith and deepened their sense of what the gospel demands. How deeply regrettable is it that Churches do not make the names of their martyrs known! According to a remark made by an orthodox friend, being tortured because of Christ and dying because of the Gospel gives one the right of entry "into the communion of saints in heaven," where there is no longer any division possible.

To this communion of martyrdom can be linked the often courageous and difficult involvement of many Christians in undertakings which have as their goal to change humanity into the-one-which-God-wills. It is certainly difficult to discern clearly the precise impact of faith on motives which compel Christians to act. Many influences enter into play. However, it is important to note a Christian conscience emerging on major questions.

5. Clearer than *communion* as a motive for action is *communion* in prayer which constitutes one of the most significant zones of *koinonia* around the Eucharist. Because in common prayer—even if it is not said in common—it is the soul of the Church which is expressed.

Augustine's remark about the prayer of "schismatics" is well known:[91] since they also are capable of saying the Our Father, they remain within

---

[90]We allude to the mysterious text of *Tradition apostolique* 9 concerning "confessors": "If a confessor has been arrested for the name of the Lord, they will not impose hands on him for the diaconate or for priesthood, because he possesses the honor of priesthood by his confession. But if he is appointed bishop, hands are imposed on him. But if there is a confessor who has not been arrested nor put in prison, nor condemned to any other punishment, but who has on occasion been ridiculed for the name of Our Lord and punished with a domestic correction, if he has confessed [his faith], let hands be imposed on him for any order of which he is worthy."

[91]It is a question of the sermon on Psalm 32 (*CCL* 38, 272-273): "My brothers, we exhort you very vigorously to the practice of charity not only towards yourselves, but also towards those

the ecclesial brotherhood despite the broken bonds and what separates them from the unbreakable unity of the Eucharist. They have broken with the community, but they certify their relationship to the Father. Here the strict logic of the Johannine letter, by force of circumstances, urging an affirmation that cutting oneself off from the community and from those responsible for it amounts to cutting oneself off from God (1 John 1:3-7), must be slightly modified.[92] There is a will to pray to God among those, and their honesty cannot be questioned who separate themselves because they believe that they are forced by their conscience to do so, and especially among those men and women who are born in the faith in communities already schismatic, centuries after the break. And everything urges us to believe that God, in the mercy-and-fidelity which defines his attitude towards his own, responds to their prayer.

In fact, all Christian communities pray to and praise the God and Father of the Lord Jesus Christ. And even when they do not pray together and in a same location for some reason, ecumenical or other, their prayer is substantially the same, even as far as the words which are used. We have mentioned the Our Father, "a prayer received from the Lord" as stated in the liturgies. What should be added to it is the old prayer in the psalms linking Christians to the most distant roots of their faith. Moreover, the contents of the prayers of intercession are identical everywhere, using different formulas but expressing the same understanding of the reality of the relationship between Christ and believers, the same will that the Kingdom of God will come. And in all beliefs there is a conviction about the essential role of this prayer, especially in difficult situations. The witness of several communities living under atheistic regimes, Ortho-

---

who are outside; whether they are still pagans, not yet believing in Christ, or whether they are separated from us, recognizing the same head but being cut off from the body. Whether one wills it or not they are our brothers. They would cease to be our brothers if they ceased to say: Our Father. The prophet said about some of them: To those who say to you: 'You are not our brothers,' answer: 'You are our brothers.' About whom was he able to say that? Would it be pagans? No, because we do not say that they are our brothers, according to the Scriptures and the language of the Church. Was he speaking of the Jews, who did not believe in Christ? Read Saint Paul, and you will see that the word 'brothers,' when the Apostle uses only that, only Christians can be understood by it. . . . But you, why do you judge your brother? And you, why do you despise your brother? And in another passage: You commit injustice and fraud, and that against your brothers! The Donatists who state: 'You are not our brothers' treat us, therefore, as pagans. That is why they wish to rebaptize us, because they declare that we do not have what they are giving to us. Their error flows from this, to deny that we are their brothers. But why did the prophet tell us, You will answer them: 'You are our brothers,' if not because we recognize in them the baptism which we will not repeat? They, therefore, by not recognizing our baptism, deny that we are their brothers; we, by not repeating it over them, but by recognizing ours, we say to them: 'You are our brothers.' They will say: 'What are you asking of us?' 'What do you want of us?' Let us answer: 'You are our brothers.' They will say: 'Leave us alone, we have nothing to do with you.' But we, we have something to do with you: we confess one single Christ, we must be in one single body, under one single head."

[92] See R. E. Brown, *The Epistles of John*, 184–187, 691–693.

dox and Catholic as well as Protestant and Evangelical, shows that several among them can survive only because of this prayer.[93]

Although non-sacramental in the strict sense, this *communion* of prayer is not something secondary or simply tangential to the ecclesial being. It is impossible, ecclesiologically, not to give it the importance that it deserves. The temptation today, even among ecumenists, is not to show any interest in it except when it is a question of a prayer made in common *hic et nunc.* Then they speak of an "event of grace." In our eyes it is infinitely more significant that for such a long time, on both sides of the walls of division, praising God and interceding in faith have never stopped. An authentic bond of *koinonia,* based on the most specific expression of the Christian faith, has, therefore, never been cut. Canonical breaks have not gotten the better of the Spirit.

6. There exists another zone of *communion,* closely linked to what we have just presented. Although it has been and remains in several places a cause of tension and conflict, accentuating again the scandal caused by division, the ardent desire to spread the Gospel is a common point in all Christian confessions. Even when it is profaned by proselytism and dreams of power, it always arises from the decision to be faithful to the will of Christ Jesus.

This universal presence of the missionary undertaking appears, therefore, as a profound *communion* in obedience to the Gospel of God. And the fact that it has always been one of the major concerns of the Churches, and has never diminished, is itself ecclesiologically also of great importance. The division of Christians has weakened the ecclesial witness, but it has never induced the Churches to stop announcing the Gospel of Salvation. That signifies that the powerful dynamism which endures since the Church during the time of the Acts of the Apostles, with its original enthusiasm, despite the barriers which have been erected, urges communities to put the concern for the Lordship of Christ over all of humanity at the very heart of its way of life. It forms one of the essential elements of *communion* with the God as it found in the Gospel. If "horizontal" unity is broken among the Churches, they remain, however, "one" in this fidelity to the *same* will of the *same* Lord Jesus Christ. They have not broken with this other major component of ecclesial *koinonia.*

We are again faced, simultaneously, with one of the greatest signs that there is no absolute break in unity and with one of the greatest proofs of the absurdity of division. Unanimous in their obedience to the will of the Lord that the Gospel be preached to the ends of the earth and until

---

[93]It is true that acts of witness come to us through channels which are often stamped with a political intention opposed to the regimes in question. Yet their unanimity militates in favor of their essential objectivity.

the end of time, if Churches do not spread division itself, they are at least responsible for the sad situation caused by it. What they display is a contrary witness, and all the while wishing to be obedient to it. . . .

7. Within this perspective, division of the Christian world into Churches which are putting up barriers among themselves, not only affective but canonical ones by which they *ex-communicate* one another, appears in its true light. The break is located within a basic unity, a gift of the Spirit, their common deep-rootedness in the mystery of God, which does not tear apart communities, ex-communicating them from one another. This common rooting in the mystery of God is the fruit of the fidelity and mercy of the God of faith. For the Roman Catholic Church, convinced that it has remained in a straight line from the apostolic community, it is a question of much more than scattered elements which would remain as drifting pieces and would continue to be somewhat active because of the pressure of some acquired habits. Rather than using the classic image of the tree whose branches have been cut off during the storms of history and continue to become green because of the sap still flowing—the old trunk still standing upright with all the force of its original sap—another image is preferable. It is the one of the river whose strong current flows along at great speed right from its source—the life-giving water of the Spirit—but which, overflowing its banks gradually losing its force all along the banks which it certainly fertilizes although without its original strength.

The assertion, which we will have to justify later, according to which the Church "lives" in the (Roman) Catholic Church, although it is not confined to its boundaries, is understood in this light. The assertion is that the (Roman) Catholic Church, because it preserves intact revealed truth and all the means to achieve Salvation, is the one where the river flows with its greatest force. In other words, the fact is that there alone the Church of God exists on this earth with all its strength and fullness. And the thinking is not so much in regards to the holiness of the members taken individually—which finds eminent witnesses elsewhere—than to the abundant means[94] and institutions of Salvation. The declaration made here is that in the (Roman) Catholic Church there exists, in spite of everything,[95] the totality of what God has offered to believers for their Salvation in Jesus Christ, for the full ecclesiality of their community and its visible communion with the other communities. But outside of the (Roman) Catholic Church is not an ecclesial void. Such is the present situation. We said earlier that the responsibility of Christians today was only

[94]We translate in this way the latin expression *ea quae sunt ad finem,* but the translation does not render the exact sense of the formula. It is a question of everything which contributes to make the Church what God wishes it to be.

[95]Vatican II did not hesitate to speak of *reformatio* (*Unitatis redintegratio,* 4, 6).

slightly implied in this division as it exists presently. The responsibility resides in the effort required to put an end to the scandal of it. Visible *communion* has become a goal to aim at. But our century is witness to the *communion* of Christians in another strong evangelical movement. It shows precisely the necessity to prepare this visible unity. This is where Hope shines forth! Human weakness remains under the control of the grace of the Spirit of Pentecost. . . .[96]

II. Church of God, "Musterion" (EP 3, 6), Divine "Communion"

What we have just discussed is valuable. But it must be examined thoroughly. To this end, the notion of *communion* must be compared with other key notions in the Scriptures. An ecclesiology which aims to understand the nature of the Church as thoroughly as possible can ill afford to ignore—despite doubts concerning their origin—the first chapters of the Letter to the Ephesians. So much more so because this epistle probably belongs to the post-apostolic generation and, thereby, becomes the witness of a faith which has started to reflect quite fully on its own implications. Beyond this, the relationships with Johannine literature—which seem more and more clear—lead us to believe that this reflection is related to questions raised about the nature of ecclesial unity, undoubtedly brought about by the appearance of the first splits.[97] Chapter four of this letter, as well as chapter seventeen of John's Gospel indicate, in fact, that this unity is already jeopardized. Perhaps this is the reason why the author makes an effort to present the Church of God in its universal dimension, its absolute *catholicity*[98] which transcends all differences, and does not restrict its attention to the situation of a local Church. The Church, as it is understood in this text, assumes and reconciles human diversity.

+ 1. This Letter to the Ephesians sees an essential link between *mystery* (Eph 1:9-10; 3:3-10 compared with Col 1:26-27 and clarified in Rom 16:25-26; 1 Cor 2:7-9) and the Church of God. All that is necessary to be convinced of this is to read its first chapters. For what is the *musterion* "revealed through the Spirit to his apostles and prophets" (3:5)? The author sums it up this way: "The pagans now share the same inheritance

---

[96]And it is important to note that this ecumenical movement rose out of the orthodox and protestant Churches, proof that the Spirit is working in them.

[97]See note 85.

[98]See the fine study by J. A. Robinson, *St. Paul's Epistle to the Ephesians,* London, 1922, 7, 14, 27, 75, 77, 78, 101, 102, 183, and F. F. Bruce, *The Epistles to the Colossians, to Philemon and to the Ephesians,* coll. "New International Commentary on the New Testament," Grand Rapids, 1984, 237–240.

(*sunklèronoma*), they are parts of the same body (*sunsoma*), and the same promise has been made to them (*summetocha*) in Jesus Christ, through the gospel'' (3:6). This is also the content of the gospel announcement (3:8-9). Several verses earlier, in a passage in which the Fathers of the great Tradition recognize one of the most important declarations of the New Testament about the nature of the Church, it was stated:

> But now in Christ Jesus, you who used to be so far apart from us have been brought very close by the blood of Christ. For he is the peace between us, and has made the two into one and broken down the barrier which used to keep them apart, actually destroying in his own person the hostility caused by the rules and decrees of the Law. This was to create one single New Man in himself out of the two of them, and by restoring peace through the cross, to unite them both in a single Body and reconcile them with God. In his own person he killed the hostility. Later he came to bring the good news of peace, peace to you who were far away and peace to those who were near at hand. Through him, both of us have in the Spirit our way to come to the Father.
>
> So you are no longer aliens or foreign visitors; you are citizens like all the saints, and part of God's household. You are part of a building which has the apostles and prophets for its foundations, and Christ Jesus himself for its main cornerstone. As every structure is aligned on him, all grow into one holy temple in the Lord; and you, too, in him are being built into a house where God lives, in the Spirit (2:13-22).

It is a question of the same reality.

The major themes of People (aliens, fellow-citizens), family of God, Temple, New Man, Covenant, Body of Christ—all those which describe the Church—merge together here, although that of Body stands out as the most central one, when these lines are put back into their context,[99] because the epistle organizes the vision of the Church, the Body of Christ, as "the fullness of the one who fills the whole creation" (1:23), "the Savior of his whole Body" (5:23). The link between the Body of Christ and *mystery* in this résumé gets to the heart of the entire vision contained in the letter: "There is one Body, one Spirit, just as you were all called into one and the same hope when you were called. There is one Lord, one faith, one baptism, and one God who is Father of all, over all, through all and within all" (4:3-6). In this perspective, the Church of God appears as the fulfillment of the *mystery,* in other words, the accomplishment in Jesus of the eternal design which forms the course of revelation and whose purpose is to join humanity together again, to reunite the universe. The Church belongs, therefore, as we said earlier, to the very reality of the *humanity-according-to-God.*

[99] See Markus Barth, *Ephesians 1-3,* coll. "The Anchor Bible," New York, 1980, 199, 4. See Id., *Ephesians 4-6,* 462–472.

2. In order to really understand the nature of the Church of God, it is not sufficient to speak of a joining together again or of a reuniting. The Letter to the Ephesians demands that we focus as much attention on the human situation which rectifies this reunification as on this reunification considered by itself. It is a question, in fact, of a work of God but with its basis in the human drama. Humanity is divided, cut off by a wall, a *mesotoichon* (2:14), which is nothing other than hatred. The term indicates that this division is at work within the walls of the same house. This is the human tragedy from the time of the story of Cain and Abel. And the division of humanity, which the Jews put into two blocks, the People and the pagans, only helps to exacerbate this spiteful situation. In its own way, the law itself shows the breaking up of the world into two portions, one of which is declared cut off from the blessings of God. What was the fruit of divine love for the chosen people has become, by the almost compulsive power of hatred, an occasion for contempt in regard to peoples who are "aliens with no part in the covenant with the Promise" (2:12). The word which we use to translate hatred (*echthra*), is to be taken in its strongest sense.[100] It signifies a hatred which is filled with intolerance, falsehood, always looking for an occasion for a quarrel, the refusal to recognize anything kind in the other person, segregation, hostility, war, and the will for revenge. It is on this course—the one where the Bible sees the consequence of human sin and its being put into action—that is woven the history of a world which goes from war to war and builds its peace only on the balance of fear. It is remarkable that the Letter to the Ephesians denounces this hatred between the two portions of humanity (2:14) before speaking of the hatred of humanity itself for God (2:16; cf. Col 1:21; Rom 8:7). The first is like the *sacramentum,* the symbol of the second.

The mystery whose fulfillment is the Church, in Christ, produces, therefore, the joining together again of humanity by the destruction and the abolition of hatred. It comes about historically on the Cross: "He reconciled them both [the two parts which were enemies] in a single Body with God, through the Cross. In his own person he killed the hatred" (2:16). Of what was divided, Christ on the Cross "makes the two into one" (2:14); of what was a humanity torn apart, he "creates one single New Man" (2:15). What was separated, he "reconciles" (2:16); what was burning with hostility, he "pacifies" (2:17). From the humanity which is living out its drama he makes the humanity-which-God-wills; a People in which we no longer speak of aliens or foreign visitors, a city in which all are fellow-citizens, a family of God which is no longer broken, a structure in which

---

[100]And (despite the suggestion by E. Haupt, *Der Brief an die Epheser*) we do not agree that there is any interpolation there, falsifying the general sense of the passage.

all form one house of God in the Spirit" (2:22), one single Body. What is the Church of God? The extent of the humanity where, by the Blood of Christ, which was *far apart*—in the strong sense that the bond which hatred gives to this term—has become *very close* (2:13).

But then, to become through the Spirit at baptism a member of the Body of Christ and to become identified with him through the Eucharist, is to enter into the dynamism of a reconciliation which wishes to be put into action continually, to win the entire world so that the eternal design of the Father can be effected in it since this eternal design embraces every divine work. Although the term *koinonia* is not used in this context, putting together the emphases which concern unity (2:14, 15, 16, 21, 22) and interruptions which took place during the reconciliation process permits, however, a better understanding of the fundamental basis of ecclesial *communion. Communion* is not the same as a gathering together of friends. It is something very different. It is a coming together in Christ of men and women who have been reconciled. It is *communion* in the victory over hatred *(echthra)*. This victory is achieved by the Cross of Christ. However, in the individual and in the world there are forces of evil which do not cease to stir up everything, working even in the community where they "toss" them one way and another, and wish them to be carried along by every kind of "doctrine" (4:14). That explains why every break in unity in the ecclesial Body represents an insult to the power of the Cross and to the action of the Spirit who is always at work. By this fact, division touches the *musterion*. Therefore, in no way should one be a part of it.

3. Read in the light of *mystery*, ecclesial *communion* proves to be the bearer of God's desire. The reunification of the universe, whose incorporation of Jews and pagans into one single Body of Christ (4:12) represents both the leaven and the substance, must *already* change history. If, therefore, the Church is the fact of making the Gospel of God an actuality, and through it the eternal *musterion*, the fate of the world finds its basis in baptism. The Letter to the Ephesians makes this clear.

The Church in this world is nothing more than the concrete portion of humanity inscribed into the sphere of reconciliation opened up by the Cross. Viewed from an historical perspective it proves to be the work of the Spirit taking human tragedy and immersing it in the power of *communion* and the peace of the Cross so that, in spite of "the Sovereignties and the Powers who originate the darkness in this world, the spiritual army of evil in the heavens" (6:12), the design of the Father will come to fruition. In another context, the Gospel of John spoke of the gathering together in unity "the scattered children of God" by the forces of evil (John 11:51).

It is there that the Christian commitment finds its specific meaning. And the call to "preserve the unity of the Spirit by the bond of peace" (4:3), which puts together the allusion to "the unity in our faith and in our knowledge of the Son of God" (4:13) by a life "in an authentic love" (4:15) and mutual forgiveness (4:32), assumes its true dimension.

It is an expression of the doxology. Continually "the praise of the glory" of the Father (1:14), "the glory [of the Father] in the Church" (3:21), "the action of grace in God the Father" (5:20) are expressed by the author. The Church exists so that the glory of God may shine forth, but in a humanity founded on reconciliation and peace. The glory of God and fervent involvement for the success of his plan, praise of the glory of the Father and a very costly action in order to join humanity together again, are the two inseparable sides of the coin of anxiety that the Church faces. This anxiety expresses its being. Here, although the Letter to the Ephesians does not depend on this language, is where the interior depth of ecclesial communion is revealed.

Communion is *before God,* in fact, both supreme grace and glory to shine forth, *charis* received and *doxa* to be spread; victory over hatred and *Agape* to be proclaimed. In brief, it is a *sacramentum* of the *mystery* eternally hidden in the secret of God. The Church is here on earth the one which cannot divide its involvement for the reconciliation of humanity—which is its mission, by virtue of its *communion* with the living God—from the continual quest for the glory of God. According to the assertion by Irenaeus, "the glory of God is man as a living person and the life of man is the vision of God: if the revelation of God in creation already gives life to all creatures who live on the earth, how much more does the manifestation of the Father by the Word give life to those who see God."[101] To work for a *living* humanity—which possesses the good things of life which are, according to Scripture, brotherhood and peace—is certainly to work for the glory of God, whether one knows it or not. But the Church must be aware of the fact that its involvement reaches its full completion only if it is done *before God.* This is what the Orthodox call "the liturgy behind the Liturgy." It must be done in the world, *before God.*

4. It is necessary to understand the full significance of this term *before God.* It goes beyond involvement for the sake of the brotherhood that we have just described. It is all embracing. And by it the Church is already putting into practice in this world its eschatological being. Because it is *already* called to live within the consciousness of the deep bond which makes everything a *communion* with God. In fact, it is not an already given reality that, subsequently, God would assume by uniting himself with it. The Church is not an appendix added to the glory of the creative

---

[101]*Adv. Haer.* IV, 20, 7.

work. It is this creative work as it is immersed in the vitality of mercy, fidelity and tenderness which are attributes of God. Irenaeus said it perfectly in his presentation of "summing up." With the Fathers it must be affirmed that when the Church in this world stands *before God,* in praise and obedience, contemplating him in a clouded but real way that faith allows and by serving him, then the Church is already within the final act of its life, in *communion* with eternal life *in Christo.* In order to be convinced of this the Johannine texts must be carefully examined.

Johannine literature is not acquainted with the notion of *musterion.* However, if we compare this literature with its vision of *communion,* then the relationship of the Church with the very being of God takes on a new dimension. In fact, the reality which establishes *communion* is not simply Salvation as it is received *hic et nunc,* nor as eternally willed by the Father. It is this Salvation as accomplished in and by the *communion* of the Father, Son and Spirit. Because if the Son is the one whose eternal being consists in living "turned towards the Father" (1:2), he is also the one whose earthly existence, oriented towards the accomplishment of the Father's will, has been only to serve the salvific design of the Father (therefore, of the *mystery,* as the Letter to the Ephesians states) through the power of the Spirit. Christians have fraternal *communion* (1 John 1:3, 6-7)[102] because all share what has been within the *economy* of Salvation the full *communion* of Christ Jesus in the will of the Father, this *communion* itself rooted in the eternal "circumincession" of the Father and the Son. Ecclesial *communion* expresses, therefore, an association with the completeness of the divine *koinonia.* This completeness implies both the eternal relationship of the Father and the Son—the latter "receiving" and accepting everything that the Father is and wills, hence also, the *mystery* "kept secret for endless ages" (Rom 16:25)—and the relationship of obedience between the Father and the Son incarnate—the latter having as food only "to do the will of the one who sent [him] and to complete his work" (John 4:34). The Church is *before* God by *communicating* with the Being and the attitude of the Son *before* the Father.

So, examining carefully the notion of *mystery* identified in the content of the Gospel of God, what we have discovered about the nature of the Church appears in all its richness. The *communion* of Christians is inseparable from that of the Father, Son and Spirit. Its total ecclesial reality, being and action, is understood only in this light. The mission of the Church of God on earth is itself nothing else but the passage into the Body, the obedience of the Head, of the Son incarnate devoted to the accomplishment of the eternal *mystery* which is the design of God. And this obedience has "glorified" the Father (John 17:4; 13:31-32; 14:13).

---

[102]Here the expression *koinonian echein* signifies preserving *communion,* but as a good always *received.*

Chapter seventeen of John's gospel—which speaks, not of having *koinonia* but of *being* one *hen einai*—must in this perspective, be considered as the major revealed text about the inner depth of the *communion* which is the Church of God. It is so much more possible that the author puts these words on Jesus' lips for the very precise purpose of reminding his community, tempted to split up, not only of the price paid but the deeprootedness and the ultimate consequences of unity (*hen einai*).[103] This unity does not consist simply of a bond of love among the disciples of Christ Jesus,[104] even less of a solidarity that rests on the fidelity of all to the teachings of the Master. The idea expressed in the Qumran texts by the Hebrew term *yadah* underlies the Johannine thought:[105] it is a question of a very concrete communion, based on the presence all persons of one and the same reality. For the Johannine Gospel, unity of the disciples has its source only in God and can be derived only from the Father. It originates in the relationship of immanence which is divine life. We read, in fact, "that they are one as (*kathôs*) we are one" (17:11), "they do not belong to the world as (*kathôs*) I do not belong to the world" (17:14, 16), "as (*kathôs*) you sent me I send them" (17:18), "that all may be one as (*kathôs*) you, Father, are in me and I am in you" (17:21), "that they may be one as (*kathôs*) we are one" (17:23), "with me in them as (*kathôs*) you in me" (17:23). But it is not by chance that the conjunction which we translate by "as" is here *kathôs* and not *hôs*. Because as a general rule hôs signifies an analogy based on imitation, external resemblance (so when we say "she has a red garment like her brother," "he commits sin like his neighbor"), whereas, ordinarily, *kathôs* evokes the analogy which arises from a rapport of causality or origin between the two elements in question ("he is intelligent like his father," "she has black hair like her mother"). In our context, *communion* of the Father and the Son is much more than the model of fraternal *communion*; it is the source, the origin, the locus of it. That gives the special commandment "love one another as (*kathôs*) I have loved you" (13:34)—an exceptional seriousness and explains why it is called special (unique).

In light of this notion of *mystery* and what is found in Johannine thinking, ecclesial *koinonia* can, therefore, be defined as the sign of trinitarian *communion* in the fraternal relationships among the disciples of Christ.

---

[103]See R. E. Brown, *The Community of the Beloved Apostle,* which shows the context, but also the important study by E. Käsemann, *The Testament of Jesus according to John 17,* Philadelphia, 1968 (we are only acquainted with the American version), 56–57. The position briefly explained by T. E. Pollard, "That They All May Be One (John XVII, 21) and the Unity of the Church," *Expository Times* 70, 1958–1959, 149–151, often invoked in ecumenical discussions, does not seem to us to have much foundation.

[104]As E. Käsemann, *op. cit.,* shows it very well.

[105]See the study by M.-E. Boismard, "The First Epistle of John and the Writings of Qumran," in James H. Charlesworth, *John and Qumran,* London, 1972, 156–165 (160–161).

Early on, Churches perceived that it implies this *communion* as much in its meta-historical reality (*theologia*) as in its presence in the midst of Jesus Christ's mission (*oikonomia*). We have observed that this immanence takes note of the authentic nature of the mission: "as (*kathôs*) you have sent me I send them." Viewed in its faith context, the Church of God is nothing else but the *communion* of the disciples of Christ Jesus as, through the Spirit, it is understood in the whole relationship of the Father and the Son.

5. In our presentation of *mystery* we have hardly mentioned the Spirit. However, we have always spoken of him. Because he is the one who, as the power of God, lives inseparably associated with the Father for the accomplishment of the *mystery*. Evangelical texts state that Jesus was conceived by the Spirit, anointed by the Spirit at his baptism, inhabited by the power of the Spirit in his ministerial acts, raised by the Spirit on Easter morning, giver of the Spirit on the day of Pentecost. Without the active presence of the Spirit, the Church of God would not exist because the Gospel of God would not be put into action. This presence constitutes, in our opinion, the milieu where it germinates, is born and developed. The Letter to the Ephesians brings out this all encompassing relationship of the Spirit with the Church when the hymn which opens the letter speaks of the "seal of the Holy Spirit" (Eph 1:13-14; cf. 4:29) or when it affirms that the pagans are called "to become a house where God lives in the Spirit" (2:22), that "in the one Spirit" all have access to the Father (2:18), that there is "only one Body and one Spirit" (4:4). This letter is closely allied to the Johannine tradition which, in texts too well known to be explained here (John 7:37-39; 14:16-17; 15:26-27; 16:13-15), underlines the essential link between the work of the second Paraclete (Advocate) and the advent of the community of believers.

In its deepest roots, because of the Spirit who joins it to the *mystery,* the Church is, therefore, by its very essence charismatic (in the classic sense of this term, which must be reevaluated because of the distortion of the term today, due to new "enthusiastic" groups). Also, because the Holy Spirit is at the origin of the Church and is the essence of its milieu, could it not be defined uniquely, even primarily, in terms of the institution it calls for, as every community wishing to live in peace and to endure throughout the ages.[106] The Church could not minimize this by any legislation. However, within the Church it is the Spirit who oversees and guarantees everything. In addition, the early community is convinced that even the apostolic Word, which reveals to it the contents of the Gospel of God and gives it the true sense of its accomplishment through the Lord

---

[106]And it calls for this strict canonical regulation on the level of the first documents of the New Testament.

Jesus Christ, has certainty only because it is transmitted through the Holy Spirit (1 Cor 2:4-5; 1 Thess 1:5). The structure of the Church is justified only by its relationship and service to the action of the Spirit, whether it is a question of sacraments, of ministry or of canonical regulation: "Those who are moved by the Spirit of God are sons, of God" (Rom 8:14). Every institution which does not reflect or which no longer contributes to this service of the Spirit has no place in *communion*.

III. Church of God
and Kingdom of God

Narrowly linked to the "mystery," the Church receives from the Spirit the mission to preserve the offer of Salvation as an ongoing reality throughout history until the end of time. It must also remain in *communion* with the story of humanity and its crying out to another world. This *communion* is not a secondary characteristic of the Church's identity; it is essential to it. But then what link is there between the ultimate vocation of the Church—the full actualization of the "mystery"—and this rooting of it in the concrete reality of human history? This question reverts to the difficult problem of the rapport between the Church of God and the Kingdom of God.[107]

A. Church of God and Kingdom

1. The relationship of the Church, *communion* of Churches, with the *mystery* explains its link with the Kingdom. It must be perceived with the acute understanding proved by Tradition. It has always had a keen intuition of the intrinsic relationship uniting Church and Kingdom but has expressed it in the life of the Church more than in perfectly clear concepts. In fact, it is especially its great Eucharistic Liturgies which bear witness to this aspect of its faith. At the holy Table, where it receives with the Body and Blood of the Lord the rewards of eternal life,[108] the Church becomes known in fact through its communion with the Kingdom. The eschatological world unites it with the glorified Lord in his dwelling place. There it discovers not only what its destiny is and what it ardently desires

---

[107]On the link between Church and Kingdom, see the remarks by R. E. Brown, *The Churches the Apostles Left Behind*, 51-53, 137-139. During the first centuries, the question of the Kingdom was linked especially to that of the relationship between Kingdom of God and Kingdom of Christ. Commenting on 1 Cor 15:24-28, some Fathers—among whom is Marcel d'Ancyre whose positions will play a major role in the tensions of the fourth century until the council of Sardis (343)—had advanced the idea that the Royalty of Christ would cease with the Parousia. See Leslie W. Barnard, *The Council of Sardica 343 A.D.*, Sofia, 1983, 30, 36, 74-75, 89-91. Paul's text wishes to emphasize that the Kingdom of Christ is identical to that of the Father.

[108]See J.-M. R. Tillard, *L'Eucharistie Pâque de l'Église*, coll. "Unam sanctam," 44, Parish, 1964, 175-242.

but, at the same time, the profound reality which *already* lives in it. As a prayer in the Byzantine office states referring to Holy Communion: "May these mysteries increase your divine grace in me and give me life in your Kingdom."[109]

The Gospel-Kingdom link is basic. The Gospel of God is nothing else, in fact, but the Gospel of the Kingdom (Matt 24:14; Mark 1:14-15; Luke 4:43; 8:1; Acts 8:12). In reality, the fulfillment of the eternal design of the Father becomes identified with the coming of this Kingdom, which is at the heart of every earthly work of Jesus (cf. Matt 12:28; Luke 17:20-21). Also the object of apostolic preaching is to announce the beginning of this Kingdom which has been sealed by Easter (cf. Matt 24:14; Acts 1:3; 8:12; 19:8; 20:25; 28:23, 31) and to indicate the means required to benefit from it. However, this *already* tends towards a surpassing or going beyond it. Because using the historical term, "coming with his Kingdom" (Matt 16:28; 25:31; cf. 13:41-43), the Lord Jesus will give back this Kingdom to God the Father "so that God may be all in all" (1 Cor 15:23-28). The messianic banquet—the one which the Eucharists on the earth were announcing and bringing about in human history—will be the eternal feast of the Church of God (Matt 8:11; 22:1-14; Luke 14:15-24; 22:30; Rev 19:9).

2. We are speaking of Kingdom. We must be precise. In fact, the term *basileia* can be translated in two ways. In one sense it designates the Reign of God, the active exercise of the divine Kingship. It seems that this is ordinarily how it should be understood. However—especially in the later writings of the New Testament—it signifies also the area, the human domain, the community where this Reign is recognized and accepted. There are numerous cases. It is then a Kingdom, like the one that the vision of the Son of Man brings out in Daniel (Dan 7:13-14, 22, 27). But since *basileia* designates, therefore, the area where the Gospel of God is *already* being accomplished and *already* producing its fruits of grace, questions must then be asked about the authentic relationship which is established between the reality of the Kingdom and the being of the Church, a communion of communions, *Church of Churches*.

It is true that Johannine literature, taken by itself, could lead one to believe that this question is secondary. Everything found there revolves around the union of believers with Jesus, the place par excellence of the Reign of the Father with whom he is only one (John 14:1-4; 22-26; 1 John 2:28). Besides, it ignores the term Church and uses the expression Kingdom of God (John 3:3, 5; 18:36) only two times. But it seems obvious to us that the Gospel according to Matthew insists that we do not separate the Church and the Kingdom of the Son of Man (Matt 13:37-43):

[109]E. Mercenier and F. Paris, *La Prière des Églises de rite byzantin,* Chevetogne, 1937, 308.

This Kingdom exists, *aliquo modo,* already before the final judgment which will do a sorting out, because then only the just will enter into the Kingdom *of the Father* (13:43). The comparison between *Ekklesia* and *basileia* in the confession of Caesarea (16:18-19) is an important sign in this sense.[110] Without being able to affirm that in Matthew the Church and the Kingdom *of the Son* are explicitly and formally the same, everything requires us to recognize that they are not mutually exclusive. It does not speak of the Kingdom without the idea of Church being directly projected. Perhaps it is impossible to elaborate further on this discreet sentence in Matthew, but it already says a lot.

The Letter to the Colossians leads to an analogous judgment. It perceives Christian life in the tension between a participation *already* come true in the Resurrection of Christ and the full manifestation of this state at the time of the final manifestation of Christ himself (Col 3:1-4; 2:12; cf. Eph 2:6). It speaks of the entrance of believers into "the *Kingdom of the Son* that he loves" (1:13), of membership "in the inheritance of the saints in light" (1:12), of apostolic involvement "for the *Kingdom of God*" (4:11). But the expression *Kingdom of the Son,* the meaning of *basileia*—which clarifies the image of inheritance (cf. Eph 1:14-18; Acts 20:32; 26:18; 1 Pet 1:4)—seems closer to the idea of the area, of the domain where the power is exercised than to the exercise of this power itself. It must be admitted, however, that it is still difficult here to speak of an equivalence between the Kingdom of the Son and the Church as the Body of Christ (Col 1:18) without making minute distinctions. And that is true although the Letter to the Ephesians, whose relationship to the Epistle to the Colossians is obvious, connects very closely belonging to the Church, the Body of Christ, to the fact of being "a fellow-citizen of the saints" (Eph 2:19) and mentions in a full ecclesial context "inheritance in the Kingdom of Christ and of God" (5:5). The Church as the Body of Christ and as the Kingdom look at the same relationship between Christ and his followers from two different angles; one refers to belonging to Christ, the other to the consequences of this belonging. The Church will inherit the Kingdom. However, to the extent that the baptized, participating in the grace of the Resurrection, are *already* "hidden with Christ in God" (Col 3:3), it can be said that the Church has *already* within it the substance of its inheritance, the heart of the Kingdom. The Kingdom is established in it.

There is a narrow relationship, therefore, which unites Church and Kingdom; a relationship which is a progression from one to the other, which will not be finished until the course of history has been completed. *Al-*

---

[110]See also P. Bonnard, *L'Évangile selon saint Matthieu,* 245, for whom the Church is here the messianic community which will proclaim the Name of Jesus.

ready, however, where Kingdom is spoken of the Church is outlined. Wherever the Church lives deeply to what it has been called the Kingdom is taking shape. It is *already* that part of humanity in which the gifts of the Spirit of the Lord are present, at least as a seed, found in their early form.[111]

Irenaeus is a witness to the conviction of the early centuries concerning the presence of this *already* of the Kingdom in the historical Church. It is the *already* of a *communion* with the eternal Liturgy of praise and glory which constitutes the life of God. This *communion* is expressed above all in the Eucharistic celebration. It is there, in fact, that the ecclesial community offers to the Father in the bread and cup what it has from him for its own benefit, the first fruits (*premices*) of the *New* Creation, and communicates with the eternal glorification of the Name of God in the glorification of the Name of his Son,[112] at the very moment it *already* receives the rewards of the Kingdom:

> The oblation of the Church, which the Lord taught us to offer throughout the entire world, is considered a pure sacrifice before God and which is pleasing to him. Not that he has need of a sacrifice on our part, but the one who does the offering is himself glorified in what he offers if his gift is accepted. By this gift, in fact, are manifested the honor and the piety which we render to the king, and the Lord wishes us to offer this gift in all simplicity and innocence. . . . We offer him what belongs to him, proclaiming and confessing coherently the intercession, the unity and the resurrection of the body and soul. The bread which comes from the earth, after it has received the invocation of the Lord, is no longer ordinary bread, but the Eucharist, made up of two things: one earthly and the other heavenly: in the same way our bodies which also participate in the Eucharist are no longer corruptible but bear in them the hope of resurrection.[113]

In the Eucharist, the Church then, enters into real *communion* with the liturgy at the "heavenly altar,"[114] which is the one which belongs to the

---

[111]Take note of the formulation of *Lumen gentium,* 5: "In this way the Church endowed with the gifts of its Founder and faithfully applied to preserving its precepts of charity, humility and self-denial, receives the mission to proclaim the Kingdom of Christ and God and to establish it in all nations, forming *the seed and the beginning on the earth* of this Kingdom."

[112]*Adv. Haer.,* IV, 17, 5-6 (*SC* 100, 590-594). Concerning the intradivine glorification, see also IV, 14.

[113]*Adv. Haer.,* IV, 18, 1-6 (*SC* 100, 596, 610-612).

[114]On this celestial altar which Irenaeus speaks of (*Adv. Haer.* IV, 18, 6, *SC* 100, 614-615)—mentioned in the roman canon which has become Anaphora no. 1, and this is the case from the time of Ambrose, *De Sacramentis* IV, 6, 27 (*SC* 25 bis, 116-117)—see Heb 13:10, and from Ignatius of Antioch, *Eph 5* (cf. J. B. Lightfoot, *The Apostolic Fathers,* t. II, ed. 1889, 43-44), *Magn.* 7, *Tral.* 7. See especially Origen, *Homélie sur le nom de Josué* 9, 1-2 (*SC* 71, 245-246): "In this edifice which is the Church, an altar is also necessary. Also I believe that all those who among

eschatological world, while it receives the rewards of the Resurrection in the Kingdom. It is linked to the Sacrifice of praise of the awaited Kingdom. *Already* the experience of this Kingdom joins the Church. And the Church becomes a place for this experience. The community is, at the celebration, the Church between the *already* and the *not yet: koinonia* of poor sinners inhabited by the Spirit, taken hold of by the power of the Body and Blood of the Lord which brings them together in him, communicating in a single praise of the Father with the other communities spread throughout the world, but also, as the Liturgies of the Orient so strongly testify, with the patriarchs, the saints and even the angels whom Revelation puts on the scene. Then the Kingdom is there, although still with the weight of history. Its holiness is seen as a fine thread in the coarse fabric of the human condition always in a sinful state.

Besides, in proportion to which believers are members of the Body of Christ, through the power of the Holy Spirit, by grace of their baptism the whole Church is *already* the Temple of God where this Spirit of glory dwells (1 Cor 3:16-17; 2 Cor 6:16). The Letter to the Ephesians sees there the privilege to which, like the Jews, the pagans themselves are henceforth already joined (Eph 2:19, 22). Since the time of the Cross and Pentecost, the Church is, in the midst of the world and at the heart of human history, the place where the living God is glorified. In a context reminiscent of liturgical references, the First Letter of Peter speaks of a "spiritual house" made of living stones who are the believers, where are offered "the spiritual sacrifices which Jesus Christ has made acceptable to God" (1 Pet 2:5). Johannine tradition, which considers the Body of the risen Christ to be the Temple of God surviving the destruction of the temple of historical Jerusalem (John 2:21), from which flow the living waters (7:37-38; cf. Ezek 47:1-12), enables us to discover the depth of this vision abundantly affirmed, as is readily evident, in New Testament traditions.[115] But Revelation, chanting the eternal Reign of God and the Kingdom of the elect (cf. Rev 1:6; 3:21; 5:10; 11:15; 12:10; 19:4-6), sees the heavenly City as the place where the glory of the living God is celebrated in the

---

you, as living stones, are capable of becoming so and are resolved to devote themselves to prayer, to offer to God night and day their supplications and to sacrifice the victims of their supplications, it is with them that Jesus builds his altar. . . . Therefore, they [the Apostles] who could pray with one single heart, one single voice and one single spirit, are very worthy of having to build together a unique altar, on which Jesus offers sacrifice to his Father. But we also on our side must strive. . . . to become stones for the altar." In its *koinonia* the Church is the altar. On the total vision, see B. Botte, "L'ange du sacrifice," *Cours et conférences des semaines liturgiques*, t. V. Louvain, 1929, 209-221; *RTAM* 1, 1929, 285-308.

[115]Concerning this vision of the Temple, see especially the enlightening work by B. Gartner, *The Temple and Community in Qumran and the New Testament*, Cambridge, 1965. See also R. J. McKelvey, *The New Temple*, Oxford, 1969; Y. Congar, *Le Mystère du Temple*, Paris, 1958. See among the patristic testimonies Origen, *In Mat.* 16 21 (*PG* 13, 1443), Tertullian, *Adv. Marc.* 3, 7 (*CSEL* 47, 3, 386) and the hymn *Urbs Jerusalem beata* (reflecting patristic thinking).

Temple which is the Lord and the Lamb, a Temple in which the elect are fully integrated (21:22-23; cf. 3:12; 7:15; 11:19; 14:15, 17; 15:5, 8; 16:1). *Already,* therefore, in the Temple which is the Church—formed from the cornerstone which is Christ (1 Pet 2:6) and from living stones which are the Christians—the reality of the awaited Kingdom penetrates our world.

Among the works of Augustine there is a sermon underlining, in a rare and beautiful way, how this ecclesial Temple is made not only of living stones placed one upon the other but of stones in *communion.* The Church is the Temple of the Kingdom only in its existence as *communion:*

> We ourselves are the house of God. If we are the house of God, we are built in this world to be consecrated at the end of the world. . . . What happened when the structure was raised up, is what happens now when those who believe in Christ assemble together. When we believe, it is like when wood is cut in the forest or stones are shaped in the mountains. When believers are taught, baptized, formed, it is as if they were cut down, shaped, planed by the work of carpenters and builders. However, the house of God is built only when charity enters in and brings everything together. If this wood and this stone were not joined together according to a certain plan, interwoven in an harmonious way, if they were not blended together in some way as they were put together, nobody could enter into this house. Finally, when you see the wood and the stones of an edifice well assembled, you enter it without any fear, without being afraid that it is going to collapse! Christ the Lord, because he wished to enter and live in us, as if to fashion his edifice, said: I give you a new commandment that you love one another. . . . Let your charity consider this besides: just as foretold and promised, this house is raised up throughout the whole world. . . . What we see here realized physically with walls must be realized spiritually with souls; what we look at accomplished here with stones and wood must be accomplished in your bodies with the grace of God.[116]

In its reality as *communion* concretely put into practice, the Church seems, therefore, *already* inhabited by the presence of the *res* of the Kingdom, in other words, by its profound reality, but in the hidden aspect, the humility, the fragility of the state of believers still struggling along the way.

Perhaps it is necessary to emphasize that if this relationship of the Church as *communion* with the reality of the Kingdom is realized in an eminent way in the Eucharist, it is seen also in the course of daily life. Besides, the sacrifices offered in the Temple of God and on the altar are, *in* and *by* the sacrifice of Christ Jesus, what the Letter to the Hebrews designates as the only sacrifices pleasing to God: "good works and help-

---

[116]*Sermo* 336, 1, 6 (*PL* 38, 1471-1475).

ing one another" or sharing (*koinonia*) resources (Heb 13:16; cf. Phil 4:18). And Irenaeus, where he evokes the sacrifice offered by the Church, underlines its link with the gratuitous love of the poor and the outcast.[117] The Church is in humanity the community which administers the law of the *already* of the Kingdom, the *Agape*. In contrast with earthly regimes, its power comes from the charity and the service received from the Lord, which are absorbed by it. It is, therefore, in history the community which freely accepts the Reign of God in its Lord Christ Jesus and lives *already* the consequences of the battle *already* won[118] on which the Kingdom depends. By its action, it makes real the fruit of the victory which *already* has started to invade the world. In it, besides, the mending of the human race starts to take shape; discretely the scandal of Babel fades into the background. It is inseparable from the power of this *already*. It bears the reality of it in itself, and this reality permeates it.

Assuredly, this realization of the Kingdom in the Church is that of the seed which germinates buried in the entire soil of the world (Matt 13:3-8, 18-23; 24:30; Mark 4:26-29, 31-32), of the leaven which rises in the secret recesses of the human dough (Matt 13:33), of the minute mustard seed thrown into the immensity of the field of human reality (Matt 13:31-32). However, in this way, the Kingdom is fully at work throughout our history. *Already* the community of the baptized can be said to be, without, however, being completely identical to it, "the community of the Kingdom," somewhat like the farmer says that the field which he has just planted is *already* "a field of wheat." *Already* the net of the Kingdom has been cast forth: when it is opened on the shore there will be found, undoubtedly, after sorting them out, (cf. Matt 13:47-50), a good catch of fish, among which are certainly numbered the authentic disciples who make up on this earth the ecclesial community.

3. In the field there are weeds, in the net there are fish which are to be thrown back into the sea. The Kingdom will burst forth in all its splendor only in "the new heaven and the new earth" (Rev 21:1-5). The Christian prayer par excellence that evangelical tradition dates back to Christ Jesus himself, contains this supplication: "May your Kingdom (*basileia*) come!" (Matt 6:10). Until that time the Church knows that it is the *corpus permixtum* that Augustine spoke of.[119] It must, at the same time when it asks for the coming of the Kingdom, cry out: "Forgive us our offenses" (Matt 6:12). We know what Augustine, fine tuning his earlier positions, deduced from this prayer, closely linked to the idea found in the letter

---

[117] *Adv. Haer.* IV, 17, 1-4; 18, 3, 6 (*SC* 100, 574-591, 598-607, 612-615).

[118] The vision of O. Cullman is recognized, *Christ et le temps; temps et histoire dans le christianisme primitif,* coll. "Bibliothèque théologique," Neuchâtel-Paris, 1947.

[119] See especially *De doctrina christiana* III, 32, 45.

to the Ephesians (5:25-27): "It is here below that exists the bath of re-birth through the word which purifies the Church. However, the entire Church repeats, as long as it is here below: forgive us our debts. It is not, therefore, here on this earth without stain, nor wrinkle, nor anything like that; but what it has received here below leads it to a glory and a perfection which is not of this earth."[120]

The baptized remain, in fact, in the clutches of the forces of evil. Often it happens that they succumb to it. In the Church, the most moving forms of holiness run closely parallel to the very disturbing forms of sin in the world. On another level, no one will deny that those in authority themselves do not always make decisions which keep the community on the straight path of the Kingdom. That is the case frequently despite the best intentions. We perceive, after the fact, for example, and with some discomfort, that looked at from a perspective of "defense of the Gospel," the reasons for embarking on the crusades had other results than those anticipated, and that a desire to safeguard the faith by suppressing the "Chinese rites" harmed an authentic birth of the gospel in a vast portion of the world. Living in a state of forgiveness is always necessary.

Certainly as we said earlier, it is at the celebration of the Memorial that the community is truly permeated and inhabited by the presence of the Kingdom. But the Eucharist is still only a *sacrament* of it while waiting for the great Feast at the Table of the Lord, on the day of the final fulfillment (Luke 22:16-18, 30; Matt 26:19; Mark 14:25; cf. Matt 8:11; 22:2-10; Luke 13:28-29; 14:15) put into song in Revelation (Rev 19:9). It is already the Feast of the Lamb, and the Canon found in eastern liturgies evokes the atmosphere of the Kingdom, the epiclesis contained in it.[121] However, there were very few sacraments at that time, proper to this period of waiting. We are in the era of the *not yet*. The good things announced are given: the Lord himself is united to those men and women who receive his Body and Blood in faith. Nevertheless, everything is accomplished with a sigh towards the fullness that is awaited, *achri ou elthè,* "until he comes" (1 Cor 11:26).

At the Eucharistic celebration the Church is in the presence of the Kingdom with its own state of mind in the presence of the Lord whose Body it is: he has come but he must still be manifested in his glory. In the interim the Kingdom is present and received, but in the poverty of a community still struggling in the midst of the snares in the desert, a people whose members remain vulnerable although all of them are *already* justified, a communion of men and women still weak, all the while, however,

---

[120]*Retract.* I, 7, 5; II, 18, 1 (see *Œuvres de saint Augustin,* coll. "Bibliothèque augustinienne," 12, Paris, 1950, 304–305, 396–397, and the note by G. Bardy, 566–567; compare *De haer.* 88; *De gest. Pelag.* 12, 27; *De bapt.* I, 17, 26; III, 18, 23; IV, 3, 5; VII, 10, 19).

[121]See J.-M. R. Tillard, *L'Eucharistie pâque de l'Église.*

in the Eucharist the Lord unites them and day after day they receive his Spirit. Their weaknesses, their cowardice, even their breach of faith could not render ineffectual the promise that the gates of hell would not prevail against the Church (Matt 16:18) and, nevertheless, the Kingdom here on earth is a Kingdom of sinners. This Kingdom maintains its identity in a future which is pre-formed and anticipated in the Church, in a great Benediction that God reserves for his own, whose rewards he gives in his Holy Spirit (2 Cor 11:22; 5:5; cf. Eph 1:14).

4. This presence of the Kingdom throughout history is entirely the presence in the people in the world. The weakness of the baptized is proof of it. Besides, what makes up their fidelity is not alien to the state of this world, changing in them and around them, even in the most profane areas. The Church is not *of* the world (John 17:14-16). However, its Lord wishes it to be *in* the world (17:11, 15, 18) because it is precisely there that the Kingdom is slowly born. He believes that in proportion as they are healed and renewed by the grace of the Spirit, personal values and social forms of existence which together determine the human condition, will become what God wills, and in this way come under his Lordship. The Church, as we said earlier, is indeed, nothing else but the portion of humanity which has been snatched away, in Christ, from its breaking with God and from the fraternal divisions which result from it. It is in history a small area of reconciled humanity, a fragile area as the dramatic display of schisms points out, but where, however, in spite of everything, there is no resignation to division and its causes, whatever they may be, because this humanity lives there in *communion*.

It is, besides, because the power of the Kingdom is at work in it that the Church is involved in the fierce struggle against the forces of evil which destroy humanity, preventing it from becoming the humanity that God wishes. In spite of the sometimes scandalous compromises of some of its members, in spite of the counter-testimony of so many of its cells, it remains a place where the battle is waged against idols: a pernicious use of power, of money, leading to the exploitation of the individual and to a denial of his fundamental rights as one born in the image of God. There has hardly been a period in history in which, while all Christians were dozing in a state of peaceful passivity, there has sprung up somewhere in the Church a messianic burst of indignation, a prophetic cry, a foundation, bringing back the disciples of Christ to their responsibility in these areas.[122] If it has been able to occur, for different motives, that those in the hierarchy have stifled the voices of prophets, have nipped in the bud courageous initiatives, these prophets themselves or these creative indi-

---

[122]We permit ourselves to go back to the article "Pauvreté" in the *Dictionnaire de spiritualité*, edited in installments by Beauchesne, Paris, 1985. See also the article "Pauvrete" in *Catholicisme*.

viduals were still speaking and acting within the very bosom of the Church. Their voices and their initiatives came from it and are to be credited to it. It is certainly possible, in certain cases, that Christians cause things to happen because of insights or impulses that have come from elsewhere. They become, then, probably without their knowledge, the signs of the profound link which unites Kingdom and humanity. Because in its involvement for the growth of the Kingdom, the Church owes it to itself to welcome truth and uprightness which lie hidden in the human heart, often outside of the Church, and to let them become part of the power of its Lord. It gives witness in this way that the dynamism of the Kingdom is for the full accomplishment of the plan of God in humanity.

The Kingdom is, therefore, broader than the ecclesial community. That is why in the course of history, this community is subordinated to it as the important paragraph nine of *Lumen gentium* affirms this about the messianic People whose vocation is to announce it and prepare it:

> This messianic People has Christ for its head, who was delivered up for our sins and raised for our justification (Rom 4:25), and who now, having acquired the name above every other name, reigns gloriously in the heavens. The state of this People is the dignity and the freedom of the sons of God, in whose heart the Holy Spirit lives as in his Temple. It has for its law the new commandment to love as Christ himself loved us (cf. John 13:34). Finally, its destiny is the Kingdom of God, begun on the earth by God himself and which must be expanded endlessly until, at the end of time, it will be completed by God himself, when Christ our life will appear (cf. Col 3:4), and when "creation itself will be freed from slavery and corruption, to enter into the glorious freedom of the children of God" (Rom 8:21). Also, this messianic people, although it does not include all men, and more than once it appears as a small flock, it is, however, for the entire human race a very powerful source of unity, hope and salvation. Established by Christ in a communion of life, charity and truth, it is also taken on by him to be the instrument for the redemption of all, and it is sent into the entire world as the light of the world and the salt of the earth (cf. Matt 5:13-16).

The poverty of the Church on this earth in the presence of the Kingdom is nevertheless more profound still. Because the Kingdom, here on earth, takes root only in communities of the baptized. It traces out a path for itself wherever men and women who take their vocation seriously put forth an effort to search for truth, to open themselves up to a universal love, to promote justice, to guarantee peace, to treat the poor, the despised, those on the fringe of society, refugees, with the human dignity they deserve. Everywhere that the powers of evil give way, which enclose humanity in a circle of misery and oppression, there the Kingdom *already* penetrates because there God *already* reigns, as Savior of his Creation. Even more so, contacts with the major non-Christian religions and the discovery of an immense crowd of men and women with an upright heart have brought about the discovery not only of the breadth but also the depth of this *already* of the Kingdom. It is the very profound quality of Salvation which unites the person himself and not only his work, giving back to him his true nature in the "image and likeness of God."

It is evidently clear that the ecclesial community belongs to this source. All of its dynamism and all of its power are contained in it. But this belonging is still a sad state, a refusal of full satisfaction. So much more so since it is inseparable from the requirement that we have described.

5. The inheritance of the Church will be the Kingdom of glory (Eph 5:5; cf. 1:14, 18; Col 1:12; Matt 21:43; Rom 8:17; Titus 3:6-7; Heb 6:12; 1 Pet 3-4). It is there that God will bring it together again forever.[123] But it is striking to note that the New Testament, even in the documents which treat the great hope of the Churches, uses only once the word *Ekklesia* when it evokes this reassembling of the elect. Besides, this single verse speaking of the Church in this context (Heb 12:23) is very specific because it is a question of referring to the Church of the first-born.[124] Entering into the sanctuary of God on Mount Zion and in the heavenly Jerusalem, with its myriads of angels, believers, according to the author, associate themselves with "the Church (*Ekklesia*) of the first-born" and with Christ Jesus himself (12:22-23). Exegetes have already indicated for a long time how this takes place:

> The description of the scene of the Kingdom of God where Christians are brought in is followed by a description of those representative persons who are included in it and in whose communion believers are associated. They are angels and men, no longer separated as on Sinai by signs of great terror but united in a vast assembly. . . . The second body which makes up the divine community is the "Church of the first-born." It represents the earthly element (men) as the other group (angels) represents the celestial element. Men are described as a Church, a community gathered together for the enjoyment of certain rights, just as the angels are for a joyful reunion, and they are spoken of as "first-born," enjoying the privileges not only of sons but of first-born sons. . . . Christians who believe in Christ, the living as well as the dead, are united in the Body of Christ. In this Body, we enter into communion with a society of "elder sons" of God, who communicate in the highest glory in the divine order. In this way the idea of communion of saints takes on

---

[123]See the beautiful prayer of the *Didache* 10, 5 ("gather together your Church from the four winds of the heavens—the Church which you sanctified—in your Kingdom that you have prepared for it").

[124]Exegetes do not agree on the construction of the sentence, but this point is secondary for our purpose. See B. F. Westcott, *The Epistle to the Hebrews,* London, 1889, 413–414.

an enriching distinction. But the word suggests still another thought. The "first-born" of Israel were representatives of the consecrated nation. We are then authorized to see in the first-born of the Christian Church the first-born of humanity, as preparing the way for numerous brothers into the one who is the First-born (1:6). Through them it is creation which enters into the beginning of its final accomplishment (cf. Rev 1:5; Col 1:15; Rom 8:29).[125]

Entrance into final glory is, therefore, entrance into a *communion* in which is accomplished the long retrenchment of all the stages of human history, of all responsibilities, all vocations, all dramas of sin and forgiveness, all the saintliness which *jam ab Abel justo* have sought to make our humanity the humanity-which-God-wills, and even of all the faithfulness of creatures capable of knowing, blessing and adoring the Lord of the universe. Many Fathers of the Church and ancient texts affirm that the old Adam and the old Eve, bearers of the entire human drama, belong to this *communion* with the title of redeemed and saved par excellence. Tertullian likes to imagine that Adam, "the first member of the human race and the first one to offend the Lord," restored to paradise after confessing his fault and doing penance, "does not cease to speak" of the planks of Salvation which God has offered to humanity.[126] The *Actes de Pilate* taking up the legend which is found in the *Révélation de Moïse,* puts these words on the lips of the angel of the Lord talking to Seth:

> "Tell your Father that . . . the only Son of God will descend on the earth, becoming man, and he will anoint your father with this oil [of the tree of mercy] and will raise him up. In water and the Holy Spirit he will wash him, him and his descendants. Then he will be cured of any weakness. . . . Hearing these words, Patriarchs and prophets tremble with joy.

---

[125]*Ibid.,* 413–415. See also E. C. Wickham, *The Epistle to the Hebrews,* London, 1910, 118–119.

[126]*De Paenitentia* 12, 9 (*SC* 316, 190–191) which Adv. Marc. II, 2, 10, 25 states precisely. See also Irenaeus, *Dem. Apost.* 31 (*SC* 62, 80–82); *Adv. Haer.* I, 28, 1; III, 22, 3–4; III, 23, 1 (*SC* 264, 357; 211, 438–447), Gregory of Nazianzen, *Orat.* 37, 7 (*SC* 318, 284–285), Augustine, *Epist.* 164, 6; *In Ps.* 101, 5; *Adv. Jul.* VI, 12, 22, 30 (*PL* 45, 1523, 1553, 1582); *De peccat. mer.* II, 34–55 (*PL* 44, 183); Origen (*In Matt.* 126). In apocryphal literature see especially *Actes de Pilate* 19, 1 text in F. Quéré, *Évangiles apocryphes,* Paris, 1983, 154; *Histoire de Joseph le charpentier* 28 (*ibid.,* 111); *Évangile de Nicodème* I, 3(19), 9(25); II 4(20) (*Anti-Nicene Fathers,* t. VIII, 436, 437, 456); *Révélation de Moïse (ibid.,* 569); *Apocalypse de Paul,* 51 (in E. Hennecke, *New Testament Apocryphes,* edit. by W. Schneemelcher, English translation by R. M. L. Wilson, vol. II, London, 1963, 795); *Ascension d'Isaïe* 9, 27–28 (*ibid.,* 658); *Évangile de Barnabé* 41, 124 (text in L. Cirillo, *Évangile de Barnabeé, texte et traduction,* coll. "Beauchesne religions," 2, Paris, 1977, 313). This ancient view is still that of the monk Silouane on Mount Athos, see Silouane, *Ecrits spirituels,* coll. "Spiritualité orientale," 5, Bellefontaine, 1970, 70–77. On the gnostics see J. E. Menard, *L'Évangile de vérité,* coll. "Nag Hammadi Studies," 2, Leyde, 1972, 89, 102, 120–131, 132, 139.

It is, however, the homily for Easter night, which dates from the fifth century and is sometimes attributed to Epiphanius of Salamine, which states it with the greatest depth:

> It is the first man whom he is going to look for, as the lost sheep. He wishes also to visit those who live in darkness and the shadow of death. Yes, it is towards Adam the prisoner, and at the same time towards Eve, a prisoner also, that God will proceed, and his son with him, to deliver them from their suffering. . . .
>
> The Lord advanced towards them, armed with the cross, the weapon of his victory. When he sees him, Adam, the first man, beating his breast in amazement, cried out to all the others: "My Lord with all of us!" And Christ responded to Adam: "And with your spirit." He takes him by the hand and lifts him up saying: "Wake up, O you are asleep, rise up from among the dead, and Christ will enlighten you."
>
> "It is I your God who, for you, have become your son; it is I who, for you and for your descendants, speak to you now and who, through my power, order those who are in chains: go out. Those who are in darkness: be enlightened. Those who are asleep: rise up."
>
> "I order you: Wake up, O you who are alseep, I have not created you to remain a prisoner of the abode of the dead. Rise up from among the dead: I am the life of the dead. Get up, work of my hands; get up, my likeness who has been created in my image. Wake up, go forth from here. Because you are in me, and I in you, we are one single indivisible person."
>
> "It is for you that I, your God, have become your son; it is for you that I, the Master, have taken the form of a slave; it is for you that I, who rule the heavens, have come on the earth and under the earth; it is for you, the man, that I have become as a man abandoned, at large among the dead; it is for you, who came out of the garden, that I was delivered up to the Jews in a garden and crucified in a garden. . . ."[127]

The *communion* of the Kingdom—which the Eucharistic celebration with the *Trisagion*, the remembrance of Mary, the saints of all ages, the dead, and in the East, the iconostasis—is, therefore, broader than that of the Christians with the Father and among themselves, in Christ and the life of the Spirit. It becomes wider to include all of the New Jerusalem, the City of God which constitutes by itself alone the Kingdom bathing in the divine splendor and in which the redeemed People finds its place. The Church becomes then what, throughout all eternity, God was wishing it to be in the heart of the heavenly Liturgy: associated with the *Alleluia* of all Creation. Such was its heritage.[128] Such is the Kingdom.

---

[127]*Actes de Pilate*, ed. cit., 154; *Homélie attribuée à Épiphane*, PG 43, 452, 461-464.

[128]Concerning the notion of heritage it is interesting to assemble different uses of the words *klēros* (Acts 26:18; Col 1:12); *klēronomia* (Acts 7:5; 20:35; Eph 1:14-18; 5:5; Col 1:12; 3:24; Heb 9:15; 11:8; 1 Pet 1:4); *klēronomeô* (Matt 5:5; 19:29; 25:34; Mic 10:17; Luke 10:25; 18:18; 1 Cor 6:9, 10; 15:50; Gal 5:21). Then all the facets of this notion, very rich in implications, are discovered.

Referring—one more time!—to an insight of Irenaeus, it can be said that the Kingdom in its final state is the epiphany of the "recapitulation" (*anakephalaiosis*) in Christ Jesus of all human reality and of what is joined to it in Creation. The divine economy of Salvation is accomplished only *dia chronou,* in the course of history. It includes the slow preparations during which God prepared the human race to be in harmony (*ad consonantiam*) with Salvation;[129] it passes through Israel's adventure; it flourishes in the Christian community. But *jam ab Abel justo* the reality of Christ Jesus finalizes it: at his Passover all these outlines, with their full extent and their limits, are taken on to be transfigured at his Resurrection. Moreover, since he is the Son of the Father, all these outlines are then immersed by him and in him into the trinitarian *communion,* and there will be no hesitation to proclaim that *unus ex Trinitate passus est,*[130] that all is created by him and for him. The Kingdom is the manifestation, in a *communion* of praise and happiness, of the fullness of mercy and of grace offered by the Father and the Spirit, in Jesus Christ. And it is so not as a summing up of individuals but as *koinonia, communion* of Christians among themselves and with the heavenly world, all admitted to *communicate* in the eternal *communion* of the Father and the Son in the Spirit. There the structure of *communion* of the Church finds at last its "place."

B. *The Kingdom of God within human distress*

It is impossible to think that the Kingdom of God would survive in our world by the simple interplay of social forces changing living conditions or by curing physical and psychological ills, freeing people from their anxiety. Political systems, as noble as they may be and as blessed as they may be by the ecclesial authorities, scientific techniques, as moral and as consistent as they may be with ethical norms, could not be the causes of the manifestation in glory of the Son of Man and the coming of the eternal Kingdom. Besides, movements guided by the utopia of the appearance in this world of the "Kingdom of Christ"—and whose strong summoning it would have been wrong to underestimate[131]—all call upon an inner experience which takes into account efforts spread throughout the social plane.

[129]Irenaeus, *Adv. Haer.* IV, 14, 2 (*SC* 100, 544–545): "thus, in many ways he prepared the human race in view of the symphony of salvation."

[130]See concerning this formula the letter by John II to the senators of Constantinople, in March 534 (text found in *PL* 66, 20–21 and *DS* 401.

[131]Contact with Mennonite and Hutterite groups cannot leave one indifferent. For want of this contact, read at least M. Simons, Scottdale, 1956, and P. J. Klassen, *The Economics of Anabaptism,* La Haye, 1964.

The Kingdom, as a seed today, takes root thanks to a change in the human heart, a *metanoia,* which comes from the Spirit alone. Its power is deployed wherever freedom permits itself to be taken hold of by the demand of God. This change—which can happen unexpectedly even in upright souls who are not even aware of the name of Jesus[132]—incites an individual to decisions or to a lifestyle and involvement which are breaks with modes of conduct in our societies. The Kingdom is the fine pearl or the hidden treasure (Matt 13:44) causing such an astonishment that for it one leaves everything, distributes his goods to the poor (Matt 19:21, 27; Mark 10:21, 29-30; Luke 18:22, 28-30), one looks for the perfect fulfillment of the will of the Father (Matt 5:20; 7:21), one faces persecutions (Matt 5:10-11; Acts 14:22; 2 Thess 1:5), one abandons the paths of sin (1 Cor 6:9-10; Gal 5:21; Eph 5:5). Because "it is not of this world" (John 18:36-38), and that is not only because its full realization coincides with the advent of another world or because it has no equivalent with any political regimes, national or social on our earth,[133] but also because the means for its coming are not those which are found in our world. They become deep-rooted in the new heart which is created by the grace of God alone.[134]

However, there exists a mysterious harmony, a rapport both profound and fragile, between the germination of the Kingdom, *a communion* of happiness and peace in the Spirit of the Lord, and the humanization of this world through justice and right. The Kingdom grows wherever the poor are freed from the slavery of their misery. And this misery from which they suffer is not confined to the realm of material goods.

This bond comes essentially from the fact that the Kingdom is *communion,* centered on *communion* with God. This *communion,* just like evangelical love, could not minimize adopting the fundamental attitude of God, his *communion* with the little ones: "Examining the cases of the poor and unfortunate, is not that what it means to know me?" says the God of Jeremiah (Jer 22:16), echoing an idea found in a host of biblical texts. God is on the side of the weak, the downtrodden, the needy, the unfortunate.[135] And it is not by accident that in the traditions of Exodus

---

[132]"Plato, expresses himself as a disciple of the Logos," Clement of Alexandria declares (*Paed.* I, 36, 1; 82, 3; II, 28, 2).

[133]Not even for the one which the Jewish messianic idea envisaged (cf. J. Klausner, *The Messianic Idea in Israel,* New York, 1955, 392).

[134]On John 18:36-38, see R. E. Brown, *The Gospel According to John (XIII-XXI),* New York, 1970, 867-869; R. Schnackenburg, *The Gospel According to Saint John,* t. III, New York, 1982, 246-251 (here *basileia* refers more to *royalty* than to *Kingdom;* Jesus is not a terrestrial king although his power is exercised in the world, wherever his voice is heard); C. K. Barrett, *The Gospel According to Saint John,* 2nd ed., London, 1978, 536-537.

[135]This point has been profoundly examined by J. Dupont in several works. See especially *Les Béatitudes,* t. II, coll. "Études bibliques," new edition, Paris, 1969, 19-91. See also the biblio-

(as well as those with a Yahwist-Elohistic source as the "sacerdotal" account) the God of Abraham, Isaac and Jacob starts, even before revealing his name, by expressing his *communion* with the misery of his own: "I have seen, I have seen the misery of my people . . ., I have heard their appeal to be free of their slave-drivers, I know their sufferings and I mean to deliver them" (Exod 3:7-8). "To Abraham and Isaac and Jacob I appeared as El Shaddai; I did not make myself known to them by my name Yahweh . . . when I heard the groaning of the children of Israel, enslaved by the Egyptians, and have remembered my covenant . . ., I am Yahweh and I will free you from the burdens which the Egyptians lay on you. I will release you from the slavery in which they hold you, I will deliver you . . ., I will adopt you as my own people and I will be your God. Then you shall know that it is I, Yahweh your God, who have freed you from the Egyptians' burdens" (6:3-7). It is through the deeds of his compassion that, especially in "sacerdotal" tradition, God reveals his real name, and, therefore, his identity.

In the course of Revelation, this mysterious connivance between the confidence of God about himself and his *communion* with misery is essential. And, praising the awaited Messiah, the psalmist only expresses this profound vein of faith when he evokes the one who "will defend the poorest, he will save the children of the poor, he will crush their oppressors . . ., he will free the poor man who calls to him and those who need help, he will have pity on the poor and the feeble, and save the lives of those in need" (Ps 72:2, 4, 12, 13; cf. Isa 11:1-5). A just king, God owes it to himself to raise up a Messiah who will be, like him, in *communion* with the humble, the downtrodden; he owes it "to the honor of his Reign."[136] In the normal course of things, with the powerful never stopping to exploit or crush the little ones, the transcendence of his Reign will appear as a rising to the defense of the "poor" and an involvement for the triumph of their rights. "Yahweh is righteous and merciful, our God is tenderhearted. Yahweh defends the simple" (Ps 116:5-6). That is why they must have a special place at the coming of his Kingdom. The waiting for the Kingdom, therefore, is inscribed in a dynamism of hope, subjected to an osmosis with the currents which stir up history, transporting it towards a victory over what clouds human destiny. And it is anchored in the conviction that it must be so because of God himself.[137]

Already during the time of waiting, in Israel, there is a perception besides that faith in this God who is a friend of the humble is intrinsically

graphy which we give in the article "Pauvrete" from the *Dictionnaire de spiritualité* and "Pauvres, pauvrete" from the dictionary *Catholicsme*.

[136]According to the beautiful expression of J. Dupont, *Les Béatitudes*, t. II, 79, 89.

[137]See J.-M. R. Tillard, *Appel du Christ, appels du monde*, Paris, 1978, 68-78, where we developed this point at greater length.

linked to a call for fraternal *communion*. Deuteronomy inserts in its regulations for the sabbatical year, whose purpose is precisely the restoration of the brotherhood of the people of God by minimizing the social inequalities, a clear command (paired here, it is true, with a less generous consideration towards "strangers"): "Let there be no poor among you" (Deut 15:4). Obedience to this precept implies not only that one does not exploit the weak (15:2; cf. Amos 5:11-12; Isa 10:1-2; Mic 2:1-3), but also that one's hand be open "to the brother, and to anyone who is in need and poor" (Deut 15:11; cf. Exod 21:1-11; 26-27; 22:20, 24; Sir 3:30–4:10), even to the stranger (Exod 22:20; cf. 12:48; Lev 23:22; 25:35; Deut 24:17-22; 26:12). Is not the stranger economically weak, falling because of this under the compassion of God? This will be the sign of the Covenant in the midst of the world where there will always be poor (Deut 15:11) since, as Ben Sirach points out realistically, "What peace can there be between hyena and dog? And what peace between rich man and poor? Wild donkeys are the prey of desert lions; so too, the poor are the quarry of the rich. The proud man thinks humility abhorrent; so too, the rich abominate the poor. When the rich man stumbles he is supported by friends; when the poor man falls, his friends push him away. When the rich man slips, there are many hands to catch him, if he talks nonsense he is congratulated. The poor man slips and is blamed for it, he may talk good sense, but no room is made for him. The rich man speaks and everyone stops talking, and then they praise his discourse to the skies. The poor man speaks and people say: Who is this?" (Sir 13:18-23).

How can one be astonished then that the gestures by which Jesus accomplishes and signifies the breakthrough of the Kingdom (cf. Matt 12:28; Luke 11:20) are precisely gestures of the tenderness and compassion of God towards the "poor"? The recipients of his evangelical signs are those who belong to the world of the lame, the hungry, but also—because the field of poverty keeps getting larger—those men and women who, perhaps well-off as far as material goods are concerned, are troubled in their mind or in their human relationships, plunging them into misery. Because for him also, to *communicate* with the Father is *to communicate* in his *communion* with the misery of his people, whatever those miseries might be. The coming of the Kingdom is accomplished in his encounter with those men and women who send up their cry of anguish to the Father: "Report to John what you have seen and heard: the blind see again, the lame walk, lepers are cleansed, the deaf hear again, the dead are raised to life, the Good News is proclaimed to the poor" (Luke 7:22; cf. Matt 11:4-5). Hasn't he been sent for this proclamation of the Good News, deliverance from captivity and oppression (Luke 4:16-21)? The Good News is that God reigns (Isa 52:7). He reigns by the coming of a new status for the "poor." Then they are "happy" (Luke 6:20-23).

But this *communion* of Jesus with the numberless crowd of poor—in *communion* with the attitude of the Father concerning their condition—is infinitely more profound than those gestures accomplished in favor of the destitute and the afflicted. The event in which his Lordship and his messianic role burst forth in full light, his Cross culminating in the Resurrection, is the event in which he takes upon himself the human condition in its deepest level of poverty. The Jesus whose Resurrection will manifest belonging to the mystery of God is the one who sends forth the cry of anguish in the garden of Olives and on the Cross, the one who is mocked when they make reference to his royalty (Matt 27:28-31; Mark 14:16-20; Luke 23:2-11; John 18:33-39, 7), the one who is abandoned, slandered, betrayed, the one who is seen on the edge of despair. In addition, in Luke, his last words to a man, before his final cry to the Father, are words of *communion* uttered to the thief crucified beside him: "Remember me when you come into your Kingdom. . . . Indeed, I tell you, today you will be with me in Paradise" (Luke 23:42-43). He is made Lord of the Kingdom at the supreme moment of his *communion* with the rejected, the despondent, the hated, the excluded, the scorned, the ridiculed, the martyrs.

It is the very fulfillment of the Beatitudes as contained in Luke (Luke 6:20, 22). The Kingdom is a Kingdom of the "poor," not only because they are heirs of it but also because it is by identifying himself with their fate that Jesus has overcome it. The victory which gives access to the Kingdom was that of a "poor man" who in the deepest recesses of his being was God himself, God-made-poor. The blessed of this life themselves will owe their entrance into this Kingdom to a "poor man" whose identity as Son of God does nothing to destroy it or even conceal his belonging to the line of men and women who are in the grips of distress. Happy are the "poor," they have given to the world—in Jesus, one of their own—the Kingdom where human hope is satisfied. It is through them that, in Jesus, God accomplishes the *mystery* for the benefit of all the upright of heart. They are at the heart of *communion*.

This narrow and inextricable relationship between "poor" and Kingdom at the very moment of the coming of this Kingdom is at this point essential, that is must last throughout its germination until the day that Revelation sings about when "there will be no more death, and no more mourning or sadness," the world of the past has gone (Rev 21:4). The Church must bear it.

And it is remarkable that the "summaries" in the Acts of the Apostles emphasize how in the community in Jerusalem "no one is in need" (Acts 4:34) because they live by sharing and in this way give concrete form to the ideal already announced in Deuteronomy. It is surely this *communion* of solidarity with the deprived and the unfortunate that Matthew presents as the fundamental attitude which gives direct access to the Kingdom of the Son of Man, on the day of his glory (Matt 15:31-46). Besides, the central place that alms-giving has in the evangelical regulations[138] and throughout the New Testament is well-known. Acts establishes a parallel between it and the sacrifice of the Memorial offered before God (Acts 10:4; cf. Lev 2:2, 9, 16) and the letter to the Hebrews compares charity (holding all things in common) with the sacrifices which are pleasing to God (Heb 13:16). The Fathers will put before the Christian community, sometimes with unusually harsh stress, this evangelical duty of prime importance.[139] In the Church of God, fidelity is not toyed with, they say, in a simple tête-a-tête with the Lord. It always implies a relationship with the misery in the world, with the common life of humanity. This is an essential element of the nature of *communion*.

Care must be taken, however, not to limit this attention to fraternal assistance to apply to the area of short relationships. Although this mutual help remains necessary, wouldn't it serve the purpose of excusing the limits and failures of political policies, even the most noble ones? According to a comment by Jacques Maritain, "the good news which was announced to open heaven and eternal life asks also that the life of earthly societies be transformed where there are miseries and contradictions at the heart of them," and, although the Kingdom is not meant for this world, "when it concerns the suffering found in earthly life, it must be prepared enigmatically."[140] And N. Berdiaeff, in his penetrating analysis about the relationship between Christianity and Marxism, pointed out: "All utopias . . . are judged by the absolutes found in Christianity, however, in no way must it be concluded that Christians do not have to draw conclusions about the struggle which is taking place in the world. More than this, they must decide to take part in this struggle. . . . The purpose of history is the business of God and man. . . . History, in this context, must be understood . . . in its real divine-human process, in the tragic cooperation of God and man."[141] Neither could the Church forget any longer "that between evangelization and human promotion—development,

---

[138]Especially in Luke (Luke 3:11; 6:30, 38; 11:41; 12:33-34; 14:14; 16:9; 18:22; 19:8; Acts 9:36; 10:2, 4, 31; 11:29; 24:17). See F. W. Horn, *Blaube und Handeln in der Theologie des Lukas*, Göttingen, 1983, 58-120.

[139]Concerning alms see *Didache* 1, 6; 4, 7-8; Justin, *Apol.* I, 14, 2; Hermas, *Shepherd*, Mand. II, 4-6, Sim. II 5-7; *Letter to Diognetus* X, 5-6; Clement of Alexandria, *Le Pédagogue* III, cap. 6, 35, 1-2; II, cap. 12, 120-121; Irenaeus, *Adv. Haer.* IV, 17, 1-18, 6; Pontius Diaconus, *Vita Caecilii Cypriani* 2; Basil, *Homélie* 6, 2, 7, 8; John Chrysostom, Hom. sur David 3; 34ᵉhom. sur *1 Corinthiens* 6; 2ᵉ hom. sur Lazare 4; Gregory of Nyssa, *Sur les usuriers* 6; Ambrose, *Sur Naboth le pauvre* 1, 2, 4, 53, 56, 58, 63; *In Psalm. 118* 8, 22; Augustine, *Sermo* 123; Gregory the Great, *Regulae Pastoralis Liber* 21; *Didascalia* II, 34-36, Iv, 6-8; *Vie de sainte Mélanie*, cap. 9, 15, 20, 30, 35; Cesarius of Arles, *Homélie sur la miséricorde, CCL* 103, 109-112; etc.

[140]J. Maritain, *Christianisme et démocratie*, Paris, 1943, 50-51.

[141]N. Berdiaeff, *Christianisme et marxisme*, trad. et prés. de Laurent Gagnebin, Paris, 1975, 34-35.

liberation—there are deep bonds"; that "there can be no division between the plan of Creation and the plan of Redemption which, struck by the very concrete situations of injustice which must be fought against and by the justice which must be restored," that it "is impossible to accept that the work of evangelization can or must ignore extremely grave questions causing such turmoil today concerning justice, freedom, development and peace in the world."[142]

Earlier we underlined how, as far as this purpose is concerned, the Church has become involved in the struggle against idols to which humanity remains inclined to offer sacrifice, despite the unfortunate consequences. It is no accident that the New Testament puts Mammon at the top of the list of these idols: "No one can serve two masters . . . you cannot serve God and Mammon" (Matt 6:24; Luke 16:13).[143] Numerous texts repeat this basic declaration: "The love of money is the root of all evils" (1 Tim 6:10), "the worries of this world, the lure of riches and all the other passions come in to choke the Word, and so it produces nothing" (Mark 4:18, 19), "your wealth is all rotting, your clothes are all eaten up by moths. All your gold and silver are corroding away . . . laborers mowed your fields, and you cheated them—listen to the wages that you kept back, calling out; realize that the cries of the reapers have reached the ears of the Lord of hosts" (Jas 5:1-6), "it is the rich who oppress you, it is they who always drag you into court, they who insult the honorable Name to which you have been dedicated" (Jas 2:6-7).[144]

The Kingdom of God, therefore, refuses all worship rendered to the idol Mammon, all slavery to his cause, all division in one's heart caused by giving in to the seduction of riches. Why? Because among the "gods" of this world, Mammon is the one who enslaves humanity more than all the other "gods" by handing it over to the powers of evil against which the gospel rises up. Money joins up with all sorts of sordid actions. Therefore, one cannot bow down at the same time before Mammon or the gods of his Pantheon and prostrate oneself before the Lord of the Kingdom of God. So much the more since throughout our history the claims made by Mammon and his rivals can always disturb the hearts of men. And this victory is usually won over the helpless, the simple, the afflicted—in brief, those favored by God—who suffer the consequences.

Wherever the Reign of Mammon and his equals is pushed back, it is there that a space is hollowed out for the Kingdom of God. Wherever, in the spirit of the gospel, human communities become free of the shackles

---

[142]These are the expressions of Paul VI in *Evangelii nuntiandi (n° of December 8, 1975)*.

[143]See the study by J. Dupont, "Dieu ou Mammon," *Christianesimo nella storia* 5, 1984, 441–461.

[144]The Fathers will orchestrate these declarations. See in particular the texts to which we return *supra*, note 139.

of Mammon or the consequences of his power and where the "poor" experience a situation of justice and freedom, it is there that the Kingdom of God stands out, shows itself and is recognized intuitively. Today even, the historical power of the poor—with a handful of the oppressed children of Abraham in Egypt in its mainstream and especially with Jesus in the agony in the garden and in the horror of the Cross—proclaims in this way in the Church that in the most profound depths of humanity God has sowed his Kingdom. This is sometimes a daring proclamation which will, undoubtedly, soon be buried by the uproar of a new storm: this Kingdom is not for *this* history. Nevertheless, it is being given birth at this time in history and its presence can be felt.

To express this presence scholastic theology had a very valuable expression. It would have stated that what is experienced in the twists and turns of the dynamics of history is a *res et sacramentum* of the Kingdom: *res* because the reality of this Kingdom is *already* present, *sacramentum* because although it is not in its final stages, what can be perceived gives an inkling of what it will be on the Day of the Son of Man, when "every Principality, Authority and Power," therefore, all those powers which are hostile to the Kingdom, will have been crushed (1 Cor 15:24; cf. 2:21; Col 2:15; 1 Pet 3:22). The Church of God has as its mission to be involved with humanity by its concern to *communicate* with the immense brotherhood of the poor and to give them their true place in its *communion,* a "sacrament" of the Kingdom which comes from something new which is produced within the wear and tear of the world even beyond its borders, some songs of joy and happiness which the ear of faith already hears through the cries of mourning and distress.

It is remarkable that, unequal in their understanding of the faith, Christian communities are usually united together in the effort of all those of upright heart so that societies of freedom, justice and respect for the rights of the human person will be established in our world. This is a manifestation of a level of *communion* which is always present. Their *communion* in the *communion* with the "poor" causes them to be conscious of their common membership in the Kingdom, as much as the urgent need for unity which flows from it. Would it be by the cry of the poor that the "seamless" tunic of Christ Jesus will be rewoven completely to enfold all the members of the Lord,[145] and above all, those who shiver from the cold and show the wounds of their suffering? We would then be living in the logic of the *mirabilia Dei.* . . and of the signs of the Kingdom.

---

[145]Concerning the untorn tunic of Christ which is seen as the symbol of the unity of the Church, see especially Cyprian, *De Ecclesiae Catholicae unitate* 7 (CCL 3/1, 254–255); Augustine, *In Johannis Evangelium tractatus* 118, 4 (CCL 36, 656–657), Bede the Venerable. *In Marci Evangelium exposita* IV, 15 (CCL 120, 630); Id., *In Lucae Evangelium expositio* VI, 23 (CCL 120, 403); Id., *In S. Joannis Evangelium expositio* 19 (PL 92, 911–912). On the biblical plane, see I. de La Potterie, "La tunique sans couture, symbole du Christ grand prêtre?," *Biblica* 60, 1979, 255–269.

Such is the Church of God on this earth, in its poor and fragile state. We have uncovered it as *communion.* We know now the breadth and depth of this *communion.* Unceasingly, whenever we listen to Sacred Scripture the same statements are made: it is a *communion* contained within the *communion* of the triune God, transported in the *communion* of the Son to the human condition, the fruit of the reconciliation of humanity in a *communion* of peace and *Agape,* sent into the world for this universal *communion,* structured as a *Church of Churches,* each Church being a *communion of communions.* It is necessary to expand this vision even more so that it will reveal its full richness to us.

Excursus

a. The liturgies are the major witness of it. See A. Baumstark, *Liturgie comparée,* Chevetogne, 1953, 176–177; H. Pétré, introduction to Etherie, *Journal de Voyage,* SC Paris, 1948, 67. Among the patristic texts let us limit ourselves to quoting Irenaeus, *adv. Haer.* III, 17, 2–3: "It is this Spirit that David has requested for the human race when he said: 'And by your Spirit who directs, affirm me.' It is again this Spirit whom Luke tells us that after the ascension of the Lord descended on the disciples, the day of Pentecost, with power over all nations to bring them into life and open up to them the New Testament: also it is in all languages that, animated by the same feeling, the disciples celebrated the praises of God, while the Spirit reunited the separated tribes and offered to the Father the first-fruits of all nations. That is also why the Lord had promised to send us a Paraclete who would reconcile us to God. Because, as with dry flour, without water, a solid dough and a solid bread cannot be made, so we, who were a multitude, could not either become one in Christ Jesus without the Water come down from heaven. And as the dry earth, if it does not receive water, does not give forth fruit, so we ourselves, who were in the beginning only dry wood, we could have never borne the fruit of life without the generous Rain which came from on high. Because our bodies, through the waters of baptism, have received incorruptibility, while our souls have received it through the Holy Spirit. This is why both are necessary, since both contribute to giving the life of God."

"It is precisely this Spirit who descended on the Lord, 'the Spirit of wisdom and understanding, the Spirit of counsel and strength, the Spirit of knowledge and piety, the Spirit of the fear of God.' And it is this same Spirit whom the Lord in his turn has given to the Church, by sending from heaven the Paraclete over all the earth, wherever the devil had been hurled as a bolt of lightning, according to the word of the Lord: that is why this dew from God is necessary for us so that we will not be consumed nor rendered sterile and so that wherever we have an accuser we also have a Defender. Because the Lord has confided the Holy Spirit to man, his own good, which had fallen into the hands of robbers, this man on whom he had compassion and whose wounds he himself bandaged, giving two royal denarii so that, after receiving the image and inscription of the Father and the Son through the Spirit, we might increase the denarius which has been confided to us and give it back to the Lord well multiplied."

Leo the Great (*De jejunio Pentecostes Sermo* 1, 1) calls the Apostles at Pentecost "princes of the new-born Church" (cf. SC 200, Paris, 1973, 26–27). In his second homily about Pentecost, John Chrysostom affirms: "Today we have arrived at the height of all goods, here we are having reached the motherland (*metropolin*) of solemnities, here we are ready to gather the fruits of the Lord's promise. 'I am going away, he said to us, I will send you another Consoler, I will not leave you orphans' (John 16:17). Do you see his solicitude? Do you see his unspeakable charity? Hardly several days ago he returned to heaven, he took possession of the royal throne, he took his seat at the right hand of the Father; and today he satisfies us with the coming of the Holy Spirit, and he sends to us from the heavens on high innumerable benefits. Isn't it true, I ask you, that all the necessary benefits for our salvation have been showered on us by this divine Spirit? . . . This is where all the things which contribute to the beauty of the Church of God find their source, their origin." (J. Bareille, *Oeuvres complètes,* Paris, 1866, vol. IV, 118.) In his first homily he said: "Human nature ascended to the highest throne ten days ago, and today the Holy Spirit is descending on it. The Lord takes into the heavens the first-fruits of humanity and from it he sends down the Holy Spirit. Another Lord distributes to us his benefits; because the Holy Spirit is equally Lord, the Father, Son and Holy Spirit having shared among them the economy of our redemption. Ten days had not yet passed since the ascension of Christ when he had sent us these spiritual gifts, these assurances of our reconciliation. So that we would not doubt at all and ask this embarrassing question: What did Christ go into the heavens to accomplish; did he reconcile us to the Father; did he bow down in our favor? The divine Master, to show us that reconciliation had been accomplished, immediately sent us the assurances of it" (*ibid.,* 105).

Let us quote yet *Epist* 120 of Jerome at Hedybia: "The Spirit was in the Lord and was not yet totally present in the apostles. It is for that reason that they were afraid at the time of the passion, that they denied Christ and swore that they did not know him. But, once they were baptized in the Holy Spirit and they received the abundance of his grace, they speak to the princes of the Jews with a noble pride: 'It is better to obey God than men' (Act 5:29), they raise the dead to life, rejoice in beatings, give their blood for Christ, crown themselves with their own torment. Therefore, the Spirit was not yet in the apostles, spiritual graces did not flow forth from their hearts, because the Lord had not yet been glorified. What must be understood by this glory, the Lord himself states it in the Gospel: 'Father, glorify me with this glory that I had with you before the world began. The glory of the Savior is the gibbet of his triumph'." (a less literal translation can be found in J. Labourt's, *Saint Jérôme. Lettres,* vol. VI, Paris, 1958, 146.)

b. As an example of this harmonization, let us quote only the *Catecheses* of Cyril of Jerusalem, *Cat* 17, 12–20: "[Jesus] satisfied his apostles with the company of the Holy Spirit. In fact, it is written: 'With these words he breathed on them and said to them: "Receive the Holy Spirit . . . Those whose sins you shall forgive, they shall be forgiven them; those whose sins you shall retain, they shall be retained".' This second breathing on them—since voluntary faults had erased the first—was done so that what had been written would be accomplished . . . But where did he come up from? From hell: because, as the Gospel has related, it is after his resurrection that he breathed on them. But if he gives grace then, he will squander it even more. Here is what he says to them: I am ready to give you at this moment, but your vessel is not yet empty. Therefore, while waiting, receive the amount of grace that you can hold, but wait for more of it still. 'As for you, remain in the city of Jerusalem until you have been clothed with the strength from on high.' Take one portion now; then you will obtain the fullness of it. Because the one who receives often possesses the gift only partially; but the one who 'is clothed' is covered all over by the garment. 'Do not fear, he said, the weapons and characteristics of the devil: you will indeed obtain the power of the Holy Spirit.' Remember what we have just said, knowing that the Spirit is not divided, but only the grace which comes from him." See also *Epistle* 120 of Jerome: "The first day of the resurrection they received the grace of the Holy Spirit by which they would forgive sins, would baptize and would be sons of God and would give believers the spirit of adoption . . . But on the day of Pentecost something more abundant was promised to them; that they would be baptized in the Holy Spirit, they would be clothed with the strength of the Holy Spirit permitting them to preach the Gospel of Christ to all nations . . . This promise of the Holy Spirit was fulfilled on the tenth day after the ascension of the Savior . . . when the Gospel begins the Church is filled with the Spirit so that by his grace and fervor all believers would be cleansed of their sins and that by the fire of the Holy Spirit that the Lord had said he would send, the tongue which was to preach Christ would be healed. Luke and John are not opposed to this." (This text is found in J. O. Labourt, *op. cit.,* 143–145.)

c. This relationship to Babel is found even in liturgical prayers. In the Gelasian (cf. *Liber Sacramentorum Romanae ecclesiae ordinis anni cir-*

culi, edit. Mohlberg, Rome, 1960, 100) and the Leonine (cf. *Sacramentum Veronese,* edit. Mohlberg, Rome, 1956, 27–28: *"Uere dignum: haec tibi nostra confessio, pater gloriae, semper accepta sit, de cordibus filiorum promissionis emissa: quia* (f. 20ᵛ) *nihil sublimius collatum aeclesiae tuae probamus exordiis, quam ut euangelii tui praeconia linguis omnibus credentium ora loquerentur; ut et illa sententia, quam superbae quondam turris extructio meruit, solueretur, et uocum uarietas aedificationi aeclesiasticae non difficultatem faceret, sed augeret potius unitatem: per"*).

d. Augustine, among others, knows this explanation. So, in the *Answers to the questions of January II,* 29 "The fiftieth day is also recommended in the Scriptures, not only in the Gospel which announces the coming of the Holy Spirit, but also in the former sacred books. There, in fact, after the Passover celebrated by the immolation of the lamb, we can count fifty days until the one where, on Mount Sinai, Moses, the servant of God, received the law written by the finger of God: but the Gospel teaches us that the finger of God signifies the Holy Spirit. One evangelist has this said of the Savior: 'I drive away demons by the finger of God,' and another expresses the same thought in this way: 'I drive out demons by the Spirit of God.' . . . The lamb is sacrificed, the Passover is celebrated, and fifty days after, the law is given on account of fear, written with the finger of God. Christ is put to death, as a lamb led to the slaughter, according to the words of Isaiah: the true Passover is celebrated, and, fifty days after, the Holy Spirit is given on account of love, the Holy Spirit which is the finger of God, and the reverse of men seeking their own interests, weighed down because of that with a difficult yoke and a heavy weight, and not finding any rest for their souls, because charity does not seek its own interests . . . Read Exodus, and see how many days after the celebration of the Passover the law was given. God speaks to Moses in the desert of Sinai on the first day of the third month. Mark, therefore, one day since the beginning of this third month and see what the Lord says among other things: 'Go down to the people and tell them to sanctify and purify themselves today and tomorrow; Let them wash their clothing and hold themselves in readiness for the third day, because on the third day the Lord will descend on the mountain of Sinai in the sight of all the people.' The law was given in this way on the third day of the third month. But, count from the fourteenth day of the first month, when the Passover was celebrated, until the third day of the third month, and you will find seventeen days from the first, thirty from the second, three from the third, which makes fifty days."

e. There is a similar vision found in Leo the Great. What we have is this passage from his beautiful Christmas sermon, linking this "christique" totality to the messianic vision of peace. But the context is different: "The feast today renews for us the first moments of Jesus' life, born of the Virgin Mary. And when we adore the birth of our Savior, what we are doing is celebrating our own origin. In fact, when Christ comes into the world, the Christian people begin: the anniversary of the head is the anniversary of the body. Without doubt, each one of those who are called is so in his turn, and the sons of the Church appear in different eras. However, since the faithful in their totality, born at the spring of baptism, have been crucified with Christ in his Passion, raised at his Ressurection, seated at the right of the Father at his ascension, they are born with him in this Nativity. Every believer, no matter where he live in the world, who is reborn in Christ, after abandoning the ways of sin which he has followed all his life, becomes a new man through his second birth. He no longer belongs to the ancestors of his father born of flesh, but to the line which finds its origin in the Savior, because he has become Son of Man that we might become sons of God . . . Because it is peace which produces the sons of God, which promotes love, which gives birth to unity, which is the repose of the blessed, the abode of eternity. Its proper work, its particular benefit, is to unite to God those whom it separates from the world. . . . Therefore, those who are not born of the flesh, nor of carnal desire, nor of the will of man, but who are born of God, must offer to the Father the unanimous will of sons who are architects of peace. All those who have become members of Christ by adoption must hasten to join together the first-born of the new creation, the one who has come not to do his own will, but the will of the one who sent him. The heirs adopted by the grace of the Father are not heirs who are divided or unlike one another; they have the same feelings and the same love. Those who are born again in the singular image must have a soul which resembles his. The birth of the Lord Jesus is the birth of peace. As Saint Paul says, it is he, Christ, who is our peace. Whether we are of Jewish or pagan origin, it is through him that we can approach the Father in one single Spirit'' (*Christmas Sermon,* 1, 1–3; trans. SC 22bis, 66–68, 72–74). See also the *Sermon on the Passion,* 12, 3–7; SC 74, 58, 63. This vision is the one which is found in Western thought. It will also be found in the beautiful text of the *Sermon for the Assumption* by Isaac of Stella, an English Cistercian, a friend of Thomas Becket, who died around 1168: "The Son of God is the first-born of a great number of brothers, because, being an only Son by nature, he gathered together around him through grace a multitude of brothers who are all one with him: to all those who received him, he gave the power to become children of God. Having become the Son of Man, he made the multitude of men sons of God. He gathered them unto himself, whereas he is unique by his love and power. Men, in themselves, by their birth according to the flesh, are a multitude; but by their second birth, the divine birth, they are entirely one with him. The only Christ, one and complete, is the head and the body. And this one Christ is the Son of the one God in heaven and of one mother on the earth. There are many sons, and there is only one single son. And just as the head and the body are one single son and several sons, likewise Mary and the Church are one single mother and several mothers, one single virgin and several virgins. Both are mothers; both, virgins. Both have conceived of the Holy Spirit, without carnal desire. Both have given an offspring to God the Father, without sin. One has produced, without any stain of sin, a head for the body; the other has given birth, in the remission of sins, to a body for the head. Both are mothers of Christ, but each one of these two does not give birth entirely without the other. Also it is deservedly that, in the divinely inspired Scriptures, what is said in general about the virgin mother the Church is applied in a particular way to the Virgin Mary; and what is said about the virgin mother Mary, in a particular way, is understood in general about the virgin mother the Church. And when a text speaks of one or the other, it can be applied almost without distinction and indifferently to both . . . The inheritance of the Lord, in its entirety, is the Church, it is especially Mary, and it is the soul of every believer in particular. In his dwelling in Mary's womb Christ stayed nine months; in his dwelling in the faith of the Church he will stay until the end of this world; and in the understanding and love of the believer forever and ever.'' (*Sermon 51 for the Assumption, PL* 194, 1863, 1865.) Or again in this sermon for the 5th Sunday after Epiphany: ''The Church cannot forgive anything without Christ; Christ does not will to forgive anything without the Church. The Church cannot forgive anything except in the penitent, in other words, in the one whom Christ has touched; Christ does not will to guarantee any forgiveness in one who despises the Church.''

''The all-powerful Christ can do all by himself, in other words, baptize, consecrate the Eucharist, ordain, forgive sins and the rest; but, a humble and faithful Husband, he does not want to do anything without his spouse. I say: this is a great mystery which applies to Christ and the Church. Be careful that you do not break the head of the dove, decapitate the turtle-dove, cut off the head from the body. Because Christ did not wish to be decapitated, but to be stretched out on the cross, suspended in order to unite the bottom, the top and the middle. Be careful, therefore, that you do not separate the head from the body, preventing Christ from existing whole and entire forever, because Christ exists nowhere in his entirety without the Church, just as the Church exists nowhere in its entirety without Christ. In fact, the whole and complete Christ is the head and the body, as he says: 'No one goes up to heaven except the one who descended from heaven, the Son of Man who is in heaven.' This man alone forgives sins.'' (*Sermon* 11, 15; trans. G. Salet, found in Isaac of Stella

Sermons, sc 130, Paris, 1967, 246-247, the latin text is very strong: *"Noli ergo corpori caput subtrahere, ut nusquam sit totus Christus; neque enim totus Christus, sine Ecclesia usquam, sicut tota Ecclesia sine Christo nusquam. Totus est enim et integer Christus, caput et corpus Propter quod dicit: Nemo ascendit in coelum, nisi qui descendit de coelo Filius hominis, qui est in coelo."*) See *ibid.,* 344-345, the interesting note about the Body of Christ showing the link with Augustine and evoking the very realistic texts of Isaac; see also in *Sermons,* vol. II, SC 207, Paris, 1974, note 21; PL 194, 1831-1832. That is taken up again by another Cistercian, Helinand de Froidmont, who died in 1229: *"Toties nascitur Christus quoties fit aliquis christianus,"* indeed *"haec mysterialis Christi nativitas ab initio mundi usque ad finem celebratur: sicut teste Paulo qui ea quae de passionibus Christi durant supplebat in Corpore suo, Christus nondum totus natus est"* (In *Epiphania* 2, PL 212, 525).

A repetition of this vision is found in Thomas Aquinas, even in the *Summa Theologica,* but in a different synthesis: *"Sicut naturale corpus est unum ex membrorum diversitate consistens, ita tota Ecclesia quae est mysticum Corpus Christi computatur quasi una persona cum suo Capite quod est Christus"* (IIIa, 49, 1). See also in the commentary of Col 1:24 (known undoubtedly in the *reportatio* by Reginald) this beautiful passage: *"Haec verba secundum superficiem malum possent habere intellectum, scilicet quod Christi passio non esset sufficiens ad complendum passiones sanctorum. Sed hoc est haereticum, quia sanguis Christi est sufficiens ad redemptionem, etiam multorum mundorum. Ipse est propitiatio pro peccatis nostris, etc. Sed intelligendum est, quod Christus et Ecclesia est una persona mystica, cujus caput est Christus, corpus omnes justi: quilibet autem justus est quasi membrum hujus capitis. Et membra de membro. Deus autem ordinavit in sua predestinatione quantum meritorum debet esse per totam ecclesiam, tam in capite quam in membris, sicut et praedestinavit numerum electorum. Et inter haec merita praecipue sunt passiones sanctorum Martyrum. Christi, scilicet capitis, merita sunt infinita, quilibet vero sanctus exhibet aliqua merita secundum mensuram suam. Et ideo dicis: Adimpleo ea qua desunt passionum Christi, id est, totius ecclesiae, cujus caput est Christus. Adimpleo, id est, addo mensuram meam. Et hoc in carne, id est, ego ipse patiens. Vel quae passiones desunt in carne mea. Hoc enim deerat, quod sicut Christus passus erat in corpore suo, ita pateretur in Paulo membro suo, et similiter in aliis. Et pro corpore, quod est eccelsia, quae erat redimenda per Christus."* But Thomas Aquinas states precisely, in the spirit of Augustine, that it is necessary to distinguish the Body without its Head from the Body with its Head. In this last case, Christ is a member of the "total" Body only in a particular way and one must be very prudent and precise in using such a formula (cf. *In IV Sent.,* from 49, 2, 4, 3, to 4; *De Ver.* 29, art. 4, to 6).

Augustine uses, in fact, several expressions worth recalling. He speaks of

—*Christus,* Head and Body (thus *De Gen. ad lit.* 11, 24, 31, PL 34, 441);

—*Totus Christus* (Thus *Sermo Denis* 11, 8, MA I, 50; C. Faust, 12, 39; 22, 94, PL 42, 274, 463; *De Unit.* Eccl. 4, 7, PL 43, 395; *De Trin.* 3, 10, 20, PL 42, 880. *Sermo* 129, 3–4; 133, 8; 137, 7, PL 38, 722, 742, 754; *Sermo* 341, 1, PL 39, 1493; *In Ps.* 3, 9; 56, 1; 68, 1; 74, 4, PL 36, 76, 661, 840, 948; *In Ps.* 100, 3; 118, 2, PL 37, 1284, 1514);

—*Unus Christus,* Head and Body (thus *De pecc. mer* 1, 31, 60, PL 44, 144 ; *De Trin.* 4, 9, 12, PL 42, 896 ; *De civ. Dei* 13, 23, 3 and 17, 409, PL 41, 397; *Sermo* 144, 4, 5, PL 38, 789; *Sermo* 341, 9, 11, PL 39, 1499; *In Ps* 54, 3, PL 36, 628; *In Ps.* 123, 1; 127, 3; 140, 3, PL 37, 1639, 1678, 1816);

—*Corpus Christi totum, universum* (thus *In Ps.* 118, 1, PL 37, 1589);

—*Unus homo* (thus *In Ps* 29, 5, PL 36, 219; *In Ps* 83, 5; 103, 2; 118, 6; 119, 7, PL 37, 1058, 1336, 1546, 1602);

—*Unus corpus* (thus *De continentia* 10, PL 40, 365);

—*Perfectus vir* (thus *In Ps* 90, 1; 101, 2, PL 37, 1158, 1305);

—*Una caro* (thus *Sermo* 263, 3, PL 38, 1211; *C. Faust* 12, 39, PL 42, 274).

—It is in the christological perspective concerning the assuming of the entire human nature in Christ that these lines of Hilary of Poitiers (*De Trinitate* VIII, 13–16; PL 10, 246–249) must be read: "If the Word has truly been made flesh, it is also true that we eat the Word incarnate when we communicate at the banquet of the Lord. How is it possible not to think of him living in us naturally? In fact, by his birth as man, he has taken on our carnal nature in a way that is henceforth definitive, and, in the sacrament of his flesh given in communion, he united his carnal nature to his eternal nature. It is thus that we all form one single being, because the Father is in Christ and Christ is in us."

See also Gregory of Nyssa, *Discours catéchétique* 32, 4: "The man in whom God was incarnated, the man who was raised up, by his resurrection, with the divinity, was indeed taken out of our clay. But, just as in our body the activity of one of the senses creates a common sensation in the entire organism which is joined to the member, in the same way, the entire human nature which forms, so to speak, one single living being, the resurrection of the member stretches out to the whole being, and from the one part there is communication to the whole, by virtue of the continuity and the unity of its nature" (trans. L. Meridier, coll. "Hemmer-Lejay," Paris, 1908, 145–147).

On this whole question, see the important study by L. Malevez, "L'Église dans le Christ," *Rev. des Sc. Rel.* 25, 1935, 257–291, 418–439. See also, for Cyril of Alexandria, M. de Durand, *Deux Dialogues christologiques,* SC 97, Paris, 1964, 90–98.

For a complete overview of the problem see J. Hamer, *L'Église est une communion,* Paris, 1962.

2

Church of God,
People of God in Communion

The Kingdom is for a People. In fact, throughout the long course of history, the two names go side by side. If one insists more on the human and historical density of the ecclesial reality, the other on its eschatological perspective, they both refer to one another: the People are marching towards a Kingdom, and the Kingdom is the good of a People.

Also, the necessity of an analysis requires us to treat the two aspects separately, emphasizing very forcefully the specific distinctions between them. It is important to recall right from the start that the one does not exclude the other. They are inseparable. In regard to *communion*—their common foundation—the socio-religious condition of the people of God has, nevertheless, the immense advantage of showing how the Church is deeply rooted in the totality of God's action from the time of the most distant origins of the historical incarnation of his design, therefore, the *communion* of all generations *jam ab Abel justo*. It permits, also, a better understanding of how the life which comes from the Spirit takes form only in the *communion* of all believers. The people of God is composed of men and women who together in an osmosis of charisms and functions, under the guidance of the Holy Spirit, welcome, understand, actualize, celebrate, transmit the faith which causes them to become the Church of God advancing towards that day when their Lord will give back the Kingdom to God his Father (1 Cor 15:24).

In this chapter we are going to try to understand *communion* no longer by its essential characteristics but by the dynamism which composes it. It is the dynamism of a People called to span the course of history. We will come across again the characteristics already encountered, but in another perspective.

I. The Church of God
The Entire Olive Tree Grafted Together (Rom 11:16-24)

The group of those men and women who believe in Christ is called "the Church of God" (*Ekklesia tou Theou,* Acts 20:28; 1 Cor 1:2; 10:32; 11:16, 22; 15:9; 2 Cor 1:1; Gal 1:13; 1 Thess 2:14; 2 Thess 1:4; 1 Tim 3:5-15), and it is composed of the Churches. It is important to reiterate that by this term *Ekklesia*—signifying in Greek the official assembly of the social group, the coming together in one and the same place citizens of the political community—the version of the Septuagint, in several very important passages translated it by the Hebrew *Qahal.*[1] This word designated the gathering of the believing People, called together by God[2] for an important step in its life, an "assembly of God" (Deut 23:2, 3, 4, 9; 1 Chr 28:8; Neh 13:1; Mic 2:5). They remained then together *before God,* in a state of Covenant,[3] conscious of the basic dependence of Israel in regard to the One who had called forth from the night peoples by his sole initiative. The *Qahal* was the People of God (the *'am*) but in a coming together because of its faith, ordinarily expressed by a common liturgical act.

Therefore, when the Christian community, quite early, it seems, is designated spontaneously as Church of God, it makes itself the object of this divine initiative. And if it is difficult to know what the Letter to the Galatians calls the Israel of God (Gal 6:16),[4] it is clear in return that the title of "saints" which is given to Christians—in Acts, the Pauline writings, the letters written while in captivity, the pastorals, the Epistle to the Hebrews, Jude's Letter which is in Revelation—affirms the same conviction. The Christian community is aware that it is the chosen people since the

---

[1]On this question, see the important study by K. L. Schmidt, *Ekklesia in G. Kittel, TWNT* 3, 502–539 (with the link with *Qahal,* 530–535); W. Klaiber, *Rechtfertigung und Gemeinde,* Göttingen, 1982, 11–21; H. Schlier, *Essais sur le Nouveau Testament,* coll. "Lectio divina," 46, Paris, 1968 363–369; and especially H. Merklein "Die Ekklesia Gottes; der Kirchenbegriff bei Paulus und in Jerusalem," *BZ* 23, 1979, 48–70. On the secular meaning of *ekklesia* see the article by G. G. Brandis, in Pauly-Wissowa, V, 2.

[2]The idea of "convocation" important for the Old Testament (cf. "la convocation sainte," of Exod 12:16; Lev 23:; Neh 29:1, of the priestly tradition) is in the verb *ek-kaleo,* I call, I convoque. In the New Testament the faithful will be called *klètoi* (Rom 1:6; 8:28; 1 Cor 1:24).

[3]The fine distinction between *synagôgè,* often used to translate both *Qahal* and *ekklesia* could be this reference to the "state of covenant," implying both divine initiative and the attitude of the people gathered together. They will speak of the *synagôgè* of nations, of wicked, of "animals," of mad people, of pagans (thus Gen 28:3; 35:11; 48:4; Ps 22:17; 68:31; 86:14), *synagôgè* putting less stress on the divine initiative and emphasizing especially the group, the crowd, those assembled together. But the distinction is often tenuous, see Prov 5:14 where the two terms are used interchangeably. See K. Hruby, "La synagogue dans la littérature rabbinique," *Orient syrien 9,* 1964, 473–564.

[4]The Church as such? Simply the totality of the members of Israel who have accepted Jesus as the Messiah? This last sense seems more plausible to us.

beginning of time—*jam ab Abel justo*—that God was preparing for himself for the eschatological era. It is seen as the People of saints spoken of in the book of Daniel (7:18; 8:24; cf. Rev 13) in its vision of the last days.[5] Because it is the result of what is prepared and then begins with Israel, it is radically inseparable from this beginning and from what it implies. It is not simply the People—the *laos tou Theou*—as an ethnic or social entity (cf. Acts 7:34; Rom 9:25, 26; 11:1, 2; 2 Cor 6:16; Heb 4:9; 11:25). It is so in its state of gathering and of *communion,* in its being of final grace, therefore, eschatological.[6] But if this community is perceived as the people of God in this way, it is as totally encompassed in the *communion* of Christ. It is the *Qahal* (the *Ekklesia*) of Thessalonika, of Ephesus or elsewhere, as it "is in God the Father and in the Lord Jesus Christ" (1 Thess 1:1; 2 Thess 1:1; cf. 1 Thess 2:14). It is from there that come both its unbreakable solidarity with the Israel of the Promise and its certainty of going beyond it.[7] It is the People in its "fulfillment" (its *teleiosis*) in Christ Jesus.

1. Complete *communion* with the vocation of the people of God, understood in its deepest roots and its most absolute beginnings, is obviously implied in the very title of Christ, Messiah, given right from the beginning to the Lord Jesus. To call this one Christ, as all of the New Testament traditions do, despite the diversity of the approaches of his person and his work,[8] is to affirm his link with the "Chosen People," even in those areas where, (as in the Hellenistic communities) there is hardly any

[5]The number of times the expression *toi hagioi* appears is considerable: Acts 9:13, 32, 41; 26:10; Rom 1:7; 8:27; 12:13; 15:25, 26, 31; 16:2; 15:4; 1 Cor 1:2; 6:1, 2; 14:33; 16:1, 15; 2 Cor 1:1; 8:4; 9:1, 12; 13:12; Eph 1:1, 15, 18; 2:19; 3:8, 18; 4:12; 5:3; 6:18; Phil 1:1; 4:22; Col 1:2, 4, 12, 26; 1 Thess 8:13; 2 Thess 1:10; 1 Tim 1:14; Phlm 1:5, 7; Heb 6:10; 18:24; Jude 3:4; Rev 5:8; 8:3, 4; 11:18; 13:7, 10; 14:12; 16:6; 17:6; 18:20, 24; 19:8; 20:9; 22:4.

The abundance of texts which are placed in an explicitly eschatological context should be noted. At Qumran this term is widely used to designate oneself as a member of the messianic community.

[6]See W. Klaiber, *art. cit.,* 22.

[7]H. Schlier, *op. cit.,* 364.

[8]On this diversity see especially the enlightening book by J. D. G. Dunn, *Unity & Diversity in the New Testament,* London, 1979; O. Cullmann, *Christologie du Nouveau Testament,* Neuchâtel-Paris, 1958, 97–117; V. Taylor, *The Names of Jesus,* London, 1953. In the Synoptics and in Acts it is a question again of a title for Christ, and not of a proper name. The transition is already made, nevertheless, in the last books of the New Testament. Concerning this evolution Cullmann states: "To the extent to which the early community was aware of already living in the time of the fulfillment and of itself being the 'people of God,' the chosen people, the idea was to assert itself on this people that the messianic role was fulfilled in Jesus; not according to the political scheme, but according to the scheme of the history of salvation. In order to bring to light the continuity between the old and the new convenant, they emphasized also the davidic relationship of Jesus, to which Jesus himself had attributed such little value. So, the title of 'son of David' acquired such an importance that it was inserted into the confessions of faith (Rom 1:3, Ign. Smyrn. I.1, Trall. 9.1). The profound sense of davidic royalty was made real in the reign of Jesus, raised to the right hand of God. The purpose to which this royalty over Israel tended was attained" (*op. cit.,* 116).

more interest in typically Jewish hopes and expectations. His work is inserted into the Covenant and the Promise.

In this perspective, the choice of the Twelve and its implications in the New Testament—all the way to the celestial Liturgy in Revelation—take on a particular significance. The Twelve have, beyond their close association with the ministry of the one "with whom they are associated" (cf. Mark 3:14) and of their mission to evangelize (Matt 28:18-20), an important eschatological function. This function links them to the twelve tribes of Israel: seated on twelve thrones they will judge them (Matt 19:28; Luke 22:30; cf. 1 Cor 6:2; Rev 20:4)[9] and in a Kingdom where Abraham, Isaac and Jacob have their places (Matt 8:11) with the prophets (Luke 13:28). It would be impossible to imagine a closer association with the People of the Covenant: on the Day of the Son of Man, when the economy of our history will open up into something totally new (cf. Matt 19:28), the witnesses of the Covenant at its fulfillment will be the twelve Apostles of the Lord Jesus. They are the ones who will have in their power judgment over the twelve tribes whose *communion* with God and with each other was to make up the Israel of God, always open to the unexpected in the Covenant but always faithful to its great demands. On the eschatological plane, it is in the twelve Apostles chosen by Christ Jesus that the meaning and finality of the choice by God of the Israel composed of twelve tribes is unveiled and understood. Also it is of prime importance that after the betrayal by Judas the number twelve is restored to it (Acts 1:15-26):[10] it proceeds from the profound unity in the design of God for his People, the object of the first apostolic preaching.[11]

Revelation can, therefore, in a grandiose vision, sing the glorious accomplishment of the people of God by enumerating the servants of the living God according to the tribes of the sons of Israel,[12] despite the difficulty which the infidelity of the tribe of Dan represents (Judg 18:11-31) ably replaced by that of Manasseh (Rev 7:4-17). But if messianic Jeru-

---

[9]On this question see the study by J. Dupont, "Le logion des douze trônes," *Biblica* 45, 1964, 355-392. For the whole of the link between the Twelve and Israel, see especially J. Jervell, *Luke and the People of God, a New Look at Luke-Acts,* Minneapolis, 1972, 75-112 (taken up again in an article entitled "The Twelve on Israel's Throne," with abundant notes).

[10]See P. H. Menoud, "Les additions au groupe des douze apôtres d'après le livre des Actes" *RHPR* 37, 1957, 71-80; J. Dupont, "Le douzième Apôtre (Acts 1:15-26), à propos d'une explication récente," *Nouvelles Études sur les Actes des Apôtres,* coll. "Lectio Divina," 118, Paris, 1984, 186-192 (on the subject of M. Wilcox, "The Judas-Tradition in Acts 1:15-26," *NTS* 19, 1972-1973, 438-452).

[11]Ph. H. Menoud, *art. cit.,* thinks that these Twelve are the sign of a Salvation which God intends first of all for Israel.

[12]It seems very much, in fact, that one must not see in 7:4-8 an allusion to the Jews who recognized Jesus as Christ and who would be set apart from the numberless crowd in verses 9-10. It is a question of this crowd but seen according to the basic cell which is the Israel of the Promise.

salem has on its doors "the names of the twelve tribes of the sons of Israel," it has on the foundations of its ramparts "the twelve names of the twelve Apostles of the Lamb" (Rev 21:12, 14). In the eschatological completion of God's plan, the holy City is the glorious fulfillment of the Jerusalem of Israel, thanks to the Lamb. Also the "old" realities now appear under their true light of day. Their role remains engraved in the final work, not as a souvenir in the modern sense of the term but as an eternal "memorial."[13] Even in the Kingdom of Christ Jesus (cf. 1:5-8; 5:10), it is still thanks to these realities that "one will enter through the gates into the City" (22:14). Without them this would not be the case.

Perhaps there is an indication of this in the fact that the adjective used to designate the ultimate realities, considering the realities of the old Covenant, is not *neos,* which would signify something radically new, but *kainos* (21:1, 2, 5) which indicates rather a radical change, a total renewal, in relation to something which precedes it.[14] Revelation speaks in this sense of a "new" (*kaine*) Jerusalem (3:12; 21:2), of a "new" earth and "new" heaven (21:1), of a "new" name (2:17; 3:12), of a "new" hymn (5:9; 14:3), of all things "new" (21:5), as a stunning contrast with the old order of things. Here, as when the Synoptics speak of the "new" wine (Matt 26:29; Mark 14:25), it is a question of something new but based on a contrast with something already experienced, of a magnificent flowering forth in the field of a customary continuity, of a reality coming forth from something which precedes it. With the same overtones Johannine tradition evokes the "new" commandment (John 13:34; cf. 1 John 2:7-8; 2 John 1:5) and Paul speaks of the "new" creation contrasted with the old world which has gone (2 Cor 5:17) or the regulation for circumcision which has lost its purpose (Gal 6:15). And when the epistles of the captivity set up the "new" man against the old man (Eph 4:22-24, cf. 2:15; Col 3:10-11), it is to declare a transformation, a renewal, not the pure and simple rising up of a new reality. It is the same thing for the "new" Covenant (Heb

---

[13]It would even seem that the apostles had in these texts a less defined place than that of the twelve tribes (cf. J. Massyngberde Ford, *Revelation,* coll. "The Anchor Bible," 38, New York, 1984, 333). But it is clear that "the juxtaposition of the twelve tribes and the twelve apostles shows the unity between ancient Israel and the Church of the New Testament" (R. H. Mounce, *The Book of Revelation,* Grand Rapids, ed. 1980, 379); and "here rests the problem of the relationship between Israel and the christian Church; without believing that this Church substitutes for Israel, it seems to be indicated that what is seen in "the new Jerusalem" is the fulfillment of the entire people of God . . . which includes that of Israel . . .; alongside of the names of the twelve tribes are those of the twelve apostles; the two covenants are, therefore, united" (Ch. Brutsch, *La Clarté de l'Apocalypse,* 5th ed., Geneva, 1966, 365).

[14]Concerning *kainos* and *neos,* see especially R. A. Harrisville, "The Concept of Newness in the New Testament," *JBL* 74, 1955, 69-79; Id., *The Concept of Newness in the New Testament,* Minneapolis, 1960; E. Larsson, "Christus als Vorbild," *Acta Seminarii Neotestamentici Uppsaliensis* 23, 1967, 197-210; J. Ysebaert, "Greek Baptismal Terminology," *Graecitas christianorum primaeva,* 1, 1962.

8:13; cf. 8:8; 9:15; Luke 22:20; 1 Cor 11:25). Apostolic traditions are careful to point out that this "newness" was awaited and announced by the Scriptures (cf. 2 Pet 3:15; Heb 8:8). It fulfills their expectation. In a certain way it sets it in motion.

Baptism then takes on its full dimension. On the morning of Pentecost it is present clearly as an eschatological act. To the recipients of the Promise (Acts 2:39) Peter proposes a baptism linked to conversion and to the gift of the Spirit who has been promised (2:33, 38), destined for their salvation (2:40), at the very moment when the last days are starting to occur (2:17, 21).[15] What John accomplished at his "baptism of conversion" (Luke 3:3), received by Jesus himself whose mission had not yet been revealed, is thus taken up again in the Christian baptism of Pentecost, in Jerusalem (Acts 1:4-5). This last points to a fulfillment of the Promise with a return of Israel to its true vocation, made possible by the acceptance of the apostolic kerygma which is supposed to lead it also to conversion and forgiveness (5:31; cf. 2:38; 3:19). What Luke gave as a vocation for the Baptist, "to give his people knowledge of salvation through forgiveness of their sins" (Luke 1:77), relates to what he gives for the content of the apostolic preaching entrusted with announcing "the conversion and the forgiveness of the sins of all the nations, starting with Jerusalem" (24:47).[16] The baptism of John, with its finality, is assumed in the baptism of the Apostles.

2. But since the time of Pentecost, Salvation, always offered to Israel, comes necessarily through Jesus Christ (Acts 4:12; 5:31; 10:43; 13:38-39). Also baptism itself is conferred "in his Name" (2:38, cf. 8:16; 10:48; 19:5; 22:16). His Death and Resurrection complete, indeed, the work of Salvation. The dynamism of the Promise is henceforth under their auspices. The realities of the people of God—always the object of the Promise, repeat to the Israelites the apostolic kerygma (2:39; 3:25-26; 13:32-33)—and the coming of the messianic Kingdom (Dan 2:44-45) where God "will gather together" his divided People (Jer 3:18; 31:1; Isa 11:13-14; Ezra 34:11-16; 37:15-28; Hos 2:2; Zech 9:1; Mic 2:12) depend now on what "the God of Abraham, Isaac and Jacob, the God of the fathers" (3:13; 5:30) has accomplished in his Servant Christ Jesus. They are swept up

---

[15]See the enlightening article by G. Lohfink, "Der Ursprung der christlichen Taufe," *ThQ* 156, 1976, 35–54. See also G. W. H. Lampe, *The Seal of the Spirit*, London, 1951, 33: the baptism of the apostles "is still an eschatological rite since it tends toward the final redemption yet to come when the Lord returns in glory; but compared with the baptism of John it represents a fulfillment and an accomplishment of the hope of Israel."

[16]That is emphasized by J. Dupont, "Les discours de Pierre," *Nouvelles Études sur les Actes des Apôtres*, coll., 58–111 (77).

and embodied in the Salvation of Christ Jesus, with what kinds of implications the Spirit causes to be perceived in it.[17]

A homily attributed, and rightly so it seems, to Bishop Fauste de Riez, in the fifth century, expressed marvelously both the basic continuation of the people of God in Jesus Christ and yet the overreaching quality brought about by the Cross and Resurrection. There is a commentary on the sign at Cana: "According to the Apostle, the old world has gone away, a new world is already born. In the same way that water contained in vats does not disappear, but receives in that way an existence that it did not formerly have, so also the law does not disappear, but is perfected by the coming of Christ. . . . Since the wine has run out another wine is brought in; the wine of the old convenant was good, but that of the new is better. The old covenant, the one which the Jews observe, evaporates in the letter. The new covenant, the one which concerns us, gives back to us the taste of life by giving us grace. The good wine, in other words, the good commandment, is the one in the Law which teaches: You will love your neighbor and hate your enemy. But the wine of the Gospel is better and stronger, when it teaches you: I tell you: love your enemies, do good to those who hate you."[18]

Blaise Pascal, always aware of the tension existing between "opposites," which is internal to truth, and seeing that "the Christian religion was founded on a preceding religion" showed that in "faces" destined to disappear, the "truth" which was to endure was prepared, that in "faces" which displeased God, the "truth" which would please him was clearing a path for itself.[19] The Church of God (*Ekklesia tou Theou*) is nothing else but the people of God at the end of time, "the People of Abraham, Isaac and Jacob" called together and assembled by God, the *Qahal* of God of the messianic era opened up by the Death and exaltation of the Lord Christ Jesus. It begins with the People. Also, "in one sense it was not to be established: the People of God existed from the time of Abraham in Israel; what Jesus did, is to institute it according to a new and definitve Disposition (*diathèkè*)."[20] It is in this sense that he establishes it.

The continuity is effected, moreover, in the strictest sense, by the "Rest"

[17]J. Dupont, "Repentir et conversion d'après les Actes des Apôtres," *Études sur les Actes des Apôtres,* 421–458, shows how for the Jews conversion implies repentance for the crucifixion (cf. especially 433–436), whereas for the pagans it will be a question of repentance for idolatry. That seems to us to be a clarifying point on the profound unity between the *Qahal* and the Christian *Ekklesia.*

[18]Fauste de Riez, *Hom.* 5 (second for Epiphany, *PLS* 3, 562, a translation of the *Liturgie des heures* I, 562 slightly modified.

[19]*Pensées* 619 (Brunschvicg) and 454 (Lafuma); 687 (Brunschvicg) and 272 (Lafuma); 571, 659, 675 (Brunschvicg) and 500–503 (Lafuma).

[20]Y. Congar, "Confession, Église et communion," *Irénikon* 23, 1950, 3–56 (25).

of Israel. This seems to be Paul's vision.[21] In sociological (or historical) Israel the irreligious, whom the prophets denounce, are intermingled with the modest Remainder of the just and elect.[22] This last group represents the authentic Israel, the true posterity of Abraham for whom the Promise is to be fulfilled. Paul affirms in the Letter to the Romans (Rom 11:5-26) his hope that this entire Remainder—the true Israel—will be saved, not only the small nucleus of Judeo-Christians who have accepted the apostolic kerygma, but also the others who remain faithful to their faith although still not open to the announcement of Christ Jesus.[23]

3. In Christ Jesus this "Remainder" who have been saved—to whom, it seems, the Letter of James is addressed (1:1; 2:2)—enter, nevertheless, into an inheritance henceforth destined for the whole of humanity which accepts the divine offer. The universal opening up of the Promise which certain sectors of the Jewish people had already had an inkling of,[24] comes about. According to Paul's expression in his speech at Agrippa, the Gentiles have "a share in the inheritance of the sanctified" (Acts 26:18). And in a conclusive passage about the Christian vision of the Church of God, whose perspective is too often limited by seeing in it only the pure and simple affirmation of justification *a sola fide,* explains that this widening is found entirely in the promise to Abraham:

> Take Abraham for example: he put his faith in God, and this faith was considered as justifying him. Don't you see that it is those who rely on faith who are the sons of Abraham? Scripture foresaw that God was going to use faith to justify the pagans, and proclaimed the Good News long ago when Abraham was told: In you all the nations will be blessed. Those therefore who rely on faith receive the same blessing as Abraham, the man of faith. On the other hand, those who rely on the keeping of the Law are under a curse, since it is written: Cursed be everyone who does not persevere in observing everything prescribed in the book of the Law. . . . Christ redeemed us from the curse of the Law by being cursed for our sake, since it is written: Cursed be everyone who is hanged on a tree. This was done so that in Christ Jesus the blessing of Abraham might include the pagans, and so that through faith we might receive

---

[21]We follow the position of F. Refoulé, *Et ainsi tout Israël sera sauvé.* See also Jervell, *op. cit.,* 41-74, especially 62-69.

[22]See the prayers of the synagogue quoted *ibid.,* p. 133 and the thinking of Qumran mentioned on p. 146.

[23]"The double declaration by Paul in chapters 9-11: 'It is the rest which will be saved' and 'all of Israel will be saved' is in no way contradictory: it is only the rest which will be saved, but *all the rest,* that which is already in the Church and that which is still presently hard of heart. This is the mystery proclaimed by Paul" (181).

[24]See P. E. Dion, *Dieu universel et peuple élu,* and what we have presented at length in our first chapter.

the promised Spirit. Compare this, brothers, with what happens in ordinary life: If a will has been drawn up in due form, no one is allowed to disregard it or add to it. Now the promises were addressed to Abraham and to his descendants—notice, that scripture does not use a plural word as if there were several descendants, it uses the singular: to his posterity, which is Christ (Gal 3:6-16).

There is no break with the Promise: it is widened. The figure of Abraham is not disowned; there is a focus on his faith and by that fact on his inner nature. His posterity is no longer limited to race, to circumcision attached to this race, but it is opened up on a faith rooted in his faith as "father of believers" (Rom 4:9-12, 16-25). And this faith embraces in unity Jews and Greeks (Gal 3:28-29).[25]

In this way the Church of God becomes, in Christ Jesus, the fundamental and radical *communion* of the pagans in the "posterity of Abraham," in the Promise, in the blessing linked to Abraham's faith. It is there that we find an essential and primary dimension of *koinonia,* too often ignored. Gentiles welcoming the gospel are, through the Spirit, immersed in *communion* to what were until then privileges of Israel, the inheritance of Israel, love and fidelity towards Israel, mercy and tenderness for Israel, a promise for Israel, a relationship with Israel, a hope for Israel, the faith of Israel. Their titles—children (Gal 3:26; Rom 8:16), heirs (Gal 3:29), beloved (Rom 1:7), saints (Rom 1:7), those who are called (Rom 1:6), chosen (Rom 8:33), believers (Rom 1:16)—are a *communion* with the titles belonging since the beginning, often dramatically, to Israel. What comes to mind here is the extensive development of this thought in the letter to the Ephesians (Eph 2:11-22; 3:6).[26]

The New Covenant (*kaine*) could not be understood and lived in its depth without the consciousness of this radical *communion to* Israel (and not only *with* Israel) which we have just mentioned. In the Blood of Christ is sealed a Covenant which, new by the fullness that it entails—the goods of the Spirit on which it opens up and especially the person of The One who establishes it in his own sacrifice—yet flourishes on the Covenant with the Fathers. The People of this new Covenant is not only saved by a Jew, it is also saved by his *communion* with the Promise and the destiny of the authentic Israel of God. Certainly,[27] belonging to God—the "vertical relationship" to the one who claims believers for his Name—is es-

[25]See the long analysis by F. F. Bruce, *Commentary on Galatians,* Grand Rapids, 1982, 156–157, 169–173.

[26]Markus Barth, *Ephesians, Introduction, Translation and Commentary on Chapters 1–3,* coll. "The Anchor Bible," 34, New York, 1974, 307–321.

[27]As J. Dupont emphasizes, "Un peuple d'entre les nations (Actes 15:14)," *NTS* 31, 1985, 321–335 (328–329) where he shows in this verse that Luke speaks of People in a "theological" sense.

sential here, God being able to have only one People in whom to introduce his own. Yet, according to Judeo-Christian faith, one could not in any way create an economy with the historical, "horizontal relationship." For the Church of God, the relationship with Israel is constitutive. We have shown in the preceding chapter that that is where catholicity is rooted.

4. Understood in this light, the passage from Peter's letter on the pagans which "formerly were not his people but now are the People of God"[28] shows itself extremely dense (1 Pet 2:4-10). It is not simply the major themes of Exodus, the desert, the Promised Land which are restated in a Christian perspective[29]: the very soul of Israel is adapted to the Church of God.[30] A point which is so much more important since it impels us to see in these verses the "doctrinal center of the epistle."[31]

To Gentile Christians the author of the epistle applies the great declaration of Exodus in regard to Israel. Because of the choice and the gift of the Spirit (1 Pet 1:2), the People who have been baptized (2:10) acquired through the Passover of Christ find themselves linked to God by the fact of their holiness. The People are, by this fact, *basileion* (2:9), a royal dwelling, a Temple radiating the divine glory, "a spiritual home" (2:5). Its mission in the place of those who do not yet believe will be exercised by the holiness of its life (2:11-12). And this is the basis of their daily existence which makes Christians the living stones in the building of the "spiritual home," to establish "a holy, priestly community" (*eis hierate-*

---

[28]The recipients are pagans converted to the faith, undoubtedly evangelized by missionaries loyal to James and Peter, living in the northern part of Asia Minor. See R. Brown, "Not Jewish Christianity and Gentile Christianity, but Types of Jewish/Gentile Christianity," *CBQ* 45, 1983, 74–79; R. Brown and J. Meier, *Antioch and Rome,* New York, 1983, 128–130; J. H. Eliott, *A Home for the Homeless,* Philadelphia, 1981, 270–295: F. Blanchetière, "Juifs et non-juifs, essai sur la diaspora en Asie Mineure," *RHPR* 54, 1974, 367–382.

[29]See R. E. Brown, *The Churches the Apostles Left Behind,* 77–78; M. Adinolfi, "Temi dell'Esodo nella 1 Petr.," *San Pietro; atti della XIX Settimana biblica,* Brescia, 1967, 319–336; M.-A. Chevallier, "Israël et l'Église selon la première épître de Pierre," *Mélanges M. Simon,* Paris, 1968, 117–130.

[30]On these verses, see especially, within the perspective of our reflection, J. H. Elliott, *The Elect and the Holy, an Exegetical Examination of 1 Pet 1: 4-10 and the Phrase basileion hierateuma,* Leyde, 1966, and the judgment of J. Coppens, "Le sacerdoce royal des fidèles; un commentaire de la 1ᵉ Pet. II, 4–10," *Au service de la Parole de Dieu; mélanges Charue,* Gembloux, 1969, 61–75. See also E. G. Selwyn, *The First Epistle of S. Peter,* 2nd ed., London, 1958; L. Goppelt, *Der erste Petrus-brief,* Göttingen, 1978; A. Feuillet, "Les sacrifices spirituels du sacerdoce royal des baptisés (1 Pet 2:5) et leur préparation dans l'Ancien Testament," *NRT* 96, 1974, 704–728; K. R. Snodgrass "1 Peter 2:1-10: its Formation and Literary Affinities," *NTS* 24, 1977–1978, 97–106; J. Schlosser, "Ancien Testament et christologie dans la prima Petri," *Études sur la première lettre de Pierre,* coll. "Lectio divina," 102, Paris, 1980, 65–96; P. Sandevoir, "Un royaume de prêtres?," *ibid.,* 219–230; J. Calloud and F. Genuyt, *La Première Épître de Pierre, analyse sémiotique,* coll. "Lection divina," 109, Paris, 1982, 113–134; Marc E. Kohler, "La communauté des chrétiens selon la première épître de Pierre," *RTP* 114, 1982, 1–21 (especially 12–15).

[31]P. Sandevoir, *op. cit.,* 220.

uma hagion, 2:5) offering "spiritual sacrifices" (*pneumatikas thusias*) pleasing to God through Jesus Christ (2:5). There is a fine line linking this text with Exodus.

In Exodus, Yahweh said to the Israelites: "I will count you as a royal priesthood, a holy nation" (Exod 19:6), and the Septuagint translated the first expression by *basileion hierateuma*.[32] It was a question for the Septuagint of the People in its collective being, of the community as a community, of Israel in its gathering before God. In fact, *hierateuma* clearly denotes a social body, a priestly body, a community with a priestly quality; and everything compels us to admit[33] that *basileion* is a significant, substantive "dwelling of the king" or "community of the king."[34] But the author of Peter's letter takes the two expressions found in Exodus (19:6) and inserts them in a list inspired by Isaiah (43:20-21), transferring to the Church, without doing them any violence and as if from the beginning they concerned it, the very titles of Israel.

The "priestly" vocation of Israel and its function as a witness of God living in the midst of the world seem therefore as the vocation and the function of the community of those "who have been chosen by the provident purpose of God the Father, to be made holy by the Spirit, obedient to Jesus Christ and sprinkled with his blood" (1:2).[35] It does not suffice to say that this community is a people of God; it must be made very precise that it is the People whose nature and function was already brought out in Exodus. The faint difference seems to us of prime importance.

5. It is, therefore, the Church, people of God *as such,* which, entering into the vocation of Israel, exercises the priestly function by the holiness of its life, a fruit which comes to it from the work of Christ.[36] The "priest-

[32]In Hebrew *mamlèkèt Kohanim.* On the history of the translation of this expression, see *ibid.,* 222-224; on *basileion hierateuma,* see *ibid.,* 224-228.

[33]With J. H. Elliott whom we follow (73). See also E. G. Selwyn, *op. cit.,* 166, who, especially because of Philo, proposes as a translation "palace of the king."

[34]Note the link between *basileia* and *basilikè* (basilica, dwelling).

[35]The word *ekklesia* does not appear in the first letter of Peter, but the term *laos,* people does (2:9, 10).

[36]J. H. Elliott resumes in this way the heart of Peter's letter on this point: "You have to lead a holy life of obedience, of good conduct and witness, and you can do it, because the one in whom you believe, as a holy and perfect sacrifice, redeemed you from your old and sordid way of living. He gave you a second birth, food and growth. You are in reality the community of God eschatological, chosen and holy, because the one to whom you go in faith is the Messiah, the Risen One, the stone chosen by God through which you also will receive life, election and the Spirit of holiness. Also your task as a royal house of the Spirit and a holy body of priests is to offer through the same Jesus Christ spiritual sacrifices pleasing to God" (218). And elsewhere: "The declaration *one single body of priests to offer spiritual sacrifices* designates in this way the believing community as the chosen people of God, holy and priestly whose task is communication of the word about his powerful acts and leading a holy life as witness for men and as pleasing spiritual offerings to God" (165).

hood" which Exodus speaks of in the text taken up in Peter's letter was not the one concerning the institution in Leviticus.[37] This last text refers to the liturgical and worship activity of the holy People. Israel explained the nature of it in another manner. Besides, it ordered it first of all, assigning a capital role to it in the life of the "priestly People." In the same way, the Church will be endowed with a ministry, entrusted with a particular style of liturgical or ritual activity for the good of all the People. And from the end of the second century this function will start to become clear by analogy with the institution in Leviticus, coming to speak of it then as a ministerial "priesthood."[38] That tends to create confusions. In fact there will be a gradual obscuring of the difference between the "priesthood" of the Church of God *as such* in its collective being (its profound reality of *Qahal*) and what is called the "priesthood of ministers" entirely linked to the realm of liturgical activities, of a different nature than that of holiness of life. But it is in this last one that the "priesthood" of the people of God as such is exercised.

In its fullest extent, this "priesthood" of the Church *as such* is not reducible to the power which every Christian acquires at baptism to take an active part in ritual worship, especially at the Eucharistic celebration, as a member with full rights. Neither could one speak, without making fine distinctions, about a participation in the work of the "priesthood" of Christ.[39] What is at stake here first of all is the repercussion of this "priesthood" of Christ on the "holy" community and its life. It is a priesthood of holiness, of grace received.

It is therefore clear that in this vision of the priestly People the distinction between hierarchy and other members is not taken into consideration at the outset. The aim is all-inclusive and is not based on the way in which individuals conduct themselves in this community-style, corporative, collective vocation.[40] This is admitted, all the while recognizing that it is not in conflict with this distinction, evident in the organization of the People of Israel and the importance which the letter of Peter attaches

[37]See *ibid.*, 183, 224; also A. Jaubert, *La Notion d'Alliance dans le judaïsme aux environs de l'ère chrétienne*, Paris, 1963, 394–407; J.-M. R. Tillard, "La qualité sacerdotale du ministère chrétien," *NTR* 95, 1973, 481–514.

[38]See J.-M. R. Tillard, *art. cit.*, where we have mentioned this history; see also the collation by F. Refoulé from the work of A. Vanhoye, *Prêtres anciens, prêtre nouveau selon le Nouveau Testament*, Paris, 1980, *RB* 91, 1984, 587–591.

[39]See J. H. Elliott, "Since the idea of the priesthood of Christ is developed according to the levitical scheme, whereas *hierateuma* goes back to Exod 19:6, and since 1 Pet does not put any link between the priesthood of Christ and *hierateuma* (nowhere does 1 Pet develop the idea of the priesthood of Christ), there is no foundation for the current opinion that for 1 Pet the community is a priestly body by virtue of its participation in the priesthood of Christ," *ibid.*, 220.

[40]One cannot, for example, depend on this *priesthood* to connect the growing desire for a feminine "priestly" ministry. It is a question of an entirely different register.

to the role of the presbyters to whom the community is entrusted (1 Pet 5:1-4). And if the idea of People implies a duration or a permanence of this People, whereas the leaders (even the most prestigious) disappear, it is also entirely true to think that the quality or the activity of these leaders has a sufficient impact on this permanence. Here again the drama of Israel and its kings attests to it.

The importance of the vision is elsewhere. We have pointed out the "vertical relationship" with God who, having only one People, inscribes in that People *all of his own.*[41] Israel and the Christian Church have, it is true, claimed as a privilege their belonging to the People of the living God, with the risk of seeing in "the others" inferior "religious men" or who are somewhat to be pitied. The notion of people of God has a ring of exclusivity to it.[42] More than that, too heavily conscious of the transcendence of the *communion* given in Christ Jesus and forgetting the gratitude that the Church should have for Israel—a gratitude which the letter of Peter itself highlights[43]—Christians tend to refuse this belonging to the people of God to Jews who are faithful to their faith (that Remainder which has not yet come over to Jesus Christ). And Jews refuse to do the same thing for Christians.[44] At the outset, the idea of people of God is not as ecumenical as one would like to think.

It can be affirmed, however, that the People welcomes all those men and women who live as friends of God.[45] Their uprightness, in particular their attention to the simple and the weak, is not without a link with the glorification of the living God by the care shown in his work, as their prayer is very often also. They are *his* perhaps without knowing it. If it is difficult to speak of "anonymous Christians,"[46] it must be admitted that the people of God contains areas where non-Christians find a place. Because it is as broad as the tenderness of the heart of the Father for whoever honors in his life the quality of the "image and likeness" of the one true God, Creator of humanity who, after calling Israel, sent into the world Jesus Christ his Son (Acts 10:35).[47] In weighty and detailed terminology, the constitution *Lumen Gentium* of Vatican II affirms: "To the catholic

---

[41]With J. Dupont, "Un peuple d'entre les nations (Acts 15:14)," 329–330.

[42]That is well emphasized by R. E. Brown, *The Churches the Apostles Left Behind*, 83, 121.

[43]See R. E. Brown, *ibid.,* 82–83.

[44]Johannine tradition will make the Jews the model of a "world" hostile to the truth which comes from God (John 16:8-9), children of the devil (8:44). And the end of Acts (28:28) is hardly ecumenical! Christians and Jews will argue precisely over their mutual "claim" of being the true people of God. In the face of what we have just developed, here is the fundamental break.

[45]In Peter, Paul and John only believers are called "children of God" in the strong sense of the expression.

[46]The position of Karl Rahner on this point seems to us to be awkward.

[47]See the sense of Acts 10:35 in J. Dupont, *Nouvelles Études sur les Actes des Apôtres,* 321–323.

[universal] unity of the People of God which prefigures and promotes universal peace all men are called; to this unity belong under diverse forms or are ordained both the catholic faithful and those who, besides, have faith in Christ, and finally all men without exception whom the grace of God calls to Salvation" (n. 13; cf. 14–16).

6. Perceived in its global understanding of people of God, without any consideration for the distinctions of duties or responsibilities which its life requires, the Church appears, therefore, as the community in which all share one and the same attribute, which makes them the same race, the same citizenship: the attribute of grace. And that is true no matter what titles are attached to the roles with which they are vested. Augustine's affirmation is well known:

> For you I am bishop, with you I am Christian—*vobis enim sum episco-pus, vobiscum sum christianus.* The first title is the one which represents the dignity with which I am vested; the second recalls to me the grace which I have received; one presents only dangers to me, the other is for me a name of salvation. . . . Therefore, if I am moved more by the happiness of having been ransomed with you than by the honor of having been put at your head, then, following the recommendation of the Lord, I will be more fully your servant and I will not become guilty of being ungrateful to the one who ransomed me and placed me like you among the number of his servants.[48]

This reiterates what Paul declared to the Galatians: "All you who have been baptized in Christ, you have all clothed yourselves in Christ, and there are no more distinctions between Jew and Greek, slave and free, male and female, but all of you are one in Christ Jesus" (3:27-28; cf. Col 3:10-11). The putting on of Christ is so radical, the fullness of his grace so complete, that in them differences become relative, they lose their edge, and cease to be separations. Distinctions are transcended.

Johannine tradition, which is especially attentive to the status of disciple,[49] highlights the depth of this common quality and the dignity associated with it. This emphasis is essential. The perpetual temptation—undoubtedly referred to in the Synoptics in the dreams of the sons of Zebedee (Matt 20:21; Mark 10:37)—to measure one's dignity by one's role according to hierarchical rank is in contradiction with a healthy vision of the nature of the people of God. We dare to add that it is in contradiction with what the whole of the New Testament says about the gospel spirit. "Dignity" resides elsewhere: in the fact of belonging to Christ Jesus and

---

[48]*Sermo* 340 (*PL* 38, 1483–1484), see *Sermo* 47:2; 46:2.

[49]What R. E. Brown has shown very well (see the résumé of his analysis in chapter 6 of *The Churches Apostles Left Behind,* especially 93–94, 99).

in this way being in *communion* with God. This is the great certainty that Paul presents in the Letter to the Philippians (Phil 3:8-9).

In this "community of belonging"—we prefer this expression despite its clumsiness, to the expression "Christian equality" less in line with biblical thinking—is rooted the value of the *sensus fidelium* which we will have to treat at length and which expresses the common conscience of all the faithful, hierarchy and lay together. It is there also that is inscribed the remarkably open way in which in several places Johannine tradition speaks of the role of the women in Jesus' company. It is significant, in fact, that Mary (the mother of Jesus) is right in the heart of the evangelical *semeia* (John 2:3-5), that the Samaritan woman is the first to announce Christ (4:29, 41-42), that Martha is the one who confesses the messianic role of Jesus with words that Matthew puts on Peter's lips (11:27), that Mary Magdalene is the first to have seen the Risen Lord (20:14) and the first to announce him (20:18).[50] Women are excluded from no aspect of the evangelical witness that the community is commissioned to declare. This witness is expressed by them and, at every level, thanks to them. Doesn't the evangelical testimony contain a feminine chord? It is always surprising to see this questioned, sometimes by Christians justly concerned about their promotion of women. No one will deny today the need for serious research on the status of women in the ecclesial community, a status demanding a place and functions much more significant than those granted to them and which, in our world, seem derisive. But by taking this course it will be necessary to find the way to reflect calmly, without trying to create a lawsuit, about the stakes involved in a search for uniformity which could deny—in the people of God and elsewhere—an essential level of being human, attaining in this way common witness and common expression of faith.

It is also the People as such, well within the distinction between clerics and lay, which proceeds in the world and throughout history, conscious of having a mission to fulfill in it. When discussing the Kingdom, what we said about the obligation to pay attention to human misery applies not only to the laity, who would be invested with a rather complete responsibility in this regard under the care and guidance of the hierarchy, but to the *communion* of all Christians, each one fulfilling his function but not being able to excuse oneself from an obligation in this matter. In particular, preaching by the heirarchy, at all levels and in whatever form that might take, and its effort to maintain the community in a state of ecclesial awareness are fully evangelical only if they remain in *commun-*

---

[50]That is studied by R. E. Brown, *The Community of the Beloved Apostle,* English text, 183–198 (French translation, *La Communauté du disciple bien-aimé,* coll. "Lectio divina," 115, Paris, 1983). We follow the original edition. How does it happen that this appearance of the Risen One to Mary is not on the list in 1 Cor 15:5-8?

ion, throughout the centuries, with the signs of Jesus, all involved with the problem of human misery (Luke 4:17-21; 7:22). The necessary dividing of ministries and tasks can be done only within this common preoccupation, without which there is a breaking with what already in the Israel of the prophets and Deuteronomy represented the very sign of communion with a God whom "his honor as God"[51] urges us to enter into the flesh of misery. He puts himself on the side of the poor, the simple, those on the fringe, men and women whose eyes are bathed in tears (Deut 10:18-19). This common attention is in the realm of ecclesial action what the *sensus fidelium* is in the realm of the perception of faith: an imprint of the Spirit.

It seems to us that in its analysis of the world and its evangelical word in this world, the people of God must take as its privileged area of observation and analysis the areas of poverty and misfortune more than laboratories devoted to progress. Is this too pessimistic a perspective, opposed to human optimism which faith in creation establishes? We do not think so. Here again the relationship between the Israel of God "of ancient times" and the Church of the Apostles seems essential to us. Reading, rereading and meditating on "the Law and the Prophets," the tradition of Luke, the texts of Matthew concerning the eschatological judgment, the Letter of James, especially when investigating closely their parallel in Justin, Basil, John Chrysostom, Ambrose, Melanie, Gregory the Great, one becomes convinced that the intensity of the involvement of the people of God resides more in a passionate desire to lift humanity out of its distress than in a constant mad rush forward towards more and more techniques whose only purpose is happiness and pleasure. Certainly, the two perspectives blend together. No one will deny today that progress can help overcome misery, at least a certain kind of misery. But, from its earliest origins, what the People has discovered as its mission, in the Spirit of God, has always been rooted more in a *communion* with the compassion of God, moved at the sight of the affliction "of his own," than in the desire to go to any lengths of human genius. And, according to a law of "ancient" societies,[52] this religious perception has actively shaped its collective soul to a very great depth. That explains its spontaneous resurgence during the most tumultuous periods of history. To be forced to pull this collective soul in another direction, to impose on it an attitude based not

---

[51]According to the beautiful expression of J. Dupont, already pointed out in the preceding chapter.

[52]See M. Gauchet, *Le Désenchantement du monde; une histoire politique de la religion,* Paris, 1985. According to Gauchet, in ancient societies everything is brought back to the religious perception and depends on it. It plays a structural role in the constitution of the social group. The split between altering the spiritual, the religious, the divine, the revealed and that of the secular social density is not yet made. Several theses of Gauchet are disputed.

on what lives in it since the "I have seen the miserable state of my people . . ., I have heard their cry, I am well aware of their sufferings" (Exod 3:7), but on the fascination with reason, is to do violence to it. What is at stake here is the collective soul of the People of God, of the "community in *communion* with the compassion of God" which coincides with the birth of Israel.

7. Composed of different members where great sinners and "people of holiness" are mixed together, always walking along roads in this world which are traced in sand and difficult to make out at first, exposed to assaults from "powerful obstacles," the people of God is seen, if you take all of its "citizens" together (Eph 2:19) as marked by infidelity, yes even sin. Also it is the theater where dramas are played out, divisions and schisms take place, and all of this since the history of the Kingdom of the North and the South, of Israel and Judah. Johannine literature affirms the fact that the first Christian generations had frequently occurring tensions, splits—Greek followers of Jesus and Judeo-Christians, "those who adhered strictly to John and dissidents, Christians belonging to the apostolic Churches and Johannine Christians[53]—disturbing the common witness and the common expression of the faith. And during this time the great schism between the Synagogue and the Church was ending, which had much more serious consequences than the internal breaks in each one of these groups.

All that is necessary is to study the *Report on the reformation of the Church* read in front of Paul III March 9, 1537, at the height of the Reformation which was to tear apart the Christian West,[54] in order to understand that the internal bruises inflicted on the people of God, "its wounds" according to the expression used at that time, are not something to be taken lightly. A judgment can be made about it:

> The Spirit of God who guarantees the power of heaven, as the Prophet says, has decided to restore through you *the Church of Christ which was falling, which was even crumbling,* and to prop up with your hand *this ruin,* to raise it up again to its former height and to restore to it its pristine beauty. We wish to take into consideration that this divine design will surely come about, we whom your Holiness has brought together to order for us to make you aware, without taking into account your own interest or the interest of whomever, the abuses, *these very serious illnesses from which the Church of God has already been suffering for a very long time* and notably the Roman Curia; because of them, by a

---

[53]See R. E. Brown, *The Community of the Beloved Apostle,* which strives to extricate these diverse currents and their clashes.

[54]Text found in *Concilium Tridentinum,* t. XII, 131–145.

very slow insensible process, *these mortal ills* have only been able to grow and have brought about *the ruin which is before our eyes.*

And, after alluding to the corruption of the papacy:

> From this source, like the Trojan horse, so many abuses and so many *very great evils* have spilled out into the Church and we see that they have caused it to suffer to the extent that we despair about its health, and the noise has spread even to the Infidels (let his Holiness wish to believe those who know it), who especially for this reason *make fun of the Christian religion,* so much so that *by us, yes by us, the name of Christ is blasphemed among the pagans.*[55]

These are not the words of polemicists or casual observers but an official report. The people of God is also a topic for evil attacks. It even happens that these attacks are aided by the complicity of those whose job it is to watch over it and protect it.

How then can we speak of a holy People? Because the letter of Peter in the same vein as the book of Exodus, does not hesitate to tell the baptized—whom it urges towards a more perfect evangelical life—that they are "the consecrated nation" (1 Pet 2:9; Exod 19:6). The Letter to the Ephesians, in a baptismal context, writes that Christ has made his Church holy (Eph 5:26-27). For its part, the Johannine Gospel declares the disciples as being purified (John 15:3; cf. 13:10). We have pointed out elsewhere the title of "saints" that is applied everywhere to Christians.[56] And we have recognized that the Church communicates with the holiness of Christ. What is at question here, what is on trial is the entire intensity between the intervention of God who "sanctifies" his People and the response of that People called to "be sanctified."[57] The people of God is holy (*qadosh*) because God has made his People so. He has brought them together from among the peoples and has consecrated this People for himself[58] by establishing a *communion* with it, has walked with it, has remained in it, as is signified by the cloud during the trek through the desert, the *shekinah,* and the Ark of the Covenant. Even more so, through Jesus Christ God has sealed the New Covenant in the Blood of his well-beloved Son. And through his Holy Spirit he makes believers

---

[55]Translation by G. Dumeige, in *Histoire des conciles œcuméniques,* t. X. Paris, 1975, 433–435. The italics are ours. See also *ibid.,* 435–444.

[56]See *supra,* note 5.

[57]In certain ecumenical contexts where catholic and protestant traditions are in dialog, this question of "holiness" is often a source of ambiguity, "catholics" refusing to consent to the declaration that the Church is a sinner, "protestants" refusing to affirm with fine distinctions the holiness of the Church.

[58]Fundamentally it is God alone who consecrates, he, "the Holy One."

(whose weakness is not laid aside because of all that) the Body which his grace, his mercy, his unfailing fidelity, his tenderness and his justice gather together. In this way something of himself—the essential attributes which Revelation entrusts to us of his being—is forever communicated to this People. His own holiness (the weight, the density, the power of his heart) remains implanted in history and in the destiny of the community of those whom the Letter to the Hebrews does not hesitate to call the "brothers" of the Son (Heb 2:17; 5:8). Because their sins, personal and collective neither nullify his mercy nor his fidelity, characteristic aspects of his holiness, this holiness continues to reunite "his own." And so the People lives, in spite of everything, in the embrace of this holiness. It remains the People of the Holiness of God, the holy Assembly of God, the holy Church of the living God.

But this People must sanctify *itself,* not only by uttering an abstract and easy "yes" to the proposed Covenant but by observing the requirements of it. In particular it must express in a behavior of *Agape* the *communion* into which God introduces it and adopt the ways of God as they are revealed in Christ Jesus. It is a question of the ethical posture, and no longer the theological one, of holiness. Here the People is seen as unfaithful, continually called to convert *itself,* to tear *itself* away from its sin. The Second Vatican Council can then speak of a permanent reformation which the Church needs everlastingly,[59] since it is both identified as holy and compelled to purify itself.[60]

8. The Church of God—"posterity of Abraham" Temple of "the Spirit, children of the Promise" (Gal 3:14; 4:29), people of God having "obtained mercy" (1 Pet 2:10), a wild olive tree grafted onto a cultivated one (Rom 11:24), a community of the "twelve tribes enduring since the dispersion" (Jas 1:1), "the chosen one" of God (2 John 1:13), "a chosen race" (1 Pet 2:9)—because a large part of Israel does not accept Jesus as the Christ, it lives cut off from the ancient People. The Church is even cut off from the faithful Rest who, still today, through a loving observance of the requirements of the Law, serves the God of the Fathers and awaits the fulfillment of the Promise.

There is, however, a limit to this break, and it is an essential one. In fact, we have seen that, at the Eucharistic celebration, the Church, gathered before the Father in the very person of the Body of Christ and in its certainty of being in the Holy Spirit the People that God wills (his *Qahal*), resumes the cry calling for the definitive coming of the Messiah which, since the time of ancient Israel, spans history. It is remarkable that the

---

[59]See *Unitatis redintegratio,* 6.

[60]*Lumen gentium,* 8.

four traditions about the Lord's Supper—to which can be added, it seems, the implicit witness of Revelation (Rev 22:17-21)—are stamped with a keen eschatological intensity, which arises, without any doubt, from the faith of Israel as it is renewed by Jesus in his expectation of the coming of the Kingdom. Even more so, this idea belongs to the very nature of the Memorial.[61] Because if Paul reminds the Corinthians that, at the Table of the Lord, they announce his death "until he comes" (1 Cor 11:26)— that is, until the purpose of it is accomplished, the coming that one is longing for[62]—the Synoptic traditions put on the lips of Jesus at his farewell supper words which express intensely, the hope of the future Kingdom: "I will not drink any more of this fruit of the vine until the day I will drink it again, with you, in the Kingdom of my Father" (Matt 26:29; cf. Mark 14:22). Luke, especially, clings to this eschatological perspective. He is not content to evoke the "fulfillment" of the Passover in the Kingdom of God (Luke 22:16) or the fact of drinking no more fruit of the vine "until the Kingdom of God comes" (22:18). He inserts in his text, yet modifying it somewhat, a promise that Matthew tied to the discussion which was provoked by the encounter with the rich man (Matt 19:28): "You will eat and drink at my table in my Kingdom and you will sit on thrones to judge the twelve tribes of Israel" (Luke 22:30).[63] The celebration of the Memorial is imbued with the thought of the final accomplishment of the design of God in the Covenant, of the eschatological coming of the Son of Man.[64]

The Christian community takes up the great intercessory cry of Israel by *communicating* it in its liturgy, especially its Easter liturgy. Because

---

[61]On this question, see J. Jeremias, *La Dernière Cène, les paroles de Jésus,* coll. "Lectio divina," 75, Paris, 1972; M. Thurian, *L'Eucharistie mémorial du Seigneur,* Neuchâtel-Paris, 1959, especially 171-219; Id., "Le mémorial," *Ecumenical Perspectives on Baptism, Eucharist and Ministry,* coll. "Faith and Order Papers," 116, Geneva, 1983; J.-M. R. Tillard, "Eucharistie et Église," in J. Zizioulas, J.-M. R. Tillard, J. J. von Allmen, *L'Eucharistie,* Paris, 1970, 75-135; Id., "Le mémorial dans la vie de l'Église," *MD* 106, 1971, 24-45; Id., "Faisant mémoire de ton Fils," *Parole et Pain* 9, 1972, 24-45; Id., "Catholiques romains et anglicans, l'Eucharistie," *NRT* 93, 1971, 602-656.

[62]What J. Jeremias shows very well, *op. cit.,* 301-305: *"achri ou elthè* (until he comes). This phrase is not a simple chronological reference, but *elthè* is a 'prospective' substantive, which, as it results from the omission of *an,* suggests a certain element of finality, and can consequently be rendered freely by 'until (may the moment come) he comes,' 'until (may the end be attained) he comes.' In fact, in the NT, *achri ou* with the aorist subjunctive without *an* regularly introduces a perspective of the eschatological end to be attained: Rom 11:25; I Cor 15:25; Luke 21:24" (302).

[63]See J. Jeremias, *ibid.,* 190-195, 247-260, and especially H. Schürmann, *Comment Jésus a-t-il vécu sa mort?,* 83-116, whose position is synthesized in Id., *Le Récit de la dernière Cène,* Le Puy et Paris, 1965.

[64]See the parallel with the *Didachè* 10, 5, whatever the link this may have with the Eucharist in the strict sense: "Remember, Lord, to deliver your Church from every evil, and to make it perfect in your love. Gather it together from the four winds, this sanctified Church, into your Kingdom which you have prepared."

this one asks God that there be a gathering together in the Kingdom of the Messiah, by recalling it:

> Our God and God of our Fathers, may our remembrance, the remembrance of our ancestors, the remembrance of the Messiah, son of David, your servant, the remembrance of Jerusalem, your holy city, and the remembrance of all your people, the house of Israel, rise up, happen, come, appear, be accepted, received, considered and recalled before you, for our salvation and happiness, so that we may receive your favor, your grace, your mercy, health and peace, on this feast day. Remember us, Eternal One, our God, on this day, for our good; think of us so that you may bless us; help us so that you may grant us health, and, by your beneficial and merciful word, protect us, show us your favor, have pity on us and help us; because it is towards you that our faces are turned, you who are a kind and merciful God.
>
> Rebuild, soon and in our time, Jerusalem, the holy city. Blessed may you be, Eternal One, who in your kindness will rebuild Jerusalem. Amen![65]

And again:

> May the God of mercy find us worthy of the era of the Messiah and of life in the world to come; he who is the rampart of salvation for his king, the patron of his anointed David and of his posterity forever! The one who establishes peace in his lofty dwellings will establish it also for us and for all of Israel, Amen!

Besides, the entire Passover feast—and not only the meal taken by itself[66]—is filled with the expectation of the Messiah. And it is known that Psalm 118 which ends the *Hallel,* is sung in Judaism as a messianic prophecy. The *Midrash* on the psalms contains in it the announcement of the Day of the Messiah:

> Inside the walls, the inhabitants of Jerusalem will cry out: "We beg you, Yahweh, save us!" (v. 25a), and the inhabitants of Juda respond from without: "We beg you, Lord, grant prosperity!" (v. 25b). The inhabitants of Jerusalem will declare from within: "Blessings on him who comes in the name of Yahweh!" (v. 26a), and the inhabitants of Juda respond from without: "We bless you, you who are from the house of Yahweh!" (v. 26b). The inhabitants of Jerusalem will declare from within: "Yahweh is God. He has given us light" (v. 27a), and from within the

[65] This is part of the third blessing of graces after the meal, in the *Haggada* of Easter, recited equally on some other feasts.

[66] Whereas it is not certain that the last Supper was a paschal meal—we personally lean towards the negative—too many authors, especially catholic, speaking of the Eucharist, neglect too much the climate of the totality of the paschal feast. It is this one which gives its proper color to the Passover meal.

inhabitants of Juda will respond: "With branches in your hands draw up in procession as far as the horns of the altar!" (v. 27b).

The inhabitants of Jerusalem will say from within: "You are my God! It is you whom I wish to praise!" (v. 28a), and the inhabitants of Juda will respond from without: "My God! I wish to extol you!" (v. 28b).

The inhabitants of Jerusalem and the inhabitants of Juda open their mouth and glorify (together) the Holy One, blessed may He be! and will say: "Praise Yahweh! For he is good, yes, for his love is everlasting" (v. 29).[67]

At the Eucharistic celebration, the Church testifies that it still is waiting for the Day of the Messiah, *communicating* in this way with the Hope of Israel. Concerning this waiting, the kerygma of Peter at the portico of Solomon, at the entrance to the Temple, is typical. He announces Jesus as the Messiah destined for the Israelites, whom "heaven must keep until the universal restoration comes which God proclaimed, speaking through his holy prophets" and that at that time he will send to them (Acts 3:20-21).[68] The glorification of Jesus and his enthronement as Christ (Acts 2:36) do not yet tell everything about his messianic role. What remains is the final event which New Testament traditions link either to the Judgment of humanity (Matt 25:31-46; Luke 12:8-10; Jas 5:8-11), or to the handing over of the Kingdom to God the Father by Christ "at the time of his coming" (1 Cor 15:22-28), or to the resurrection of the dead (1 Thess 4:16-18; 1 Cor 15:21-26), or to the final victory over the forces of evil (1 Cor 15:25-26), or to "the coming of the new heavens and the new earth where justice reigns" (1 Pet 3:13), or simply to the final manifestation of the glory of the Lord Jesus (1 Tim 6:14). Passover and Pentecost are "not yet" *the* Day of the Lord.[69] Their *already* is inscribed in a "not yet," also a determinant. This *already* has a messianic density, a reality of fulfillment, but always open to the last event. This one is anticipated, since the final battle is won since we are in the last phase, *already* endowed with the Spirit; however, the supplication is still heard *"Marana tha"* (Rev 22:17, 20; 1 Cor 16:22).

[67] We take up the translation of this *Midrash* on Ps 118:22 given in the French edition of the book by J. Jeremias, 307.

[68] See W. G. Kümmel, *Einleitung in das Neue Testament,* Heidelberg, 1976, 111–112; E. Rasco, *Actus Apostolorum, introductio et exempla exegetica,* fasc. 2, Rome, 1968, 238–248; J. A. T. Robinson, *Twelve New Testament Studies,* London, 1962, 139–153 (151–152); C. F. D. Moule, "The Christology of Acts," in L. E. Keck and J. L. Martyn, *Studies in Luke-Acts, Essays in Honour of Paul Schubert,* Nashville, 1966, 159–185 (167–169); R. Brown, "How Much did Jesus Know, a Survey of the Biblical Evidence," *CBQ* 29, 1967, 315–345 (332).

[69] O. Cullmann, *Christ et le temps,* which has become the classic study, showed the tension between the *already* and the *not yet.* See also Id., *Le Salut dans l'histoire,* Neuchâtel-Paris, 1966, especially 196–210, 237–264.

This waiting is joined to that of the faithful Rest, not yet come over to Christ Jesus. The account of the martyrdom of James recorded by Eusebius of Cesaerea is typical on this point. During the Passover, "while all the tribes and even the Gentiles gathered together," James is asked to make a declaration about Jesus. He does so by focusing on the eschatological Hope:

> And he answers in a loud voice: Why do you question me about the Son of Man? He is seated in heaven at the right hand of the great power and he will come on the clouds of heaven. Many were entirely convinced and glorified the testimony of James by saying: Hosannah to the son of David. Then, by contrast, the scribes and the pharisees said to one another: We have erred in obtaining such a testimony about Jesus. Let's go up, therefore, and throw him down, so that they will be afraid and not believe in him.[70]

In the Eucharist, beyond the break, the Church of God finds again the same prayer and the profound intention of faith of the entire Israel of God. Even more so, it gives to this prayer and this faith, the object of the Hope of Israel, which is also the object of its own Hope: the Day of the Messiah of God, which it knows to be the Day of the Lord Christ Jesus. The Eucharist appears in this way, as we said earlier, as the sacramental moment of *communion* with Israel, never entirely broken, a *communion* from which the Church takes its origin in the design of God. To sing in the gathering together which the Eucharistic celebration is, "we await his coming in glory," or to proclaim that the celebration take place "while awaiting that he come in glory," is to confess the deep-rooting of the Church of God in "the very mystery" (Rom 11:25) of Israel, *Church of Churches,* Church of the *Qahal.* . . . It is impossible to understand the Church without having understood Israel, impossible to live conscientiously the Christian vocation without knowing that it goes back farther than Pentecost and that it is already outlined in the adventure of Abraham chosen by God to become "the father of believers."

II. The Church of God, People of the Faith

People of God, the Church is fully itself in the Eucharistic celebration. There, its members celebrating together the Memorial of the Passover and taking part together in the "sacrifice of communion" of the New Cove-

---

[70]*Hist. Eccles.* II, 23, 13–14 (*SC* 31, Paris, 1952, 87). This "legend" must be placed in the climate mentioned by C. F. D. Moule, "Sanctuary and Sacrifice in the Church of the New Testament," 29–41.

nant, see themselves as the community of God gathered together from the midst of the world (the *Qahal*), coursing through history, to God's place of rest (cf. Heb 4:1-11). But this People is a *communion* of believers. If in its gathering together it "announces the Death of the Lord until he comes" (1 Cor 11:26), it is because it is, in the wake of Israel, welded together by faith. This is how the First Letter of Peter understands the state of the "community of the chosen ones" (1 Pet 1:22-25; cf. 5:13).

To describe the Church as a People of faith is to say that what it basically is in its being of *communion* comes from the acceptance of an offer from God. This offer contains a Promise and the assurance that what is offered will come about by the very power of the Spirit who has taken the forefront. This proposition of God, "received" in the acceptance of the faith, is expressed, preserved and transmitted in what the Bible calls the Word of God.

A. *A Word which God declares in his people*

Who says Word of God says, in the biblical context, the initiative of God breaking the silence which the drama of original sin established between him and humanity. Then he becomes part of this humanity by his design that has existed from the beginning of time—"kept silent for endless ages"—and which is the *mystery* of the Salvation of the world (Rom 16:25-26; cf. 1 Cor 2:7-10; Eph 1:9-10; 3:2-9; Col 1:26-27). This notion of *mystery* will be reconciled with the Johannine allusion of a Word eternally present in God which "will be made flesh" in Jesus Christ. Linking these two visions to the first lines of the Letter to the Hebrews—"at various times in the past and in various different ways, God spoke to our Fathers through the prophets; but in our own time, the last days, he has spoken to us through his Son . . . who sustains the universe by his powerful word"—what is evident is that it is a Word belonging to God's being who makes himself heard in the revelation of the *mystery* to humanity. Urges by polemics to distinguish *logos endiathetos* from *logos prophorikos*,[71] the Greek Fathers will express both the essential link and yet the difference between these two states of the Word of God. The revealed Word springs forth from the eternal Word. But on the one hand, the being of God transcends in an unfathomable way the created being and, on the other hand, God has "no voice that can be heard," no handwriting. Only the human creature has a voice, a handwriting. The eternal Logos by which

---

[71]This distinction has a stoic origin. It concerns the difference between the immanent *logos*— which in the human being is his reason—and the *logos,* expressed in words, images, which language uses. Philo had applied it to the divine *Logos,* going as far as identifying the "angel of Yahweh" appearing to the patriarchs with this *Logos prophorikos.* For the Fathers, see Theophilus of Antioch, *Trois Livres à Autolycus* II, 10, 22 (*SC* 20), Paris, 1948, 122-125, 154-155. On apophasis the position of Thomas Aquinas is well known, *Summa theologica* Ia, 3, prol.

the *mystery* is expressed "will be revealed," therefore, in voices, words, human signs, all of that even in Christ Jesus at the time of the incarnation. The faith, from which the Spirit will bring forth the Church, will be the acceptance of a "revelation" from God, heard, read, perceived in a human language.

It is not our purpose here to treat the question of Revelation. It is necessary, however, in the spirit of the great Tradition,[72] to discern very well the truth which has been transmitted through Revelation. This is the way chosen by God so that what reason alone cannot grasp may be known. The Holy Spirit illumines, inspires a prophet, a scholar, a writer and causes him to perceive a truth that he will faithfully transmit but in his own language and culture, adapted to his own situation and that of his readers or listeners. And ordinarily, it is by reevaluating the events of history, in the Spirit or in light of the past that the experience of a People will be clarified, by seeing in that event or experience a Word of God, the meaning of the Promise, and the precise meaning of the content of the Covenant. There is an event (perceived as created by God) and an interpretation (in the Spirit) of the meaning of this event, the intervention of God and a word concerning this intervention.[73]

This has value even for Christ in whom God reveals himself in the most complete way. His preaching is inscribed in the history and the expectations of his People. And it is especially the Christian community, brought forth by the Spirit and interpreting all his *acta et dicta* in the light of the Resurrection, which will clarify their meaning. The evangelical writings give us the words of Jesus, not verbatim, but what the apostolic Churches understood and retained of the profound meaning and finality of his life, his preaching, his work, his person. But this understanding was filtered through their surroundings, their culture, their concerns. It was already distorted by a certain interpretation. They transmit (and they alone) the Word *of* Christ while transmitting their traditions *about* Christ. This is done so well that, even in them, we hear Jesus throughout the Churches.

What this says is that the Church, a *communion* of local Churches and present in each one of them, given birth by the Word revealed by God— and God alone in his absolute and transcendent initiative—is not unacquainted, even from its beginnings, with the way in which this Word is revealed in human language. It furnishes its revelation not only with the

[72]Again followed by Thomas Aquinas but forgotten on this point after the council of Trent and even by Vatican I (in the enthusiasm of the encyclical *Qui pluribus* of Pius IX, in 1846). See H. Bouillard, "Le concept de révélation de Vatican I à Vatican II," *Révélation de Dieu et langage des hommes,* coll. "Cogitatio fidei," 63, Paris, 1972, 35–49, and V. White, "Le concept de révélation chez S. Thomas," *L'Année théologique,* 1950, 1–17, 109–132.

[73]Read the suggestive study by B. Albrektson, *History and the Gods,* coll. "Conjectanea biblica," Old Testament, Ser. 1, Lund, 1967, on the relationship between Word of God and history. The event is understood under the light of the words of Yahweh already understood.

necessary wording (whose importance is well known) and the contexts in which they were used at that time but also the ideas coming from its own experience, even its own needs. The Word of God for the Church is transmitted only by a Word in the Church, even the one which comes from Jesus, the Word of God incarnate. Beyond this, if the apostolic community did not believe in the Resurrection, the means by which it becomes a community of the New Covenant, who else would announce what "God himself told us in his Son Jesus Christ"? The impact of the Resurrection on this community is not unknown to the way in which it perceives the final Revelation through this intervention by God.

So the People of the faith is not outside the Word whose source is found only in God. Basically, this People depends on the Word since it arises totally through faith, which it alone makes possible, and the sacraments of this faith. And yet without the absolute gratuitousness of God's initiative being questioned, God wishes that it be this People, especially through its "inspired members" filled with the Spirit that his Word comes forth, that its meaning be discovered, that it be articulated, that it be made explicit, with the power of this Spirit. And that has been of value from the beginning. The Church of God is founded on a path which can come from God alone and whose meaning God has wished to reveal so that the Church will preserve it and transmit it in human terms. But it is the Church which, in this discovery of the meaning of the Word and its expression in human language, with the guarantee of the Spirit, makes the intervention of God, transcending every imagined understanding when left to its own forces, an audible then readable Word, which emerges into the world of human communication. It is truly, and in the strictest sense possible, a Word of God. And this is likewise true, and in the strictest sense possible, the Word which establishes the Church. However, it is the Word of an "event of God" (and of God alone) passing through the realm of the Word (which is human) thanks to the Spirit and to the Church which he inspires.

B. A Word which is perceived by all

1. If the Word of God is the expression in human language of the "event of God" which establishes the Church, it is necessary that the Church preserve it from generation to generation. The Church must also then make the content timely so that each era and culture find in it what is useful to it. It must also defend it against attacks from without or interpretations which change its meaning, all the while permitting a healthy pluralism of readings. Finally, it has a mission to transmit it to those men and women who do not yet know the Name of the Lord Jesus Christ. All of this implies that the Word, as it is recorded in the holy Books, could not simply be repeated in a fundamentalist manner. It is "given" (as a free gift) by God to his People with the mission to maintain it, as a continual

living entity, through the power of the Spirit. Because it is not a document to be put into the archives. It is the foundation of a people of God coursing through history with all of the twists and turns that course might take.

In order to preserve the Word, it is set down in what will become the "Scriptures" in the heart of which—in an equal way for the Old as well as the New Covenant—a determination will gradually be made about a nucleus which will be the essence of the Canon, an ensemble of normative documents, determined once and for all around the fourth century.[74] The ultimate purpose of this Canon will be to maintain all these communities in *communion* with one and the same faith, rooted in apostolic testimonies "recognized" as authentic. Through the intercession of the Word, whose link with what Jesus was and what he lived is, therefore, assured, the Church will remain attentive to what God has truly willed to declare to it in Jesus Christ. So it will be confirmed continually as to what the purpose of its faith is and to the Salvation on which the Church is based. When circumstances require it to determine the ramifications of these different interpretations, with the risk of dividing communities, and which one should have first place, it will decide in the light of all texts taken together what makes up the "testimony of the Scriptures."[75] But also, when the needs of catholicity demand that a new language be used, that the words which have conveyed the proper meaning for centuries give way to those of another culture or another context, this is the norm that will be used as a frame of reference: the essential aspect of "scriptural testimony" should not be made more suitable or agreeable in any way whatsoever. This will permit "all to be recognized" mutually in *communion* with one another, and in *communion* with the apostolic faith. It is this essential aspect of "scriptural testimony" which will compose the content of the "confessions of faith."

But it is even there that the Church has to interfere. In fact, expressed in very special categories which apply to such and such a culture, to such and such a situation, or to such and such a need, Scripture must be interpreted so that it can be understood. But this requires that other resources

---

[74]On the history of the canon, see especially *Le Canon de l'Ancien Testament, sa formation et son histoire,* Geneva, 1984; H. von Campenhausen, *La Formation de la Bible chrétienne,* Neuchâtel-Paris, 1971; R. M. Grant, *La Formation du Nouveau Testament,* Paris, 1969; E. Mangenot, "Canon des Livres saints," *DTC* 2, 1550-1605; see also "Le corps des Écritues," *Lumière et vie* 171, 1985 and A. Paul, *Le Fait biblique,* coll. "Lectio divina," 100, Paris, 1979, 151-178. On the history of the function of the canon in the Churches, see the unequal work, a collection of studies, published by J. D. Kaestli and O. Wermelinger, *Le Canon de l'Ancien Testament; sa formation et son histoire,* Geneva, 1984 (see especially the studies by D. Barthelemy, E. Junod, O. Wermelinger, P. Fraenkel).

[75]See canon 59 of the council of Laodicea (from 360) and the text of the council of Rome of 382, under pope Damasus.

be used besides what is contained in the holy Book. If the techniques of human sciences occupy an important place among these resources, this must be subordinated to the *instinctus* of the believing community, in the *sensus fidei* which resides in this community and links it to the understanding of all the generations which have preceded it since Pentecost. The Word contained in the documents of the people of God does not reveal its meaning simply by having recourse to human sciences. It contains in it a depth which comes from the Spirit and which is perceived only "in the Spirit," this Spirit which in a precise way gives life to the Church since Pentecost. Scripture is truly understood only "in the Spirit," who is "in the Church."

2. This understanding "in the Spirit," often defined in a doctrine or dogma of faith "recognized" as an authentic interpretation, which demands, even while going beyond it, recourse to human techniques, is a complex phenomenon which gets the entire people of God involved. What intervene here are both the acute spiritual discernment of the community and the determination of those who exercise a "magisterium" in it, but in an advantageous relationship. At the heart of this relationship or *communion* is the "reception," by which, on the basis of the talent of the believers (the *sensus fidelium*) a consensus is established on this interpretation proposed by those whose job it is to perceive this *sensus* and to interpret it. *Sensus fidelium* and hierarchical magisterium[76] are in perfect agreement, with a mutual understanding, respecting the competence of each other with each one being a norm for the other. This is where a basic form of *communion* is found. Because if there are ministries of truth (or a magisterium), it is only within the community, entirely endowed with the Spirit of Truth[77] and because of it fit for what Thomas Aquinas described as the understanding of the sense of the Word *per modum connaturalitatis,*[78] the intellect being inclined by instinct to adhere to what is in harmony with the true meaning of the Word of God, faith "recognizing" spontaneously its aim and purpose.[79] In a well known text and one which is often commented on, the famous article in the *Rambler* about consulting the faithful, it seems to us that Newman presented very shrewdly

---

[76]That it would be more correct to call *ordained* magisterium (linked to a sacramental ordination).

[77]Concerning the biblical bases for this vision, see especially J. Dupont, *Gnosis, la connaissance religieuse dans les épîtres de saint Paul,* Louvain, 1949; L. Cerfaux, *Le Chrétien dans la théologie paulinienne,* 431–469 (summing up several studies); I. de La Potterie, *La Vie selon l'Esprit,* coll. "Unam sanctam," 55, 1965, 85–105, 126–144.

[78]*Summa theologica,* IIa-IIae, 2, 3, ad 2; cf. Guibert, "A propos des textes de saint Thomas sur la foi qui discerne," *RSR* 9, 1919, 30–44; C. H. Joyce, "La foi qui discerne d'après saint Thomas," *RSR* 6, 1916, 433–455; S. Harent, "Note sur l'article récédent," *ibid.,* 455–467. Compare with what Diadoc of Photice says about spiritual instinct in *La Perfection spirituelle* 6:26, 30 (*SC* 5, Paris, 1955, 87–101).

[79]Without necessarily being able to express it in an adequate, rational manner.

this *communion* of the *sensus fidelium* and of the exercise of the magisterium. Perhaps, as seems certain, he has a tendency to reserve the first quality to the laity alone, while in fact it is found in all who are baptized. And he passes too easily from this *sensus* of the faithful to the *consensus* of the faithful.[80] It seems to us in fact that it is better to designate by this *consensus* the agreement among the faithful which results from the presence in all people of the spiritual reality which is the *sensus fidei* (or *fidelium*). But whatever arises from these questions of vocabulary, Newman shows very well that there is present in every baptized person a certain talent, an instinct (a *phronema*), a sense, a certainty, that he owes to his membership in the Body of Christ through Baptism.[81] This is a personal attribute, certainly, but which is nothing more than participation in an attribute of the Body of Christ as such; a quality which a person would not possess if he did not belong to the *communion* of all those who have been baptized, so that what is manifested in this *instinctus* is the conscience of the people of God *as such*.[82] Composed of individuals created again with their dignity of the image of God, his understanding of People cannot exist outside of its members or simply in certain ones. It exists in all of them, making them instinctively sensitive to what is in harmony with the nature of of the Body of Christ or to what is inconsistent with it.

The hierarchical magisterial function, given at ordination, is a function in this Body endowed with this spiritual talent. And it aims to state precisely, to make explicit, and to defend the precise object of this talent.

[80]This text and an enlightening introduction by J. Coulson will be found in the reedition done in 1961. *On Consulting the Faithful in Matters of Doctrine* was written in July 1859. See the recent article by J. Walgrave, "La consultation des fidèles en matière de doctrine selon Newman," *Concilium* 200, 1985, 35–43 (pessimistic in its conclusion). See also J. Newman, *Pensées sur l'Église*, coll. "Unam sanctam," 30, Paris, 1956, 402–439; C. Dillenschneider, *Le Sens de la foi et le progrès dogmatique du mystère marial*, Rome, 1954; H. Vorgrimler, *"Du sensus fidei au consensus fidelium,"* *Concilium* 200, 1985, 13–22 (which gives a bibliography which is solely German); E. Schillebeeckx, "Le magistère de tous, réflexion sur la structure du Nouveau Testament," *ibid.*, 23–33; J.-M. R. Tillard, "Le *sensus fidelium*, réflexion théologique," *Foi populaire et foi savante*, coll. "Cogitatio fidei," 87, Paris, 1976, 9–40; Id., "Théologie et vie ecclésiale," *Initiation à la pratique de la théologie*, t. I, Paris, 1982, 161–172.

[81]See in particular *On Consulting the Faithful in Matters of Doctrine*, ed. cit., 73–75. The *sensus fidelium* is the effect in them of their *sensus fidei*.

[82]No. 12 of *Lumen gentium* is, on this point, a main text. Integrating the vision of Augustine (*De Praed. Sanct.* 14, 27) he states: "The collectivity of the faithful *(universitas fidelium)*, having the anointing which comes from the Holy One (1 John 2:20, 27), cannot be deceived in faith; this particular gift *(proprietas)* that it possesses, it manifests by means of the supernatural sense of faith which is that of the entire people, when, 'bishops to the last of the lay faithful,' this collectivity of the faithful brings to the truths concerning the faith and to ways and customs a universal consent. Thanks indeed to this sense of the faith which is awakened by the Spirit of Truth and under the direction of the sacred magisterium which permits, if one follows it faithfully *(fedeliter obsequens)*, of receiving no longer a human word but truly the word of God (1 Thess 2:13), the people of God is attached indefectibly to the faith transmitted to the saints once and for all, it penetrates more profoundly by interpreting it as is necessary and in its life putting it into practice more perfectly."

But it is clear that it too falls under its verdict. Through all of this, without accepting, and not making allowances for some very fine distinctions, the too radical position of Komiakov—which, in order to make the agreement of the entire Church united in charity the ultimate criterion of truth, makes the role of the hierarchical magisterium extremely relative[83]—it must be recognized that a magisterial declaration in which the *sensus fidelium*[84] does not recognize what is good for it is *a priori* very awkward or even suspect. Certainly, those who exercise a magisterium do not do so as mere delegates. They receive, for this purpose, a grace from the Spirit proportionate to their function, which does not consist in simply stating in a more orderly way what others think. It is incumbent upon them to find new formulas to express the traditional faith (as at Nicaea and Chalcedon), to correct faulty practices, to treat questions whose impact is not evident to the whole community and which, however, are crucial to the life of the community. Yet the faith which they are treating is the one which belongs to the entire Church, "felt" by the *sensus fidelium*. Also, the novelty of the new formula, the correction that it imposes and the determination introduced by it, no matter how valid they might be juridically,[85] could not be presented as being outside this commonly held notion. Their adherence to this notion must be clear, for to be brief would run the risk of dividing the Christian community.[86] And a position which is too airtight between *ecclesia docens* and *ecclesia discens,* a Church which knows and a Church which follows, already represents a corrosion of the *communion* of faith, just like the distance between scholarly faith and popular faith.[87]

[83]See P. P. O'Leary, *The Triune Church, a Study in the Ecclesiology of A. S. Xomjakov,* Fribourg, 1982, especially 104–107, 115–124, and the last chapter. The views of Komiakov have been stated very distinctly especially, in the heart of orthodoxy, by Florosvsky, Afanasieff and Schmemann (cf. *ibid.,* 115–124).

[84]Not the opinion of such or such a Christian even an eminent one or of such or such a milieu, but the reaction of the "Christian conscience," not in an immediate "acceptance" but, as we see it, often over a long drawn out course (the case of Nicaea is typical).

[85]Even, in Catholic tradition, when the magisterium in question is the one exercised by the bishop of Rome. In fact, the declaration of Vatican I (*DS* 3074) on the authority of the dogmatic definitions of the bishop of Rome *ex sese non ex consensu Ecclesiae* aims at an error of the Church of France. It signifies that the validity of a definition does not depend for its confirmation on the totality of the Church and that there is no strict and absolute necessity for counsel and help from the bishops for every infallible judgment (cf. the declaration by Mgr. Gasser in Mansi 52, 1215, and the declaration by the Assembly of the clergy of 1682 in *DTC* 4, 197; *DS* 2284; see also G. Dejaifve, "Ex sese non autem ex consensu Ecclesiae," *Salesianum* 25, 1962, 283–295; H. Fries, "Ex sese, non ex consensu Ecclesiae," *Volk Gottes, Festgabe für J. Höfer,* Fribourg, 1967, 480–500).

[86]One of the sources of a certain uneasiness provoked by Vatican II has certainly been the fact that several areas perceived some of these declarations as breaks with tradition whereas they were a return to it.

[87]See J.-M. R. Tillard, *Foi populaire et foi savante,* 9–40 (where we have summed up our posi-

The act of anyone who exercises a magisterium is, therefore—while preserving his specific role—contained within the instinct of the *sensus fidelium*. There is a slight analogy here with the sacramental celebration where the minister presides—with his essential and irreplaceable role— and where his intention is entirely understood in that of the community, which is imposed on him.[88] Can it be said, by referring to an expression used to exaggerate this vision, that in this way we make the magisterium the "hostage of the opinion of the laity"? To do so would be forgetting three things: that the *sensus* in question is something else than an opinion and responds to a certainty which is often not realized but infused by the Spirit, that because they are the faithful, those who have charge of the magisterium also have this *sensus* and that they cannot stifle it in the exercise of their job, that it reverts to them in the name of this job to enter into dialog with the whole community by educating it, all the while being educated by it, as well.[89]

In order to assign this mutual dialog its proper place ecclesiologically— one in which the study of situations and practices counts as much as the study of doctrinal contents—Newman called attention to the very nature of the Church, a *communion* of "varied, irreducible functions, in conflict with each other in the pursuit of their own goal, but by this very act, creating a balance, mutually preserving each other from harmful excesses and joining them all together in the one divine center."[90] What should be mentioned more precisely is this idea of conflict, certainly inevitable but not customary and as an integral part of the *conspiratio* of the faithful and the shepherds.[91] Take into consideration, nevertheless, this *communion* of all the parties which make up the Church, each one having its specific feature and yet depending on the others in the very exercise of this specific feature. The authority of those who exercise the magisterium does not come from the faithful, yet it draws its credibility from the *sensus fidelium*.

Undoubtedly such a *communion* will be seen as an abstract ideal, somewhat romantic, not applicable to a Church with universal dimensions. One can point to "the often superficial and elementary consultation of the faith-

---

tion). On the other distinction, see L. Boff, "La distinction entre *Ecclesia docens* et *Ecclesia discens* est-elle justifiée?," *Concilium* 168, 1981, 85–92.

[88]See J.-M. R. Tillard, "A propos de l'intention du ministre et du sujet des sacrements," *Concilium* 31, 1968, 101–112.

[89]See the brief study by L. Sartori, "Critères pour un appel adéquat au *sensus fidelium,*" *Concilium* 168, 1981, 99–108.

[90]J. Walgrave, *art. cit.,* 38. See the important *Preface to the Third Edition of the Via Media* (in 1877).

[91]See *On consulting the Faithful,* 71, 106. On the way in which this *conspiration* is put into operation under Pius XII, see J.-M. R. Tillard, *Foi populaire et foi savante,* 12–19.

ful before the dogma of the Assumption was defined," by explaining that "good intentions were rendered fruitless by concrete reality." But here everything holds up. The Church of God is a *communion* of local Churches. It is basically at the level of the local Church that what we have presented can and must be put into practice,[92] not as a Church conceived as a uniform and homogeneous entity. And it is in the synodal *communion* of the responsible hierarchies of individuals of these local churches that the osmosis described spreads to the outer reaches of the *catholica,* where each one receives from others and gives something back to them.[93] The *communion* of faith which establishes the *communion* of the Churches depends, for its groundwork, on this synodol *communion.* It is this synodal *communion* which states, re-expresses, in the language and needs of each locality what the *communion* of the apostolic Churches has bequethed. In this way the Churches are permitted to "recognize" their faith in that of others and to enrich one another as much on the plane of understanding the revealed Word as on the plane of its defense, of making it explicit, of conveying it in new areas of life in the world.

3. We speak of "recognition" of the faith. But history shows that there has been a slow evolution in the perception of what gives official weight to the declaration of faith worked out in the *conspiratio* of the hierarchically responsible individuals, exercising a magisterium at all levels,[94] and the totality of the people of God. This evolution is parallel to that of the concept of obedience[95] in which the sense of listening has been overpowered by the sense of submission. In the early centuries, the weight of authority for a formula came above all from the strength of the truth contained in it and whose *sensus fidelium* perceived the value, pushing the community to submit to the demands that it implied. Gradually the position was

[92]Which is not without requiring, on the one hand, the return to dioceses of more human size and, on the other hand, putting into place instruments for dialog and mutual listening.

[93]The extraordinary synod of 1985 permitted a quick grasp of this process in a "dialog of experiences" opening up on a re-reception of several of the major conclusions of Vatican II but reinterpreted in light of the *sensus fidelium* by bishops exercising their magisterium.

[94]On magisterium, see F. A. Sullivan, *Magisterium, Teaching Authority in the Catholic Church,* New York, 1983; Y. Congar, "Pour une histoire sémantique du terme *magisterium,*" *RSPT* 60, 1976, 85–98; Id., "Bref historique des formes du magistère et de ses relations avec les docteurs," *ibid.,* 99–112; A. L. Descamps, "Théologie et magistère," *ETL* 52, 1976, 82–133; R. E. Eno, "Ecclesia docens: Structures of Doctrinal Authority in Tertullian and Vincent," *The Thomist* 40, 1976, 96–115; D. van Den Eynde, *Les Normes de l'enseignement chrétien dans la littérature patristique des trois premiers siècles,* Gembloux-Paris, 1933; A. Vacant, *Le Magistère ordinaire de l'Église et ses organes,* Paris, 1899. On texts from Vatican I consult especially P. Nau, "Le magistère pontifical ordinaire au premier concile du Vatican," *RT* 62, 1962, 341–397; M. Caudron, "Magistère ordinaire et infaillibilité pontificale d'après la constitution *Dei Filius,*" *ETL* 36, 1960, 393–431.

[95]See J.-M. R. Tillard, "Obéissance," *Dictionnaire de spiritualité,* t. XI, 535–563.

taken to attach this authority above all to the hierarchical position earnestly taken which proclaims and teaches. Certainly this hierarchical position must be taken into consideration, certain members of the hierarchy receiving from the Spirit the mission and grace to preserve the Church in the authentic understanding of revealed truth. Nevertheless, their function consists in permitting the Word to shine forth in all its brilliance and, through the strength of the Spirit, to be imposed by itself. Obedience to what they have determined, acquiescing to their decisions, stems basically from listening to the truth in question not primarily from consideration of their hierarchical rank and their power.[96]

The ordained hierarchical magisterium has as its usual agent the bishop of the local Church, in *communion* with the bishops of the other Churches but also in close solidarity with what ancient Tradition calls its *presbyterium*. This last term comprises the very slender network by which, on the one hand, the questions, the difficulties, the *praxis,* but also the convictions of the *sensus* of the community give way to the bishop and by which, on the other hand, the decisions of the bishop (those which are his personally as well as those of the whole episcopal body of which he is a member) are not only communicated but explained, interpreted, if necessary, to the community. In a healthy ecclesiology of communion, the vital osmosis of the faith is at work there, especially at the time of the Eucharistic celebration where the proclamation and the explanation of the Word occupy an important place. And when the bishops of the same area, the same nation, of the same continent or of all the nations gather together to treat in a collegial manner the Church of God, its cohesion in the apostolic faith, its inculturation, remedies which might be applied to the division of Christians, they do it as links in this very slender network which the ministerium is in a constant symbiosis with the communities. The weight of their magisterial word stems certainly and undeniably from their own mission as those who are responsible, accomplished with special assistance of the Spirit, but it also stems from the fact that its content is in harmony with what, instinctively, their Churches feel, in their *sensus fidei.*

For reasons that we will have to make more precise, Catholic tradition maintains that in certain circumstances and under certain conditions the Bishop of Rome can impose an infallible judgment on an important point relating to faith or to evangelical life. As Head of the episcopal college, he exercises then the authority with which the Spirit has endowed him. Because if he is head of the college, he is so as bishop and under this title acts only in solidarity with all his brothers in the episcopate.[97] It is not

---

[96]See the constitution *Dei verbum,* 10, of Vatican II.

[97]We know the traditional declaration about the unity of the episcopate and the fact that this

his personal point of view but that of the entire college, even more so that of all the bishops who, since the beginning of the Church, have been in communion with the apostolic college, that he expresses then. Besides, although it may be related to a previous consultation of the entire episcopate,[98] the Bishop of Rome can make a pronouncement then only after having "listened" and investigated the faith of all the Churches confided by the Spirit to the episcopal college. He "defines" not his faith but that of the local Churches.

In these Churches there are theologians.[99] It is well known that, undoubtedly in the prolonging of the didactics which the New Testament speaks of, some Christians—often those who have not been ordained like Justin, or Origen at the beginning of his activity[100]—have exercised a scholarly ministry, not a hierarchical one, since the beginning. Thomas Aquinas, in a text that is often quoted,[101] recognized the existence of two chairs: the *cathedra pastoralis* of those who exercise what we have called the hierarchical or ordained magisterium, and the *cathedra magistralis* of the theologians and scholars.[102]

It is evident, and even a superficial reading of history bears this out, that between these two magisterial chairs tensions break out. But far from being *a priori* deplorable, they respond to what Newman described as the

---

is exercised by a bishop only in solidarity with the whole group. That will be at the heart of the doctrine of Vatican II on the episcopal ministry. The best known old expression of this situation is that of Cyprian (*Epist.* 66, 8, 3; *De Unit.* 5).

[98]The definitions of Pius IX and Pius XII depended on this consultation which a Vatican I doctrinal commission *(deputatio de fide)* refused to introduce into the final text as a condition required for the validity of the definition.

[99]In addition to the studies by Congar , Deschamps, Eno cited above, see on this question of "magisterium" the theologians J.-M. R. Tillard, "Théologie et vie ecclésiale, II. Du ministère des théologiens au magistère doctrinal," *Initiation à la pratique de la théologie*, t. I, Paris, 1982, 173-182; H. Vorgrimler, *art. cit.*; E. Schillebeeckx, *art. cit.*; H. Küng ed., *Fehlbar? Eine Bilanz*, Zurich, 1973; A. Dulles, "The Two Magisteria; an interim Reflection," *Proceedings of CTSA* 35, 1980, 155-169; R. Brown, "The Dilemna of the Magisterium vs the Theologians; Debrinking Some Fictions," *Chicago Studies* 17, 1978, 282-299. The positions of H. Küng against the monopolization of the official teaching by the hierarchy are well known (cf. a discussion of these views in F. A. Sullivan, *op. cit.*, 35-51).

[100]If Eusebius is to be believed, *Hist. Eccles.* VI, 3; VI, 15; VI, 19; VI, 23 (*SC* 41, Paris, 1955, 86-90, 109, 113-119, 123-124). See the study by Th. Schaeffer, *Das Priester Bild im Leben und Werk des Origenes*, Francfort, 1978, 103-115. On the didascals, see especially, A. Lemaire, *Les Ministères aux origines de l'Église*, coll. "Lectio Divina," 68, Paris, 1972, 181-182; H. Küng, *op. cit.*, (which envisages a quasi-"succession" in the didascalia); J. Fitzmyer, "The Office of Teaching in the Christian Church, according to the New Testament," *Teaching Authority and Infallibility in the Church*, coll. "Lutherans and Catholics in Dialogue," 6, Minneapolis, 1980, 186-212.

[101]Very well studied by Y. Congar (*art. cit.*), this text is the *Quodlibet* III, 9, ad 3; also *In IV Sent.*, d. 19, 2, 2, 1 qa 2, ad 4.

[102]See R. Guelluy, "La place des théologiens dans l'Eglise et la société médiévale," *Miscellanea in hon. A. de Meyer*, Louvain, 1946, 571-590.

inevitable discord yet necessary for an agreement which is richer in its subject matter,[103] creating a mutual balance. Because it is not a question of two activities destined to remain parallel or to be swallowed up by one another.

The hierarchical magisterium, based on an ordination, has for its principal function to "preserve" the faith that its predecessors, preaching from its *cathedra,* have taught to its Church or its Churches, by assuring a faithful "tradition" (*paradosis*) coherent with the apostolic Word and by it suitable for safeguarding ecclesial *communion.* Also, listening to the competence and the requests of theologians, he assumes everything which (in his pastoral prudence) seems to him to be an interpretation or an harmonious opening to truth itself, intervening if he judges that such a position would ruin the faith, watching over the reaction of the community when facing proposed opinions. It is not up to him to dictate such or such an interpretation but to remain open to what theology brings to the understanding of the dictum of faith and to let it go through its own instructional process.

The magisterium of theologians strives to discover the meaning of the Word, to disclose possible and established interpretations, to show the fragility of a particular official interpretation which scientific discoveries compel us to re-examine, and to open up new avenues. It especially falls on him to let questions of world-wide interest enter into the Church's thinking, by weighing them, by showing the seriousness of them and by indicating their foreseeable impact. On this plane he is like an antenna without which the people of God would risk casting itself into a vague, ambiguous or fanatical little corner, incapable of taking on authentic progress and questions which are pertinent to human intelligence. In relationship to the ordained magisterium, its attitude must be, of course, one of welcome, with the conviction that its own word does not have, in regard to the common good of the people of God, the same guarantee as the pastoral judgment, that it is an instructional process *in* the Church and not in the strict sense an instructional process of the Church in the strong sense which we have defined in examining carefully the interaction of the *sensus fidelium* and the hierarchical magisterium. Its function aims, in fact, at clarifying and nourishing both. However, the theologian must show to those who exercise the hierarchical magisterium that there exists several valid theologies, therefore, that the one from which they are inevitably drawing their inspiration is not necessarily the only one and, perhaps, is not the best one. By breaking, in this way, the monolithic character of inspired theology, it helps both the *sensus fidelium* and the ministerial

[103]See again the *Preface to the Third Edition of the Via Media* (of 1877).

judgment to make the distinction between faith of the Church (of which there is only one) and theologies in the Church (of which there are many).

The tension between the more pragmatic function of the *cathedra pastoralis* and the more contemplative function of the *cathedra magistralis* subsides during privileged moments of which Vatican II is the most recent example.[104] The "discord" (as Newman views it)—sometimes being expressed by a condemnation of certain theologians—of the turbulent research of preceding decades has become "agreement" in texts of the hierarchical magisterium of the episcopal college as such. Theology has been "received" by the organization thanks to which the entire Church stays in the succession of the apostolic faith. No one will deny that in this marvelous event of *communion* questions and interpretations of theologians of local Churches,[105] in a state of tension with positions held by Roman preparatory commissions but, just like them, listened to by the entire Catholic episcopate, weighed and judged in an open dialog, have played a role not only unappreciated (as it has become routine to declare) but necessary. On the occasion of the episcopal synod of 1985 it was said and resaid, with reason, that Vatican II had been an "event of episcopal *communion.*" It is necessary to add that it was also an event of *communion* of all perceptions, listening, searching and tensions thanks to which the Church of God is preserved in the apostolic faith, yet all the while opening itself up to the problems, the needs, and the sufferings of the world to which it is sent for the purpose of Salvation. Vatican II has been in large part an event of acceptance. It was there that the seal was put on a long search, conducted in theological honesty.

This recent experience shows, beyond the strict problem of theologians, that what affects the truth of the faith is the concern of all the people of God. In the decision of the bishops, as in the research of theologians, it is the entire ecclesial body which searches and proclaims for itself the truth which gives it vitality.

C. A Word which is "received"

Communion among all members of the people of God, based on the *sensus fidelium,* which we have disclosed in the advent of the revelation in human language, then in the preservation, understanding, defense of this Word of God, acts also on the level of its "reception." This belongs to the process by which the contents of this Word, but stated precisely

---

[104]But at the Council of Trent the role of theologians was equally very important.

[105]Let us think of the effort of the Church of Milan, whose publications by the Instituto Paolo VI have given us the documents, and to the one of the Church of Bologna, accessible in the beautiful book by G. Lercaro, *Per la forza dello Spirito,* Bologne, 1984.

and declared by those who have as their mission to exercise a magisterium in the Church by virtue of their ordination, is imposed on the Christian conscience, takes on substance there, becomes one of the points of doctrine which the *sensus fidei* "will recognize" henceforth or will not "recognize" in a particular opinion, affirmation or current. And if the "reception" is not what gives credence to the declaration by the hierarchical magisterium, it does, however, give the certain confirmation that in this declaration truth was found. And so, through *communion* truth "is created."

1. It is hardly possible today to page through a magazine which is somewhat specialized in ecclesiastical history or ecclesiology without finding in it an allusion to "reception." This term designates one of these fundamental ecclesial realities, always present in the life of the people of God but which an era suddenly becomes keenly aware of, urging that it give particular attention to it and bring it to the forefront. This was the case, for example, in the last decades for an entire vocabulary centered on "community" and which gradually invaded ecclesial language: there is talk of "Christian community," "liturgical community," "prayer community," "community proceedings" where formerly the talk was of parish, congregation, office, participation. Once certain immoderations were calmed and the excesses of what had been able to become almost a way of life were done away with, there usually remains a profound impression of it in the ecclesial soul: it has been reminded of an important aspect of the grace-filled being, modifying its look.

2. The Churches owe especially to the ecumenical movement, and in a particular way to the studies of the commission, Faith and Constitution, this re-emergence of the idea and of the need of "reception."[106] Linked first to a reflection on the authority and acceptance of the major conciliar decisions, the research was gradually centered on the welcome, by the Churches, of the doctrinal *consensus* worked out by the ecumenical commissions officially mandated.[107]

---

[106]It seems to us correct to affirm that this re-emergence is tied to the conferences or "consultations" (Oxford, Badgastein en Autriche) on the councils of the early Church and to research elicited by Faith and Constitution in the years 1965 to 1970. The idea broke through officially at the time of the meeting of the commission Faith and Constitution in Louvain, in 1971. See, on the one hand, the important ensemble *Councils and the Ecumenical Movement,* coll. "World Council of Churches," 5, Geneva, 1968 (with the studies of L. Stan, W. Küppers, St. L. Greenslade), the special edition of *The Ecumenical Review* 22, 1970, on Chalcedon (with the studies by Mesrob Ashjian, J. Coman, A. Grillmeier, E. R. Hardy), the report published in *Irénikon* 44, 1971, 349–366. See, on the other hand, for the meeting in Louvain, *Faith and Order Papers, Louvain 1971* (in particular, p. 29, which treats the process of acceptance of councils by the local churches).

[107]On this complex question of reception see especially: E. W. Kemp, *Counsel and Consent, Aspects of the Government of the Church as Exemplified in the History of the English Provincial*

Some have been able to think that they were assisting at a gradual movement towards a new understanding of "reception."[108] But it is rather a change in context. In the ecumenical perspective it is a question of what must permit groups who are implicated not only in welcoming—in certain cases for the first time in an explicit way—points which have been judged to be central to the unity of faith and life but also to recognize that they are unanimous on these points. In the case of former councils,

Synods, London, 1961; M. Dombois, *Recht der Gnade. Ökumenisches Kirchenrecht I*, Witten, 1961, 825-836, 864-865; P. Fransen, "L'autorité des conciles," *Problèmes de l'autorité*, coll. "Unam sanctam," 38, Paris, 1962, 59-100; *Councils and the Ecumenical Movement*, coll. "World Council of Churches Studies," 5, Geneva, 1968 (articles by L. Stan, W. Küppers, S. L. Greenslade); special edition of *The Ecumenical Review* 22, 1970, 348-423 (articles by A. Grillmeier, E. R. Hardy, J. Coman, M. Ashjian); A. Grillmeier, "Konzil und Rezeption. Methodische Bemerkungen zu einem Thema der ökumenischen Diskussion," *Théologie und Philosophie* 45, 1970, 321-352 (reprinted in *Mit ihm und in ihm. Christologische Forschungen und Perspektiven*, Fribourg, 1975, 303-334); C. Andresen, *Die Kirchen der alten Christenheit*, Stuttgart, 1971; *Louvain 1971*, coll. "Faith and Order Papers"; Y. Congar, "La réception comme réalité ecclésiologique," *RSPT* 56, 1972, 369-403 (summarized in *Concilium* 77, 1972, 51-72, and to be read in the continuation of Y. Congar, "Quod omnes tangit ab omnibus tractari et approbari debet," *Rev. hist. droit. franç. et étr.* 36, 1958, 210-259); K. Krikorian, "La réception des conciles," *Istina* 18, 1973, 378-402; J. B. Bauer, "The Reception of the Councils," *Wissenschaft und Weisheit* 2, 1974, 94-102; W. Wilhelm, *Bemerkungen zur Rezeption auslandischen Rechts*. Jus commune V, Francfort, 1975, 122-137; W. Hryniewicz, "Die ekklesiale Rezeption in der sicht der orthodoxen theologie," *Theologie und Glaube* 65, 1975, 250-265; A. Lumpe, "Zu *recipere* als gültig aunchmen annehmen, anerkennen im Sprachgebrauch des römischen und Kanonischen Rechts," *Annuarium Historiae Conciliorum* 7, 1975, 118-135; H. Muller, "Rezeption und Konsens in der Kirche. Eine Anfrange an die Kanonistik," *Osterreichisches Archiv für Kirchenrecht* 27, 1976, 3-21; Id., "Der Anteil der Laien an der Bischofswahl," *Kanonistiche Studien und Texts* 29, Amsterdam, 1977; G. Gassman, "Rezeption im ökumenischen Kontext," *Okumenische Rundschau* 26, 1977, 314-321; F. Wolfinger, "Die Rezeption theologischer Einsichten und ihre theologische und okumenische Bedeutung: von der Einsicht zur Verwiklichung," *Catholica* 31, 1977, 202-232; Id., "Rezeption, ein Zentralbegriff der okumenichen Diskussion oder des Blaubensvollzugs. Ein Vergleich zweier Veroffentlichungen," *Okumenische Rundschau* 27, 1978, 14-21; K. Schmidt-Clausen, "Die Rezeption okumenischen Bewegung," *ibid.*, 1-13; H. Sieben, *Die Konzilidee der Alten Kirche*, Paderborn, 1979 (especially 53-55, 178-181, 515), to be connected with Id., "Zur Entwicklung der Konzilidee," *Theologie und Philosophie* 45, 1970, 353-389; 46, 1971, 40-70, 364-386, 496-528; D. Ramos-Lisson, "Communio y recepcion de canones conciliares de los sinodos hispanicos en los sigles IV y V," *Annuarium Historiae Conciliorum* 12, 1980, 26-37; P. Lengsfeld and H. Stobbe, *Theologischen Konsens und Kirchenspaltung*, Stuttgart, 1981; Emilianos Timiadis, "Reception, Consensus and Unity," *The Greek Orthodox Theological Review* 26, 1981, 47-61; E. Lanne, "La réception," *Irénikon* 55, 1982, 198-213; A. Houtepen, "Reception, Tradition, Communion," in M. Thurian, *Ecumenical Perspectives on Baptism, Eucharist and Ministry*, coll. "Faith and Order Papers," 116, Geneva, 1983, 140-160; W. G. Rusch, "Baptism, Eucharist, Ministry and Reception," *Dialog* 22, 1983, 85-93; A. Papaderos, "Quelques réflexions sur la réception," *POC* 33, 1983, 186-189; G. Denzler, "Autorité et réception des décisions conciliaires dans la chrétienté," *Concilium* 187, 1983, 25-34; E. Kilmartin, "Reception in History, an Ecclesiological Phenomenon and its Significance," *Journal of Ecumenical Studies*, 21, 1984, 34-54 (see also in this number the articles by G. Wainwright, V. Chandran, W. Lazareth, R. Trubhovich); J. Zizioulas, "The Theological Problem of Reception," *Bulletin du Centro pro Unione*, 26, 1984, 3-6; cf. especially *La Réception de Vatican II*, edited by G. Alberigo and J.-P. Jossua, coll. "Cogitatio fidei," 134, Paris, Cerf, 1985.

[108] As some seem to insinuate, especially among the Orthodox or Catholic ecumenists, for instance, A. Papaderos, *art. cit.*, 189-199.

each Church was to place itself simply, with its tradition, before the affirmations of organizations intrinsically linked to its being. In the ecumenical undertaking, one group must make a pronouncement about the compatibility of its own understanding of the faith not with that of an organization internal in its structure and charged with taking care of its fidelity but with that of an instance created for the particular circumstance and added on. Besides, the texts on which this group is called to make a pronouncement are proposed to it with the authority of a commission of experts, several of whom, by definition, come from other beliefs which are not yet in true communion with it. Moreover, in the agreements or consensus the visions of these "others" have also been integrated. The authority in question does not, therefore, have the weight of a "magisterium." Its views can only challenge each group by asking it to question itself in light of the gospel and its own tradition.[109] It is a question of a challenging authority, not of the decision-making kind. So that "reception" then has two different stages. First of all, what is necessary is to accept (or refuse) the content of the challenge, especially if it implies a change in ways of thinking or acting as a group, because a relationship to the gospel is recognized in it (or not recognized in it). Then it is necessary, if the response is positive, to incorporate it into the life of each community. This second stage of "reception" counts much more than the first. Because the end result of a welcoming of texts is "reception" into the life itself.

The second stage that we have just brought up unites with, it seems to us, the ordinary function of "reception." The ecumenical outlook complicates the process. It stresses the customary function of "reception" in the life of the people of God. And it permits it to be grasped right away.

3. If closing the parenthesis, we examine in a more precise way the process of traditional "reception," we discover that it is a fact of *communion*. That is so much the more important since it marks out the great stages of history of Revelation and then of the Church. Because the first Chris-

---

[109]Here is found the difficult problem of the authority for the decisions of the Ecumenical Council and its organisms, on which they pronounced in Toronto in 1950 (see *The Church, the Churches and the World Council of Churches, Minutes of the Central Committee, Toronto 1950*, Geneva, 1950; see also article nine of the "Rules of the World Council of Churches," *Breaking Barriers, Nairobi, 1975*, 333). But the question is still not resolved in a satisfying way. See our study in *Cristianesimo nella storia*. In regard to bilateral agreements the question has yet a more particular horizon. Let us give an example. The Anglican Churches having to make a pronouncement on the ARCIC (Final Report), will they accept a modification of their version of ecclesial unity because the conviction of the Roman Catholic Church, which the experts have integrated into their doctrinal agreement, will seem to them to be a true answer to the will of Christ? It is the first moment of the "reception" of the report of the mixed commission. But once the decision was made by competent Anglican authorities, it will be necessary to suppose that it is positive, to translate it into facts, which will demand that all Anglicans "receive" it.

tian generations "receive" the Old Testament, in spite of the knowledge that they have something that surpasses this by the Word and the Passover of Christ Jesus, and despite the Jewish opposition and even hatred. In the Spirit, they understand that everything is accomplished "according to the scriptures."[110] The Johannine writings, not very favorable towards the Jews,[111] emphasize nevertheless, the depth of this link (2:15; 10:35; 11:51; 12:13-15, 38-41; 13:18; 15:25; 17:12; 19:24, 28, 36, 37). It is the same thing with the Letter to the Hebrews, filled with quotations from the Old Testament, and yet careful to show that the institutions of the Old Covenant were only rough outlines (Heb 8:5; 10:1), a preparation become antiquated (8:7, 13; 9:10), therefore, suppressed (10:9). And Revelations, which refers to the Jews as "the synagogue of Satan" (Rev 2:9; 3:9), describes, however, the realities of the eschatological world only in images and themes which show that it is a question of the flowering of what the Old Convenant was, only the seed and the promise. As for Paul presented in the Acts of the Apostles, very pessimistic because of the closed attitude of the Jews to Salvation through Jesus Christ (Acts 28:25-29), he does not persist any less in "trying to convince them by speaking about Jesus, arguing from the Law of Moses and the Prophets" (28:23; cf. 17:1-4).[112] The "reception" of the Old Testament by the new-born

[110]See the small book by C. H. Dodd, *According to the Scriptures,* London, 1952 (numerous reeditions). As a scriptural witness of the importance attached to the understanding of the "holy Letters," see especially 2 Tim 3:14-17 (cf. 2 Cor 2:14-18). It is known that the determination of the canon of the Old Testament will be finished only after the beginnings of Christianity. Towards the end of the second century, books such as *Hénoch* or *l'Ascension de Moïse* are still often taken as scriptural. See, written in collaboration, *Le Canon de l'Ancien Testament sa formation et son histoire,* Geneva, 1984. The worship of the synagogue will play a great role in this process of canonization and Christians will adopt in their own liturgy books which the Jews read in the synagogue.

[111]The Jews have the devil for Father (John 8:44), the feasts of the Old Testament have become the feasts of the "Jews" (5:1; 6:4; 7:2), the Law has become the Law of the Jews (8:17; 10:34; 15:25), the Sabbath has become their feast (cf. 19:31), they have chased the Christians from the synagogues (9:22; 12:42; 16:2). All that brings up a question of distance, but which implies no break with Scripture.

[112]Concerning Paul's thinking, let us go back to F. Refoulé, *Et ainsi tout Israël sera sauvé,* which we follow. Concerning an evolution of Paul's thought in this area, see R. E. Brown and J. P. Meier, *Antioch and Rome,* (especially R. E. Brown, *passim*). On the total aspect of the problem of the relationships between Jews and Christians as shown in the New Testament, see in addition texts mentioned here in the letter of James (1:1; 2:1-26; 5:16-18); the letter to the Ephesians which is witness to an irenic view (2:11-22); the letters to Timothy which evoke tensions affecting respect for the Law (cf. 1 Tim 1:4-11); the first letter of Peter (1:10-2, 10); the Gospel according to Matthew whose declarations give witness to a certain osmosis between Synagogue and Church and leave one to think that the break is not total to the point that some believe that Jews and Christians have been able to frequent for some time the same places of worship (compare 5:18; 10:5; 24:20; 27:53 and 8:10-11; 10:17, 23; 12:9-21; see also the problem posed by 18:17); writings by Luke (Luke 1:6-17, 26-35, 54-55, 67-79; 2:22-32, 37-42; Acts 2:46; 3:1; 5:42; 13:14, 42; 14:1 and especially 24:14; cf. J. A. Fitzmyer, *The Gospel according to Luke I-IX,* New York, 1981, 9-10). It would be necessary also to examine carefully the theme of the "fulfillment" of the Scriptures in the totality of the New Testament (cf. C. H. Dodd, *op. cit.*).

Church is, without doubt, one of the most determinant factors in the make-up of what was to become the Christian idea. It implants the Cross, Easter and Pentecost in the totality of the design of God. All it takes to be convinced of this is to read the kerygma in *Acts,* in particular Peter's speech after the miracle of the Portico of Solomon (3:13-26). Jesus Christ's work becomes not a point of departure but a "fullfillment," a *teleiosis.* We have already reflected on the implications of this vision.

But "reception" is at work also even within the New Testament. Paul's case is typical. He interprets the "Handshake of communion" (Gal 2:9) which James, Cephas and John, the pillars, extended to him as well as to Barnabas, as a "reception" of the "gospel that he will preach among the pagans" (Gal 2:2), a "sign" of the apostolic grace which is his (2:9), quieting his fear "of running or having run in vain" (2:2). This will permit him to resist courageously those who, following Peter, "were not respecting the true meaning of the Good News" (2:14). Certainly, he knows that his gospel comes from God (1:12), that what he has "received" (*parelabon,* 1 Cor 11:23; 15:3) goes back to the Lord himself, whatever might be the extraordinary way by which that has overtaken him. Nevertheless, he knows also, through the Spirit, that there can be only one gospel (Gal 1:7-9): its course aims at the integration of his message with that of the first witnesses, so that this unity of the gospel will be guaranteed. Also, in the brief confession of faith in his First Letter to the Corinthians (1 Cor 15:3-8), it is this message of the primitive community as such that he "receives" and makes his own. Otherwise it would divide not only doctrine but Christ himself (1 Cor 1:10-17).

Soon the Churches will put into operation some kind of selection process among the whole body of writings presenting themselves as witnesses of the primitive faith. Almost spontaneously, a nucleus of them will come to the fore by common agreement,[113] but some documents which find favor in certain areas will be refused; there will be some hesitation concerning others. The *Didache,* the *Letter of Clement,* the *Letter of Barnabas,* the *Shepherd of Hermas,* included at first, will finally be thrown out, whereas

---

[113]The witness of Justin on the examples reveals the first stage (cf. *Ap.* I, 66, 67; *Dial.* 100–106). The role of Marcion is known, who died in 160, with his "non-reception" of the Old Testament, in this need of precision in regard to the list of holy Scriptures. Irenaeus of Lyon (with his knowledge of the Acts of the Apostles as a normative text) is the witness of another stage. At the turn of the third century, the gospels, Paul's letters, Acts, the first letter of Peter are already "received" in the quasi-totality of the churches, and the first Johannine epistle begins to assert itself everywhere. The African provinical councils of 393 and 397 know the list which will make up the scriptural canon. The declaration of Irenaeus (between 180 and 190) is of prime importance. He declares that among the criteria for authentic *knowledge* it is necessary to count on the "unchangeable preservation of the Scriptures." He explains that this involves three elements: "an integral account, without addition or subtraction, a reading exempt from fraud and in accord with these Scriptures, a legitimate interpretation, appropriated, exempt from danger and blasphemy" (*Adv. Haer.* IV, 33, 8, trans. A. Rousseau, *SC* 100, Paris, 1965, 821).

the Letter of James, Revelation, and the Letter to the Hebrews will be retained although not without some difficulty. The last two Johannine letters, the Second Epistle of Peter and the one by Jude will also have difficulty being included everywhere on the list. "Received" in its final form in the fourth century, the scriptural canon will be "re-received" at certain crucial times for the unity of the Church. This will be the case in Florence in the decree for the Jacobites, when at Trent faced with the Reformation, a "reception" which, in treating the faith, the Council of Vatican I will adopt.[114] It is important to underline that in these conciliar actions they speak explicitly of "reception."[115]

There is, therefore, a very complex history behind this slow "reception" of the books which make up the rule of faith itself. Three points must be raised. The "reception" of some books and the "non-reception" of others seems at the start less of fact, the consequence of the consciousness of a sort of internal evidence by which a particular book asserted itself and another one did not. What is at stake here is an instinct about the faith. Elsewhere, this instinct is manifested in the lives of the communities. Finally, the definitive list is established thanks only to the interplay of relationships between Churches, certain ones sharing with others their own richness. The process is one of communion.

These three observations are found later in the acceptance of the major conciliar decisions. It happens that, by a sort of horizontal communication, the declarations of one provincial council gradually make an oil-stain and are "received" by other councils of the same type, sometimes by a general council.[116] This phenomenon, well proven, seems to us ecclesiologically very significant. We will come back to it. What is also significant is the fact[117] that in the patristic era the "reception" is seen not as the simple juridical course of acquiescence to the decision of legitimate authorities but as a slow "spiritual" process permitting truths thus declared to pass into the life of the local Churches. In this way, moreover, is ex-

---

[114]The decree for the Jacobites is from 1442; at Trent it is a question of the fourth session (1546); at Vatican I it is the second chapter of the Constitution *Dei Filius* (cf. *DS* 1334, 1501–1505, 3006). At the time of the Reformation, the canonicity of certain books was questioned.

[115]An attentive study of the discussions of Trent is very enlightening here. The terms *receptio, susceptio* (which will be retained in the body of the decree of April 8, 1946) are those which designate the process in question. See *Concilium Tridentinum*, t. V, Fribourg, 1964, 3–104, for *receptio* 4, 5, 6, 7, 9, 10 *(de receptione traditionum apostolicarum)* 11, 13, 18, etc.; for the final decree see also *DS* 1501, 1504.

[116]See the situation for some Spanish councils, examined very well by D. Ramos-Lisson (cf. the article of the *Annuarium Historiae Conciliorum* 2, 1980, especially note 107). See also the case of the Council of Orange (from 529), where only about ten bishops were present, whose declarations about grace guided the Council of Trent (*DS* 370–397). See the article by W. Küppers (especially note 107).

[117]Well accented by Y. Congar, "La réception comme," 391–401. See also H. Muller, "Der Anteil der Laien an der Bischofswahl," (especially note 2).

plained in large part the tortuous road that declarations as important as those of Nicaea and Chalcedon took in order to be accepted.[118] Official acceptance by the heads of communities transmitting conciliar actions was the mechanism for an incorporation of truth by the people of God. Every "reception" is inscribed in this way in the Spirit's pedagogy communicating what the Johannine Gospel calls the "good" of Christ (cf. John 16:14), access to the "complete truth" (16:13).

4. It is clear in the life of the Church of God, in its areas of organic unity as in those where the desire to weld together again in *communion* is hard at work, that the process of "reception" holds an essential place. In order to determine the nature of it, it will be necessary to return once again to the nature of *koinonia*.

In the Church of God—which exists because it "remains" in the "communion" of the Son with the Father and the Spirit (cf. John 14:10-14, 20-23; 15:10-11; 17:10-11, 21-24)—nothing exists which is not "communion," beginning evidently with love. That brings in also in a very full way the Word of truth, which is not reduced to a pure intellectual proclamation. It is inseparably Word pronounced and Word accepted, Word declared and Word "received," announcement and *Amen* declared on this announcement, to the point that one cannot be in the truth without also "putting it" into action (cf. John 3:21; 1 John 1:6). The Truth according to the gospel is not struck down. One permits oneself to be convinced by a Spirit, in a way that this truth becomes part of us. Because the action of the Spirit of truth contains both the course of the person who announces or declares and the attitude of the person who accepts. And its acceptance indicates not only hearing, but listening by "receiving" with one's whole being,[119] in a freedom which God respects.

---

[118]Nicaea (and Constantinople) are accepted by Chalcedon. In 597, Gregory the Great will give witness again to a reservation about the Council of 381 (Constantinople). The history of post-Chalcedon is extremely complex. See all of the studies on Chalcedon gathered together in *The Ecumenical Review* 22, 1970. See concerning the complex history of the reception of Nicaea, A. de Halleux, "La réception du symbole œcuménique, de Nicée à Chalcédoine," *ETL* 61, 1985, 5-47.

[119]This vision is especially certified in the Johannine writings. See F. M. Braun, *Jean le théologien*, t. II, coll. "Études bibliques," Paris, 1964: "To listen to him [Jesus], is to recognize him as the Son of God . . . from there comes the fact that for some, they are the cause of salvation, for others, condemnation" (140). In his posthumous book, D. Mollat, *Études johanniques*, Paris, 1979, 62-75, 85-90, shows how in Johannine tradition Word and call are one, the Word bearing a power which urges one to get involved in the salvation it proclaims, to the point that "to reveal itself is to convert men to the truth" (65), which makes the Word a "saving work." Truth is the meeting of Revelation and adherence to this Revelation. Speaking of faith he adds that, for John, "faith is a decision, an option, an involvement in following Jesus, a break with the world, an heroic confession of the truth" (85). But John also accents a vision of the truth which is not abstract, which other scriptural texts certify, although less vigorously. See A. Vanhoye, *Situation du Christ, Hébreux 1-2*, coll. "Lectio divina," 58, Paris, 1969, 52-117 (especially 52-54,

Perhaps the dynamism of the faith itself will be recognized in this presentation of the "reception," which belongs, just as the announcement does, to the full truth of this Word. In the Church, the Word is, indeed, Word of truth in the full sense only if it expands into faith in the man or woman who welcomes it. Correlatively, the faith exists only if a word of God has been not only listened to but "received" and therefore, appropriated.

Taken in this very broad sense, encompassing the entire life of the Church, "reception" designates the process by which either an individual or the people of God as such makes a word which is declared to it truth (in the full sense) of one's faith, integrated with what that individual recognizes as the authentic expression of the Revelation. It can be described as an entrance into the *Amen* where faith comes to light. In the biblical ideas, the expression "this is true" is in fact the action—bored into by the power of the Spirit—which changes what was until that time only a word objectively true (in its noetic content) into a word of life-giving faith. Because the assent to this *Amen* transforms what he "receives" into much more than words, idea, "propositions," in brief, into an understanding in the Western sense of this term, he makes it a communion with the God and Father of Jesus Christ (cf. 2 Cor 1:18-20). According to the great intuition of Thomas Aquinas, faith emerges much beyond the formula of believing. Its object is the divine reality itself (the *res*), in other words, precisely the eternal communion of the Father, the Son and the Spirit,[120] but as a bearer of what Pauline tradition calls the *mystery* (Rom 16:25; Eph 1:9; 3:3-9; Col 1:26-27; cf. 1 Cor 2:7-9), the gathering together of all into the one Body of Christ. Then, through the density of such a formula, it is the very love of the Father, revealed and incarnated in Jesus, which reunites either the individual or the believing community. The letter of the gospel is "received" (Gal 1:9; 1 Cor 15:1), but, in the gospel, Jesus Christ the Lord (Col 2:6).[121] And by "receiving" the Lord one "receives" the Kingdom which he has taken possession of (Heb 12:28; cf. 1:8). In its proper perspective, the Johannine Gospel in its Prologue also identifies the "reception" of the Word (John 1:11-12, 16), Word made flesh, with the "reception" of divine life.[122]

Perhaps, in order to understand this idea, it is necessary to recall that in every acceptance of the Word, the heart, in the sense used by Pascal, plays a primary role. The Spirit opens the intellect at the very moment

---

insisting on the fact that the biblical Word is a "word of someone to someone"). See also, G. Kittel, art. "Legô," in *TWNT* 4.

[120]"*Actus credentis non terminatur ad enuntiabile sed ad rem,*" *Summa theologica* IIa-IIae, 1, 2, ad 2.

[121]The context is that of the apostolic proclamation (cf. 1:25-29; 2:1-5).

[122]In all these cases the verb used is *paralambanein, lambanein.*

when he opens the heart. The individual or the community says "yes" rationally to propositions or formulas by judging the objective content of them. But it is because the individual perceives them, with his heart, as illuminating the being and the design of God and not because they would enrich his intellectual knowledge. He "receives" words which help him to enter better into the unfolding of the *mystery*. This "reception" is in no way a cold judgment on an assertion presenting itself as dogmatic, or a verdict of inflexible orthodoxy. In its basic biblical sense, which we are examining at the moment, it deals totally with what permits one to discover or better perceive what in a formal way makes the content of Revelation a *Good News*.

It is understood then why "reception" is a spiritual phenomenon, normally associated with a prayer experience. We do not think we are mistaken by stating that truths as central but equally as difficult to get to the heart of as those which treat the mystery of the Trinity have penetrated the life of the Churches only because of the liturgy. The *lex orandi lex credendi* also has this meaning. The faith could not inhabit the people of God without the epiklesis of liturgical prayer.

5. In fact, "reception" shares in the essence of faith which is based on communion. That explains why one cannot understand the nature of it if one adheres to its purely juridical or institutional aspects. It is one of the dimensions of the ecclesial deep-rootings of belief. Because although it is in every believing person the fruit of a personal and secret action of the Spirit, in no way could faith be reduced to individualistic perspectives, made into something completely private. This extends to everything which springs from it.

In the Covenant, the first partner of God is none other, in fact, than the Church *as such*.[123] God speaks to all the People, and he is revealed not to such and such a person or in such and such an era but to the whole. His dialog does not wish to be held in private. Also the promises are addressed to the "holy community." Moses, Jeremiah, John the Baptist,

---

[123]This is a point on which Catholic and Protestant traditions are not in complete agreement. But ecumenical dialogs of recent years have made it evident that in spite of everything there is agreement on essential points. Certainly it is necessary to recognize that already on the level of the New Testament Johannine tradition puts more emphasis on the relationship *of each Christian* with the Lord Jesus than on the *collective* dimension of the life of faith. The *personal* relationship of love with Jesus has more importance than the pure and simple belonging to the community (the word Church does not appear in Johannine literature, except in 3 John 6, 9, 10), and the emphasis on the relationship of Jesus with "his own" (cf. John 13:21, 34; 15:9, 13; 17:23; 1 John 3:16-17) outweighs it. Yet, the Johannine Gospel is also the New Testament document which gives in the theme of the vine (15:1-17), in that of the shepherd (10:1-18), in the prayer in chapter 17, an extremely profound vision of the *collective* dimension of the life "of his own" (see also 1 John 1:3, 6-7), inserting personal relationship into a wider perspective. See on this R. E. Brown, *The Churches the Apostles Left Behind*, 84-101.

Jesus himself are confidants of Yahweh or of the Father only in order to hand over to the entire People the secret of God and to assemble the "Israel of God" into a common Amen uttered to the message contained in these promises. They are mediators. In the strict sense, there is no individual faith. All faith is ecclesial, belonging to communion by its very essence. Its subject is the Church in its being as *koinonia*. Also every act of faith flows from the man or woman who believes. Personal faith is a communion with the faith which is contained in the entire Body, an insertion of the individual *Amen* into the great chorus of the Church (cf. Rev 5:4; 7:12; 19:3; 22:20). When Irenaeus writes that the Spirit of God is the water which makes the powdery flour one single dough for one single loaf of bread,[124] he is probably also thinking of this reality of faith as it relates to community. One believes personally but one does so only within the context of Church.

Since faith in the life-giving Word is, therefore, carried only by the Church in its essence as communion,[125] the two moments which make it a Word of truth—announcement and acceptance—must involve the whole Body. Some in this Body will have as their mission to declare it in its objective truth. The subsequent assent by the faithful is not, as we said, necessary for the help of the Spirit to be guaranteed for those whom the Lord charges with the ministry of the Word, for their interpretation or explanation to be authentic, and valid, objectively correct.[126] Besides, since evangelical truth is by definition a transmitted truth, it is very necessary that the instances entrusted with its transmission be also those which, to their own extent, can discern the real content of it. And even when they only express what they gather from the life of the People of God or "receive" from the *sensus fidelium,* they have in this way a sort of creative priority. However, as exact as it may be objectively, this content floats in some way in so far as it has not entered into the *Amen* of the people of God, into the structure of ecclesial faith, in so far as the community which perhaps carried it along has not consciously appropriated it.

Undoubtedly the best analogy for understanding this difficult compenetration and complementarity of ministers of the Word and of the entire People is still the relationship of the presider and the congregation at the Eucharistic celebration. It is certainly the minister who, by the epiklesis and the recalling of the Words of the Lord, can give to the faithful the Body and Blood of Christ. But his act is enclosed in the act of the

---

[124]*Adv. Haer.* III, 17, 2 (*SC* 34, Paris, 1952, 305-307).

[125]This is the total, universal Church which cannot err. See O. Rousseau, *L'Infaillibilité de l'Église,* Chevetogne, 1963.

[126]See the illuminating study by H. Bacht, "Vom Lehramt der Kirche und in der Kirche," *Catholica* 25, 1971, 144-167.

entire congregation, culminating in the *Amen* which closes the Anaphora and which the one who accompanies the reception of the Eucharistic bread and cup prolongs. Without the acceptance of faith which the *Amen* expresses, there is no authentic communion—according to Augustine and Thomas Aquinas—hence no full effect of the sacrament despite the presence of the Lord in the Eucharistic species: *crede et manducasti.* This is likewise true in the "reception" of the Bread of God which is the Word.

"Reception" does not indicate that a particular position presented as a declaration of faith has been taken in a way that justifies the imposition by those responsible for it. It is not from it either that a particular official proposition maintains its objective accuracy or not. But it says that the Church has accepted this declaration—which, evidently, implies that the Spirit acclaims its truth—and has integrated it into its life by seeing in it a wholesome doctrine, a positive property for its structure in fidelity to the gospel. It has made a truth of it. Because the Spirit gives to communities and to the faithful the *sensus fidei* permitting them to appreciate the benefit to them of the official propositions, to make a judgment about their relationship to the concrete structure of the Church of God under such a circumstance and in such a place.

As a consequence, it is clear that adherence is then ordered by the authority of the truth itself. In fact, since truth is at stake here, this authority could not, after all, come from outside. It is the contents of the truth itself which makes it imperative. It is convincing, recognized, "received." It has every priority.[127] Human instances, as lofty as they may be, are at its service, under its control. They also "receive" it. "Reception"—which in our case springs from the action of the Spirit—makes the Church a Body "united in faith and the knowledge of the Son of God" (Eph 4:13), where all charisms come together "for each separate part to work according to its function" and which "realizes its own growth in order to build itself up in love" (Eph 4:16).

To this dynamism of truth *as such* is attached also everything which concerns a certain dimension of ecclesial discipline. Too much has been written in recent years about the *praxis* of the faith for us to repeat it here.

---

[127]Y. Congar often quotes, in contrast with this vision of the early centuries, a text of Thomas Stapleton (who died in 1598): *"In doctrina fidei non quid dicatur sed quis loquetur a fideli populo attendendum est"* ("in what concerns the doctrine of faith the faithful people must consider not what is said but the one who is speaking." *De principiis fidei doctrinalibus,* 1572, lib. X, cap. 5). See Y. Congar, *L'Église de S. Augustin à l'époque moderne,* Paris, 1970, 371. Compare with the recognized authority in the symbol of Nicaea and which comes to it from the harmony of its content with the faith of the Apostles; compare also with "Peter has spoken through the mouth of Leo," indicating the acceptance of the *Tome à Flavien* by the Fathers of Chalcedon. Concerning the transcendence of the content in regard to the authority who speaks, the thought of Maximus the Confessor (*PG* 90, 145–148) is known.

Ecclesial life does not rest on an abstract acceptance of doctrine. Doctrine must be embodied in a concrete *communion*.

"Reception," therefore, as we describe it, could not be confused with a purely subjective measure, provoking a tension between hierarchy and faithful people. In reception, the reference of prime importance is always to teaching and to practice of the faith, taken in its link with the tradition of the apostles,[128] which takes into account the primary role of the bishops—entrusted by a special title with Tradition—at the basis of the dynamism which helps to unleash, through a very explicit presentation of the "content" of faith or a kind of highlighting, certain imperatives which flow from it.

6. If "reception" takes place in reference to the apostolic witness, it is in its relationship with today, even when the area spoken of is discipline. In fact, it is a question entirely of a moment inscribed on the course of Tradition (*paradosis*), belonging to the economy of the Spirit by which, the "once and for all" of the apostolic faith must invade all times, be sowed in all cultures and local situations. "Reception" puts into practice and makes possible the catholicity of the one faith, in every sense of the word catholic: qualitative, historical, geographical and cultural catholicity. It causes the *entire* faith to reside in such Church, but also that this faith be in *all* facets of humanness and throughout *all* of history. Through it, the Spirit takes care so that in the complex twists and turns it remains what *comes* from the apostles. It is, therefore, both a guarantee of orthodoxy and a support for the creativity of the Spirit, by force of adaptation. Because if Chalcedon "receives" Nicaea and Constantinople, if the Fourth Council of Toledo (in 589) "receives" Nicaea, Constantinople, Ephesus, Chalcedon,[129] it is not simply to place itself in a line of continuity with the past. It is also in order to give apostolic Tradition its rich catholicity, by permitting it to expand in a new context. Theology today speaks here of acculturation, of rendering the one faith into the compost of peoples, human traditions, and old religious subject matter.[130] A difficult undertaking! It is evident that it could not be done unilaterally by

---

[128]See H. Sieben, *"Die Konzilidee der Alteu Kirche,"* 511–516.

[129]Mansi 9, 987. These councils of Toledo (between 400 and 701) are, one knows, one of the most important sources for understanding the conscience of the Church in this era. That gives to the formula of "reception" of the old Councils in 589 its entire depth *"Consentione nostra vera esse probavimus."* Compare the attitude of the fourteenth Council of Toledo (in 684) in regard to the decisions of the third Council of Constantinople (of 681). For monotheism, one judges the new texts in light of what has been "received" from the past, one "receives" them to the extent to which they are not in disagreement with the decisions of the old councils and are in harmony with them (see H. Sieben, *op. cit.,* 341).

[130]See J.-M. R. Tillard, "Pluralisme théologique et mystère de l'Église," *Concilium* 191, 1984, 109–120.

way of authority.[131] Whether it is a question of disciplinary canons, of liturgical forms or doctrinal expressions, it is necessary that it pass through the soul of the peoples. "Reception" assures this passage, which is one of the forceful lines of Tradition.

7. It can happen that propositions which are objectively exact, doctrinal affirmations which are validly taken and legitimately promulgated, ideas accepted and spread by those who are responsible for the communities, canonical decisions, are not filtered either into the life of all the Churches, or into certain local Churches, or at the very least they are stored away for the time being. And that happens without the least desire to refuse or disregard authority. According to its own tradition, to its concrete situation, a Church will perceive that a particular point is not in full harmony with its spirit, without denying that elsewhere it might be beneficial.

The resistance by the Church of Milan under the direction of Charles Borromeo, after Trent, concerning making the liturgy uniform, is an example of the integrity of such reaction.[132] In a more radical and complex way, the difficulty of Carolingian Christianity regarding decisions of the Second Council of Nicaea concerning the veneration of icons (787) came not from contempt but from the fact that they did not seem in full harmony with the practice and teaching of all the Churches.[133] Under our

---

[131]As examples of badly executed liturgical acculturation show, by a lack of authentic "reception," given by E. J. Kilmartin, *art. cit.,* 40–44.

[132]The problem was on the frontier of what is disciplinary and doctrinal. See the illuminating study of P. Prodi, "Charles Borromée, archevêque de Milan, et la papauté," *RHE* 62, 1967, 379–411 (especially 393–397). It is true that this Church in Milan has a long tradition of freedom on this point, certified already with Ambrose in *De Sacramentis* (III, 1, 5, *SC* 25 bis, Paris, 1980, 95, 5): "We are not ignorant of the fact that the roman Church does not have this custom, although we followed its example and rite in everything. However, it does not have this custom of washing feet. Perhaps it was done away with because of the great number. There were some who tried to excuse it by saying that one must not do that in the course of the mystery, not at baptism, not at the time of rebirth, but feet must be washed as one does for a guest. But one rises out of humility, the other out of sanctification: 'If I do not wash your feet, you will have no part with me.' I do not say that to criticize others, but to justify the office that I fill. I desire to follow the roman Church in everything; but yet we are also endowed with human reason. Also what is observed elsewhere for the best of reasons, we preserve it also for the best of reasons."

"It is the apostle Peter himself whom we follow, it is to his fervor that we are attached. What does the roman Church respond to that? Yes, it is surely the apostle Peter himself who suggests this declaration to us, he who was bishop of the roman Church. It is Peter himself when he says: 'Lord, not only my feet, but also my hands and my head.' See his faith. The refusal that he put forth first of all came from his humility, the offer that he made of himself afterward came from his fervor and his faith."

[133]After this Council the question of the "reception" of the East will no longer be asked. On his decision, see *Libri carolini* IV, 28. Leo IX will have a moe positive vision in 1053 (Mansi 19, 663), taken up at Trent (*DS* 1823); see C. Silva-Tarouca, *Institutiones Historiae Ecclesiasticae,* Rome, 1933, t. II, 49. Here the stakes are doctrinal but also concern discipline. As far as

eyes, whereas large sections of decisions of Vatican II were put into practice very quickly—those which concern the liturgy, ecumenism, the renewal
of religious communities—others have remained in the background and
are at great risk of not being contained in Denzinger kinds of collections
in future centuries. Since we were involved we know very well that, without any doubt, that is explained by other reasons than a refusal of obedience and is on an equal footing with a deep veneration for the work
of Vatican II. Non-reception is not the same as rejection.

In fact, according to the statement by Y. Congar, "reception" of a council is practically equal to its efficacy.[134] This remark is applied, besides,
to the "reception" of every important decision of a hierarchical instance.
But one must, examining the past after several centuries, recognize that
it is a question of a complex process of actualizing the Word in history.
One is in the realm of the biblical *Dabar,* which is power for an effect
of creation or Salvation (cf. Isa 55:10-11), but is so only by osmosis with
the Spirit, in unforeseen ways. And this Spirit is in every baptized person. That is why, as we said earlier, actualization appeals to the *sensus*
of communities and their members. But the diversity of places and times
is so immense. If it is then clarifying to state that there exist very few cases
of absolute non-reception, some Churches having found something good

this is concerned, already a century earlier the bishop of Rome Sergius, a Syrian, had not "received" the canons of the famous synod of Constantinople of 692, called council *in Trullo* or
Quinisexte, not only because of the revival of canon 28 of Chalcedon and powers given at Constantinople, but also because they were loosely tied to the West, even aggressive (see on these canons
the important article of V. Laurent, "L'œuvre canonique du concile *in Trullo* [691–692], a primary
source of the right of the eastern Church" *Revue des études byzantines* 23, 1965, 7–41). Leo the
Great had received Chalcedon only *"in sola cause fidei"* (*Epist.* 141, 1 *PL* 54, 1029), excluding
disciplinary decisions. On the doctrinal plane, one knows the stirrings that created in Africa, in
Milan and in Aquila the hesitant "reception" of the council of 553 on the *Trois Chapitres* (between 553 and 555) by pope Vigile. Stranger yet, one knows that in 597 Gregory the Great will
hesitate again on the "reception" of the canons of the Council of Constantinople of 381, accepting only what concerns the condemnation of the Pneumatomaches or Macedonians (cf. *Rég.*
VII, 321, *MGH,* EPPI, 479). Concerning the questions of the "reception" of the canons, canon
3 of the Council of Constantinople of 381, on the rank given to the bishop of the New Rome
(Constantinople), plays an important role. Until then, in fact, Alexandria was seen as the most
important See in the East. In 451, the famous canon 28 of Chalcedon recognizing the privileges
of Constantinople will be contested by the roman legates. Leo the Great "will not receive" it.
In the sixth century, in 545, Justinian will declare that the bishop of Constantinople comes immediately after Rome and before all the other bishops (*Novellae* 131, 2). The bishop of Rome,
Gregory the Great, will protest again in the seventh century against the use of the title "ecumenical patriarch" used by the patriarch of Constantinople as an official title, and he will explain
himself on this in a letter to Eulogius of Alexandria and Anastasius of Antioch. But in 1439, in
the *Décret pour les Grecs,* the Council of Florence after having strongly declared "the primacy
over all the earth" of the bishop of Rome, will add: "We declare again the order of the other
venerable Patriarchs, transmitted in the canons: the patriarch of Constantinople is the second
after the very holy roman Pontiff, the one of Alexandria is third, the one of Antioch is fourth,
the one of Jerusalem is fifth, all their privileges and rights being evidently safe" (*DS* 1308). See
J. Gill, *The Council of Florence,* Cambridge, 1959, 284.

[134]"La réception comme réalité ecclesiologique," 374–399.

for them in what the whole sometimes remained quite indifferent to, a pluralism is discovered in "reception".[135] Besides, "reception" of several essential doctrines germinated after they had been buried away for a long time. They had to be subjected to reviews, clarifications, and corrections. Churches reacted by making a judgment in light of their tradition. It took nearly sixty years of often troubling discussions for Nicaea to be "received." And would it have been without the decision of the Council of Constantinople (381), itself rather in limbo until its "reception" at Chalcedon? Some apparent non-receptions can be revealed after the event as providential elements of the patient economy of the Spirit. They were done in the ways of God.

8. It is not sufficient, however, in the ecclesiological perspective which is our particular one, to scrutinize "reception" uniquely in this relationship which goes from those who, with their ministerial charism, proclaim or promulgate a doctrine or a decision to those who permit this doctrine or decision to take on life. There exists also an acceptance by osmosis, from one local Church to another local Church. The present ecumenical juncture gives to this question of "reception" a totally new importance. Yet it belongs to the fabric of the life of the Church of God as much as what we have just examined carefully.

Since the Church of God is a communion of local Churches, a *Church of Churches,* ecclesial unity is established, in fact, on two levels, radically inseparable, which compenetrate one another. There is certainly the welding into a single body ministers who "represent" each Church, preside at its Eucharist and watch over it, in communion with the faith and practice of all those who, since the time of the apostolic group, have been anointed with the Spirit for this service. We speak then of an episcopal college, especially since Vatican II. The Catholic Church has, besides, the certainty that the Bishop of the Church of Rome possesses in this college, by will of the Lord, a special function to safeguard his brother bishops— and through them Churches which they "represent"—in authentic visible *communion* that Jesus Christ wills (cf. John 17:21-23). But this first level, linked to the hierarchical structure of the Church, is inseparable from the *communion* of communities themselves in faith over which, according to the very sense of the term *episkopè* which defines their function, ministers watch and whose mission it is to promote.

[135]It would be exciting to make, for example, an inquiry on the "reception" of the decarlation *Dignitatis humanae* of Vatican II on religious freedom. Is it "received" in the same way—twenty years already after its promulgation—in the United States and in Ireland? Is it read in the same way by insisting on the same points in Western countries and behind the iron curtain? A dossier which we are putting together on this subject reveals a wide range of distinctions, showing that "reception" passes through a diversity of situations which it is sensitive to.

The faith of the bishop is, in reality, that of his Church. In old practice, besides, his Church presented him for ordination because it recognized in his faith the deposit transmitted to it and preserved by it. He is not to change this faith but to affirm it, nourish it, spread it and, especially under certain difficult circumstances, to permit him to triumph over its storms. But the fact that the Churches are, in their communion of faith and life, one single and unique Church of God, marks their reciprocal relationships. It is put into practice and expressed by their mutual "reception": they mutually "receive" each other as Church. The exchange of synodal letters assures and maintains this "reception,"[136] eminently attested to in the Eucharistic concelebration of ministers, when they happen to be gathered together. But this "reception" is not static. It implies a mutual gift. We have already pointed out the current diffusion, by a sort of spiritual capillary action of decisions of local synods of one Church to its neighbors, sometimes even to all of the Churches. Since in every local Church gathered together for a Eucharist it is the Church of God which is present,[137] the good of one of these Churches is a good of the Church of God in general, where every other local Church can also find its own good.[138] Besides, this good could only be authentically a good of the Church on the precise condition that all Churches can recognize in it what they also have from the Spirit. This possibility of "reception" of doctrine, of canons, liturgical forms, decisions of one Church by the others has always been perceived as a very basic consequence of *communion* in faith. It is even by communication of the sentence of a local Church that some excommunications have been able to become effective everywhere.[139]

---

[136]See Y. Congar, "La réception comme réalité ecclesiologique," 381 and notes 29, 30.

[137]*Lumen gentium,* 26, a fabric of partistic allusions, says it by speaking of the bishop, in very rich terms.

[138]*Lumen gentium,* 13, recalls it by presenting the catholicity of the People of God. The text states: "By virtue of this catholicity, each one of the parties brings to the others and to the entire Church the benefit of its own gifts, in such a way that all and each one of the parties grow by a universal and mutual exchange and by a common effort towards a fullness in unity. . . . That is why there still exists legitimately, in the heart of the communion of the Church, some Churches enjoying their own traditions—without prejudice from the primate of the Chair of Peter who presides at the universal gathering of charity, guaranteeing the legitimate differences and sees to it at the same time that, far from causing any harm to unity, these particularities on the contrary are advantageous to it. It is from this fact, finally, among the diverse parts of the Church, that there are bonds of intimate communion with regard to spiritual riches, apostolic workers and material resources. The members of the people of God are called indeed to share their goods and to each one of the Churches is applied in an equal way the words of the Apostle: 'Let each one put at the service of others the gift he has received, like good stewards responsible for all the different graces of God (1 Pet 4:10)'."

[139]For Marcion's case, see H. Marot "Conciles anténicéens et conciles œcuméniques," *Le Concile et les conciles,* Paris, 1960, 19–42 (23).

It is not a question of one Church copying what is lived or affirmed elsewhere or of wishing to impose on another local Church its own ways of doing things. "Reception" does not mean servility. Usually, of course, when a local synod or someone responsible in the Church (especially in his profession of faith) declares "having received" the decisions of a universal council, they accept the terms, the expressions of it. There is no playing around with certain words, the turbulent history of the *homoousios* is evidence of that.[140] But when a Church "receives" the life, practice, doctrine, discipline of another Church, it does so in a judgment which accepts diversity, pluralism of expressions and forms.[141] This "reception" depends on the conviction which establishes catholicity: the unity of faith and ecclesial life does not call for a uniformity, putting between parentheses or denying the richness proper to each race, temperament, culture, religious site, or history. Earlier we spoke about acculturation.

According to the image found in the *Catecheses* of Cyril of Jerusalem, the gift of the Spirit which, at baptism, creates the Church is like water:

> It is different in the palm tree, different in the vine, it makes itself everything to all. It has only one way of being, and it is not different from itself. Rain is not transformed when it falls here or there. But, by adapting itself to the make-up of the creatures who receive it, it produces in each one what is suitable to it. The Holy Spirit acts in this way.[142]

The Church "is not different from itself," "is not tranformed" when it is in Jerusalem, Antioch, Rome or Corinth. However, it prays there under forms which can be different in Jerusalem and in Corinth, it expresses in each place its faith with formulas or words which can be different in Antioch and in Rome, it rules its life in each place with a discipline which can be different in Rome and in Jerusalem. The same baptismal water of the same Spirit can cause the same Church to germinate in the immense variety of human areas, all tributaries of the vast deployment of Creation, itself a work of God. In this way it makes it catholic. When it seems desirable to enrich itself by making its own good from what another Church has in its life of faith, it often becomes necessary to retranslate it in the language of its own culture or the particularities of its own soul. "Reception" emerges then in a creativity thanks to which the power of the Passover embraces the work of Creation.

---

[140]On the question of words and their importance, see the letter by Athanasius on Nicaea, in PG 25, 415–476 (453).

[141]See J.-M R. Tillard, "Pluralisme théologique et mystère de l'Église."

[142]*Cat.* 16, 11–12, text in J. Bouvet, *Saint Cyrille de Jérusalem, catéchèses baptismales et mystagogiques,* Namur, 1962, 368. On the attribution of these texts to Cyril, see A. Piedagnel, introduction to the *Catéschèses mystagogiques, Sc* 126, Paris, 1966, 14–40 (the question of authenticity is asked about the subject of the five mystagogic catecheses, not the prebaptismal ones).

We find a good example of this creative "reception" in the way in which the *sequela Christi*—developed well before Anthony[143]—passed from the East to the West and there was incarnated into an infinite variety of foundations, according to temperaments, places, needs and times. And it is important to note that here the process unfolded, usually, without the hierarchy having been involved at the start. It approved, "received," what one or several persons had initiated, officially declared that there was a good for the Church there, integrated the witness and the involvement of these groups into the mission of the people of God, watched that nothing harmed the faith and practices found in the gospels. This is a marvelous example of the compenetration of the two levels, both required, which we spoke about earlier—the level of those responsible for "communion," and the level of living forces of the people of God without being able to say which one should, by nature, set things in motion.

In this way an authentic "reception" is accomplished. Reference to the apostolic community, assured by the episcopate, guarantees evangelical truth by the adaptation or, as we would say today, by the acculturation of what is "received" besides in order to be appropriated by a particular Church. But the creative dynamics must come from the very soul of this Church, moved by the force of the Spirit.

9. It is necessary to bring out at this time Catholic conviction concerning the particular ministry of the Bishop of Rome, which we are going to examine at length. It is too easy to affirm in a peremptory way that it is "alien to those things which have been presupposed in an ecclesiology of communion" or yet that it "contradicts the aspirations of local Churches for a recognition of their identity and of their proper vocation." History shows that down through the centuries an effective recognition of the particular function of the Church of Rome and its bishop has been able to create a harmony with a wholesome practice of the *communion* which we have just described. Chalcedon, with the role which the *Tome of Flavian* of Leo plays there and for all of that, the reception by Rome *in sola causa fidei*[144] gives evidence of it. Besides, the opening of Vatican II to the ecclesiology of communion was accompanied by a profound rereading of the central affirmations of *Pastor aeternus*.[145] The pontificate

---

[143]See J.-M. R. Tillard, *Devant Dieu et pour le monde, le projet des religieux,* coll. "Cogitatio fidei," 75, Paris, 1974, 153–223; Id., *Il y a charisme et charisme,* Bruxelles, 1977, especially 67–102.

[144]*Epist.* 114, 1, *PL* 54, 1029. And let us remember that at that time it was not normally the Bishop of Rome who convoked the council.

[145]On this subject see what Father Congar (*RSPT* 68, 1984, 449–456) says about the position which we have developed in *L'Évêque de Rome,* Paris, 1982. We do not quite understand how, in an article published November 14, 1984 in the *Osservatore Romano,* Mgr. Maccarone could think that we scorned this rereading. We present it as the essential point making of Vatican II the council which leads Vatican I to its completion. Undoubtedly, several of our expressions were clumsy. We thank our friend Mgr. Maccarone for having pointed them out to us.

of Paul VI appears more and more as an undeniable example of the unique role that the Bishop of Rome can fulfill in the Church when he courageously puts the weight of his office at the service of decisions of the council which he has lived through with his brother bishops and with whom he wishes to remain in solidarity.[146]

The Latin West, it is true, when it had to be given without the East present, in its general councils, doctrinal and disciplinary norms that its life required, did so in a tributary fashion by the polarization of authority on the Bishop of Rome, characteristic of the ecclesiology which for several centuries was rooted in it.[147] Its conciliar decrees were promulgated by the pope *sacro approbante concilio*,[148] which explains that Christians "separated" from Rome had had the sad impression that in these councils, without being denied,[149] the thought and the decision of the episcopal body became the material for the decision by sovereign authority. This is why the formula used by Paul VI for putting the seal of his authority on the conciliar documents appeared as an important sign in shaping Western ecclesiology at Vatican II.[150]

> The whole and each one of the points which have been enacted in this [Constitution] have pleased the Fathers of the Council. *And we,* by virtue of the apostolic power which We have from Christ, *in union with the venerable Fathers,* We approve them, resolve and decree in the Holy Spirit, and We order that what has thus been established in Council be promulgated for the glory of God.
>
> > Rome, at St. Peter's,
> > I, Paul, bishop of the catholic Church.
> > [the signatures of the Fathers follow][151].

[146]Would Vatican II have been "received" as it was in areas as crucial as the liturgy and ecumenism without Paul VI?

[147]The gap with the East, dug for a whole number of reasons, kept getting larger for all that. The response of the patriarchs of the East to the invitation from Pius IX, before Vatican I, is evidence of it (cf. Mansi 40, 377–418). Under Leo XIII the response of the patriarch Anthime VII to the letter *Praeclara gratulationis* of June 20, 1894 will be also very rude (text found in *Revue anglo-romaine* 1, 14 December 1895, 81–92).

[148]For Florence, see *Conciliorum œcumenicorum decreta,* ed. 1962, 499, 509; for Trent, *ibid.,* 775; for Vatican I, *ibid.,* 787.

[149]That is clear at Trent, for example, where the episcopate expresses itself and decides with a great freedom left to it by Rome. The influences come from elsewhere.

[150]See the important study by G. Alberigo, "Una cum patribus, la formula conclusiva delle decisioni del Vaticano II," *Ecclesia a Spiritu Sancto edocta, Mélanges Gérard Philips,* Gembloux, 1970, 291–319. See also, for one more complete, the text by Mgr. Vincenzo Carbone, dell'Archivo del Concilio Vaticano II, "L'azione direttiva di Paolo XI nei periodi II and III del Concilio Vaticano Secundo," part V, formula per l'approvazione dei documenti, in the *Acta* of the conference of the Instituto Paolo VI on *Paul VI et les problèmes ecclésiologiques du concile,* held at Brescia from 19 to 21 September 1986, forthcoming.

[151]*"Haec omnia et singula quae in hac (Constitutione) edicta sunt, placuerunt Sacrosancti Concilii*

The heading for each document should be added here:

> Paul, bishop, servant of the servants of God, in union with the Fathers of the Holy Council, so that the remembrance will be maintained forever.[152]

The formula of Paul VI is certainly a pontifical formula. But it inserts this pontifical authority in the collegial reality of the episcopate and its conciliar workings. This is where it receives its interest and its balance. It is a question of Roman authority exercised *in council* and not, as one would have thought concerning the approbation of Pius IX, *thanks to the council*. The experience—still present in the memory of several—of the council itself shows that in spite of tensions as those which were provoked by corrections asked for in the final text of the decree on ecumenism[153] or by *Nota praevia* of the constitution on the Church, the formula expresses the attitude which was that of Paul VI during all of Vatican II. Acting formally with an explicit understanding of his own mission, the Bishop of Rome has, however, lived Vatican II as a member of a council of bishops—*concilium episcoporum est,* declare the acts of Chalcedon[154]—knowing how to accept that certain of his suggestions will be rejected,[155] in full collegial solidarity.

"Reception" of conciliar decisions by the Bishop of Rome, required in his eyes and in those of his Church so that they will have authority,[156] appears in the formula that we are commenting on as the seal of their ecumenicity.[157] It is not *above* the "reception" by each one and the whole

---

Patribus. Et Nos, Apostolica a Christo Nobis tradita potestae, illa, una cum Venerabilibus Patribus, in Spiritu Sancto approbamus, decernimus ac statuimus, et quae ita synodaliter statuta sunt ad Dei gloriam promulgari iubemus.
    Romae, apud S. Petrum, die
        Ego Paulus catholicae Ecclesiae Episcopus.
        (Sequuntur Patrum subsignationes)."

[152] *"Paulus episcopus, servus servorum Dei, una cum Sacrosancti Concilii Patribus, ad perpetuam rei memoriam."*

[153] See the study by P. Duprey in the *Acta* of the conference of Brescia (cf. note 150); see also J.-M. R. Tillard, "Œcuménisme et Église catholique, les vingt ans du décret sur l'œcuménisme," *NRT* 107, 1985, 43–67, and *Irénikon* 37, 1964, 50–53.

[154] See P. R. Cren, " 'Concilium episcoporum est'; note sur l'histoire d'une citation des Actes du concile de Chalcédoine," *RSPT* 46, 1962, 45–62.

[155] In particular in the case of an amendment for the last lines of no. 22 of *Lumen gentium.* see G. Alberigo and F. Magistretti, *Constitutionis dogmaticae synopsis historica,* Bologne, 1975, X, 22, 192–195, 456.

[156] That is argued since the time of Damasus.

[157] See A. Grillmeier, "The Reception of Chalcedon in the Roman Catholic Church," *The Ecumenical Review* 22, 1970, 383–411, which shows it very well. The formula of Leo for Chalcedon is clear: *"ego mea consensione firmavi" (Epist.* 162, *PL* 54, 1145). See also the famous letter of Gelasius I, written in 495, to some bishops: ". . . *synodum male gesta [est] contra Scripturas,*

body of bishops (with the local Churches that they "re-present"). It is *in it,* as the core which makes it one single word, perhaps as the stitch for the differences which were able to manifest themselves during the course of discussions. In this way, it transmits to its universal expression what has been an authentic collegial course, oriented towards the good of all Churches. And it guarantees that what will be found in each one will be, in every truth, faith or practice of the universal Church, of the *Church of Churches.*

In fact, it has been asked if support for the verdict of the majority of votes is sufficient for a difficult ecclesial decision to be able to be effectively recognized everywhere.[158] This question is often asked by the orthodox. But "reception" by the Bishop of Rome in his role as mark and cement of collegiality, relying on the help of the Spirit—since it is a question then of "affirming [his] brothers" in their faith (Luke 22:21)—and being able to judge as far as the common good is concerned the diverse aspects of a complex question, is it not presented as an act in which the *prudentia*[159] of the college as such is embodied? On condition, of course, that the voice of the other bishops has not been stifled, that it has not been a simple instrument in view of the decision of another. By nature, every council *episcoporum est.* Catholic ecclesiology specifies that it is a question of bishops as *college,* with *in* it—and not *above* it—the specific function of the Bishop of the Church of Rome, guardian of the witness of Peter and Paul. "Reception" by the Bishop of Rome is a "yes" *in* the college. But the "yes" has the power and the function of sealing, by opening up explicitly and without any ambiguity for the good of the universal Church, the "yes" of this entire *college.* In this way he brings it to its full ecclesiality. It is not simply the "yes" of the spokesman for the other bishops. It implies qualitatively more than the sum of their "yes," although it supports the same reality and agreement with them. Exactly as the universal Church is something else than the sum of the local Churches since it is in each one and since each one is Church only because it is in this way in it. In fact, it is not sufficient for the Churches that a "yes" be stated for a legitimate doctrine or for an exact juridically precise detail.[160] In order for it to be fully ecclesial it must be stated for

contra doctrinam patrum, contra ecclesiasticas regulas, quam tota merito Ecclesia non recepit et praecipue sedes apostolica non probavit," ". . . *per bene gestam synodum, id est secundum Scripturas sanctas, secundum traditionem patrum, secundum ecclesiasticas regulas pro fide catholica et communione prolatam,* quam cuncta recepit Ecclesia, quam maxime sedes apostolica comprobavit" (*Ep.* 26, 6, *CSEL* 35, 380k, sqq.).

[158]See the remarks by Mgr. Emilianos Timiadis, *art. cit.* (note 107). The discussions on the *pars sanior* are known; see the *Régle de Saint Benoît,* chs. 64 and 65, and the *Decretum* 61, ch. 14.

[159]On the beautiful sense of the term, *recta ratio agibilium* (cf. *Summa theologica,* IIa-IIae, 47, 8).

[160]In the actual state of the division of the People of God, each group adheres to correct doctrines—Trinity, divinity of Christ, baptism—without that being sufficient for full communion.

a truth or a norm of *communion*. By stating explicitly—and it must be done so—his own "yes," but by stating it in the "yes" of the one whose grace and mission it is to gather together the Church of God in a visible *communion,* each bishop makes his approval a "yes" to the truth of the very act which is a creation of unity. According to the great intuition of the first Johannine letter, "to live the truth" and "to be in communion with one another," in the light, cannot be separated (cf. 1 John 1:6-7).

The process of "reception" by which the ecclesial Word becomes, by entering into the flesh of the Churches and by putting it into practice in them, a life-giving truth, a founder of the *communion* of faith, is in this way pre-formed in council in the proceeding of those who are responsible for these Churches. This makes it already this *symbiosis* of the diversity and unity which we call catholicity.

D. A Word which belongs to the memory of the Church

Every explicit rendering or definition of faith "received" by the Churches acquires from this "reception" a particular status. It enters into the traditional body of knowledge. It becomes a constitutive element of Tradition.

1. Speaking of Tradition, in this context, is not to speak of a collection of documents or of texts which have become reference works to be consulted, just as it is not (in another realm) to speak of rites to be copied, in the way in which lovers of folklore restore the feasts of yesteryear. Tradition is the memory, continually alive, of the people of God marching through history, the dynamism (*paradosis*) thanks to which in all generations, under all skies, the same life is lived, enriched certainly but unchanged in its essence. It is not something to be relegated to the archives but the profound unity and cohesion of a living Body, almost as old as the world itself—*jam ab Abel justo*—identical to itself throughout all evolutions, transcending in its very essence the interplay of causes and effects which establish and undo human groups. What Lévinas says about Judaism is analogically valid for Judeo-Christianity in its entirety: because inhabited and carried on by Tradition, it is "a non-coinciding with its time, in coinciding. . . . The simultaneousness of youth mindful of the present and impatient to change it and of old age having seen everything, going back to the origin of things."[161] So the inner essence is affirmed and maintained against the intoxication of a resignation before the immediate, always destructive of identity. Tradition pays inseparable attention to the present and "distance" in regard to this present, involvement in history and making a judgment about it, a permanent reprisal of an idea which

---

[161]E. Lévinas, *Difficile liberté, essais sur le judaïsme,* 3rd ed., Paris, 1976, 297.

is valuable for all times without being destroyed during any one of these times. Because it is a past which goes beyond the present, a center which is previous to it, remaining while everything changes, and yet gathering what the march forward brings that is authentic in the sense of the Word. Memory in the biblical sense of the term[162] is not simply storage of the sediment of the past. It is also the humus from which life never stops borrowing. As the memory of the Church, Tradition represents the permanance of a Word which is always alive, always enriched, and yet radically always the same, where the Church never ceases to nourish its faith.

2. But this memory, both transcending today and always open to the efforts of time, allows an integration of a number of traditions in one single Tradition. This is how one sees a pluralism of expressions born, translations deeply rooted in cultures, social contexts, historical heredities, all the while remaining in full *communion* with one another and with those who since the beginnings have preceded them, several having disappeared but not without leaving their mark on the Christian conscience. We find thus—but this time on the level of the Word—the essential question of catholicity.

Catholicity—*communion* of the infinite multitude of human forms in the unity of faith—is besides on this point coextensive with the Church that it seems already there where (in the Holy Spirit) the People of God expresses in its own words, signs or rites, the truth which God has revealed to it by his saving intervention. That the Word of God, since the beginning of Revelation, is expressed not in a single tradition but in *several* traditions (Yahwistic, Elohistic, sacerdotal, then Pauline, Johannine, hierosolymite, Antiochine, Roman, then Alexandrine, Latin. . .) is the evident manifestation that this Word is declared from the beginning "in a catholic manner," in other words, by espousing the human law of the diversity of lands and by expressing itself in this diversity. It is born "catholic." Adaptation to languages or to different contexts is not something which would happen after the fact. It is the question of a situation which is "connatural." Tradition of the Word (the *paradosis*) happens at the outset in *several* traditions. That is based on the fact that it is destined for all. The Bible is a fabric of traditions, just as, in a parallel way, the liturgy where it is put into practice will take shape spontaneously in a wide

---

[162]The root ZKR (from which comes *zikkaron*, which is translated by memorial) is one of the richest on the ecclesiological plane. See Brevard S. Childs, *Memory and Tradition in Israel*, coll. "Studies in Biblical Theology," 37, London, 1962; W. Schottroff, *Die Wurzel ZKR im Alten Testament*, Mayence, 1961; Id., *Gedenken im Alten Testament*, Neunkirchen, 1964; H. Gross, "Zur Wurzel ZKR," *Biblische Zeitschrift*, 1960, 227–237; P. H. A. de Boer, *Gedenken und Gedächtnis in der Welt des Alten Testaments*, Stuttgart, 1960. For a more sacramental vision, see M. Thurian, *L'Eucharistie*, Neuchâtel-Paris, 1959 (especially 21–49). This vision of memory is found in the entire work of the writer E. Wiesel.

fan of liturgies and like the reflection on its content will be done in a variety of schools. Since it is the passing into human language of the sense of divine initiative and intervention, the Word of God cannot be expressed only in *some* languages, *some* mentalities, *some* cultures, *some* traditions. It is in the *communion* of all of these, in fidelity to the one Spirit in the service of the unparalleled design of the Father, that the sole Word of God will be woven in some way.

Earlier, we mentioned the role of the community in the emergence of the Word. Even the most personal prophet, Jesus himself, we said, communicates his message only as a link with what his community already knows, already hopes for, has experienced.[163] His teaching is a symbiosis of tradition and inspiration, of collective remembrance and personal conviction. That is to say that the particularity of *its* tradition—implying language, customs, legislation, mentalities, and hopes, always colored by political situations—conditions *its* way not only of delivering but even of understanding what God reveals. *The traditions* enter therefore, into the very texture of what *the Tradition* preserves, transmits, makes explicit. If it transcends them, it could not be by denying them: it depends on them.

3. It is clear, however, that if there were not this common "remembrance" which is *Tradition,* enclosing by releasing from it a meaning common to all *traditions,* the diversity of these latter ones would quickly lead to confusion and even division. Babel would rise up, walls of reciprocal misunderstanding would be built up. *Tradition* perceived in its function of *remembrance*, integrating, in an unbreakable unity and yet forever welcoming, all authentic readings of the Word—with the guarantee of the Spirit who preserves the Church indefectible—makes up, therefore, the basis of the unity of faith. The ordained ministry of *episkope,* the servant of the *communion* of the Churches among themselves and charged with assuring internal *communion* for each community, is inscribed in his embrace. He operates, in fact, on the basis of the faith "received" from the community which he serves and that it must transmit intact, after having embodied and expressed it in its context and its own soul. The succession of ministries is done within *Tradition* and in reference to it.

Far from being a reducing agent, therefore, and of leading to a levelling off or to the imperialism of a single reading of the Word, Tradition is shown in this way essentially as a liberating element. It makes possible a wide range of languages without its causing any danger to the living unity of faith. Even more so, this liberation of languages, always on the basis of the essence which comes from beyond them and which integrates them

---

[163]That is true of Paul himself, so attentive yet to emphasize his link with the Risen One, which makes of him an Apostle although he is not one of the Twelve. See 1 Cor 15:3, 8.

without being destructive, opens up a *communion* of an extreme depth, something which Christians are little aware of. Contained in my faith life today is the drama of Israel, the fruit of costly discussions at Nicaea and Chalcedon, what Francis of Assisi brought to fruition concerning the secrets of evangelical poverty, what thousands of unknown believers have testified to as to the power of hope in their answers to their persecutors. And our successors, in their turn, will be enriched by what, for example, in their own context, African Christianities and Latin-American ones work out before our eyes. The *communion* of the saints is not enclosed in the realm of merits or of prayer. Where it finds its validity already is in the fundamental plan of faith. It owes it to Tradition. The Word of God to which I subscribe strikes me with the patina of all the generations which have given it its human shape, have put it to work in their lives, and have investigated closely its meaning. In brief, it does not bring me to a solitary face to face with God but in this density of human and fraternal communion of believers, *jam ab Abel justo* which *Tradition* guarantees, preserves, examines thoroughly and transmits.

4. It is not useless to resume this long exposé. The faith is "received" and "preserved." Its essence even demands it. It can be only gift and a welcoming. Since the adventure of Abraham, the entire life of the People is enclosed in an offer from God, dealing with a salvation which is put into operation by the Spirit. This offer is made thanks to what Judeo-Christian Tradition calls the Word of God, which "reveals" the existence of a salvation and discloses the contents of it.

There are stages in history concerning this Word. But the coming of Christ Jesus—which Johannine tradition designates as the Word made flesh—does not sweep away what preceded it.[164] On the contrary, it is inscribed in the great "prophecy" of the Scriptures by revealing in them—since they are fulfilled in it—an unsuspected sense, some hidden riches. In light of the new and highest norm which the person and work of the Lord Jesus represent, the Word in its entirety is taken up again, reread. That will lead first of all to the writing down *of the* apostolic witnesses in Jesus, culminating in the promises, then in the determination of the texts "received" as a normative expression *of the* apostolic Witness, and of other documents until that time considered not being privileged to be counted among the canonical Scriptures.

Besides, the life, thought, cohesion, defense of the Church demand an interpretation of this Witness and its being made explicit in confessions

---

[164]The reaction in regards to Marcion (towards 150) is here very revealing. Because Marcion refuses, among the Christian documents, those which seem too close to Judaism, Luke and several epistles of Paul escape his verdict. The reaction of Christian milieux in regards to this position implies certitude about the link between Christianity and Jewish tradition. See G. Bardy, "Marcion," *DBS* 5, 862–881.

of faith, doctrines, dogmatic definitions, all made in reference to it. The apostolic Witness is not transmitted by simple repetition. Its transmission always implies interpretation. This is where the need arises for a magisterium, the call for a guarantee of the Spirit.

With its *instinctus fidei* the community itself plays a role in the "reception," already from what will become the Scriptural canon—whose composition has never been decreed by a council but has been decided by the life, especially liturgical, of the Churches—then of the conciliar and synodol decisions. And it is especially by this life itself that the truth so "received" will bury itself in the memory of the people of God as a Wisdom in which the future will never cease to be reborn and from which it will never cease to borrow. Through Tradition, which the Spirit guarantees, the Word declared "once-and-for-all" lives and travels through history. The People of faith is the Church of God in all its fibers. But these are fibers of *communion*. There is nothing in the faith which is foreign or simply parallel to the working of solidarity and of mutual dependence which we have uncovered as the soul of *communion*. Not even the Word. *Communion* gives to the Word its vigor. Irenaeus felt it:

> The preaching of the Church presents in every respect an unshakable stability, remains identical to itself and benefits, as we have shown, from the witness of the prophets, apostles and all their disciples, a witness which embraces "the beginning, the middle and the end," in brief, the totality of the "economy" of God and his operation infallibly ordained for the salvation of man and establishing our faith. From then on, this faith, which we have received from the Church, we preserve it with care, for unceasingly, through the action of the Spirit of God, such a deposit of great price enclosed in an excellent vessel, rejuvenates and causes a rejuvenation of the very vessel which contains it (*Adv. Haer.* III, 24, 1).

III. The Church
"Sacrament" of the Faith

The Church of God arises from the Spirit of Pentecost taking "the good of Christ Jesus," the Risen One, in order to communicate him. Since God respects human freedom, this communication passes, as we have seen, through the welcoming of the faith. There, the people of God are not passive.

Welcome and reception are, however, only one facet of the essential function of the community in the area of faith which causes it to exist. Because it receives it in order to communicate it, so that it spreads throughout the world and lives down through history. But this communication is not accomplished simply by passing on the holy Book in which the contents of the faith of Israel and the apostolic witness are preserved. It demands as well something other than pure and simple preaching of the Word based on the Scriptures. It passes through the very life of the local Churches.

The Church is, in fact, in its web of communion, the locus of truth,[165] hence of faith. There is a profound link between the contents of this faith and the way in which each believing community puts into practice in its daily life in the world and celebrates in its liturgical gathering the gift received from God. Every local Church has the vocation to be the-announcement-of-the-facts, the revealing event, of the faith that it confesses. It realizes this vocation in the witness (the *martyria*) of its *communion,* the involvement of its members, and its Eucharistic celebration. Brought to life by the Word, it gives life to it in return: "The mouth of the Father has given life to a pure Word, a second Word appears born of the Saints, constantly bringing to life Saints, it is itself reproduced by the Saints."[166]

A. *The Church proclaims the faith by its communion*

In order to perceive well this essential point for an ecclesiology of communion, it is important to grasp the basis of the bond which joins the content of the confessed faith and the lived reality or that which is put into practice in *communion.* In other words, it is necessary to understand how what is found at the heart of the confession of faith is precisely what is translated into *communion.* Then only does one understand how the Church is "sacrament" of the faith.

The confession of faith belongs to the most profound being of the Church. That is why it constitutes an essential aspect of mission. This mission is theocentric or it is not properly evangelical. But it is impossible to confine the "confession of faith" in one or the other area of ecclesial life, even in one of the *ore confitetur.* Its forms are multiple, pervious to one another and complementary. Great care must be taken to avoid identifying, without making fine distinctions, "confession of faith" and a "formulation of common faith." The latter represents only a form of the former one and even is only its instrument. Neither could one reduce "confession of faith" to "profession of faith *ore*" (by the lips). In 2 Cor 9:13, in fact, the *homologia* itself declares more than an oral affirmation. And already in the New Testament the *martyria* includes an essential reference to faith: it states the seriousness of it in human life. This seriousness is that of *communion.*

---

[165]See Irenaeus, *Adv. Haer.* III, pref. (*SC* 211, Paris, 1974, 18–19); V, pref. (*SC* 153, Paris, 1969, 11–15).

[166]Hippolytus, *Comment. sur Daniel* I, 10, 8 (*SC* 14, Paris, 1947, 89).

When it confesses its faith, a Christian community explicitly affirms the certitudes which it recognizes as the ultimate foundation of its existence, the explanation of its behavior, the inspiration for its involvement in the world. Because, for a Christian community, to proclaim what it believes is to reveal its justification and the source of its obedience to God. From there arises the importance of every confession of faith. The specific characteristics of the group are revealed in it.

a. The first certitude integrated into the Christian confession of faith is that God offers a Salvation to which all are invited. But this Salvation is accomplished on two planes which are inseparable. If it concerns the personal destiny of those men and women who welcome it, nevertheless, it includes a divine will for the whole of humanity, indeed Creation. Because the reality into which believers are sure of being introduced by accepting the offer of God is none other than the Kingdom opened by Christ at his Passover and which projects them, integrates them into a fullness which does not reduce itself to their own accomplishment.

It would be easy to show how Christian Tradition in its entirety has made Good News of the Kingdom and Good News of Salvation synonomous. Since the latter is identified with the victory of God negating the forces of death which prey upon humanity, the Fathers understood that its final event was to coincide with the moment when Christ "hands over the kingdom to God the Father, after having done away with every sovereignty, authority and power" (1 Cor 15:24-28). Besides, wasn't the Good News reinforced by the signs of Jesus freeing those men and women "whom the devil held enslaved" (Acts 10:38; cf. Matt 12:28; Luke 10:18)? Individual salvation is inscribed in the heart by the comprehensive intervention of God against the Reign of evil, causing the advent of his Kingdom.

Because the Kingdom comes from this victory of God and because we do not have a full experience of its nature, its characteristics can be imagined by comparison with the situation of humanity still in the grips of perverse powers. This is also the way that the Gospel according to Matthew uses in its version of the Beatitudes (Matt 5:3-11).[167] And Revelation mentions the new world only by contrasting it with the works of the great prostitute or the empires of the Beast. But it is probably in the Letter to the Ephesians that the contrast is the clearest, in an explicit relationship with the nature of the Church of God (1:22; 3:10, 21). It is a

---

[167] "Jesus describes here not some human qualities proper to certain categories of people who would have thus certain natural dispositons for the Kingdom of Heaven, but some human *situations* which provoke, in those who live them, a waiting, a hope, and which create in these same individuals a manner of being, an attitude both interior and practical resulting from what they lack," H. Roux, *L'Evangile du Royaume,* 2nd ed., Geneva, 1956, 52.

question of the contrast, that we mentioned, between a world where walls of separation have been built up, barriers of division, pockets of hatred, and what has been made possible by the Blood of Christ (2:12-17).[168] A new possibility of existence is offered, characterized by the quality of peace which the destruction of hatred has established. It is actualized in a concrete reconciliation with God (2:1-5) and with one another (4:32), based on forgiveness.[169]

In such a context it is clear that the personal Salvation of those men and women who "were dead because of their sins" (Eph 2:5) and "by nature children of anger" (2:3) could not be conceived as cut off from the universal reconciliation accomplished by God. One is saved by being integrated into the plan of God (the "mystery") whose aim, we know, is none other than the gathering together of the entire universe "under one single head, Christ" (1:9-10). Salvation is not reduced to purely individual categories. And when it is defined in terms of reconciliation, it is impossible to think only of reconciliation of the individual with God and his immediate circle. This personal gift of grace is intrinsically tied to the total economy of the "recapitulation" (the *anakephalaiosis*) in which the bits of torn humanity are joined together again,[170] reconciliation with God and universal reconciliation representing the two aspects of an indivisible economy of grace.

We have recalled how the Fathers saw the manifestation of this truth in the account of Pentecost which they interpreted in relationship with the drama of Babel. They deduced from it that personal Salvation is inscribed in the collective Salvation of humanity: the individual and the multitude are inseparable.

b. The other truth which the confession of faith contains concerns the source of this Salvation. It is acquired by Christ and actualized by the Spirit. The first generations are even convinced not only that Salvation comes from Jesus Christ but that "there is no Salvation elsewhere except in him, because there is under heaven no other name offered to men who is to save us" (Acts 4:12). The old confession inserted in the Letter to Timothy certifies that "there is only one God, and there is only one mediator between God and mankind, himself a man, Christ Jesus, who sacrificed himself as a ransom for them all" (1 Tim 2:5-6). And Johan-

---

[168]See Markus Barth, *op. cit.*, 307: "Paul evokes the image of two old enemies entering together into the temple for worship more than he praises the warmth of the spirit of fraternity."

[169]"The material with which he [Jesus Christ] creates the new man consists of the Jews and Gentiles who are both dead in their sins and are hostile to each other and to God" (*ibid.*, 310). See also H. Schlier, "L'Église d'après l'épître aux Éphésiens," *Le Temps de l'Église*, 169–193; Id., "L'unité de l'Église dans la pensée de saint Paul," *ibid.*, 291–309.

[170]H. Schlier, *loc. cit.*

nine tradition puts this affirmation into the mouth of Jesus: "No one can come to the Father except through me" (John 14:6).[171] In the kerygma in Acts, this conviction is born of the certitude that God has exalted Jesus and has made him Lord, a title that he alone shares with God himself. But, as the liturgical hymn in the Epistle to the Philippians underlines, this title is totally dependent on what he has done (Phil 2:6-11).[172]

Christ is the only one who brings humanity a Salvation which coincides with the opening of the Kingdom. Certainly, other heroes have given their community joy, freedom, peace and prosperity. But they have not gotten for it full Salvation, the one which is rooted in the remission of sins and comes from reconciliation with God.

It is to maintain this exclusive role of Christ that theologians have spoken of the implicit belonging to his Salvation of all those men and women who, perhaps not knowing his Name, act in such a way that they are of his Kingdom. Because he is the Lord and, as such, is associated with the Lordship of God over every creature, his influence can be exercised outside of the community which confesses his Name. Christian communities are more and more convinced that Salvation can exist, for example, in the great non-Christian religions.[173] However, it is impossible for them to deny that even in this case it comes from Christ and is made possible by his Lordship. The Salvation of the world is in Christ and nowhere else. It is actualized by the Spirit of Christ and only by this Spirit.

c. In the New Testament, the Pauline and post-Pauline doctrine concerning the Body of Christ wishes to illustrate this fact.[174] To be saved is tantamount to being inserted in a Body which Christ saves and in which

---

[171]The Christian experience is not solely that of an "imitation" of Christ. It is also that of the recognition (all adoring) of the fact that everything which is lived on the plane of salvation "comes from Christ Jesus." From this comes the difficulty raised by the idea of "anonymous Christians." There are some "anonymous saved." Are there any "anonymous Christians"?

[172]Certainly the obedience of Christ does not force the hand of God and K. Barth is right to object to a strict interpretation of *dio kai* in the sense of merit. Yet what is given to humanity is linked to the course of Christ. It is the sense of *dio kai,* "in consequence of. . . ." It seems difficult to us to see in the second part of the hymn a free gift from God which would be absolutely without any link with what was expressed in the first part. In the great movement of divine gratuitousness is inscribed the movement of the communion of the Lord Jesus with the course of God. See R. P. Martin, *Carmen Christi, Philippians II, 5-11 in Recent Interpretation and in the Setting of Early Christian Worship,* Cambridge, 1967, 231-235; Id., *Philippians,* Grand Rapids, 1982, 100-101, 109-116 (goes back to the rabbinical idea that the just who suffers will be the one whom God avenges). See also L. Ligier, "L'hymne christologique de Phil 2:6-11, la liturgie eucharistique et la bénédiction synagogale 'nishmat Kol hay'," *Studiorum paulinorum congressus internationalis catholicus 1961,* Rome, 1963, 65-74.

[173]See an echo of that in the discussions of the synod of 1985.

[174]See C. F. D. Moule, in several very dense pages of *The Phenomenon of the New Testament,* London, 1967, 21-42.

they become members of one another (Eph 4:25; 5:23).[175] New life is received from the Spirit, which is none other than that of the Body (4:16). And the Letter to the Ephesians ends its meditation on the work of reconciliation by Christ with these verses, essential for a proper understanding of Salvation, which we have examined at length, where the aim is collective at the outset:

> He wished out of the Jew and the pagan to create one single New Man in himself, and by restoring peace through the cross, to unite them both in a single Body and reconcile them with God. . . . So you are no longer aliens or foreign visitors: you are citizens like all the saints, and part of God's household. You are part of a building that has the apostles and prophets for its foundations, and Christ Jesus himself for its main cornerstone. As every structure is aligned on him, all grow into one holy temple in the Lord; and you, too, in him, are being built into a house where God lives, in the Spirit (2:15, 22).[176]

For these first generations Salvation comes therefore from Christ but in his role as Head of a Body, a builder of unity, a cornerstone of a building.

This is also clear in the First Letter of Peter expressing Salvation in collective terms, which come from the old heritage of Israel:

> He is the living stone, rejected by men but chosen by God and precious to him; set yourselves close to him so that you, too, the holy priesthood that offers the spiritual sacrifices which Jesus Christ has made acceptable to God, may be living stones making a spiritual house. . . . You are a chosen race, a royal priesthood, a consecrated nation, a people set apart to sing the praises of God who called you out of the darkness into his wonderful light. Once you were not a people at all and now you are the People of God; once you were outside the mercy and now you have been given mercy (1 Pet 2:4-10).[177]

---

[175]See Markus Barth, *Ephesians 4–6,* coll. "The Anchor Bible," 34A, New York, 1974, 512–513: "It is as if the hand were a member of the eyes."

[176]See Markus Barth, *Ephesians 1–3,* 307–311: "The *new man* is created to be a social reality; the new existence is a social existence" (311). In addition: "The members of the Church are not equalized, brought to one level, all dressed in one uniform in such a way that they become a *genus tertium* which would be different both for the Jews and the Gentiles. On the contrary, the Church consists of Jews and Gentiles reconciled with each other by the Messiah who came and died for both. By his origin and constitution, the *new man* is a community of several persons. He is neither an individual nor a conglomerate of identical individuals. He is an organic body made up of distinct members not an amalgam, a social structure not a shapeless mass, a permanent and mutual meeting, an exchange, an amazement of free persons, not a tiresome collective uniformity" (310). See also F. F. Bruce, *The Epistles to the Colossians, to Philemon and to the Ephesians,* Grand Rapids, 1984, 291–307.

[177]See the bibliography given above.

Johannine tradition itself, in spite of its insistence on the personal relationship of the disciple with Christ, presents him as the Vine whose disciples are the branches (John 15:1-7), the Shepherd of the whole flock (10:3). The collective dimension of Salvation is too central to be ignored.[178]

In brief, the faith confessed by the Churches rests on a grace which could not be reduced to its effect in each individual who believes. All are said to be integrally dependent on a Salvation which implies the establishment of a new collective situation. This situation comes from Jesus Christ. His Cross, that the power of the Spirit transfigures and impregnates with the creative power of God, breaks down the walls which isolate individuals and groups. To be saved is to enter into the welding together of humanity, made possible by the initiative of God taking hold in Christ of all the broken pieces and reconciling them to one another.

2. It is around this acknowledgment (confession) of the Name of Jesus, Lord and Savior, that every Christian community is gathered together. Baptism is fulfilled in an explicit reference to the saving act of Christ Jesus; the Eucharist is celebrated "in memory" of him, "until he comes" (1 Cor 11:26); preaching never ceases returning to the profound meaning of his life and to the content of his message. Without this all-embracing relationship to Christ and his work, a local Church would cease to be formally Christian. Also, its internal life and its involvement in the world, so that the humanity-which-God-wills might become a reality, must manifest and affirm what it confesses as the Salvation accomplished through Jesus Christ and to which it declares itself linked, since it *already* enjoys its fruits. In other words, the nature of Salvation—therefore, the essential content of faith—must be able to be seen in its internal life and actions.

If, therefore, Christian communities possess characteristics which contrast profoundly with those which Johannine tradition calls the "world" and in harmony with what they proclaim as the content of Salvation, this situation will be an indication of what Salvation implies concretely and the sign that it is *already* at work. It will manifest it. Faith confessed in words will be seen then expressed in the ecclesial reality. This is where the sacramental aspect of the Church of God lies.

a. We find in this sacramental aspect *communion* (*koinonia*). It stands out in fact as the essential characteristic, making a contrast between the concrete state of humanity and the Salvation testifed to by those men and women, baptized in Christ, who have become "children of the Kingdom."[179]

---

[178]That is emphasized quite well by R. E. Brown, *The Chruches the Apostles Left Behind*, 84-85.

[179]Concerning *koinonia* as such, consult the bibliographical references given in the first chapter. Add for the point of view developed here, the short synthesis of Ralph P. Martin, *The Family and the Fellowship, New Testament Images of the Church*, Grand Rapids, 1979, 34-35.

—The most striking difference is perhaps the one which contrasts the "catholicity" of the Church and the state of the world where walls of hatred continue to be built up, to become perfected and armed. Already on the Pentecost of the pagans, represented by Cornelius, there is an astonishing discovery that "the gift of the Holy Spirit is now poured out on the pagan nations," that they receive the Spirit just as the Jews do, that Gentiles can be heard "speaking strange languages and proclaiming the greatness of God" (Acts 10:44-48). Also when Paul writes that "there are no more distinctions between Jew and Greek, slave and free, male and female, because all are one in Christ Jesus" (Gal 3:28; cf. Col 3:11), he is stating in plain language one of the essential elements of Salvation.[180] The Spirit of Christ unifies Christians in a unity so that their differences are absorbed into the power of a common belonging to the one who on the cross destroyed what transformed differences into divisions. So he saves them from "this perverse generation" (Acts 2:40), the one represented by our earth immersed in the confusion of Babel, as the Fathers will declare.

—It is not by chance that the first description of the Christian community follows immediately the account of Pentecost (Acts 2:42-47). The word *koinonia* (*communion*) is found in it. Many interpretations have been given concerning the meaning of this word in this context, connected with the other terms which go side by side with it.[181] We have seen that the most exact one seems to be the one which evokes life through sharing, *communion* in the mutual caring for the good of others. It states precisely, in fact, that Christians "were united, held all things in common (*hapanta koina*), sold their property and their goods in order to share the proceeds with all according to the needs of each one." And it is clear that it is again a question of this *koinonia* (*communion*) in the second description of the same community several pages farther on: "The whole group of believers was united, heart and soul; no one claimed for his own use anything that he had, as everything they owned was held in common (*panta koina*)" (4:32). We discover here the indication of an attitude of mutual caring, expressed in the concern for others, especially for those in need, and rooted in the common union with Christ Jesus. Here, *communion* or at least the

[180]See F. F. Bruce, *Commentary on Galatians,* Grand Rapids, 1982, 187-190.

[181]See on the question of "summaries," in the perspective of this chapter, L. Cerfaux, "La première communauté chrétienne à Jérusalem," *Recueil Lucien Cerfaux,* t. II, Gembloux, 1954, 129-154, and J. Dupont, "L'union entre les premiers chrétiens dans les Actes des Apôtres," *Nouvelles Études sur les Actes des Apôtres,* 296-318; Id., "La communauté des biens aux premiers jours de l'Église," *Études sur les Actes des Apôtres,* 503-519; A. Rasco, *Actus Apostolorum; introductio et exempla exegetica,* t. II, Rome, 1968, 271-330; G. Ghidelli, "I tratti reassuntivi degli Atti degli Apostoli," *Il Messagio della Salvezza,* t. V, Turin, 1968, 137-150; L. Cerfaux, *La Communauté apostolique,* Paris, 1953.

fact of sharing by putting all in common (*panta koina*), expresses, "demonstrates" the unity into which Salvation thrusts believers. The collective dimension of Salvation appears essential there. It is, with prayer and hearing the apostolic word, the characteristic element of the new life brought to the world by the Cross and Resurrection. The Letter to the Hebrews—also using the word *koinonia*—will state that charity and community-style mutual aid are "sacrifices which please God" (Heb 13:16).[182]

—Paul, speaking explicitly of *koinonia* (*communion*) in the context of the collection of money for the poor of Jerusalem (Rom 15:26; 2 Cor 8:4; 9:13), brings out two important points. He shows, first of all, that sharing is not limited to the internal life of each community and does not answer only a generosity and interdependence created by the needs of the immediate area. It spreads out to include a generous solidarity of local Churches *as such*. The universal solidarity of believers says much more than the certitude that all have become brothers and sisters, more than a common feeling of belonging to the same Christ Jesus. It includes the constant preoccupation with the needs of other Christians and their community. This concern is expressed in a costly sharing of goods (a *koinonia* according to Rom 15:26; 2 Cor 9:13) with men and women in need. It follows that all Churches are united in their generosity, each one *communicating* with all the others—being in *koinonia* (2 Cor 8:4)—"in this service of the poor." It is a question of a universal attitude. Even more so, the response of poor Churches to this *communion* will be their action of grace and their prayer. The Church of God is revealed in this way as a fabric of *communion*. There is the source of its joy, peace, even its life.[183]

The contrast is striking with what happens in our world where too often greed, thirst for power, desire for money cause individuals and groups to become wrapped up in their own interests. It suggests that this *communion* is a Salvation. Because if it is true that most dramas and conflicts which wound our world rise out of egoism and a lack of solidarity, and if it is accurate to say that humanity by itself cannot overcome this weakness, then *communion* where it exists, gives witness to the central affirmation of faith: a Salvation is offered, and it comes from God.

Let us add that the law of forgiveness, without which no *koinonia* of hearts could exist, plays an important role here. The difference in the behavior of our societies is too evident for us to make this more explicit.

---

[182]See especially J. Moffatt, *A Critical and Exegetical Commentary on the Epistle to the Hebrews,* coll. "The International Critical Commentary," Édimbourg, 1924, 237–239; and H. W. Montefiore, *Commentary on the Epistle to the Hebrews,* London, 1964, 247–248 (which insists on the link between material contribution and *communion* brought about by the Holy Spirit).

[183]On Paul, see A. George, "La communion fraternelle des croyants dans les épîtres de saint Paul," *Lumière et vie* 16, 1967, 3–20.

But forgiveness is one of the constitutive elements of compassion, necessarily implicated in *communion*.

But Paul, always in the context of collection of money, underlines another point also. He writes that *koinonia (communion)* between those who are in need and those who help them establishes a channel for *communion* with Christ himself, a *communion* with his own generosity: "Remember how generous the Lord Jesus was: he was rich but he became poor for your sake, to make you rich out of his poverty" (2 Cor 8:9). *Communion (koinonia)* in the service of the saints (8:4-5) is, therefore, rooted in the service of Christ.[184] But this service is the great truth found at the heart of the confession of faith. So the only way to understand the justification and the source of Christian *communion* is to have recourse to the central affirmation of faith. In another context, the Letter to the Ephesians will state something similar, in relation this time with forgiveness: "Forgive each other as *(kathos)* God forgave you in Christ; imitate God since you are children he loves, live in love as *(kathos)* Christ loved us and gave himself up to God for us" (Eph 4:32–5:2). Why is there Christian *communion*? Because that is where Jesus Christ is.

b. This *communion* with Christ has, however, a link still more basic and complete with faith. It is not enough to say that at the heart of faith is the conviction that Salvation comes from Christ, who acquired it. What must be added is that sharing, mutual concern, and putting things in common which characterize community and make a *communion* of it depend basically not only on the action of Christ Jesus but also on the reality that God gives to it. There is *communion* because all have a share in this unprecedented reality. For them, there lies the need to lead a life of brotherhood, with a concern for others, a responsibility for their lot, a dependence on others. Subjective *communion* or *koinonia* (in the network of fraternal relations) is the consequence of objective *communion* or *koinonia,* in other words, participation in the same and unprecedented reality of grace present in Christ Jesus.

—We have shown at length that the most vigorous affirmation of this function of Christ as creator of *koinonia* was in the few verses where Paul

---

[184]See J. Dupont, "Pour vous le Christ s'est fait pauvre," *Assemblées du Seigneur* 44, 1969, 32-37. For another perspective, see C. K. Barrett, *The Second Epistle to the Corinthians,* London, 1976, 222-224; see also Ph. Edgcumbe Hughes, *Paul's Second Epistle to the Corinthians,* Grand Rapids, 1962, 299-301, which emphasizes how the generosity of Christ transcends everything that Christians can do on their part, and how their generosity is an entry into his proceeding since "every sacrificial gift belongs to the very essence of divine grace" (299). For the whole question of collections, see L. W. Hurtado, "The Jerusalem Collection and the Book of Galatians," *Journal for the Study of the N.T.* 5, 1979, 46-62; Klaus Berger, "Almosen für Israel," *NTS* 23, 1976-1977, 180-204; D. R. Hall, "Saint Paul and Famine Relief; a Study in Galatians 2:10," *Expository Times* 82, 1970-1972, 309-311; K. F. Nickle, *The Collection: a Study in Paul's Strategy,* London, 1966; C. H. Buck, "The Collection for the Saints," *Harv. Theol. Rev.* 43, 1950, 1-29.

speaks of the bread and cup of the Supper of the Lord to the Church at Corinth, divided into rival groups (1 Cor 1:10, 13; 3:4; 11:17-22).[185] All are united in one single Body[186] because all partake of the same bread and the same cup, *communicating* in this way in the Body and Blood of Christ (1 Cor 10:16-22).[187] This is the source of all the links and all the steps towards fraternal solidarity which demands this unity. But this source pre-

[185]Concerning this quotation, see J. Moffatt, *The First Epistle to the Corinthians,* London, 1947, 8-13. J. Dupont, "Réflexions de saint Paul à l'adresse d'une Église divisée," in L. de Lorenzi, *Paolo e una chiesa divisa,* Rome, 1980, 215-231.

[186]X. Léon-Dufour, "Corps du Christ et Eucharistie selon saint Paul," *Le Corps et le Corps du Christ,* coll. "Lectio divina," 114, 1983, 225-255 (234-236) emphasizes that Paul does not yet state that they are "the Body of Christ which is the Church."

[187]Positions differ on these often examined verses. So see X. Léon-Dufour, *ibid.,* 235-236, who comments: "The risen Christ is the sovereign Savior, the one whose 'blood' poured out is universally efficacious, and who exercises by reason of his lordship his power over all men 'who are saved': his unifying action transforms not only individual existence but that of the community. From then on, what establishes this community is not so much the fact of being united around one table, it is the unique character of the Bread which is received there; it is, through this gift, Christ the Lord in person. Such is the function of the Eucharist which Paul emphasizes here. He does not seem to have directly in mind the theme of unity among the faithful in the sense of good understanding or mutual help, but the very existence of the new community in Christ (cf. in 8:6: '. . . Christ through whom we are'). In addition to the intimacy with the Lord produced in whoever eats the eucharistic bread, it is the entire community which is bonded together in this way: 'We are one single body'; the community exists in regard to other communities which could boast about belonging to such or such a God, not as a simple sociological or religious entity, but as a community whose principle of cohesion is directly Christ alone: it cannot return to belong to anything else, and whoever is a member of it participates both in Christ and his community." Compare this with the interpretations by C. K. Barrett, *The First Epistle to the Corinthians,* London, 1968, 230-238: "The interpretation of *koinonia* would be oversimplified if the word meant that all, by drinking the same cup of wine, drink together the Blood of Christ. As the parallelism between verses 16a and 17 shows, Paul is thinking about the sharing which all Christians enjoy, and which they enjoy together, and which is the sharing of all the benefits which are guaranteed to them by the Blood of Christ. . . . The cup which we bless is the way by which Christians participate together in the benefits of the passion of Christ; yet this participation is not impersonal since both Christ and Christians are persons." See also J. Héring, *La Première Épître de saint Paul aux Corinthiens,* Neuchâtel-Paris, 1959, 84-86; H. Schlier, "L'unité de l'Église *loc. cit.,*" 292-293, who writes: "The body of Christ on the cross is present by the power of the Holy Spirit in the bread at the supper of the Lord. The new dimension and the new life that it establishes are brought together and present in it. Those who receive him in the bread, brought together by him and in him, proclaim themselves his members and in them appears at that time the sacramental body of Christ crucified as his 'bodiness,' his body. In them is formed the open existence whose design was traced by Christ on the cross. It is by virtue of this design that the power of the sacramental body fortifies and brings together in life, in this vital space of the Church in which power is continually conferred. In them is built the body of Christ on which they live and which, by his presence in the sacramental body, builds incessantly the body of the pleroma of Christ, the Church"; J. Moffatt, *op. cit.,* 134-142: "Our communion is participation in the crucified body of Christ (cf. Rom 7:4), broken for us in sacrifice, but there is a mystical body, unbroken, in which we have communion with him and among ourselves. . . . By *participating,* Christians share *all* and enjoy *all* of his life, the life which creates and sustains brotherhood when it joins us together through his sacrifice." For the classic catholic exegesis, see especially L. Cerfaux, *La Théologie de l'Église suivant saint Paul,* 202-203; P. Benoit, *Exégèse et théologie,* 107-163; P. Grelot, "Le repas seigneurial," *La Pâque du Christ, mystère du Salut, Mélanges offerts au père F.-X. Durrwell,* coll. "Lectio divina," 112, Paris, 1982, 203-236.

cedes the network of mutual relationships and exchanges that, with the power of the Spirit, the community weaves together in order to be truly the Church which God wills. If Christians must live in *communion* it is, as Paul recalls at the beginning of the letter, because "God has called [them] to *communion (koinonia)* with his Son Jesus Christ, our Lord" (1 Cor 1:9). The Letter to the Philippians will speak of *communion (koinonia)* of the Spirit (Phil 2:1; cf. 2 Cor 13:13), the Letter to Philemon of a *communion (koinonia)* of faith. There it is still a question of the recollection of the gift of God, always primary, thanks to which all live in *communion* because they have been absorbed into the *communion* of Christ Jesus.

The author of the first Johannine letter will be more radical (basic). He writes: "What we have seen and heard we announce to you also, so that you also might be in *communion (koinonia)* with us, and our *communion (koinonia)* is with the Father and his Son Jesus Christ" (1 John 1:3; cf. 6:7). The origin, the cause, the ultimate basis of our *communion* is none other than the Father, in God. Even if he does not use the word *koinonia* but the expression "to be one," the Johannine Gospel is still more bold. According to it, the unity of the disciples is that which corresponds (*kathos*) to the unity which exists between Jesus and the Father, and which is founded on the reality of God. Even more so, it is inscribed in the community of love uniting the Son to the Father (John 17:20-23). It is rooted, therefore, in what exists in God "before the world was" (17:5).[188] Also it is, for all the world to see, the confirmation of what the confession of faith proclaims: that the Father loves the disciples of Christ Jesus as he loves the Son, that the Father has sent the Son so that these disciples may have a part in his eternal *communion* with the Son.

When, gathered together around the Table of the Lord, for the Memorial, communities proclaim his death "until he comes" (1 Cor 11:26) and share his Body and Blood, they manifest this origin of their *communion* in the *communion* of Christ, himself in *communion* with the Father.[189] There would be no way, in fact, to doubt that their liturgical gathering in the same place and for the same celebration makes their *communion* visible. But also it is for them an affirmation of its source. It reveals their

---

[188]See R. Schnackenburg, *The Gospel according to St John,* t. III, New York, 1983, 180–191 ("it is a unity which penetrates believers by coming from on high and pushing them also to become one in fraternal love"). See also Ralph P. Martin, *op. cit.,* 86–96; J. F. Randall, "The Theme of Unity in John 17:20-23," *ETL* 41, 1965, 373–374; on the context of the first Johannine letter, see P. Perkins, "Koinonia in 1 John 1:3-7, the Social Context of Division in the Johannine Letters," *CBQ* 45, 1983, 631–641. Concerning its sense, see especially C. H. Dodd, *The Johannine Epistles,* 3rd ed., London, 1953, XLIV-XLVIII, 6–16; R. Brown, *The Epistles of John,* New York, 1982, 170–171, 676–677.

[189]See J.-M. R. Tillard, "Eucharistie et Église," in J. Zizioulas, J.-M. R. Tillard, J. J. von Allmen, *L'Eucharistie,* Paris, 1970, 75–135.

faith in the place of the Father, of Christ and of the Spirit at its origin and in its perpetuation. It is besides what, without any difference, the words and the rites of the liturgies proclaim explicitly.

But at the same moment, by preaching and sharing the bread and cup as also by the experience of being together, this Eucharistic celebration communicates to believers the very *communion* that it signifies. It gives them what they are, said Augustine. But this gift goes beyond them because it can be said that, because it testifies to the importance of Christ in the life of normal and reasonable human beings, it communicates to the world at least one question: "Why is Christ so important for these people?"

—Such *communion* is the result of a long "economy" (*oikonomia*), gratuitous, of God, starting explicitly with the call of Abraham but already proceeding *jam ab Abel justo*.[190] And it is by grace alone that the pagans themselves are joined to the inheritance of Israel, becoming thus *sun-koinonoi* (Rom 11:17). However, even on this radical plane, *communion* with Christ is not pure passivity.[191] Chapter three of the Epistle to the Philippians puts some words on the lips of Paul which express the desire for a *communion* (*koinonia*) with the sufferings of Christ (Phil 3:10). Without using the word *koinonia,* the Letter to the Galatians ends with the mention "the marks on my body are those of Jesus" (Gal 6:17; cf. Col 1:24).

Christians receive from the Spirit the vocation to be together (cf. 2 Cor 1:7; Phil 1:5) in *communion* with Christ in his courageous and costly involvement for the coming of the Kingdom. What we call today the apostolic task of the community and its effort for the renewal of human society are not a Christian realm added over and above *communion*. They come, we have shown, from its most profound root: *communion* with Christ himself.

In this perspective, the activity of the Church must be seen as an epiphany of the intensity of Christ's involvement for the Salvation of the world. Here we are, again, at the heart of the confession of faith. What the ecclesial body accomplishes in *communion* (*koinonia,* cf. 2 Cor 1:7; Phil 1:5), suffering, persecutions, distress, agonies, jobs, announcing the gospel, responsibilities (cf. Gal 2:9), is the illustration and the deployment

---

[190]See the declaration by Flavius Josephus, *Contre Apion,* II, XXIII, 196: "We are born for *koinonia* and the one who prefers it to his won interest will be the most pleasing to God" (translation by L. Blum, coll. "Les belles lettres," Paris, 1930, p. 93). This finds in the Christian reality an unsuspecting going beyond by old Israel. See also the well known text of Philo, *De decalogo* 14, where the sense is not as rich.

[191]That is emphasized by F. F. Bruce, *Commentary on Galatians.* For Paul, "the personal appropriation of love manifested for the human race in the gift which Christ makes of himself is as real as his consciousness of his union of faith with Christ as source of his new life" (184).

of the depth of the love of God for humanity and the world, accomplished in Christ Jesus. Head of the Church, he is *hic et nunc,* in the Holy Spirit, manifested by his Body. *Communion* in the involvements and tribulations of communities, their participation in a common and unique enterprise which is none other than the Salvation of the world, demonstrate that one cannot belong to Christ without being inhabited and urged on by his obedience to the love of the Father for his Creation. Christian faith implies a *communion* with the intense concern of God for the world which has come from him. The unfathomable depth of this "divine torment" is measured both by the multiplicity of the apostolic tasks, the works of compassion, energies expended for the health of our earth, and by their *communion* with the indivisible and singular obedience of Christ to the design of the Father. All that shows, confesses in action, the God of faith.

c. If what we have just developed is correct, it can be concluded, with an anxious eye on the situation of divided Christianity, that as long as those who are responsible for communities refuse to shake "the right hand of *communion (koinonia)*" (Gal 2:9),[192] the faith itself will be harmed. In fact, it could not be announced in a persuasive way by communities confessing their *communion* with Christ while they refuse to take the necessary step towards a full and total fraternal *communion.* The seriousness of faith demands the search for unity.

It is equally necessary to recognize that our communities are far from realizing the ideal *communion* that we have described. Even within each confession there are divisions. And solidarity among members of the same Eucharistic gathering is often a word, not a reality, not even an ideal to which they are moving. *Koinonia* remains for each local Church a goal to be fully realized. We have described what the result could be!

However, in a more confident perspective, it can also be affirmed that wherever *communion* is taking shape, being developed locally—even if still somewhat imperfect, especially because it does not have its universal dimension—it manifests by its own standard the content of faith. And at the same time it inscribes in Salvation those men and women who live it. In fact, to strive to live locally, even very simply the "confessional" brotherhood of compassion, care for one another, sharing, generous involvement, prayer, liturgy, into which one is introduced by *communion* in Christ, is already in the place where one is, an escape from the isolation of Babel, until the day of the final victory of Christ over all the powers which are hostile to the Reign of God. Even though wounded, *communion* is not, however, nonexistent. The Spirit preserves it as a spark which could ignite the universe.

---

[192]On this "right hand of *koinonia,*" see F. F. Bruce, *op. cit.,* 121–125.

The discovery made here is that ecclesial *communion* is a "sacrament" of Salvation. It manifests and actualizes the object of faith. Paul, in the Second Letter to the Corinthians ends his appeal for the collection with a remark in this sense: "By offering them this service you show them what you are and they glorify God by your obedience in professing (*homologia*) the Gospel of Christ and for the generosity of your *communion* (*koinonia*) with them and with all" (2 Cor 9:13).

B. The Church and the "martyria" of its members

1. From Pentecost to the Parousia, unified in *communion,* the Church, therefore, is in a state of acknowledgment (confession). By its very being it always remains called to *martyria*. Earlier we were able to say that it exists *for* the glorious confession of the Name of God in the midst of the world, this confession being, besides, what, through the power of the Spirit, leads men and women to the faith whom the gospel has not yet reached. It is defined as inseparably doxological and missionary. It is so in the *communion* of vocations. The supreme act of this confession is *communion* with the Cross of the Lord by martyrdom. In the great liturgical Tradition the title of confessor of the faith designates the martyr.

The fact that the people of God, torn apart and divided, still has martyrs today, in all Churches and ecclesial communities, must be taken very seriously. Martyrdom transcends confessional barriers. In it all recognize their deep faith. Does it not seal, in the most realistic way, Christian *confession* of the God and Father of Jesus? The oneness of the Church, preserved by the grace of the Spirit in spite of breaks and schisms, has its initial sign in one baptism but its supreme act is in one martyrdom. Undergoing death for Christ breaks down all walls of division. We should point out that in some regions this *confession* by martyrdom causes the faith, right before our eyes, to become a power which challenges, whereas before there was a tendency to consider it an *opium*. Power of God in the sin of the world. . . .

The notion of witness (*martys*) and that of confessor of the truth are, as far as Tradition is concerned, linked very closely together. That is clear, despite the difficult question of knowing what distinction and what relationship the first generations establish between bearing witness to a fact and bearing witness to the truth implied in it.[193] Certainly the apostolic

---

[193]In addition, see especially E. Lohmeyer, "Die Idee des Martyriums im Judentum und Urchristentum," *Zeitschrift für systematische Theologie,* t. V, 1927, 237–249; de H. Lietzmann, "Martus," in Pauly-Wissowa, XIV/2, and de Strathmann, "Martyr," *TWNT,* 4, 477–520, the essays of A. A. Trites, *The New Testament Concept of Witness,* coll. "Monograph series—Society of New Testament Studies," 31, Cambridge, 1977; Id., " 'Martus' and Martyrdom in the Apocalypse; a Semantic Study," *NTS* 15, 1973, 72–80. Also, L. E. Heck, *Mandate to Witness— Studies in the Book of Acts,* Valley Forge, 1964, 60–61. Reference the older studies of R. P. Casey, "Martus," in F. J. Foakes Jackson and Kirsopp Lake, *Beginnings of Christianity* 5, London,

group is, for the rest of history, the "eye witness" of the public life of Jesus (Luke 1:2; John 15:27; Acts 10:39) and especially the only one which can testify to the Resurrection (Luke 24:48; Acts 1:22; 2:32; 3:15; 4:33; 5:32; 13:31). But it is certain that on Pentecost its witness is thoroughly penetrated by "confession" of the truth that it declares inseparable from these facts. In Paul's prayer, Steven is called witness especially because at his death he affirms the truth of Christ (Acts 22:20). His death puts the seal on this confession, which is not without a link with what in another context Revelation says about Jesus himself: if he is the first witness, the faithful and true witness (Rev 1:5; 3:14), it is because he has confessed to the point of shedding his Blood, the truth of the Father. Also Christians are those who "bear witness to Jesus" (Rev 12:17; cf. 1:10; 19:10).[194] This is their Salvation.

But Christians are also those men and women who know themselves to be called to enter into this testimony, to be in a state of *communion* with it. Realistically, *communion* in the testimony that Christ gave is costly. It is done especially before courts where the powerful of the world sit (Matt 10:18; Mark 13:9; Luke 21:13). It can lead to death, to *martyrdom*. But thanks to it the truth of Christ remains "proclaimed to all the peoples" (Matt 24:14). *Martyria* is, through the power of the Holy Spirit, an association with the dynamism of Salvation which must, since Jerusalem, reach all the limits of the earth and of history (Matt 10:28; 20:14). In this way Christians participate in the great struggle of the last days which is to end with the glorious coming of the Son of Man (Matt 10:23) and their entrance into his Kingdom (Matt 25:34; cf. Luke 22:28-30). Their *communion* in the glory of the Lord Jesus will come from what, afterward, they will have confessed of the truth of the living God in the face of the world, in spite of persecutions, sufferings, contempt and death. They will have *communicated* in his *parrhèsia*.

2. Such is the lot of all believers. They must know that they can be one day or another led to give the supreme witness of the gift of their life (cf.

1933, 30–36. E. Stauffer, *New Testament Theology*, London, 1955, 185–188; E. Gunther, "Zeuge und Martyrer," *Zeitschrift für die neutestamentliche Wissenschaft* 74, 1956, 145–161; C. Spicq, *Notes de lexicographie néotestamentaire*, coll. "Orbis biblicus et orientalis," 22/2, Fribourg, 1978, 533–538. On the history of martyrs, see especially W. H. C. Frend, *Martyrdom and Persecution in the Early Church*, Oxford, 1965; A. Kubis, *La Théologie du martyre au XXᵉ siècle*, Rome, 1968; Massimo Toschi, "Poverta e Martyria," in B. Calati, B. Secondin and T. P. Zecca, *Spiritualità, Fisionomia e compiti*, Rome, 1978–80, 177–186. For a complete view, see B. Gherardini, "Il martiria nella moderna prospettiva teologica," *Divinitas* 26, 1982, 19–35; M. Pellegrino, "L'imitation du Christ dans les Actes des Martyrs," *VS* 98, 1968, 38–54; W. Rordorf and A. Solignac, "Martyre," *DS*, t. X, 718–738. W. Rordorf, "Aux origines du culte des martyrs," *Irénikon* 45, 1972, 315–331.

[194]See A. A. Trites, " 'Martus' and Martyrdom in the Apocalypse; a Semantic Study," 74–75.

Heb 12:1-4). But in the Church of God, and very early,[195] Christians have felt a particular call, urging them to live in a state of radical witness where in a certain way the vital powers of their person are reserved to the affirmation of the "one necessity." This is such that it is worthwhile for a person to prefer it to everything else. Therefore, individual and in numerous cases collective existence is organized in terms of this choice. In this way are born hermits, cenobites, "virgins," monks, mendicant orders, then congregations or apostolic families, all grouped under the label, which is too vague, of "religious life."[196] These Christian men and women strive, by the example of the apostles, to "follow Christ" by adopting a style of life which is, within the Church itself, a living "memorial" of his witness (his *martyria*). For that they make a vow of their entire self.

This vow of oneself is accomplished within a certain state of the three great dynamisms which are at the root of the human person: the dynamism of sexuality, that of ownership, and that of self-affirmation. These men and women do not marry. They will not have descendants to carry on their bloodline, their name, or their remembrance in this world. They will die alone, mourned very little and soon forgotten! By all of this they testify through action that this temporal history is not the sum total of humanity, that it is not the absolute. And they challenge the involvement of their brothers and sisters, Christians, too, in the struggle against death in this world. Because the human species, as every living species, is tenacious. It wants to endure. This perpetuation goes through the complex interplay and mixture of *eros* and *thanatos*.[197] Without any of this preventing them from being men and women in the fullest sense and without destroying the richness of their emotion and their heart, some Christian men and women choose to put these things not at the service of procreation but at the service of the Kingdom of God in a gratuitous love especially of the weakest, the poorest and the unloved members of society. They *already* focus the attention of their life in this way on what the Gospel according to Matthew presents as the eschatological encounter with the Son of Man (Matt 25:31-46). Others strive through constant prayer and

---

[195]Certainly well before Anthony, usually considered as the point of departure of this style of evangelical life. See J.-M. R. Tillard, *Devant Dieu et pour le monde, le projet des religieux,* coll. "Cogitatio fidei," 75, Paris, 1975 (especially 94–196); Id., *Il y a charisme et charisme,* Brussels, 1977 (especially 67–102).

[196]We have evoked this history in lengthy sections in the introduction to the collective work *Religieux et moines de notre temps,* Paris, 1980, 9–34.

[197]On the link between *eros* and *thanatos,* see J. Ruffie, *Le Sexe et la mort,* Paris, 1986 (especially 17–22), and already the classic analysis of S. Freud, *Abrégé de psychanalyse,* translation by Anne Berman, Paris, 1955, 8–9; Id., "Le moi et le ça, les deux variétés d'instincts," *Essais de psychanalyse,* translation S. Jankélévitch, Paris, 1972, 210–219; G. Bataille, *L'Érotisme,* Paris, 1957, 62–70; J. Rostand, *Bestiaire d'amour,* Paris, 1958, 74–76; E. Morin, *L'Homme et la mort,* Paris, 1970; Rollo May, *Love and Will,* New York, 1969, 106–111.

contemplative praise, to live *already* the great Liturgy of adoration and glory announced in Revelation (Rev 19:1-10). This is the *already* of the Kingdom which these Christian men and women put forth.

Moreover, in a world where possession of material goods and rank in financial circles count above everything else, these men and women decide to renounce personal fortune, and the accumulation of material goods. They put a radical distance between themselves and the insidious worship of Mammon and his rivals in their lives (Matt 6:24; Luke 16:13). Repeating the words of Jesus to the rich young man (Matt 19:19-22; Luke 18:22), they signify then that "the treasure in heaven" *already* wins out in this world over everything else (cf. Luke 18:29-30), that it is enough to fill a life.[198] Besides—along the line of the "summaries" in the Acts of the Apostles which Tradition has never stopped mentioning—they strive to build a community of common life and sharing, each one renouncing personal gain. If consequently "none of their members is in want" (cf. Acts 4:34), they are also capable of coming to the aid, gratuitously, of the poor and unforunate in our societies. Communion with human misery, where we have disclosed at the beginning of our reflection a major line of the ecclesial being, is for several of these religious families their justification. They have been founded for the love, healing, education and promotion of the weak and ordinary. Many do not separate this goal from a realistic communion with the condition of the poor. In this way they remind other Christians of the evangelical command about involvement in the fight against misery, usually associated with the appetite for power, which Jesus himself attacked. But they are for the world also a sign of the true nature of the design of God that the Church has a mission to preach and serve.

These men and women take it upon themselves, besides, to live, through obedience, in a state of dependence. When we know the force in each person of the appetite for power, we can better appreciate the meaning of this choice. Because by it a person refuses to build his life uniquely according to his own dreams. In community, the will of the other, his call, his needs, the indication of a Word of God addressed to me in his look of distress or joy, words of reproach of one or another person, must, as much as my own desires point out what my options are. Besides, for the common good of fraternal communion or fidelity to the group in its mission, those who are responsible for this mission can, according to what the Rule prescribes, ask me to give up such and such a job or benefit to take on a particular responsibility, to change my environment. Here again the perspective is never purely individual.[199] Monastic or religious obe-

---

[198]See J.-M. R. Tillard, "Le propos de pauvreté et l'exigence évangélique," *NRT* 100, 1978, 207-232, 359-372.

[199]See our article "Obéissance," *Dictionnaire de spiritualité.*

dience specifies that in the design of God relationship with others must always be based on what it takes from Christ Jesus: it has authority over one's entire life. This is the law of kenosis.

Therefore, in a global plan of existence which, down through the centuries and with very different methods, has never stopped re-emerging,[200] men and women acknowledge in the most existential way possible, in the very heart of ecclesial life and in the midst of the world, the transcendence and the profound sense of the object of faith. Even more so, they do so by setting forth the *already* of the Promise, the anticipation of the content of hope. Certainly, the austerity of such an undertaking requires the recognition that there will necessarily be failures,[201] that the ideal which is aimed at will always be beyond communities and individuals. However, knowing that not all these ideals are realized, the conviction of the value of the project and its accord with the ecclesial vocation shines brightly. This can be compared somewhat to the event of a martyr's death—but under a very different form and which is not inscribed in the same urgent or absolute context—fullness is given in a very concrete way to the confession of faith. It is not made only with the mouth. It passes also through "flesh and blood," here by the three great dynamisms of sexuality, ownership and power.[202]

But we have pointed out that men and women religious did not cut themselves off from solidarity with humanity, especially with the needy and the suffering. In their desert surroundings, hermits weave baskets for the poor; Basil makes these communities places of welcome and help for those in misery.[203] They renounce the enjoyment of the basic goods of this life; they do not renounce procuring them for those who, without them, would wallow in misery. They try to enter into the *already* of eschatology;[204] yet they are still troubled by the full entry of Salvation into a world *not yet*

[200]It is remarkable that it is reborn at the present time in milieux which came out of the Protestant Reformation.

[201]It is sufficient to read, in order to be convinced of it, the *Rapport sur la Réforme de l'Église* read in front of Paul II March 9, 1537: "Another abuse to be corrected in religious orders. Many are so distorted that they are a great scandal for seculars and their example is particularly harmful. We estimate that it is necessary to abolish all conventual Orders seeing to it that no injustice is done to anyone, but forbidding them to receive novices. In this way, without injustice to anyone, they would be quickly destroyed and they could be replaced by good religious. We think that it would be very good to remove from their monasteries all the young who are not yet professed." (Latin text in *Concilium Tridentinum*, XII, 131–145; translation by G. Dumeige, in *Latran V et Trente*, coll. "Histoire des conciles œcuméniques," 10, Paris, 1975, 440.)

[202]Concerning the strength of witness which does not pass through the spoken word, see 1 Pet 3:1, not studied enough for this perspective. See the short remark of J. Calloud and F. Genuyt, *La Première Épître de Pierre*, coll. "Lectio divina," 109, Paris, 1932, 165.

[203]See J.-M. R. Tillard, "La pauvreté religieuse" *NRT*, 92, 1970, 806–848, 906–941.

[204]They will speak of life opening up Paradise, not without some exaggeration.

won over to the powers of the spirit of justice, peace, love and still controlled by the forces of evil. This testifies to the complex situation of the Church of God, coursing through human history. But it is also stated that this situation has its source in the God of faith: a God who *already* is given to those men and women who welcome him but letting them *communicate* in his universal design of kindness for this world which he has created. Monastic or religious life seems as a declaration (word) of faith.

In this declaration to the world, expressed in the heart of an effort towards what Tradition calls sanctity, is hidden a call fully evangelical that must be emphasized. Men and women religious indicate discretely to the world that relationship with a transcendent power is as necessary to it as the relationship to its intrinsic powers. Burying oneself in a myopic way in the quest for progress without placing it on a level which goes beyond it is tantamount to playing with apprentice sorcerers. We experience this in the face of the anguish of millions of our contemporaries. What is necessary is an attention here and there to the immediate course of things, a renouncing of the attraction of "always-more," a supremacy of the need for success.

But religious life is a word (utterance) in the world by being a word in the Church. By its emphasis on demand, it is indeed a word which wakes up the Church, bringing it back to the radical choice between God and Mammon, recentering it on its true values. Perhaps even, in certain cases, it is an instrument of the Spirit to prevent the Church from being too talkative. The words of the Church, the great themes that it develops and declares to the world are fruits of the Gospel. But these fruits spoil quickly if they are cut off from the tree whose sap they live on. It is not by chance that the great ecclesial awakenings have usually been inspired by religious. And the role which these have played close to us in certain situations in Latin America have certainly permitted ecclesial words on the solidarity and the preferential option for the poor[205] to be made concrete.

It is clear that this word is understandable only to the extent that it is declared in the Church, becomes an integral part of the *communion* of all testimonies and confessions, neither above the others nor parallel to them.[206] It is regrettable that in the West for several centuries the testimony of religious and monastic families has been isolated, perhaps because of a certain mistrust by some bishops in their regard: what affects the universe of charisms often upsets those responsible for peace and the institution. On their side, it is true, these families are perceived as autocratic groups, scarcely having any need for the parochial or diocesan community for their own fidelity. They felt themselves necessary for others but

---

[205]An expression taken up again in the final text of the extraordinary Synod of 1985.

[206]This is one of the central points of our book *Devant Dieu et pour le monde.*

not seeing well enough how others were necessary for them. The present crisis in recruitment has had the advantage of making the local Church more interdependent and of breaking down too many walls which made their evangelical life unintelligible, the word of their testimony unheard. For everything misfortune has its benefits.

C. *The Church confesses the faith in the Eucharistic celebration*

At the center of the state of confession thus magnetized by martyrdom is the *Memorial* of the Martyrdom of Jesus, the Eucharistic celebration, a liturgical celebration of the Death and Resurrection of the Lord. The Eucharist which is *the* sacrament of *communion* constitutes the liturgical act par excellence of the *confession of faith*. Here again everything comes together.

1. The Eucharist, in fact, makes the *confession of litugical faith* of prime importance, by the fact that it is the *Memorial* of the paschal mystery of Christ Jesus. In our view, this point is essential.

To the Corinthians Paul writes: "Every time you eat this bread and drink this cup, you are proclaiming *(pataggellete)* the death of the Lord until he comes" (1 Cor 11:26). The term used is *pataggellein*. But the word contains several of the overtones found in *martyrein* and *exomologein* (cf. Phil 2:11).[207] The words fit very well together. It is there that baptismal *confession* results in a common confession, in sacramental union in Christ. That is why normal Christian initiation seals the rites opened up by baptism in the Eucharistic celebration of the Memorial. But the Memorial has its central support essentially in the announcement, the confession of the Death of the Lord. It is that just as much as presence of the Body and Blood of the Passover. The present agreements about the Eucharist represent already besides this fact an opening towards a "common confession of faith" in one of the fundamental realms of the ecclesial confession of the living God.

More widely, the entire anaphora (Canon), concludes with the *Amen* which is an affirmation of faith, equivalent in fact to a development or an orchestration in words of the confession of the anamnesis (recalling). The great liturgies give it as content all the deeds of God, from Creation to the eternal glory of the chosen, by making them like an unfolding *Credo*. The Liturgy of the Word, with its proclamation of Scripture and often its recitation of the Nicene Creed, is connected besides to this central Eucharistic "confession" of the anaphora (Canon).

---

[207]See C. K. Barrett, *The First Epistle to the Corinthians,* 270, 271: "It seems certain . . . that it must signify to proclaim, to announce with words from the mouth. That means that when Christians had a meal in common, they recalled aloud the event on which their existence is established." Cf. also Günter Bornkamm, *Paul,* London, 1971, 193; H. Schürmann, *Comment Jésus a-t-il vécu sa mort?,* 115; J. Jeremias, *The Eucharistic Words of Jesus,* London, 1966, 106–107, 253.

The Eucharistic proclamation of the faith is accomplished, besides, *before God*. It is doxological, turned towards the glory of the Father. By this aspect again, it represents the conclusion of the ecclesial confession of faith. Because, let us repeat it, this confession of faith is not at first a pragmatic goal. It is always a gratuitous reminder of the marvels which God has done, in order "that the Father may be glorified."

2. But as a gathering of believers in a given place, the Eucharistic celebration becomes also, *before the world and for the world,* a confession in action of the Salvation brought about by the Father, in Jesus Christ, through the power of the Spirit. The dimension "confessing before the world" of the Eucharistic assembly attracted attention already in Justin's time.[208]

Such a "confession" has three profound implications. Indeed, the simple fact that Christian communities rooted in different cultures, representing different social contexts, linked to different expressions of faith, adopting different liturgies, mutually *recognize* their Eucharists constitutes a confession of the universality of Salvation. By their Eucharists in *communion,* Christians not only declare *before the world* that they believe in the gospel but also certify that in his Son, Jesus Christ, God has broken down the barriers which divide humanity. To gather together (every race, rank, culture and sex) for the *Memorial,* is to confess, by this step itself, the importance and the sense of what is commemorated. And *to recognize* in the Eucharist of another gathering made in another context the same reality as the one that is being practiced there where one is present is tantamount to confessing the universality of the Salvation coming from God. The vow in chapter seventeen of the Johannine Gospel is thus fulfilled, with its insistence on the wish "that all may be one so that the world may believe that it was you who sent me."

Besides, the Eucharistic epicleses seem to find their inspiration in this chapter seventeen. The Eucharistic celebration realizes the profound wish of Jesus, a wish where the quest for the glory of the Father and the truth about the Salvation of the world are in a state of osmosis. And the words of the entire anaphora (Canon), by stating in detail the acts of God, making explicit the sense of the sentences which the author puts on the lips of Jesus: "I have made your name known to the men you took from the world to give me" (17:6), "the words that you gave me I gave to them and they have truly accepted that I came from you and have believed that it was you who sent me" (17:8), "consecrate them in the truth, your word is truth" (17:7), "may they be so completely one that the world will real-

---

[208]See in *Apol.* I, 65–67 the way in which from the celebration of the Eucharist he justifies the faith of Christians.

ize that it was you who sent me and that I have loved them as much as you loved me" (17:23), "these have known that you have sent me" (17:25).

3. Besides, gathered around and nourished at the Table of the Lord, the Christian community finds in the celebration the strength necessary to be truly, a *witness* of the Lord Jesus Christ in the world, both as a community and in each one of its members. The well-known formulas of Augustine express it very well: "you are what you have received," "your own mystery is present on the altar," "you say *Amen* to what you are."[209]

But the Christ of the Death and Resurrection, whose Memorial is being enacted, is precisely the Son in the supreme act of *martyria*. It is in this act, indeed, that he gives all his strength to what Johannine tradition expresses in an extremely profound way: "It is not we who have loved God but it is he who has loved us and has sent his Son to be the sacrifice that takes our sins away" (1 John 4:10), "he loved us first" (4:19). And "there is no greater love than to give his life for those whom he loves" (John 15:13). The Death of Jesus is the great confession of the Father who dominates history. But it is remarkable that chapter four of the first Johannine letter, joining the faithful to the *Agape* of God in Jesus, uses vocabulary from the "confession of faith" (4:2, 3, 14, 15 . . .).

The "confession" of the Father by Jesus has, however, passed through the precise service of the Good News, which has led him to the *martyre* of the Cross. According to Luke, as early as the scene of the preaching in the synagogue (Luke 4:16-30), he identified himself with the love of the Father for the poor, sinners, those injured by fate. He has served the divine will of conversion of all hearts in fraternal love and justice. For its part, the Eucharistic community knows that it is urged by the power of the sacramental Body and Blood, to this *martyria* of the God who, since he revealed himself to a People, has shown himself decidedly "on the side of the poor." But who is not poor in some area in his life?

4. It is in the function of this common confession of Eucharistic faith and its carry over into the life of the believer by a *martyria* going if necessary all the way to the gift of one's life that the need for a formulation of the common faith that is celebrated and lived arises. The baptismal Credo is the synthesis of what will be made explicit day after day in the testimony of all the baptized, united in the *communion* of one single faith.

It is important, however, to agree on what is at stake. It would indeed be a grave error to seek to enclose the Christian faith in certain formulas and a style of language that is stiff. The reality of the faith transcends any formula, however appropriate it might be. It judges it. A formula can only be an instrument at the service of a *res* which it never succeeds

---

[209]See in particular *Sermo* 227.

in encompassing perfectly. One could not make it absolute, seeing in it *the* "confession of faith." The great Tradition knows several Credo, having authorized all of them.

The perspective in which it should be placed can only be the one which serves catholicity, in a Church which is *Church of Churches*. A sufficient formulation of faith is needed so that within the necessary variety of verbal expressions, cultural contexts, religious rootings in the traditions of peoples, liturgical forms, embodiments in human problems, the Churches know that they refer to the same gospel and that they know why it is so. The situation which finds us divided for centuries has created so many ambiguities and suspicions that we understand better the necessity of being able to recognize one another in the same and identical faith.

The formulation of the common faith appears therefore as the sign and the guarantee of catholicity, as it demands both unity and diversity, knotted together in a way that is radically indissoluble. Whoever confesses the Credo states his Christian identity and every local Church putting it in its Liturgy declares itself in *communion* with the great Tradition. Whatever their differences may be, all Churches which proclaim it show themselves in *communion* on what is essential. Then one is sure that the *Amen* of all the Eucharists is said in the same faith, that the *martyria* of all the witnesses of the Gospel is lived because of the same attachment to the same Lord and to his Father.

It is this *communion* which, expressed in the fullest way at the Eucharistic celebration in the great *Amen* which seals the anaphora (Canon), even carries over into personal prayer. Cyprian expresses the very soul of Christian prayer when he writes, commenting on the Lord's *Prayer*:

> Above all the Doctor of peace and the Master of unity did not wish prayer to be individual and private, so that while praying each one prays only for oneself. We do not say: My Father who is in heaven; nor: Give me today my bread; each one does not ask that his debts alone be forgiven, and it is not for him alone that he begs not to be led into temptation and to be delivered from the Evil one. For us, prayer is public and has a community element; and when we pray, we intercede not for one person alone but for all the people; for we, a whole and entire people, are one.
>
> The God of peace and the Master of harmony, who taught unity, wished that one alone pray for all, as he has borne all men himself alone. . . .
>
> We declare that the Apostles and disciples, after the Ascension of the Lord, pray in the same way. It is said: "All of one heart persevered in prayer, with the women, with Mary, who had been the mother of Jesus, and with his brothers." With one and the same heart they persevered in prayer; by their fervor and mutual love they gave witness that God, who causes conciliatory men to live in one and the same house, admits

into his eternal dwelling only those whose prayer expresses the union of souls.[210]

By investigating the nature of the people of God we have discovered to what depth the Church is created through *communion*. That goes all the way into its faith. Thought about in what is sometimes called its horizontal dimension, its life is nothing else but the fruit of a constant interplay of gift and welcome, of proposition and "reception." There is nothing in it which is not *communion*. More than this, with its dynamism, this *communion* spans the centuries—*jam ab Abel justo*—gradually integrating all generations of believers but also the multitudes of men and women of upright heart who are inhabited by the Spirit of the Lord. For goodness and generosity which germinate in this world—in the usual sense of this word, which is not the one found in the Johannine Gospel—are not enclosed only in the lodging of the community of the baptized. Yet this community possesses, by its "reception" of the gospel and the gift of Christ Jesus, the reality on which can be built the only *communion* which answers the deep wish of humanity. And it gives witness to it by being its *sacramentum*.

[210]*Dom. Or.* 8. Translation by M. Reveillaud, *Saint Cyprien: l'oraison dominicale, texte, traduction, introduction et notes,* Paris, 1964, 87–89. As a note, the translator reverts to texts of Luther and Calvin decidedly inspired by Cyprian (*ibid.*, 169–170).

3

The Service of Communion

We have recognized in *communion* the profound being of the Church of God. Church of Churches, it is a *communion* of *communions,* linked to God who is revealed as the eternal *communion* of three Persons. And the Church is led to *communicate* as a servant for the expansion of Salvation. An always fragile *communion,* as we have said, and, putting the divine being aside, continually put to the test. In its members, the Church remains locked in battle with the powers of evil. Each one confesses it at the moment in which he receives the bread and cup of the Lord: "I am not worthy . . ., say a word and I shall be healed." With communion God gives, in his goodness, what is necessary for its preservation and its growth.

I. The Ministries
for the Communion of the Churches

A. The ministries and the sacerdotal community

1. At the heart of the power and fragility of *communion* are inscribed the ordained ministries, the only ones we will speak about in the beginning, to avoid any ambiguity. Because it is both a gift of the invisible God and the visible actualization of this gift in human beings, a reality proper to each local Church (in the imbroglio of the attitudes of its members towards each other) and a common reality in all the Churches (in the interplay of their mutual relationships), *communion* necessitates that on the part of God one puts it in contact with the sources of grace, then that one maintains it there and guides it there. This "preservation," this "support," this "direction," this "attention," this "surveillance," in the name of Christ and his Father, is what is called ministry, *episkopè*. Since in each

of the local Churches there is *catholica*,[1] it is understandable that this ministry, in its different forms, will have as its goal both the communion which is each community and the *communion of communions* spread thoughout the earth and which must "be recognized" in each other. Besides, since in the Church of God everything is *communion,* this ministry itself will have a structure which is based on communion. There will be a ministry of *communion* and a *communion* of ministries. In this sense, we will speak, in the singular, *of the* ministry in the Church.

2. In reference to the Lord and his Father *communion* is primary. It is the goal that is pursued. We have shown that, far from implying a contempt of persons and their destiny, this emphasis on communion defines, on the contrary, the divine proposal for their Salvation. Because if God establishes Christ Jesus as Head of a Body, cornerstone of a building (Eph 2:20), the New Adam of a race (1 Cor 15:45), it is inseparably in terms of everything and individuals.[2]

The First Letter of Peter conveys, we said, a main and precise detail in this sense. The community which the ministry has an obligation to preserve (cf. 5:1-4) is "the chosen race, the royal priesthood, the holy nation, a people set apart to sing the praises" of God (1 Pet 2:9-10). These expressions designate the people of God (2:10) in its community essence *as such,* its *collective* vocation, its *entire* mission. It is constructed *in toto* as a sacerdotal body. This is, indeed, what establishes the community of the eschatological God by the totality of its life in the Spirit, led faithfully to God and, thus, in a perpetual situation of sacrificial offering, in the biblical sense of this term.[3] The priesthood is, let us repeat, the primary important attribute of the community *as such.*[4]

The sanctification of its members and the spiritual quality of the community are therefore in symbiosis (harmony). The "spiritual sacrifices"

---

[1] It seems that the adjective *katholikè* is for the first time applied to the Church by Ignatius (*Smyrn* 8:2) so attached to the unity of the local church. The *Martyre de saint Polycarpe* (8:1) will state precisely that it is the Church throughout the whole inhabited world (*oikoumenè*). But it does not think about what would be the sum of the local churches.

[2] Chapters 2 and 4 of the letter to the Ephesians are a typical witness of this link between "saved" persons and the Body of Christ *as such* (2:16; 4:4, 12, 16), the family of God *as such* (2:19), the construction of God *as such* (2:20-22).

[3] See R. de Vaux, *Les Institutions de l'Ancien Testament,* t. II, Paris, 1960, 209-211.

[4] Prosper D'Aquitaine will say: *"Totus populus christianus sacerdotalis est"* (*Psalm. Expos. 131, PL* 51, 381). For an entire vision of Scripture, see J. Delorme, "Sacrifice, sacerdoce, consécration," *RSR* 63, 1975, 343-366. On the theological interpretaion of the letter of Peter, see in the bibliography already given, especially J. Coppens, "Le sacerdoce royal des fidèles; un commentaire de la I P 11: 4-10," and the book by J. H. Elliott, *The Elect and the Holy. An Exegetical Examination of 1 Peter 2:4-10, and the Phrase basileion hierateuma;* see also P. Grelot, "Le sacerdoce commun des fidèles dans le Nouveau Testament." We ourselves have studied this point in J.-M. R. Tillard, "La qualité sacerdotale du ministère chrétien" (see F. Refoulé, "Prêtres anciens, prêtre nouveau," *RB* 91, 1984, 587-591).

which weave together the life of each baptized person and which are spoken of in Peter's letter, the offering of each person "as a holy and living sacrifice pleasing to God" (Rom 12:1-2) which Paul mentions,[5] the sacrifices of good works and sharing mentioned in the Letter to the Hebrews (13:16) find their consistent and authentic Christian value only in the heart of *communion*. They are acts of a believer who is *one* living stone in the spiritual home (2:5) which God builds up on the cornerstone of Christ Jesus (2:7). The temple thus constructed, there is the place for the liturgical service of God,[6] the community; there is the *sacerdos*.

Ministry exists in light of this priesthood of the *sacerdos* community. It is the servant of the Spirit of Christ for priestly and theocentric *communion* which is the local Church in its profound being and life. Also it could not be understood outside of the constant reference to this total community sense formed by the Spirit. It is not sufficient then to hold that "no one is minister for himself." What must be added is that the ministry manifests its nature only in the act of the *whole* community where it is at work. To consider it simply in its own activity, isolated from the symphony of activities created by the Spirit, is to subject oneself to a gross misunderstanding.

3. Besides, if very early the ministry seems turned essentially towards the Eucharistic celebration, it is because it is the central act of the community *as such*. Gathered together for the sharing of the Body and Blood of the Lord, the community is then a *communion* where not only the grace but the function of each one find their sense and completion in the totality where they are inserted dynamically. Ignatius of Antioch reflected on the local Church in this gathering where all act *together,* celebrate *one single* Eucharist,[7] but each one according to his rank, without confusion of roles. The congregation, wherever it is determined to give each member the place belonging to him, is not only the *sacramentum* of the communion of believers in the one Body of the Lord. It is also that of the communion of charisms, circumstances, functions, services, ministries in the one and indivisible Church of God, therefore, in the one and indivisible "priestly

---

[5]Concerning Pauline thinking in this area, see A. M. Denis, "La fonction apostolique et la liturgie nouvelle en esprit. Étude thématique des métaphores pauliniennes du culte nouveau," *RSPT* 42, 1958, 401–436, 617–656; C. K. Barrett, *The Epistle to the Romans,* London, 1971, 230–236; see the intervention of Chr. Evans, and the discussion which follows it in L. De Lorenzi, ed., *Dimensions de la vie chrétienne,* coll. "Serie monograph, de benedictino," sect. Bibl. œcum., 4, Rome, 1979; M. Löhrer, "Seipsos hostiam viventem, sanctam, Deo placentem exhibeant (Rom 12:1): note alla quaestione del rapporto fra culto e vita cristiana nel contesto del Sacerdozio comune," *Lateranum* 47, 1981, 106–110.

[6]In his interpretation of *Basileion hierateuma,* J. H. Elliott shows that *Basileion* refers here to the royal dwelling, to the temple radiating glory.

[7]See *Eph.* 4:1-2; 5:2-3; *Symrn.* 8:1-2; *Magn.* 7:1-2; *Philad.* 4:1.

body" whose daily existence nourished by the Eucharist is the "spiritual sacrifice" which glorifies God.[8]

4. In this symphony—to revert back to the image of Ignatius—ministry is revealed as an integral, essential part of the terrestrial wandering Church. It is in its place, in no way above and outside of the whole, or even as the function which would claim for itself alone the priestly quality, in the sense that the letter of Peter[9] gives to this adjective. It is a question of a function given to the local Churches in light of a specific activity which others would not be able to exercise, but which, nevertheless, exists for the priestly act of the whole and becomes real in this act.[10]

Tradition has instinctively shown itself conscious of the fact that in the liturgical celebration the minister is only a concelebrant, and that applies also to the Eucharist. According to the formula by Guerric, in the twelfth century, "the priest does not consecrate alone, he does not offer alone, but the entire assembly of believers consecrates and offers with him."[11] Such a consciousness is very old. From the time of Justin, the action of "the one who presides at the assembly of the brothers," at the time of the Eucharist which he describes two times,[12] is inscribed at the heart of a whole list of functions. He mentions "the one who reads," "the ministers called deacons," all the people present (*pas ho paron laos*) who "utter the exclamation: Amen" (65:3). Added to this are common prayer said out loud (65:1; 67:5), attendance at which is according to the need made possible by the generosity of the assembled faithful (65:5; 67:1, 6). The act of "the one who presides" does not amount to the celebration

---

[8]This is what the epiclesis asks, entirely oriented towards the transformation of life. See our study J.-M. R. Tillard, "L'Eucharistie et le Saint-Esprit," *NRT* 90, 1968, 363–387. See also the study by P. McGoldrick, "The Holy Spirit and the Eucharist," *The Irish Theological Quarterly* 50, 1984, 48–66.

[9]As also Rev 1:6; 5:10, and without doubt 20:6. On these texts, see the interpretation by A. Vanhoye, *Prêtres anciens, prêtre nouveau selon le Nouveau Testament,* Paris, 1980, especially 291–340: "In these circumstances which made Christians appear as victims and as condemned persons, John invites them to recognize proudly that they are in reality priests and kings, in other words, that they have a privileged relationship with God and that this relationship plays a determining role in the history of the world" (339). This book by P. Vanhoye, so detailed, seems to us however that it does not distinguish enough the point in Peter's letter and that in the letter to the Hebrews in its synthetic vision of the Christian *sacerdotium*.

[10]We know that Johannine tradition, centered on the relationship of the believer with the Lord Jesus and the position as "disciple," leaves the question of ministries somewhat in the dark and does so in spite of the importance granted to the sacraments by which Jesus gives and nourishes "life." Consider above all the *Agape* relationship uniting Jesus (and the Father) to his own. Chapter 21, despite its epilogue-like form, uniting in Peter love and function (21:15-19) takes on in this way a particular emphasis.

[11]*Sermo* 5, PL 85, 87. Consult the study of Y. Congar, "L'Ecclesia ou communauté chrétienne, sujet intégral de l'action liturgique," *La Liturgie après Vatican II,* coll. "Unam sanctam," 65, Paris, 1967, 241-282. See also L. Bouyer, *L'Église de Dieu,* Paris, 1970, 356-357.

[12]*I Apol.,* 65-67.

of the "day of the sun" for him alone (67:3). The organization of the Christian Initiation, since the preparation for baptism until what follows it, expresses the same vision of the interaction of ministries in a common act of the Church. Among the witnesses of this "baptismal discipline" who have come down to us, one could take as a good example the liturgy of Antioch.[13] The prayer of the congregation for the catechumens, the role of the Christian "guarantors" of the faith of these catechumens at their enrollment, the action of the exorcists, the intervention of the elders at the time of the renouncement of Satan which follows the commitment to Christ, their anointing of the catechumens on the forehead, the function of the deacons and deaconesses for the anointing of the whole body, the sign of the bishop (or the elder) and his word during the triple immersion, the kiss of peace by the congregation, the Eucharistic celebration[14] are the elements of a unique ecclesial proceeding, the one which "makes" catechumens Christians. Throughout the unfolding of this rite, the central act of the bishop does not make up the totality of the ecclesial intervention. It is, literally, the community *as such* which joins together members and ministers who play the essential and unique role there which presents itself to them.

We find the same thing in the celebration of the sacrament which gives the community its ministers. Not only does the community during the first centuries have something to say about the choice of its shepherd,[15] but

[13]We refer to the excellent synthesis by P. A. Wenger, in his introduction to John Chrysostom, *Huit Catéchèses baptismales, SC* 50, Paris, 1957, 66-104.

[14]Elsewhere the rite of *consignation* is added, sometimes started by the presbyters and finished by the bishop. As is found in *The Apostolic Tradition* by Hippolytus, 21-22. For the anointing (of chrismation) in Jerusalem in the fourth century, consult the *Catecheses mystagogiques* attributed to Cyril of Jerusalem, *Cat.* 3, 1-7, 4, 7-8 (*SC* 126, Paris, 1966, with notes by A. Piedagnel, especially 122-123, note 2 which compares with other traditions). For the Church of Milan, see Ambrose, *De Sacr.* 2:24; 3:1, 8, 10; *De Myst.* 29, 42, with the commentary by dom Botte). For the Church of Hippo, see in *SC* 116, Paris, 1966, Augustine, *Sermons pour la Pâque, Sermo* 227, with the introduction by S. Poque, 36-37, and 37 note 1.

[15]The witness of Cyprian is important here, as in *Epist. 67:3-5; 43:4; 45:3; 55:8*. On this question of elections see J. Gaudemet, *Les Elections dans l'Église latine des origines au XVIe siècle*, Paris, 1979; R. Gryson, "Les élections ecclésiastiques au IIIe siècle," *RHE* 68, 1973, 353-402; Id., "Les élections épiscopales en Orient au IVe siècle," *ibid.*, 74, 1979, 301-345. Let us note that the declarations go much higher than one would ordinarily think. If the *Letter of Clement to the Corinthians* (around 95) contains the famous paragraphs (42 and 44) concerning the succession for historical continuity, it mentions uniformly in two passages which seem to us to be more and more clear the "authority" of the local church in the choice and support of its ministers. Those given the responsibility of the episcopate are those who have been established by the Apostles then by "other eminent men," but "with the approbation" of the whole Church (44:3) and also who know how to conform "to the orders of the multitude" (54:2) when they feel that their presence becomes harmful (see A. Jaubert, introduction to Clément de Rome, *Épître aux Corinthiens, SC* 167, Paris, 1971, 85-86). We are already within the logic of the *"nullus invitis detur episcopus"* of Celestine (*Epist.* 4, *PL* 50, 434) and of the famous declaration of Leo the Great in *l'Epistola* 14, to Anastase: *"Cum ergo de summi sacerdotis electione tractabitur, ille omnibus praeponatur quem cleri plebisque consensus concorditer postularit: ita ut si in aliam forte personam partium*

he is ordained during a Eucharistic celebration where the congregation plays a key role. The ceremonial of episcopal ordination handed down by the *Apostolic Tradition* of Hippolytus is well known:

> Let the one be ordained as bishop who has been chosen by all the people, [who is] irreproachable. When his name has been spoken and he has been accepted, the people (*populus*) will gather with the presbyterium and the bishops who are present, on Sunday. With the consent of all, let these impose hands on him and let the presbyterium stand without doing anything, let all keep silence praying in their heart for the descent of the Spirit. After that, let one of the bishops present, at the request of all (*ab omnibus rogatus*), pray by imposing his hand on the one who is made bishop, saying . . . when he has been made bishop, let all offer him the kiss of peace (*omnes*) . . . .[16]

This rite puts on stage two groups of actors. It is not reduced to an impersonal act which would imply only the bishop pronouncing the prayer of ordination and the ordained. It takes place among the group of bishops—witnesses of the living presence of apostolic Tradition in their own community and charged with transmitting the "power of the sovereign Spirit" for the apostolic ministry—and the community. Since this community does not yet have its bishop it is made up of the presbyterium and the rest of the people of God. The "descent of the Spirit" takes place during the prayer of the community. This composes its climate. It is besides during this prayer that, through the mediation of the epiclesis and the act of one of the bishops, God in some way will respond. The liturgical act of this bishop will seal the adherence of the ordained to the group of those who exercise on the part of God the *episkope* for the Church. Besides, the first act of the newly ordained will be to preside at the Eucharist where the community will express and nourish its own reality. Ordination implies, therefore, the community as actor. And it is not because this role does not belong to the agent who serves formally as instrument for transmitting the power to exercise the ministry which is secondary and therefore, negligible. The prayer of the people and the consecrating epiclesis fit together even in the rite of ministerial ordination. The prayer

---

se vota diviserint, metropolitani judicio is alteri praeferatur qui majoribus et studiis juvatur et meritis: tantum ut nullus invitis et non petentibus ordinetur; ne civitas episcopum non optatum aut contemnat, aut oderit; et fiat minus religiosa quam convenit, qui non licuerit habere quem voluit" (PL 54, 673). In addition, this major role of the community works also in the difficult question of ordinations of individuals forced to receive the rite. For the facts in question, see Y. Congar, "Ordinatione invitus, coactus, de l'Église antique au canon 214," *RSPT* 50, 1966, 167-197.

[16]*Trad. Ap.* 2, translation by B. Botte, *SC* 11 bis, 40-43. It has often been studied by Herve Legrand, in particular in *Initiation à la pratique de la théologie,* t. III, Paris, 1983, 194-209.

of the people prolongs in some way the role that it has already played in the declaration of the faith and dignity of the "designated minister."[17]

The ministry appears, therefore, at the outset, inseparable from what the letter of Peter sees as the priesthood of the community *as such,* which concerns life in its daily existential dullness, lived *before God* for his glory. And that applies to the liturgical celebrations which are acts of this concrete life which should not be cut off artificially from the rest. It is exercised in ecclesial *communion.* It has a proper role within it.

B. The ministry in the ascendancy of apostolic witness

1. In order to understand what ministry has to do specifically with ecclesial *communion,* it is necessary to return to what Acts, presenting the manifestation of the Church on Pentecost, emphasizes about the relationship between Christ the Lord, the apostolic group and the new-born Church.[18] The group, made up of "Peter and the eleven" (Acts 2:14) appears in this context charged with the unique role of witness of the Resurrection of the Crucified. This role consists of communicating, revealing, with the news of this Resurrection opening up access to the benefits of which it is the source (those of the Spirit of eschatological times), the cause and the nature of the means for Salvation. It is in this way that it belongs to the essence (being) of the Church. So it enters into Revelation.

This group, in fact, goes back to Jesus. And the election of Matthias proves the importance that being rooted in the experience before the Cross has for the community (Acts 1:21-22). The realism of the witness depends

[17]On this question, read A. Santantoni, *L'ordinazione episcopale,* coll. "Studia anselmiana," 69, Rome, 1976, especially 125-137. Note that the local Church will have a certain right to look at the faith of its bishop. In the interrogation which *L'Entretien d' Origène avec Héraclite* (SC 67) reports and where the orthodoxy of the local bishop is questioned, "all the Church is there listening" (§1, cf. p. 16-17).

[18]The interesting study by M.-A. Chevallier, "Pentecôtes lucaniennes et Pentecôtes johanniques," shows that the major characteristics of the account in Acts 2 are found again in the ensemble of other accounts, in spite of the great diversity of frameworks:
—the communication of the Spirit is the fact of the Risen One identified as the Crucified;
—it is linked to the mission assigned to the Twelve;
—it has a distinct finality: it is a gift made to the Church so that it may be the Church, an eschatological people. Let us quote this paragraph which forms a synthesis: "If we come back . . . to the fourth gospel, we discover a fissure which is entirely analogous. John 20, we have seen, is parallel to Luke 24, it is the gift of the Spirit by the Risen One to the group of the apostles in view of their missionary witness. The Johannine equivalent of the gift of the Spirit to the Church as a grace characteristic of the eschatological people is found in John 19:30, when Jesus as he is dying inclines his head towards the group which has been "drawn" by the "glorified" crucified one and "transmits the Spirit" to it which "rested on him." There, as in Acts 2:39 and 41-47, is profiled, behind the first elements of the "family of the Lord," the crowd of those who will be called according to John 12:32s. There is, as in Luke, a distinction between two aspects of the communication of the Spirit, with appropriation of the first among them, the missionary impulse, to the group of Twelve, and of the second, the eschatological gift, to the people of believers in general" (310).

on it (2:32; 3:15; 4:20, 33; 8:25; 10:39-42; 13:31). Despite its direct origin, even the apostolate of Paul does not coincide totally with that of the pentecostal group. This is what is insinuated in the speech at Antioch of Pisidia found in Acts (13:31) and what the author gives as the aim of the witness of the apostle. It places less weight on the identity of the Crucified and Risen One than on the "fulfillment of the Promise" (13:32; cf. 26:22), the "messianic role of Jesus" (18:5), the "Good News of God's grace" (20:24), the "will of the God of our ancestors" (22:15, 18), the "cause of Christ" (23:11), the "vision received from the Lord" (26:16), the "Reign of God" (28:23). What is noticed here are the expressions and the tenacity with which Paul, in his letters, means to show that despite everything he is a true apostle (1 Cor 9:1; 15:8-9; Gal 1:16-17; 2:7-8). But, however eschatological and authentic his being sent is,[19] however secure his investiture is, the witness of anyone at all who has not "accompanied" Jesus before the Cross (Acts 1:21-22) needs to find a confirmation in what the witnesses of the facts in question certify. Doesn't the short kerygma in the First Letter to the Corinthians (1 Cor 15:3-5) refer back to what Paul received from the tradition which precedes it?[20] Because it is through the apostolic witness, conveyed through the power of the Spirit, that we know what happened to Jesus, what God accomplished in him, the words of the Lord himself which permit us to undertand why. Salvation is then recognized as a gift not coming from a vague and abstract source but from the Father in and through Jesus Christ, faithful Servant of the Good News of God. This relationship to the *acta et dicta* of Christ Jesus is essential. It is fundamentally for this reason that the Church is said to be founded on the apostles (Eph 2:20).

An object of Salvation, the Church itself is known, indeed, by the apostles to be totally dependent on the divine initiative and an action of the Holy Spirit over which it has no control, deeply indebted for its existence on Jesus Christ alone. The apostolic cell—whose place in the heart of the ecclesial being was shown on pentecost—is much more than the instrument which announces the Good News or brings the means of Salvation. It is also the sign, the *memorial* of the rooting of Salvation in the

---

[19]See the study by Anton Fridrichsen, "The Apostle and his Message," *Uppsala Universitets Arsskrift*, 1947, 3–23. It is remarkable that Acts does not make Paul an Apostle in the sense where he claims this title for himself in the epistles; nor do they emphasize his doctrinal authority but his missionary activity. The contrast with Paul's place in the Pastorals is clear (cf. 1 Tim 2:7; 2 Tim 1:11). The terms used by Paul to describe his vocation are often borrowed from vocation accounts of the great prophets.

[20]J. Murphy O'Connor, "Tradition and Redaction in 1 Cor 15:3-7," *CBQ* 43, 1981, 582–589; see also J. Schmitt, "Les discours missionnaires des Actes," *RSR* 69, 1981, 165–180 ("une sélection d'énoncés kérygmatiques déjà reçus," 171); Id., "Le milieu littéraire de la tradition citée dans 1 Cor 15:3b-5," in E. Dhanis, *Resurrexit*, Vatican, 1974, 169–184; J. Kloppenborg, "An Analysis of the Pre-Pauline Formula in 1 Cor 15:3b-5 in Light of Some Recent Literature," *CBQ* 40, 1978, 351–367.

diakonia of Christ Jesus. The recalling of this relationship necessarily precedes the progress of every believer and every community. It is an essential dimension of Salvation because it inserts it in its concept of Incarnation. The baptized are Body of Christ only by remaining dependent on what the Lord was and what he did, by taking their essence from him, from his life, his Cross and Resurrection. To eliminate this relationship would be to fall into the illusion of the Gnostics.

The apostolic group is, therefore, in its very being, the *memorial* group of the "established relationship" with Jesus. It is besides, the established judge of the messianic community and through it linked to the eschatological judgment, according to Matthew (19:28), or more widely to the Kingship of the Lord Jesus over the people of God, if Luke must be believed on this point who places it in a full Eucharistic context (26:30), which is replete with meaning.[21] This eschatological role is not without a relationship with the mission of being a depository of the fundamental witness which this group alone is capable of rendering: Jesus has been crucified, *we are witnesses of it,* he is raised, *we are witnesses of it.* The deposit (the *parathèkè*) which the pastoral letters will speak of (1 Tim 6:20; 2 Tim 1:12, 14) comes from this group, from its understanding (in the Holy Spirit) of the content and the object of the faith.[22] The entire life of the Church will be founded on the faithful transmission (*paradosis*),

---

[21]See J. Schlosser, *Le Règne de Dieu dans les dits de Jésus,* t. II, coll. "Études bibliques," Paris, 1980, 584–589; H. Schürmann, *Le Récit de la dernière Cène,* Paris, 1966, 43–50.

[22]On this notion of *paranthèkè,* not examined very extensively, see P. Medebielle, "Dépôt de la foi," *DBS* 2, 374–395; S. Cipriani, "La dottrina del Depositum," *Analecta Biblica* 17–18, Rome, 1963, 128–140; C. Spicq, "Parathèkè," *Notes de lexicographie néotestamentaire,* coll. "Orbis biblicus et orientalis," 22/2. Fribourg-Göttingen, 1978, 651–655. On the notion of "rule of faith," see especially P. T. Camelot, "Le magistère et les symboles," *Divinitas* 5, 1961, 607–621. In Acts, Paul's speech to the presbyters (Acts 20:28), whose tone closely parallels the one in the Pastorals, does not speak of "deposit of faith." Let us note that the idea of *orthodoxy* is intrinsically linked to that of "deposit of faith." The idea of orthodoxy is of prime importance in the unfolding of the history of the Church. Certainly the New Testament itself is a witness to a rather wide diversity in the way of approaching and understanding the person and the work of Christ Jesus (see the beautiful book by J. J. Dunn, *Unity and Diversity in the new Testament,* London, 1977). Yet a line of strength is extricated from it, a nucleus becomes precise, permitting one to judge the authenticity of such or such a presentation, of such or such a way of proclaiming the Gospel of God, and of refusing or at least putting certain currents in doubt. A certain diversity will be able to be reconciled with communion in the same faith. But beyond certain limits the diversity will also be able to lead to a break in the communion of faith. R. E. Brown, *The Community of the Beloved Apostle,* thinks that the Johannine community is the witness of a break caused by the emergence of non-orthodox positions, vigorously refused by the original group (1 John 2:19). Recognized as orthodoxy is what responds to the intelligence which the first witnesses (the apostolic group) had of Christ Jesus and his work. This is where orthodoxy is rooted. It is a will to be faithful to the authentic "truth" of Christ. The study by R. H. Fuller, "New Testament Trajectories and Biblical Authority," *Studia Evangelica* 7, Berlin, 1982, 189–199, an understanding of how it is the "deposit" attested to by the first witnesses which makes up the dynamic nucleus on which orthodoxy depends. The views of W. Bauer, *Orthodoxy and Heresy in Earliest Christianity,* translation am., Philadelphia, 1971, no longer create unanimity today.

faithful protection and faithful preservation of this deposit (what has been entrusted): it gives its faith to it. This is surely what the author of the Second Letter to Timothy seems to express: "I have no doubt at all that he [Christ Jesus] has the power to preserve what has been entrusted until this day [of judgment] . . . guard this precious deposit with the help of the Holy Spirit who lives in us" (2 Tim 1:12, 14).

This is what establishes the importance of what will be called the Tradition in which we have recognized the dynamic thread of the life of faith because its content is precisely this apostolic deposit, the fruit of what, inseparably, Christ and the Spirit have turned over to the apostolic community (cf. John 16:13-14)[23] but "once-and-for-all." Tradition (*parado-sis*) is in fact the perpetual remembrance, preserved by the Spirit, of the *acta et dicta* of the Lord Jesus, of what he was and also the understanding which the apostles had of the work which God accomplished in him. It is, therefore, *communion*—here is the word which recurs—throughout the ages, with what has made up the experience of the Apostles. The "succession" of believing generations will happen in this remembrance of the apostolic witness. If it happened that a group separated itself from this witness, it would cease to be in *communion* with the core of the Church because to be Christian signifies by definition to be a believer, therefore, to adhere to a truth which is known only because it has been transmitted (cf. Eph 4:21; Col 2:7). Without tradition (*paradosis*) there is no faith.

All life in Christ, besides, depends on what the Letter to the Romans calls the "creed you were taught" (Rom 6:17). But this remains such only to the extent where it passes unchanged, always identical, no matter who the preacher is, what words are used, the context or the particular era.[24]

---

[23]In an immense dossier on the biblical vision of Tradition let us take out the note by C. Spicq, "Paradidômi," *op. cit.*, 22/3, supplement 1982, 506–515, with this excellent paragraph of synthesis: "In the New Testament, it is first of all divine revelation which is transmitted: 'All has been transmitted to me by my Father . . ., and no one knows the Son except the Father . . .' It is a question 1) of revelation . . ., 2) of transmission of a knowledge . . ., 3) total or universal, the totality of revealed doctrine. According to Luke 1:2, the evangelical facts have been transmitted to us . . . by 'those who were from the beginning eye witnesses and servants of the word.' Believers are those who accept this witness: 'You have obeyed with your heart the rule of doctrine which has been transmitted to you . . . I praise you that in all things . . . you hold to the traditions as I transmitted them to you,' (1 Cor 11:2); the traditions of the universal Church, to which every believer must submit, are those of doctrinal teaching, morals and discipline, and even uses and customs (dress of women at liturgical gatherings). When it is a question of a worship tradition and especially of an article of faith—for example, the institution of the Eucharist—the Apostle must be careful that he does not take credit for it [by a personal revelation], and he emphasizes the origin of it: 'I have received . . . coming from the Lord . . . what I have transmitted to you . . .' Likewise the most original and essential article of the Credo: Christ the Redeemer: 'I have transmitted to you in the first place what I myself received . . . that Christ died for our sins . . . and that he was raised.' Finally, the entire contents of the faith, in other words all the truth revealed by God, is transmitted to the faithful by an unchangeable tradition, such a deposit which is confided *ne varietur*" (508–510).

[24]Concerning the expression *typos didaches* in Rom 6:17, see F. W. Beare, "On the Interpreta-

Vincent de Lérins will have done nothing more than express this basic intuition when he writes in the *Commonitorium*: "Guard this deposit, what has been confided to you and not what you have invented, what you have received and not what you have thought . . . You are not the author but the guaradian, you are not the founder but a disciple . . . You have received gold, give back gold . . . Teach that just as it has been taught to you. And while you express yourself in a new way do not utter new things."[25] Within the diversity of expressions and the ways of making things explicit, the one and the same truth must endure and be passed on, the one which comes from the apostles.

2. It is in this relationship to apostolic tradition (*paradosis*), hence to the faithful succession within the apostolic deposit (*parathèkè*), that the institution of the ministry must be placed. The place that reference to the guarding and transmission of the "Salutary doctrine" holds in the whole of the New Testament relative to beginning ministries, whose complete characteristics it is impossible to discern with precision has been quite well neglected.[26] The well known view of Irenaeus follows the straight line on this point of departure:

> This is where the charisms of God that are necessary to teach about the truth were deposited, in other words, around those in whom succession in the Church since the apostles, the unquestionable integrity of the conduct and incorruptible purity of the word are gathered. Those men guard our faith in the one God who has created everything, they make our love grow towards the Son of God who accomplished such great "economies" for us, and finally, they explain to us the Scriptures with all sureness.[27]

tion of Romans VI, 17," *NTS* 5, 1959, 206–210; J. Kurzinger, *Typos didachès* und der Sinn vom Rom 6:17," *Biblica* 39, 1958, 156–176; J. Murphy O'Connor, *Paul on Preaching*, London-New York, 1963 229–232; S. Lyonnet, *Exegesis Epistulae ad Romanos V-VII*, Rome, 1961 48–49. J. Dupont, *Gnosis*, Louvain-Paris, 1949, 214–215, note z emphasizes that it is not a question of a pure and simple transmission of the Good News but of a teaching where the moral dimension of the Christian life is assumed. See also J.-P. Audet, *La Didachè, instructions des apôtres*, coll. "Études bibliques," Paris, 1958, 117.

[25]On this whole problem, see the dossier assembled and presented by W. Rordorf and A. Schneider, *L'Évolution du concept de Tradition dans l'Eglise ancienne*, coll. "Traditio christiana," 5, Berne-Francfort, 1982.

[26]See A. Lemaire, *Les Ministères aux origines de l'Église*, coll. "Lectio divina," 68, Paris, 1971. As witnesses of this emphasis let us quote, in addition to the Johannine epistles (see R. Brown, *The Epistles of John*, coll. "The Anchor Bible," 30, New York, 1982 and Id., *The Community of the Beloved Apostle*), in the Pastorals 1 Tim 1:2, 3-7; 2:7; 3:9; 4:1-2, 6-7, 13, 16; 5:17; 6:1, 2-4, 12-13, 20-21; 2 Tim 1:5, 12-14; 2:2, 9, 14-18; 3:7-8, 10, 14-17; 4:1-5, 7, 17; Titus 1:1-4, 9, 14; 2:1, 3, 10, 15; 3:1, 8-11, in the catholic epistles 1 Pet 1:12, 22-25; 2:2; 4:6-11; 2 Pet 1:2 (?), 12-20; 2:1-21; 3:16-18.

[27]*Adv. Haer.* IV, 26, 5. It is interesting to note also the emphasis of the first generations on the quality "disciple." See Justin (*Dial.* 17, 1, 35; cf. 1 *Ap.* 61), Irenaeus (*Adv. Haer.* IV, 17,

According to the Letter to the Ephesians (4:7-11), isn't the goal of ministry precisely "unity in our faith and in our knowledge of the Son of God" outside of the drifting in of false doctrines? It seems clear to us first of all to search there, in this fidelity to the Revelation made in Jesus Christ but known only through *communion* with the apostles, the reason for ministry in the Church after Pentecost.

Already, in fact, the last generation of the New Testament era is shown filled with this concern. It must take a practical orientation before the disappearance of the first witnesses and the necessity to provide subsequently for the life of the Church. According to all evidence, the delay of the Parousia requires this generation to think about a future whose length of time could not even be guessed at. It will become impossible to find later witnesses having "heard," "seen with their eyes," "touched with their hands," "reflected" (cf. 1 John 1:1) on the announced reality. There was in the apostolic witness an irreplaceable "once-and-for-all." Yet the deposit (*parathèkè*) of this witness will be able to be confided to trustworthy men, officially invested with *ad hoc* authority and assured of the help of the Spirit. They will have to "watch over" it, and in this way over the Churches whose life basically depends on faith. They will become by this fact the first ones responsible for the "tradition" (*paradosis*) of the true faith. This certainly will precede them. They themselves will receive it from their community, "preserved" by their predecessors.[28] However, they will be the guarantors of its being rooted in the apostolic witness. If this function does not assure the quality of life in the community by itself alone, it is, nevertheless, perceived as what maintains in this quality of life the fundamental stratum of fidelity to the Lord Jesus Christ.

A similar source of ministry in the tradition of the apostolic faith, through an osmosis with the fidelity of the local Church—because it is this one which preserves the deposit to be transmitted—seems to us coherent with several elements of this period of transition. It is first of all in a straight line of the prime importance accorded to the Word in all the sources of the New Testament, the Johannine record included, which seems, however, the least "missionary."[29] It is then in harmony with a fact which is often pointed out: the emphasis passes gradually from the unifying influence of the apostle going from community to community

5; 26, 2; V, 5, 1; 34, 3; 36, 2), Origen (*Com. sur Jean* VI, 59), etc. This emphasis is, in the New Testament, the one found in Johannine literature insisting more on the grandeur conferred by this *condition* of disciple than on that which the functions confer.

[28]This is what, several centuries later when the liturgical forms are set, will show the judgment of the community about the faith of the one who must be ordained. See in C. Munier, *Les Statuta Ecclesiae antiqua,* Paris, 1960, 75-78, the regulation for examining the future minister.

[29]See the beautiful study by E. Molland, "L'antiquité a-t-elle eu un programme et des méthodes missionnaires?," *Miscellanea Historiae Ecclesiasticae,* t. III, Louvain, 1970. See the commentary made on it by P. Jacquemont, J.-P. Jossua, B. Quelquejeu, *Le Temps de la patience,* Paris, 1976.

to a desire for structuring of the local Churches, each one of which becomes responsible for its faith.[30] It allows for an understanding of the reticence of the texts—up to Clement of Rome, around 96—on the major role (presidency) of the Eucharist. It agrees with the unending link established between the community organization, so important in the Pastorals where it appears as one of the functions of the ministry, and fidelity to the Word.[31] It squares off with what the First Letter to Timothy states about the presiding role of the presbyters "who are assiduous in the ministry of the word and in teaching" (1 Tim 5:17) and with the explanation a little later of Clement where the appointing of ministers by the apostles then their successors is not cut off from "the approval of the entire Church."[32] This explanation for the final justification of ministries is, besides, within the logic of an articulation between kerygma and *didachè* within the teaching of the faith, that can be revealed since the beginning of evangelization. The kerygmatic announcement of the apostle which is passed on and justified must, to reach its goal fully, spread out through a word of edification for the community.[33]

If the faith must be maintained and spread, it is understandable that the "planting" (1 Cor 3:6) having been assured by the preaching (*kerygma*) of the apostle communicating the deposit of faith, the principal concern of the Churches after his death and that of his collaborators is the faithful preservation of its witness for all generations "until the Day of the Lord" (cf. Tim 1:12). The once-and-for-all in the apostolic charge tends to be fixed on the *first* apostolic preaching which is the promoting one. Contact with it will be continued in two ways. The written account of remembrances transmitted by "those who were eye witnesses from the beginning and have become servants of the word" (Luke 1:1-2; cf. Acts 1:1-2) will crystallize it in what will become the Scriptures, the normative witness. In relationship to this norm ministry will see to the guarding of the deposit of faith. It will be in this way the *vicar* charged with the radiance of what will remain *the* basic ministry—that of the apostles—until the end of time, throughout history as it courses along and is subjected to continually new circumstances. Its task will be the preservation, the

---

[30]See J. Zizioulas, "Episkopè et episkopos dans l'Église primitive," *Irénikon* 56, 1983, 484–502 (487); A. Faivre, "Les communautés paléochrétiennes," *Lumière et vie*, 167, 1984, 5–25 (9); E. Molland, *op. cit.*, "Le phénomeène est net dans les épîtres pastorales" (see R. E. Brown, *The Churches the Apostles Left Behind*, 31–46).

[31]See already for apostolic practice J.-P. Audet, *La Didachè, instructions des apôtres*, 117–118. See the short work by C. H. Dodd, *The Apostolic Preaching and its Developments*, London, 1951.

[32]42:1-5. See the commentary by A. Jaubert, *op. cit.*, 84–86.

[33]See J.-P. Audet, *op. cit.*, 117, and for the general context P. Bonnard, *Jésus Christ édifiant son Église*, coll. "Cahiers de l'actualité protestante," 21, Neuchâtel-Paris, 1948.

making explicit, the interpretation, the realization and the transmission of the apostolic Word, in the local Churches.

We do not know and we will probably never know, what precise forms this ministry takes at the outset. A collegial type of presbyteral ministry, especially in the Judeo-Christian communities, was able to coexist, in particular in the Greek world, with an organization centered more around a person,[34] we should say more episcopal. The problem of a possible survival of a collegial presbyteral type in Alexandria is known,[35] and the views of Jerome are not perhaps as personal as was stated.[36] The episcopate in the sense that Ignatius of Antioch gives to it, and which will assert itself, was able to rise up gradually from the fact that one of the ministers took the central place in the college of presbyters, then gained distinction from the others by becoming holder of the authority.[37] We do not even know the real origin, the precise meaning and universality of the rite officially conferring this ministry; the reference to the Jewish *semikhah* seems to be insufficient.[38] However, one thing is indisputable: there is an adherence to the fact that this ministry officially has the guarantee of the Spirit and the assurance that the life-giving strength of the Spirit accompanies it. This Spirit is evidently that same one which was with Jesus during his ministry (Luke 4:1, 14, 18; Acts 10:37) and with the apostles (Acts 4:8; 13:9; 2 Cor 3:8).[39]

[34]See E. Griffe, "De l'Église des Apôtres à l'Église des presbytres," *Bull. de litt. ecclés.*, 1977, 81–102; J. Zizioulas, *art. cit.*, 488, denounces, with reason, the expression "monarchical episcopate."

[35]See the discussion of this problem in J. Lecuyer, "La succession des évêques d'Alexandrie aux premiers siècles," *Bull. de litt. ecclés.*, 1969, 80–99; Id., "Le problème des consécrations épiscopales dans l'Église d'Alexandria," *ibid.*, 1964, 241–250.

[36]On Jerome, read Y. Bodin, *Saint jérôme et l'Église,* coll. "Théologie historique," Paris, 1966, 196–204; P. Batiffol, *Études d'histoire et de théologie positive,* Paris, 1904, 267–280. Letter 146 is at the heart of the debate.

[37]On this process, see P. Nautin, "L'évolution des ministères aux IIe et IIIe siècles," *Revue de droit canon* 23, 1973. For the face of the bishop by Tertullian, see F. Refoulé, *Traité de la prescription contre les hérétiques, SC* 46, Paris, 1957, 61, note 2. It must be noted that the dossier of Qumran attributes to the "overseer" a task similar to the one the pastoral epistles will attribute to the *episcopos,* called also "shepherd." It may be that there was some influence there; see R. E. Brown, *The Churches the Apostles Left Behind,* 33. In 1 Tim 5:17, it is possible to read already a diversity in the function of the presbyters, a greater esteem being given to those who "preside," distinguishing them from the others.

[38]Among the numerous studies on this subject, let us cite Lawrence A. Hoffman, "L'ordination juive à la veille du christianisme" and E. J. Kilmartin, "Ministère et ordination dans l'Église chrétienne primitive, leur arrière-plan juif," *MD* 138, 1979, 7–48, 49–92; Also J. Colson, "Désignation des ministres dans le Nouveau Testament," *MD* 102, 1970, 21–29; Kurt Hruby, "La notion d'ordination dans la tradition juive," *ibid.,* 30–56; A. Ehrardt, *The Apostolic Ministry,* coll. "Scottish Journal of Theology, Occasional Papers," 7, Edimbourg, 1958; Id., "Jewish and Christian Ordination," *Journ. of Eccles. History* 5, 1954, 125–138; E. Ferguson, "Jewish and Christian Ordination; Some Observations," *Harv. Theol. Rev.* 56, 1963, 13–19; Id., "Laying-on of Hands; its Significance in Ordination," *JTS* 26, 1975, 1–12; J. Newman, *Semikhah,* Manchester, 1950.

[39]On this point, see J.-M. R. Tillard, "Ministère ordonné et sacrifice du Christ," *Irénikon* 49, 1976, 147–166 (156–166).

We cannot trace the stages leading from this era at the beginning to the situation found in later centuries. Yet, it seems clear to us that this evolution, as far as institutions and rites are concerned, is placed inside the plan, perhaps implicit but real, which we have presented. It is that plan to introduce "servants" of the Church of God into the *communion* of the apostles (and of those associated with them) so that the Church remains within the dynamism of what the Spirit has "delivered" by them (*paradosis*), always faithful to the deposit of faith (*parathèkè*) and obedience to what it implies.[40] So the particular vocation of the apostolic group, an integrating part of the Church at its birth, will be continued without losing anything of what these "witnesses" had to realize "once-and-for-all," the make-up of the deposit of faith. Thanks to its *vicars,* the life of the Church will unfold in an integral way *in* their witness. Irenaeus, who will draw up a list of bishops succeeding each other in the See of Rome, will speak of those to whom the apostles are "confiding the Churches themselves, leaving them as successors, transmitting to them their own teaching mission, in a way that the tradition of the Apostles can always be found there."[41]

In this way our ministers appear and their function of *episkopè* is explained, in relationship to the founding of the Church of God. In the New Testament, the verb *episkopeo* always contains as a harmonic the idea of a gratuitous visit to a person towards whom one has some responsibility and whom "one is going to see" (Acts 7:23; 14:36). It is *to watch over* someone by *seeing* to his lot, to cover with a look full of understanding and kind consideration an important situation by *seeing to* what things are and to what they should be. *Episkopè* designates the function especially concerned by this "looking after . . .," this "watching over . . .,"

[40]On obedience to the faith, see J.-M. R. Tillard, "Obéissance," *Dictionnaire de spiritualité,* t. XI. 535–563.

[41]*Adv. Haer.* III, 3, 1-3, *SC* 211, 30–38. This text is a key document. We are right at the heart of what will be called "apostolic succession." This aims at guaranteeing the link, essential to ecclesial life, between the "once-and-for-all" of the apostolic witness and today. That seems evident for the pastoral epistles. There is a "succession" of ministers, and Irenaeus will be able from this perspective to draw up a list of bishops *"succeeding one another"* on the seat of Rome (Adv. Haer. III, 3, 1-3). The bishop "succeeds" his predecessor in the role of presiding and in the teaching of the "sound doctrine" on which his local church establishes its life. He is servant and sign of unity not only by linking his church to everything which has been taught and lived since apostolic times but also by preventing it from being eaten away from within by forces which are not orthodox. Two important points must be mentioned here. Johannine literature, attentive also to the tradition received from the beginning (cf. 1 John 3:11), insists above all on the role of the Paraclete and his influence in the hearts of believers (John 14:26); here again it is scarcely ministerial. On its part, Acts insists more on the continuity in the life of the Churches than on the succession of ministers: there is continuity between what Paul does and teaches and what Peter does and teaches, and what is in continuity with what Jesus did and taught. Moreover, there is continuity between the tradition of Jesus and that of Israel. See R. E. Brown, *The Churches the Apostles Left Behind,* 63–65, and F. A. Fitzmyer, *The Gospel according to Luke I-IX,* New York, 1981, 9–10.

this "consideration . . .," what the Spirit of God accomplishes in the Church since Pentecost. If one can speak of the function of the "head," it is not in the usual sense of this word in our political societies. Rather it is a question of a diaconate of total consideration for a group for which one is responsible "to look after." The letter of Peter, again, clarifies the authentic nature of this responsibility when it makes Christ Jesus the *episkopos* (1 Pet 2:25) and the supreme shepherd (1 Pet 2:25; 5:1-4), gives as a model to those to whom God's flock is "confided," because Christ is not only the one who leads. He does it while knowing his flock thoroughly, by taking care of the weaker ones and those who are threatened in a special way (cf. John 10:1-9; Ezek 34:1-22), especially by giving up his life for his own (John 10:11, 15, 18). His "watching over" the flock, being aware of the weaknesses and dangers, is directed entirely by his love.

The Christian minister exercising the *episkopè* has, therefore, at the heart of his function, the responsibility of guaranteeing the apostolic character of what is being practiced in his Church. He does it especially in two ways. The first is the conduct of the community in its fidelity to what the apostles did and wished, according to their knowledge of the thinking of Christ. It is not the minister's mission to take everything upon himself. Yet, he must "preside" at the ecclesial *communion* and exercise a *leadership* there. The other way for him to guarantee the apostolic character is the "reception" of the "services," of the initiatives and intuitions of other members of the community. In other words, his responsibility is to coordinate, but by "verifying" them, which means by judging them in the light of the apostolic Tradition and by declaring that they are in conformity with this Tradition and authorized *by it,* charisms assuring the building and the vigor of the ecclesial *communion.* They are the ones, we will see, who permit the continual adapting of this ecclesial *communion* to the needs of today, its continual response to the needs of times and places. The ordained minister—the one we are speaking of—guarantees that this *aggiornamento* remains in the understanding of what the apostolic community understood and transmitted of the *acta et dicta* of the Lord. He is there in order to put on what remains the only seal capable of authenticating what the community is practicing: the apostolic witness on which the Church of God coursing through history is based.

C. Ministry and Eucharistic communion

In the course of establishing ecclesial ministry, two elements on which the New Testament record was shown to be silent became evident very soon. The first is important: presiding over the Eucharistic celebration appears as arising from the ministry which we have just described. Probably already evident in the allusion by Clement to the presbyters in which *episkopè* implies according to him the presentation of the gifts (the *dona*), this Eucharistic function of the ministry becomes central in the vision of the local Church presented by Ignatius of Antioch.[42] It is no accident that those who ascribe to Eucharistic ecclesiology find their inspiration in Ignatius and the typical expression, truly normative of the nature of the Church.[43]

But in order to interpret objectively the thinking of Ignatius, it is important to note that the one he calls bishop is in fact the person whom he sees at the center of the life of the local Church. According to him, everything which concerns it, including the exercise of the ministries of presbyter and deacon, is "in the thinking of Christ" only when accomplished in communion with the bishop.[44] The Eucharistic celebration being the gathering together of the entire community around Christ, "head" of his People in the double sense of the word *kephalè*,[45] it becomes normal then that the one who presides at it be that same person who presides daily over its unity and its charity.[46] Ignatius proceeds from the "unitive" function of the bishop to his "Eucharistic" presidency, and not *vice versa*. In other words, he perceives in the structure of the celebration the moment in which the very reality of the local Church is shown in its undeniable truth, because the Church comes from God who gives Salvation by reestablishing *communion,* which has its main axis in the gift of the Son. The first one responsible for *communion,* the bishop—who for Ignatius "takes the place of God" in it—is at the height of his function when, surrounded by presbyters "who take the place of the senate of the apostles,"[47] he presides at the celebration where the Flesh and Blood of the Lord are given for the sake of unity.[48]

It is possible that the record of Ignatius is neither as old nor as coherent, nor even as objective as was spontaneously thought on the basis of the witness of Eusebius.[49] Yet there could be no doubt at least about the

---

[42]For Clement, see 44:4, and the note by A. Jaubert, *op. cit.,* 173, with the introduction *ibid.,* 82–83; for Ignatius, see *Smyrn.* 8, 1-2.

[43]See N. Afanassief, *L'Église du Saint-Esprit,* coll. "Cogitatio fidei," 83, Paris, 1975 (cf. preface by dom. O. Rousseau, p. 10); J. Zizioulas, *L'Etre ecclésial,* Genève, 1981 *(passim),* and especially "Episkopè et Episkopos dans l'Église primitive," *Irénikon* 56, 1983, 484–501.

[44]The texts are abundant. See *Smyrn.* 8:1-2; 9:1; *Eph.* 2:2; 4:1; 5:2-3; *Magn.* 2:1; 3:1-2; 6:1; 7:1-2; *Tral.* 2:1-2; 3:1-2; 7:2; *Philad.* 3:2; 4:1.

[45]"Head which is source of life (for some medical schools), the head which bears the authority. See L. Cerfaux, "La théologie de l'Église suivant saint Paul," 280–283. See also P. Benoit, *Exégèse et théologie,* 131–134.

[46]See *Smyrn* 6:2; *Tral.* 3:1-2; *Philad.* 2:1; 7:2; *Magn.* 7:1-2.

[47]*Magn.* 3:1-2; 6:1; *Rom.* 9:1 (on the bishop); *Magn.* 6:1 (on the presbyters).

[48]*Philad.* 4:1; *Smyrn.* 7:1.

[49]For several years the origin, the context, even the authenticity of the Ignatian dossier have again been questioned. Also the declaration of Eusebius (*H. E.* III, 36) is contested by several. So R. Weijenborg, *Les Lettres d'Ignace d'Antioche, étude de critique littéraire et de théologie,*

ancient character of this presiding over the Eucharistic celebration by the bishop alone when the image of the bishop is starting to be clarified or the one to whom he will have given the responsibility of it.[50] There is, of course, Tertullian.[51] But Origen is clear. Around 250 we find in Cyprian the firm evidence of an extension of this presidency to the presbyters, with the assistance of a deacon, under certain circumstances.[52] And the problem that will soon be created by the "pretention" of some deacons, thinking themselves capable of this presidency is well known.[53] But in all these cases the situation occurs within the circle of ordained ministers, in the sense in which we speak of them. It seems to us also that the climate mentioned in the record by Ignatius—and here the precise date has little importance—is the one which renders the best account of why this prerogative of presiding at the Eucharist is reserved solely to the minister charged with preserving and consolidating ecclesial *communion,* in the wake of the apostolic mission.

It must be added that this prerogative accompanies and conditions the development of a "levitical" vocabulary, seeing in the Christian ministers "priests" of the clergy put in charge of ritual actions. At that time they speak of ministerial "priesthood." But they are no longer at the fundamental level where the community *as such* is priestly by the daily sacrifice of its existence led before God, according to the intuition of the epistle of Peter. Now what is called priestly is the function of a group of baptized persons especially set aside for the performance of official acts of the liturgy.[54] The New Testament was not aware of this use.[55] Ignatius himself did not make his bishop an *hiereus.* Whatever his personal thinking might

---

French translation by B. Heroux, Leyde, 1969; H. J. Sieben, "Die Ignatianen als Briefe; einige formkritische Bemerkungen," *Vigiliae Christianae* 32, 1978, 1-18; R. Joly, *Le Dossier d'Ignace d'Antioche,* Bruxelles, 1979 (suggests that the theme of union with the bishop should have been added); J. Riuscamps, *The Four Authentic Letters of Ignatius the Martyr,* coll. "Pont. Inst. Orient. Stud," 213, Rome, 1980 (Ignatius would be in reality a deacon); B. D. Dupuy, "Aux origines de l'épiscopat, le corpus des lettres d'Ignace d'Antioche et le ministère de l'Unité," *Istina,* 1982, 269-277 (an interesting synthetic essay).

[50]*Smyrn.* 8:1.

[51]*De exhortatione castitatis* 7 seems to insinuate the equality between the laity and members of the hierarchy. But there is the opposite declaration in *De prescriptione haer. 41, 6-8.* See M. Bevenot, "Tertullian's Thoughts About the the Christian Priesthood," *Corona Gratiarum, Mél. E. Dekkers,* Bruges, 1975.

[52]*Epist.* 5:2. The multiplication of rural communities plays, with the persecutions, a decisive role in this extension of the presiding function. See dom Botte, "Caractère collégial du presbytérat et de l'épiscopat," *Etudes sur le sacrement de l'ordre,* coll. "Lex orandi," 22, Paris, 1957, 97-124 (especially 104-105).

[53]See the regulation of the synod of Arles in 314, in canon 15 (or 16), in Mansi 2, 473.

[54]See J.-M. R. Tillard, "La qualité sacerdotale du ministère chrétien," especially 497-514.

[55]The analyses of P. Vanhoye do not seem to us to be convincing because they appear to assimilate too much the perspectives of the letter to the Hebrews to those found in Peter's letter.

be, and it is difficult to determine, Tertullian is, however, already a witness of this change in vocabulary.[56] Very soon the ordination prayer of the bishop found in the *Apostolic Tradition* of Hippolytus which conveys Roman discipline from the beginning of the third century will be filled with priestly images and words.[57] In Alexandria, Origen is not at all uneasy about applying priestly titles to the Christian minister, which he often explicitly compares to the levitical model.[58]

If we mention again this breakthrough in priestly-ritual vocabulary to designate ministers, it is because of old misunderstandings which die hard.[59] Presiding at the Eucharist is inseparable from the charge to preserve the local Church in its priestly character, in other words, in the *communion* which the first Tradition qualifies as "priestly" according to the sense with which it is used in the letter of Peter. But the priesthood of the community *as such* is not absorbed in what comes to be described as a ministerial "priesthood," united to presiding at liturgical or sacramental celebrations and above all at the Eucharist. And although the Eucharistic celebration cannot be effected without the minister, it is important to repeat that the role of the minister is to permit the community *as such* to exercise *the* priesthood there.

Even in this realm, this necessity of the intervention of the ordained minister comes from the need to put the community in *communion* with the group of apostles and the "once-and-for-all" link of this group to Christ. From the Last Supper to the last Eucharist which the Church will celebrate in history, there is only one Eucharist; exactly as from the first evangelical "teaching" to the last evangelical Word which will be uttered on this earth there is only one Word—that of the deposit of the apostolic faith—continually repeated, unaltered, through the power of the Spirit. The Eucharistic celebration is inscribed in the same economy as the *paradosis* of the deposit of faith. It demands the same guarantee of being inserted in the experience of the apostolic group, beyond the walls of space and time. That takes up the realism of the rooting in the historical "once-and-for-all."

[56]See M. Benevot, cited in note 51. The sacerdotal vocabulary is *Adv. Jud.* 6, 1, 14; *De Baptismo* 17, 1-2; *De Praescriptione haer.* 41, 6; *De Pudicitia* 20, 6-13; *De exhort. cast.* 11, 1-2; *De Monogamia* 12; *De Virg. velandis* 9, 1.

[57]See the article by P. M. Gy, "Les anciennes prières d'ordination," *MD* 138, 1979, 93-122 (especially 119-122).

[58]See *Hom. in Jos.* 2, 1, *SC* 71, 116; 6, 6, *SC* 71, 210; 17, 3, *SC* 71, 379-381; *Hom. in Lev.* 6, 6, *SC* 286, 291-293; *Hom. in Jerem.* 11, 3, *SC* 232, 419-423; *Hom. in Num.* 2, 1, *SC* 29, 83; 10, 1, *SC* 29, 88-189. Has this evolution been favored by the influence of Jewish sacerdotal groups converted to Christianity? Has it been provoked by the destruction of the Temple? See A. Faivre, "Le texte grec de la Constitution ecclésiastique des Apôtres 16-20 et ses sources," *RSR* 55, 1981, 31-42.

[59]They are manifested in certain reactions to the agreement of Lima (1982) on Baptism-Eucharist-Ministry.

Because it is thus a *vicarial* service of the apostolic witness which establishes the faith, ministry is essential to the local Church. God gives it to the Church, with his guarantee, through ordination. Accomplished by a minister himself put into this apostolic ministry, this rite is indeed centered on an epiclesis for the gift of the Spirit. A Eucharist follows. It is celebrated in true *communion* with that of the apostles and all those which, from Pentecost to the Parousia, have been celebrated and will be celebrated. There is then on the *sedes* (the seat) of this local Church a pastor—whom the first centuries very soon call the bishop—capable of preserving it in its apostolic faith (which it has recognized in him), to gather it together for the Eucharist, and through it to maintain this local Church and to make it grow in its *koinonia*. It is thus assured of remaining in the true tradition of the apostles (*paradosis*). United around the one who is seated on his *sedes,* celebrating the sacrament of unity, it will not break with the succession (*diadochè*) of all its generations throughout Tradition. Ordained ministry and fidelity of the community to the apostolic deposit together assure, in a radical way, the full apostolic *communion* of this local Church. This *communion,* in fact, is not reduced in anything at all to the single ministerial line but, on the contrary, finds its substance in the coincidence of the local Eucharist with the apostolic Eucharist.[60]

In each local Church the apostolic Church is recognized in this way. It is not sufficient, therefore, for the Churches to have validly ordained ministers, devoted and good, directly involved with the problems of the world and the needs of humanity. It is necessary that pastors be in the "apostolic continuity," in a way that, in their very special context and their own historical situation, the Churches remain in the "apostolic Tradition." The expression "apostolic continuity" should be noted very carefully. What we include here is certainly "apostolic succession," but understood in a much broader context: "continuity" of teaching of the faith, "continuity" of sacramental life, "continuity" of the inspiration of its mission, "continuity" of the preservation of the community in the preferential option for the poor (testified to throughout Tradition), "continuity" of solidarity with the other Churches, "continuity" in the faithful transmission of what "has been received from the apostles." In brief, ministers are necessary who watch (*episkopein*) that the local Church remain in *communion* with the apostolic community. And this *communion* is, we repeat, a *koinonia* which travels through and through history and links *hic et nunc* the different geographical places. The truth (or validity) of ordination of the minister is inscribed in this whole, which is the number of characteristics indicating the identity of the original apostolic com-

---

[60]This vision of succession appears to us exposed in a way which has not aged in two studies which are somewhat old: E. Lanne, "Le ministère apostolique dans l'œuvre de saint Irénée," *Irénikon* 25, 1952, 113-141, and F. Refoulé, *op. cit.,* 45-66.

munity. And it is ordained in it. It is a guarantee in view of this "continuity." Every history of the Church, without speaking of the strange situation of the *episcopi vagantes,* shows that the "validity" of an ordination could be only an instrument of witness where there would not have been an insertion into the "continuity" of apostolic *life* of a Church. The ministers succeed one another, but in the "apostolic continuity" of the local Churches.

Its pastor being linked, in his ministry, to the apostolic group, the deposit of apostolic faith remaining faithfully preserved, defended and transmitted to it, a local Church is by that very fact in *communion* with other Churches in an identical situation. The *communion* of Churches is brought about, in fact, by this shift of the relationship to the foundation which the apostles are. It implies both the identity of faith with theirs and the common rooting of ministry in their historical "once-and-for-all." It can happen that this communion exists and yet is not expressed, because one or the other essential elements required for its visibility is lacking. But as soon as a Church, discovering its own faith and an identical ministry to its own in another community, can "recognize" in this other community an authentic Church, in the very depths of its being, both of them are in *communion.* They are so objectively, even if they are not so visibly in their reciprocal relationships.

The explicit will of Christ is certainly that the communion of the Churches be visible, for the glory of the Father and "so that the world will believe" that the Son was sent (cf. John 17:21-23), and consequently will believe in the gospel of God. Up against the divine design such a visibility has nothing accidental nor accessory about it. It is an imperative. But two groups can be Churches in an authentic way without so much as making their profound identity visible by establishing outside links of communion. Everything impels us to affirm that this is the case, for example, between a Catholic Church and an Orthodox Church. They are two sister Churches, yet "separated." In this perspective, the drama of division and reestablishment of unity appear under a new light.

In fact, the question of the necessary visibility of interecclesial *communion* and that of the existence of this *communion* should be distinguished theologically. This point seems very important to us in regards to an ecclesiology of communion. The visibility of *koinonia* among Churches belongs, according to all evidence, to the fullness of the Church in this world. But it exists among communities where each one is already in itself constituted as Church thanks to its inclusion in Tradition (*paradosis*) by fidelity to the full deposit of faith and the apostolic character of its ministry, guaranteeing in particular the authenticity of its Eucharist. If that is true, it must be concluded from the the (Roman) catholic point of view that communion with the See in Rome is essential to the visibility of ecclesial *koinonia* but yet is not the absolute condition for claiming the title of Church,[61] because wherever a *true* Eucharist is celebrated, presided over by a *true* minister inserted into the apostolic succession, there exists there a true Church. It may be that this Church is not integrated in the visibility of communion, which is a serious limitation and, without any doubt, an ecclesial deficiency in formal contradiction with the will of Christ. Therefore, it is not fully the Church that it should be. Yet, it is already Church. And it is by virtue of this title that it is destined to enter into visible *communion*.

D. The ministry and "representation"

A second aspect of ordained ministry has gradually emerged and taken on importance in the evolution of the first centuries. It arises from another plane than presiding at the Eucharist. The community is conscious of being represented and supported in its ministry. It sees him as its agent for fraternal relations which will be established with other local Churches. He writes to them, visits them, supports them, and brings them assistance.[62] Later, it is to a high degree through him that it will be present and active in the councils.

a. It is clear that already with Ignatius and Irenaeus ministers seem invested with this role of ambassador, spokesman. Soon, at the time of divisions and schisms or at the moment when reconciliation takes place, breaks and healings will come about in the interplay of relationships among pastors. Even more so, a Church will be, at this point, linked to its minister, and ordinarily the other Churches will judge it according to the orthodoxy or fallacy of this minister.

It could be justified by the fact that other faithful either are disinterested in dogmatic questions or do not understand the stakes involved relevant

---

[61]Two texts of Vatican II give evidence of it. On the one hand, the decree on ecumenism does not hesitate to call Churches the communities of the East, and it does this in the usual way (so *UR* 14, 15, 16, 18), going as far as stating precisely: "These Churches, although separated, have true sacraments, especially by virtue of apostolic succession, priesthood and Eucharist which unites them intimately to us" (*UR* 15). On the other hand, the *nota praevia* feels the need to be precise, in a *nota bene,* where an important theological question remains "in what concerns the power which is exercised in fact by the separated Eastern Churches," hence, outside of the hierarchical communion with the bishop of Rome. Since Paul VI and Athenagoras it has become ordinary to speak of sister Churches (see E. Lanne, "Églises sœurs, implications ecclésiologiques du Tomos-Agapis," *Istina* 48, 1975, 47–74). Besides, in a bold formula (which is inspired by the Council of Florence), Vatican II speaks of a wall which separates the Eastern Church from that of the West (*UR* 18). Let us add that Vatican II names implicitly as Churches the communities of old type catholics. Read the article already cited by J. Hamer, "La terminologie de Vatican II et les ministères protestants." For the background of the vision of the sister churches, also see M. Fahey, "Ecclesiae sorores ac fratres, in the Pre-Nicene Christian Era," Proceedings of the 36th Annual Convention of the CTSA 36, 1981, 15–38.

[62]See D. Gorce, *Les Voyages, l'hospitalité et le port des lettres dans le monde chrétien des IVe et Ve siècles,* Paris, 1925.

to these questions. The *sensus fidelium* is not always and everywhere expressed with the same vigor. But one can suspect that there is another reason as well. It is the one which explains that today the break between Churches is accomplished because of a break between ministers and that in an inverse sense, for all Christian groups, the "recognition" of the apostolic character of ministries of a community is equivalent to the "recognition" of the ecclesiality of this community. One can no longer call upon the ignorance of the faithful in this matter. It is significant that on this subject under Leo XIII the thorny Anglican question was examined exclusively from the angle of episcopal ordinations.[63]

Here again, Irenaeus seems to be the most important witness. He associates, in fact, a "representation" of a special type to the function of the "presbyters, who are disciples of John," and to the role of certain persons who have had a direct contact with the apostolic group and acquired by this fact a particular authority.[64] He himself, besides, belongs to those who have heard Polycarp and preserved not "on paper but in the heart" the *memory* of his teaching.[65] Apostolic truth is "represented" in these men.[66] In order to find the true Church this is where one must look. Besides, in a parallel way to the emerging of the episcopate as the principal ministry, there is produced an amalgam of this "representation" with the theme of the bishop as the "representative of Christ."[67] If the bishop is the image of Christ and if, as far as the faith is concerned, he bears his people, Ignatius, for example, can deduce from that as an ecclesial rule that, "wherever the bishop appears, there also is the people, in the same way that wherever Christ is, there also is the catholic Church."[68] In his exalted state reserved to the episcopal function—"he takes the place of the all-powerful God"[69]—the *Didascalia* also contemplates in the bishop the vigor and quality of the community. It is in him like the river is in

---

[63]And at the moment when ARCIC-I began its work, at Windsor in 1970, several members of the commission were sceptical concerning the proposition of an examination of the "dossier of division" opening up the framework of ordinations. What we will make explicit seems important to us for a rethinking of the difficult problem concerning the reconciliation of ministries.

[64]See *Adv. Haer.* II, 22, 5; III, 2, 2; IV, 27-32; V, 5, 1; V, 30, 1; V, 33, 3; V, 36, 1-2; *Dem. de la préd. ap.* 3, 61. See on this point R. Berthouzot, *Liberté et grâce suivant la théologie d'Irénée de Lyon*, Paris-Fribourg, 1980, 27-29, which seems convincing to us.

[65]As Eusebius points out, *Hist. Eccles* V, 20, 6.

[66]And thus *Adv. Haer.* IV, 26, 5.

[67]See the suggestive study by O. Perler, "L'évêque représentant du Christ selon les documents des premiers siècles," *L'Épiscopat et l'Église universelle*, coll. "Unam sanctam," 39, Paris, 1962, 31-66. For the prolonging of this view, see B. D. Marliangeas, "In persona Christi in persona Ecclesiae, note sur les origines et le développement de l'usage de ces expressions dans la théologie latine," *La Liturgie d'après Vatican II*, coll. "Unam sanctam," 66, Paris, 1966, 283-288; Id., *Clés pour une théologie du ministère, in persona Christi, in persona Ecclesiae*, coll. "Théologie historique," 51, Paris, 1978.

[68]*Smyrn. 8, 2.*

[69]*Didascalia* II, 26, 2-8.

the source from which it flows, the child in the father, the people in the king, the effect in its cause. Wherever the bishop is, it could then be said, is where is manifested what the Church receives, in the name of God. A tough notion certainly. Yet, in it an intuition breaks through which, when refined, will be able to lead to something else than an autocratic vision of the ministry.

The most well-known expression of this representation is still Cyprian's. To the argumentative Florentius Puppianus he writes that "the bishop is in the Church and the Church in the bishop,"[70] to the point that "if someone is not with the bishop he is not in the Church." Speaking of the martyrdom of the bishop in the presence of all the people, he specifies besides that "what a bishop says at the moment of his confession under the inspiration of God, he says it in the name of all."[71] Between the bishop and the local Church there exists a dynamism of mutual inclusion which means that in the voice of the bishop is heard that of the entire local Church.

There is probably a relationship between this inclusion, or "representation," and the law of every society which wishes that the people, the nation, the group, be projected in its chief, that it be a question of a natural chief, one who has been elected or designated.[72] It is equally in the orbit of the phenomenon of the "corporative personality," a concentration of a social whole in one of its members, a crystallization in this one of the idea that the group has of its own nature, in a way that it can "be recognized" in him.[73] This demands, it is true, that the influence of this individual have an impact on the origin of the group. But we have underlined the vicarial link uniting the ministry of the bishop with the function "of the Apostles." But these, undoubtedly, play a role if not in the very birth of the Church at least at its birth, by the make-up, "once-and-for-all," of its initial and normative cell.

The relationship to the apostolic nucleus of the Church is what establishes, it seems to us, in its true depth the "representation" of the ministry and what corresponds to it, in other words, the inclusion in it of the

---

[70]*Epist.* 66, 8 ("*scire debes episcopum in Ecclesia esse et Ecclesiam in episcopo*").

[71]*Epist.* 81, 1–2; cf. *Epist.* 77, 22.

[72]On the comparison of the ecclesial "representation" with that of political regimes, see the short work of Carl Schmitt, *Römischer Katholicismus und Politische Form*, coll. "Der katholische Gedanke," t. XIII, Munich, 1925, especially 40–53 (from Dostoievsky).

[73]See H. Wheeler Robinson, "The Hebrew Conception of Corporate Personality," *Zeitschrift für die oldtestamentliche Wissenschaft* 66, 1936, 49–61; R. Aubrey Johnson, *The One and the Many in the Israelite Conception of God*, Cardiff, 1942; Id., *The Vitality of the Individual in the Thought of Ancient Israel*, Cardiff, 1949; J. de Fraine, *Adam et son lignage, études sur la notion de "personnalité corporative" dans la Bible*, Desclée, 1959; H. H. Rowley, *The Re-discovery of the Old Testament*, London, 1945; H. Wheeler Robinson is often cited on this idea. Also, in *The Religious Ideas of the Old Testament*, London, 1952, 87–91, 163–164, 185, 203–206.

community. Irenaeus' vision, which we mentioned, and the ecclesiological *ethos* of the first centuries convince us of this. For the first postapostolic generations, the bishop is the one who, having as his proper task to watch over (*episkopein*) what has been given to the apostles—therefore, the deposit of faith and the authentic tradition of Christian realities—is perceived as the bearer of the knowledge that he teaches and "incarnates." If you wish to find the true doctrine of this Church, look at the bishop, is what they could have said after Irenaeus,[74] not because of the ignorance of the other members but it is a little like if you wish to find the true philosophical doctrine of a particular School look at its Master. This "representation" is so much the more assured in the first centuries which at the time of the choice of the bishop the local Church gave its opinion on the conformity of its faith with the one which he professes, a faith that it intends to preserve and transmit by having given to him all its fruit.

There will be found in the theme of the bishop as spouse of the local Church[75]—as an icon of Christ the Spouse—understood in light of the anthropology of the first centuries, where it is present, a symbolic expression of this solidarity between bishop and Church. It takes into account the "representation" of the bishop. Ambrose of Milan, perhaps, expresses in the simplest way the nature of the link between each bishop and his Church when he writes: "Particular Churches, made fruitful by the Spirit

---

[74]*Adv. Haer.* IV, 26, 1-2.

[75]This theme spans the centuries. In the tridentine context, the expression is found in *Consilium delectorum cardinalium et aliorum praelatorum de emendanda Ecclesia, S.D.N. Paulo III jubente conscriptum et exhibitum,* III, 1, in V. Schweitzer, *Concilium Tridentinum,* t. XII, Fribourg, 1966, 138. At the Council of Trent, see the text of *Concilium Tridentinum,* t. IX, 179, 15-21, 32-52. He is the future Innocent IX. We will find it, for example, with Mgr. Pie, the bishop of Poitiers whose role at Vatican One is well known, in two major circumstances, one where he resumes his episcopal activity, the other where he refuses to move on to another See. See Mgr. Baunard, *Histoire du cardinal Pie,* 1-2, Paris, 1886, 241, 455: "Your Excellency will feel that there are more reasons than are necessary for me to take refuge behind authority and the protection of the holy Canons which forbid, as a general rule, leaving one's Church for another. From this point of view, not only my conscience would not permit me, but it would order me to answer: *Uxorem duxi, habe me excusatum"* (457). For the acts of witness of the oldest tradition, see J. Trümmer, "Mystisches im alten Kirchenrecht. Die göttliche Ehe zwischen Bischof und Diozese," *Österreichisches Archiv für Kirchenrecht* 2, 1951, 62-75. The image will be applied to the relationship between the bishop of Rome and the entire Church. So we have Humbert de Romans, *Opusculum tripartitum, Liber de his quae tractanda videbantur in Concilio generali Lugduni celebrando 1274,* who writes, in an ecumenical context: "The Pope is the husband of the universal Church. In the heart of the Church two sons are fighting, the Greek one and the Latin one, as in the heart of Rebecca Jacob and Esau. Could the husband worthy of this name and with a good heart be aware of this situation without experiencing pain nor be anxious about his wife who would be a prey to such a grave torment?", Pet 2, cap. 16 (text in Ortuin Gratius, *Fasciculus rerum expetendarum et fugiendarum, 2 — Appendix ed.,* London, 1690, 219-220; see Edward Tracy Brett, *Humbert of Romans, his Life and Views of Thirteenth Century Society,* coll. "Studies and Texts," 67, Toronto, 1984, 176-194, and especially the old study by H. J. Omez, "Un opuscule du bienheureux Humbert de Romans, 1273," *Documents de la Vie intellectuelle* 1, 1929, 196-211.

and by grace, are visibly united to a mortal pontiff."[76] By this nuptial image is shown that there can be only one bishop per community.[77] It can be equally understood why, as a canon of Nicaea specifies,[78] a bishop could not cross over to another more dignified community without sinning: the union is indissoluble.[79] Very often wearing the episcopal ring passes besides for his sign, and this is true right in the pontifical formula.[80] The symbolism of this marriage—going back to the marriage of Christ and the Church—is so imperious that it explains, while making all other reasons relative, why the bishop cannot while he is living ordain his successor: he would lead his Church into infidelity by giving it a second spouse.[81]

But this symbolism, replaced in the sociological context of the first centuries of the Church, implies a juridical relationship. In this era, in a gen-

---

[76]*In Lucam* II, 7, *SC* 45, 74. In the same vein, see Pacien (de Barcelone), *Hom. sur le baptême* 5, 7, *PL* 13, 1092-1094.

[77]See Eusebius, *Hist. Eccles.* VI, 43, 11.

[78]Canon 15. See also canon 14 (or 13) *Canons apostoliques*. The Council of Antioch in 341, canon 21 (Mansi 2, 1317), the Council of Sardica 343 (stamped by the position of Osius of Cordoba, C. H. Turner, *Ecclesiae Occidentalis Monumenta Juris Ant.*, I, 2/3), take it up again (but see Socrates, *Hist. Eccles.* VII, 35-37, *PG* 67, 818-826, which provides a series of exceptions). For the West, see particularly the severe position of the bishops of Rome, Damasus (in Théodoret, *Hist. Eccles.* V. 11, *PG* 82, 1221) and Leo the Great (*Epist.* 14, 8, *PL* 54, 674).

[79]Every moving on to another seat is an adultery, as the Council of Alexandria emphasized it in 339 (Mansi 2, 1285-1287), Evagrius The Scholastic in his *Histoire ecclésiastique* (*PG* 86, 2526), among many others. For the West, see Jerome *Epist.* 69, *PL* 22, 658-659, etc. Mgr. Pie writes: "I am bound to Poitiers, . . . Scripture said: *Alligatus es uxori: noli quaerere solutionem.* Are you bound to a wife, do not look to be unbound. It is not you, my friend, who would like to preach divorce to me. The Church, besides, is too pleasant company for you to be able to decline the requirements of this marriage, a true type of Christian marriage, such as you have the good fortune of knowing." (Mgr. Baunard, *op. cit.*, 241.)

[80]This is where the explanation comes from (probably from Hugues de Saint-Victor) *Speculum Ecclesiae* 6 (*PL* 177, 354), that of Innocent III (*De Sacra Altaris mysterio* I, 46, 60, *PL* 217, 770, 796), that of Thomas Aquinas (*In IV Sent.* 24, 3, 3, c.). The pontifical formula of Leo XIII is still: *Accipe annulum, fidei scilicet signaculum quatenus sponsam Dei, sanctam in delicit Ecclesiam, intemerata fide ornatus, illibate custodias,* where the designation for *a* local Church has disappeared. What has remained is the present formula. See Bonaventure, *De Perf. evang.* art. 3, q. 4 (*Quaracchi* 5, 192); Thomas Aquinas, *Contra Impugn.* 4.

[81]The importance given to this "regulation" comes from the fact that it is in agreement with the end of canon 8 of Nicaea. See canon 23 of the Council of Antioch of 341 (Mansi 2, 1317), answering canon apost. 76, and which will be revived in the West (so we have canon 17 of the collection, probably from the eighth century, published in Migne, *PL* 96, 1283): "It is not permitted for a bishop even at the end of his life to set up and consecrate another bishop. If the case presented itself the ordination would be null and void. Ecclesiastical law must be observed according to which another bishop can be appointed only by the council and the opinion of the bishops who, after the death of the predecessor, have the right to present the one whom they judge worthy" (canon 23). The case of conscience of Augustine is known by Possidius, *Vita* 8, and letters 31, 4 and 213, 4-6 (in *PL* 33, 123-124, 967-968). He was ordained while Valerius was living who made him his co-bishop, because both of them were unaware of the law. But he refuses to ordain Heraclius, designated as his successor; he keeps the function of presbyter for him, all the while letting him get closely involved with his worries. He will be ordained after his death. That is important to take note of for the sense of the "apostolic succession."

eral way,[82] the civic and juridical status of the wife is integrally dependent on the authority of the husband, whatever the vast field and honorable magnificence of her social activities might be.[83] She is "represented" in her husband. Often, what is seen there is a consequence of her inferior status. In rabbincal traditions, for example, she does not participate by herself in public life[84]: it is in and through her husband that she exists juridically. It is normal, then, that the bishop is put into the role of husband, the one who "represents" the local Church, his wife. Much more than these nuptials are the icon of those of Christ—which, in Tradition, includes in him all those who belong to him—and those of the Church. It would seem that today that would be an annoyance. We have another experience of the relationship between husband and wife, at least in the West. This foundation of representation is then contested and discarded. It would be regrettable, still, to forget the intuition of it. It is valuable.

b. After recognizing this, let us note that "representation" for the Church is not especially juridical. It arises fundamentally from *communion,* first of all, as the local Church is, through the bishop who bears the Church in him, joined to the apostolic group. The Church feeds on the relationship to this group whose faith it preserves and confesses. But there is more. In the link between the bishop and the apostles, is joined the link between the apostles and Christ himself, whom they "make present" to the Church. Because for Tradition the "representation" of the ministry has another side, that which makes it a "representative" not of the community which it "includes" but of Christ mysteriously present and efficacious whose icon he is. The image of nuptials was revealed here as valuable. It helped understanding and interpreting the theological basis and not first of all the juridical one of the ministerial "representation."

Besides, the New Testament vision of Christ-the-Spouse (Eph 5:25-32; 2 Cor 11:2; Rev 19:7-9; 21:2, 9; 22:17) emphasizes, undoubtedly, with more force than the vision of Christ-the-Head, how, although in ecclesial *communion* there is no separation of Christ and the Church, there is not, however, a confusion of roles.[85] The wife meets the husband. We have

[82]But see the important exceptions, imposing by their sheer number, which C. Spicq raises, *Saint Paul — Les épîtres pastorales,* 4th ed., entirely redone, t. I, coll. "Études bibliques," Paris, 1969, 387-388, note 3 (to be compared with 386, note 4). See also A. J. Festugière and P. Fabre, *Le Monde gréco-romain au temps de notre Seigneur,* t. I, Paris, 1935, 128-135 (for Rome); F. Buffière, "Situation de la femme athénienne au IVᵉ siècle et féminisme de Platon," *BLE,* 1981, 165-186.

[83]Read in particular P. Grimal and R. Flacelière, *Histoire mondiale de la femme,* Paris, 1965, and the note by C. Spicq cited above.

[84]See J. Jeremias, *Jérusalem au temps de Jésus,* Paris, 1967, 471-472.

[85]On this theme, very often raised in ecclesiology, let us return to the beautiful letter of Bossuet to "une demoiselle de Metz," letter 4 (in *Œuvres complètes,* 1879 ed., t. XI, 278-282), from

pointed out that this situation implied for biblical anthropology a dependence.[86] The Church always remains, especially in the *communion* which establishes its being, in a radical dependence on Christ its Spouse. As Ambrose said, it can operate and live only if it is continually made fruitful by the Spirit and the grace which Christ gives it.[87] Even more so, it remains as an object of grace where it puts into operation its vocation of spouse and mother.

It is this radical dependence on Christ which is made real in the relationship of the Church to the apostolic group and to the ministry which is derived from it. In fact, whatever the exact origin of the term *apostolos* might be and the meaning given to it by the New Testament,[88] one point

which we extract this passage: "Man chooses his wife, but he is formed with his members; Jesus, a special man, chose the Church; Jesus Christ, the perfect man, was formed and completed to be improved every day in the Church and with the Church. The Church as wife is for Jesus Christ by his choice; the Church is for Jesus Christ by a very intimate operation of the Holy Spirit. The mystery of election by the involvement of promises appears in the name of wife; and the mystery of unity, consummated by the infusion of the Spirit, is seen in the name of body. The name of body makes us see how much the Church is for Jesus Christ; the title of wife makes us see that she has been a stranger to him and that it is voluntarily that he has sought her. So the name of wife makes us see unity through love and will; and the name of body helps us to understand unity as natural, in such a way that in unity of body it seems to be something most intimate, and in the unity with the wife something most sensitive and tender. In the end, it is only the same thing: Jesus Christ loved the Church and he made it his spouse. Jesus Christ carried out his marriage with the Church and made it his body. There lies the truth: 'Two in one flesh,' 'bone of my bone and flesh of my flesh,' that is what was said of Adam and Eve, and 'it is' says the Apostle, 'a great sacrament in Jesus Christ and in his Church.' So the unity of body is the last seal which confirms the title of spouse. Praise to God for the series of these truths which are always admirable" (281). For the biblical vision, see in particular, among a wide choice of studies, E. Cothenet, "L'Église Épouse du Christ," in A. M. Triacca and A. Pistoia, *L'Église dans la liturgie,* Rome, 1980, 81–106, especially for the conclusion which demands (104–106) that the expression be stated with its fine distinctions on a biblical base: "The Church is none other than Jesus Christ continued." The author shows that Scripture highlights "the personality and the responsibility proper to the Church," "fully distinct from her Husband" (compare, in another perspective, Y. Congar, "Dogme christologique et ecclésiologie; vérité et limites d'un parallèle" *Sainte Église,* coll. "Unam Sanctam," 41, Paris, 1963, 69–104. See also J. Cambier, "Le grand mystère en Ép. 5:22-33," *Biblica* 47, 1966, 43–90. For the totality of the Old Testament context, see A. Feuillet, "Développement dans l'Ancien Testament de l'allégorie nuptiale entre Dieu et Israël," *Carmel* 37, 1985, 2-17; Id., "Les épousailles messianiques et les références au Cantique des Cantiques dans les évangiles synoptiques," *RT* 84, 1984, 181–211, 399–424; Id., "La femme revêtue du soleil et la glorification de l'Épouse du Cantique des Cantiques," *Nova et Vetera* 59, 1984, 37–67, 103–128.

[86]This point has been studied a great deal for some years and the bibliography is immense. Let's be content with referring to L. Monloubou, "Modernité de la femme biblique," *BLE* 82, 1981, 243-262; K. Stendhal, *The Bible and the Role of Women,* Philadelphia, 1966; R. Loewe, *The Position of Women in Judaism,* London, 1966; R. de Vaux, *Les Institutions de l'Ancien Testament,* t. I, Paris, 1958, 37–91.

[87]*In Lucam* II, 7; *SC* 45–74. *De Mysteriis* and *De Sacramentis* (whose ambrosian authenticity has been put in doubt) are very marked by this perspective, in the context even of Christian initiation. Thus *De Sacramentis* IV, 5; V, 5-11, 14-17 (*SC* 25 bis, 104-105, 122-125, 126-129), *De Mysteriis* 35-42, 54-56 (*SC* 25 bis, 174-179, 188-191).

[88]We do not have to enter into this debate. See, especially, the most representative works on the positions. So J. Dupont, *Le nom d'apôtres a-t-il été donné aux Douze par Jésus?,* Bruges,

at least is commonly admitted today. This term retains some components of the Jewish notion of *shaliah,* in particular the idea that through the *apostolos* is joined the one who sends him. The apostle is sent only to act for this other person, entirely taken over by his constitutive relationship to the sender (cf. Matt 10:40; 18:5; Mark 9:37; Luke 10:6; John 13:20). As a consequence, through the apostle (and the one who takes up the relay for certain conponents of his mission, those which are destined to last), the Lord himself is united. If, therefore, the minister holds first place in his Church, it is because in his word or his gesture—necessarily linked to the apostolic witness Christ on whom everything depends—becomes present and efficacious, as a source of grace. He is the icon of this presence. He exists only in the relationship of total transparency and radical dependence that this implies. Vicar of the Apostles, he is also this by their privileged relationship to the one who "sends" them as his "representatives." A title of glory? Rather a crushing responsibility.

E. The ministry and collegial solidarity

1. Speaking of the apostles, we have been careful to use the expression: the apostolic group. It can be surprising, the more that one wonders if the apostolic perception of group was so important. It is necessary, indeed, to recognize that the pastoral letters express themselves as if Paul alone counted in the eyes of several Churches.[89] Read carefully, they create the impression that—while placing him with the knowledge of the ancient Scriptures (2 Tim 3:15-17)—it is Paul's teaching alone that Timothy and Titus must faithfully preserve and transmit (2 Tim 3:10-14; Titus 1:1-9). His teaching seems to be sufficient. No reference is made to other apostolic witnesses of the orthodox faith. The apostolic character seems to be concentrated in Paul "herald, apostle and teacher of the Gospel" (2 Tim 1:11) to the pagans (1 Tim 2:7). But Paul is not one of those who have been witnesses of the ministry, death and Resurrection of the Lord Jesus Christ. Reference could be made to a "personal apostolic vein" linked directly to the perception which Paul has of Christ, and certain sentences of the letter to the Galatians urge him to it (Gal 1:15-17).

There is no other case than Paul's. The Acts of the Apostles are careful to underline that Peter goes to Cornelius—for an initiative which will be

1956; G. Dix, "The Ministry in the Early Church," in K. E. Kirk, *The Apostolic Ministry,* London, 1946, 183–303; Id., "The Christian Schaliach and the Jewish Apostle, a Reply," *Theology* 51, 1948, 249–256; L. Cerfaux, "Pour l'histoire du titre *apostolos* dans le Nouveau Testament," *Recueil Lucien Cerfaux* 3, Gembloux, 1962, 185–200; J. Roloff, *Apostolat-Verkundigung-Kirche,* Gütersloh, 1965; W. Schmithals, *The Office of Apostle in the Early Church,* New York, 1969; C. K. Barrett, *The Signs of an Apostle,* Philadelphia, 1970; brief synthesis in S. Brown, "Apostleship in the New Testament as an Historical and Theological Problem," *NTS 30, 1984, 474–480.*

[89]See R. F. Collins, "The Image of Paul in the Pastorals," *Laval théologique et philosophique* 31, 1975, 147–173.

the great turning point of evangelization—under the sole impetus of the Spirit, without the other Apostles being consulted or even advised (Acts 10:19-20). The author points out that "the apostles and brothers of Judea" will learn about it after the incident has taken place, which will surely upset some of them (11:1-3, 18). On its part, Johannine literature, which certifies the existence of the Twelve (John 6:67-71; 20:24) without knowing the term "apostle,"[90] clearly puts the emphasis on the personal relationship of the disciple with Christ Jesus and on the role of the Spirit. Hardly any "collegial"[91] anxiety is perceived there.

It would be incorrect to understand the collective dimension of the initial apostolate according to the democratic scheme of a group making *as a group* decisions to which then each member would conform. Each of the apostles presented in the New Testament enjoys the broadest power of initiative, evidently within fidelity to the recollection of the *acta et dicta* of the Lord Jesus Christ. In other words, the Spirit does not guide him simply because of decisions of the apostolic group *as such*. Besides it is necessary to be realistic. It was not common for the apostles to meet, after the dispersion of most of them, to make major decisions which had reference to the mission of the Church or when they were faced with internal problems such as those which the *Letter of Clement* will soon point out.

However, even as far as Paul is concerned, related New Testament documents, as much as the Pastorals, by his person and his heritage show him anxious to inscribe his ministry in that of the great apostles. We have already pointed out this fact. The letter to the Galatians (1:18-19; 2:1-11) mentions the visit to Cephas and to James, the meeting with the "mainstays" who are James, Cephas and John. The First Letter to the Corinthians testifies to a "reception" of the common apostolic teaching (1 Cor 11:23; 15:3-7; cf. 7:10, 12). In addition, the Paul found in Acts is, with "Barnabas, several others" and Peter himself, one of the principal actors at the meeting in Jerusalem which makes laws concerning the mission (Acts 15:2-4, 12, 22, 25, 35; cf. 21:18-26). This active participation forbids making him a sort of non-conformist arguer, a missionary sniper or parallel preacher. In this perspective, the importance that he gives to the collection for Jerusalem (Rom 15:26-28; Gal 2:10; 1 Cor 16:1; 2 Cor 8:1-9, 15; Acts 24:17), therefore, for a Judeo-Christian Church, takes on a new light. His "apostolic" preoccupation is inserted into that of the other responsible persons. And it is better understood when he permits himself to write to the Church in Rome which he has not established.[92]

[90]John 13:16 cannot be invoked as an exception, because the sense is clearly that of *sent* in the common sense of the term.

[91]See the remarks of R. E. Brown, *The Churches the Apostles Left Behind,* New York, 1984, 90-95.

[92]For the motivations for this letter to the Romans, see R. E. Brown in R. E. Brown and

The meeting in Jerusalem, considered by itself, is without any doubt the most revealing scriptural episode of apostolic planning and of what we call today the "collegial" quality of major decisions. The insistence of Luke, presenting the episode as an apostolic verification of the turn which the mission took—a turn which questions the future of the faith—gives it a somewhat normative character. This has been put on a parallel with what is found in the "summaries" concerning the early community (Acts 2:42-47; 4:32-35; 5:12-16). It is in this way that great Tradition will understand it. When it is a question of the identity of the Christian community, of what touches at the roots of the faith, no one is free to make decisions about these things as he pleases; it must be done with recourse to the unanimity of the apostolic witness. It is important to point out that in the case we examined which took place in Jerusalem the question lays claim to a central point: the relationship to be preserved with the ancient inheritance in the land where faith in Jesus Christ took root and which "is fulfilled" in this faith. The opening up to the pagans, and hence the catholicity of the Church of God, depends on this attitude towards the faith of the ancestors. It is wrong to speak here, as is sometimes done, about a "disciplinary decision." It is a question of a judgment formally dogmatic, under the garb of practical regulations. What is at stake is Christian identity.

2. We are led to distinguish from this, more clearly than is usually done, two areas in the mission of the apostolic college as the New Testament presents it.

a. There is first of all, and this is of prime importance, the intransmissible function of witnesses, attached to the Twelve *as such*. Chosen and gathered together by Jesus himself, they are taken as a whole and in their unanimity the group charged with giving witness to what the one whom they have seen and touched (1 John 1:1; 2 Pet 1:16) said and did and to what happened to him after his death when "God raised him up." Their witness can only be a common one because their experience of the key moments in the life of Jesus has been a common one (cf. Mark 3:14; Matt 10:1; 11:1; 19:28; 26:14, 20; 28:16; Luke 6:13; 8:1; 9:1; 18:31; 22:3, 14, 28; 24:9, 33, 36-53; John 6:67-71; 20:24; Acts 1:1-8, 12-14). The first chapters in Acts usually present them collectively, as a group expressing itself through its spokesman Peter (cf. 2:14, 37; 4:34; 5:12, 18, 29, 40; 6:2, 6; 11:1; compare with Gal 1:17), when it is a question of witness.[93] And when

---

J. P. Meier, *Antioch and Rome,* New York, 1983; Id., "Not Jewish Christianity and Gentile Christianity but Types of Jewish/Gentile Christianity," *CBQ* 45, 1983, 74–79. Paul would try to present *his* theology to a Church which remained faithful to its Jewish roots, in the line of thought found in James and Peter.

[93]The decision of Acts 6:2 is explicitly motivated by this mission of witness.

Paul is writing to the Galatians perhaps he is making a reference to this solidarity when he mentions his progress in "communion" near the "mainstays" who are James, Peter and John (Gal 2:1-10). One point is certain: it is about this witness of the faith of the apostolic group *as a group* that the author of the Letter to the Ephesians is thinking when he reflects on the house of God "which has for its cornerstone Christ Jesus himself" and "the apostles and prophets for its foundations" (Eph 2:20).[94] Revelation, in its turn, will not separate the apostolic group when it describes the messianic Jerusalem: The city walls stood on twelve foundation stones, each one of which bore the name of one of the twelve apostles of the Lamb (Rev 21:14).

Cyril of Alexandria, noting that Thomas, although absent from the house on the evening of the Resurrection, has also received the Spirit, explains this apparent anomaly by emphasizing that it was a question of a gift, not given individually but for the group *as such,* "not only for those who are present then but for the multitude of holy Apostles," in the same way in which the Spirit of the seventy elders in the desert was also given to those who were not yet in the Tent "but were counted among those already enrolled" (Num 11:16), Eldad and Medad.[95] Until now we have insisted too much on this point so it is not necessary to dwell on it any longer.

To this collective mission of witness, given "once-and-for-all," for the everlasting foundation of the faith another one must be added. It carries a judgment with it. And this judgment concerns *koinonia.* Essentially its object is an appreciation of, a verdict on, types of behavior or teachings which must be evaluated in light of what God has revealed in the Lord Jesus or what must be coordinated in order to safeguard *communion.* Here it is more a question of pastoral reflection and prudence than of witness. There is a return to decisions or tensions, such as those which figured in the documents concerning the crisis in Jerusalem. But because they involve in a very grave way the faith and the authenticity of *communion* whose preservation was confided to the apostolic group *as such,* it is the obligation of this group to speak out. Linked to the mission of giving witness which this group has *as a group* and which it exercises by the simple fact that it exists, this second function is exercised only when circumstances warrant it. We said earlier that each apostle usually has the personal latitude which his job requires and does not have to depend on decisions taken by the whole group. It can happen, however, that one finds oneself up against crucial problems which demand recourse to a collegial judgment

[94]For this verse, see J. Pfammatter, *Die Kirche als Bau,* coll. "Analecta gregoriana," Rome, 1960, 78-97.

[95]*In Joan. Ev.,* lib. XII, *PG* 74, 717-720.

because the totality of ecclesial life is in question. On this level of decision-making concerning communion *as such,* the function of each apostle implies an essential and necessary reference to the judgment of the apostolic group *as such.*

This symbiosis of the "collegial process" (in its two moments of witness and judgment) and of the personnel (being deployed in its full scope) seems to us to define exactly the ministerial situation which the New Testament permits us to catch a glimpse of. The personal dimension of the apostolate opens up a large field of creativity and prevents thinking about a "pastoral concept" which is stereotyped. The radical dependence on the area of giving witness as a group *as such* and the recourse to its judgment when ecclesial *communion* is being questioned, guarantees the link with the "once-and-for-all" of the Event of Christ Jesus.

3. Ecclesial ministry, by its being rooted in the mission of the apostolic group where we see its justification, will necessarily be the bearer of the symbiosis of the personnel and the "collegial element" which we have just examined. And it will come into play in both areas in question.

a. There will be, first of all, for those whom Tradition will designate very early by the term "bishop," an absolute unanimity in the confession of the apostolic faith, relaying the apostolic witness. This unanimity, liturgically vouched for by the intervention of bishops of neighboring Sees at the time of an episcopal ordination, spans the centuries since the Credo professed today and is the very same one which, in their great gatherings, since Nicaea, the bishops have never stopped announcing. A breakdown in solidarity over this Credo would be tantamount to being cut off from the rooting in the apostolic witness and from what Irenaeus described as the certain charism of truth, "the incorruptible purity of the word," the certainty in regard to the explanation of the Scriptures, the holy Word, assuring "succession in the Church since the Apostles."[96] Therefore, it is no accident that every conciliar gathering takes place around the confession of the Credo.[97]

b. Besides, by instinct—as their reaction will show when faced with the Montanist crisis in Asia Minor, hence from 172 or even 156 if Epiphanius must be believed here—in the face of heresies which were corroding *communion,* bishops of such or such a country, sometimes accompanied by members of their Churches, would gather together despite the distances involved to resolve the crisis together. And the custom of sending syno-

---

[96] *Adv. Haer.* IV, 26, 2-5.

[97] That explains that the commission on Faith and Constitution of the ecumenical Council of Churches decided to give for axis to its research on the confession of faith the study of the Nicaean-Constantinople creed.

dal letters to the Churches in other regions will seek to link all the communities together for the decisions in question.[98]

Peace in Constantine will allow enlarging such a gathering to the dimensions of *oikoumene,* when the vastness of the problem seems to demand it. Then, together, the episcopate will discuss, judge and decide, confident of being aided by the Spirit. And instances will be seen in these "ecumenical" councils making pronouncements about ecclesial faith, in certain cases in a decisive way, on a line (analogically) with what the gathering in Jerusalem had been. The decisions of the seven ecumenical councils in matters of faith continue to be imperative precisely because in them is perpetuated, through the solidarity of the episcopal "college," the progress of the apostolic "college" putting to work its "collegial" responsibility. These decisions come from the refusal to let each bishop alone regulate questions which have an impact on the fidelity of all Churches to the witness that the apostles were called to make together, inseparably and unanimously.

One of the most tragic consequences of the great split between the East and the West will be the impossibility of a meeting of all the bishops to face some serious questions, while remaining convinced—at least until the Reformation—that on both sides of the "wall of separation" spoken of by the council of Florence[99] the episcopate continues to exist. The Church will be wounded by it until its conformity in the apostolic *oikonomia.* On the catholic side, in fact, there is a persistence to recognize that, through the sacrament of their ordination, the bishops on the other side of the "wall" are truly linked up with what we have described as the primary and fundamental register of episcopal solidarity, a solidarity which spans the centuries. They prove it besides by their firm adherence to the content of the apostolic faith such as was confessed and defended by the councils of the undivided Church.[100] However, it can be declared—with a sadness which is not imagined—that, cut off from communion with the Bishop of Rome, with no link to the episcopal "college," full exercise of this solidarity escapes them. Since the split, they are absent from the "collegial"

---

[98]See P. Nautin, *Lettres et écrivains chrétiens des IIe et IIIe siècles,* Paris, 1961. Y. Congar, "La réception comme réalité ecclésiastique," *RSPT,* 56, 1972, 369–403 (381) cites some cases. So for the solution of the paschal question in Palestine, Eusebius, *Hist. Eccles.* V, 23, 2-4; for the synods of Alexandria on Origen (in 230 and 231), Jerome, *Epist.* 33, 4 (*PL* 22, 447); for the Council of Carthage of 252, Cyprian, *Epist.* 41, 42, 55; for the synod of Antioch of 268 which deposes Paul of Samosata, Eusebius, *Hist. Eccles.* VII, 30, 17; for the Council of Arles of 314, text found in Mansi 2, 469–471.

[99]In *Laetentur coeli* (sixth session) cf. Mansi 31, 1026. This text is revived at Vatican II in *Unitatis redintegratio,* 18. See J.-M. R. Tillard, "Œcuménisme et Église catholique," *NTR* 107, 1985, 43–67 (56–59).

[100]This notion is imprecise. In fact before 1054 there were some blocks already detached. But it is not a question of a break between the East as such and the West as such.

gatherings where the catholic episcopate makes the second register of its solidarity real, in the face of crises which continue to threaten *communion*. But then these councils are no longer ecumenical in the full sense of the word.[101] And one can only dream about what would have been the contribution of the East in the debates at Trent and at the Vatican councils.[102]

4. If on this second register of *episkopè* "collegial" solidarity—with the "collegial" responsibility that it implies—finds its specific and full action in the "ecumenical" council[103] which other forms of conciliar progress announce,[104] it radiates also—and that is true since the first centuries—in more spontaneous progressions and more customary structures . Although having neither juridical status nor the guarantee of uprightness from the ecumenical council, these realizations of episcopal solidarity and of its "collegial" responsibility are not, however, merely accessory. Through them pass both the spirit and the efficacy of what will be called collegiality. This produces its fruits in it. They rise from this sphere.[105]

a. In fact, the affirmation by Cyprian on the oneness of the episcopate is well known. And it is clear that the vision found here goes beyond the conciliar action as such. This is before the time of Nicaea!

> There is among the bishops only one single Church, only one single soul and one single heart . . . Through the institution by Christ there

[101]It is more exact to call them "general councils" of the Western Church, following the distinction made by Paul VI on the occasion of the anniversary of the Council of Lyon (cf. *DC* 72, 1975, 63-65).

[102]The interventions of the melchite patriarch Maximos IV Saigh at Vatican II made one feel the richness of this contribution. See M. Villain, "Un prophète: le patriarche Maximos IV," *NRT* 90, 1968, 50-65. See also *Voix de l'Église en Orient, choix de textes du patriarche Maximos IV et de l'épiscopat grec-melchite catholique*, Paris, 1962.

[103]*Lumen gentium* expresses itself in this way: "The supreme power which the college enjoys in regard to the universal Church is exercised solemnly in the ecumenical council. . . . The collegial power can be exercised in union with the pope by the bishops residing on the surface of the earth, provided that the head of the college calls them to act collegially or at least that he gives to this common action of the dispersed bishops his approbation or his free acceptance in order to make it a true collegial act" (22). So many studies have appeared on collegiality that it appears useless to us to refer here to titles, that it suffices to point out the totality *La Collégialité épiscopale, histoire et théologie*, coll. "Unam sanctam," 52, Paris, 1965. For the historical consciousness about the authority of the council, see in Leslie W. Barnard, *The Council of Sardica 343 A.D.*, Sofia, 1983, how the eastern bishops continually invoke this in order to resist the way which the Bishop of Rome readmitted into communion bishops deposed by the council (thus we have 63-70, 83-84).

[104]Before Nicaea regional synods and the links which they weave are a formal exercise of episcopal solidarity, because this is exercised also at the immediate level. Concerning these synods, see E. Lanne, "L'origine des synodes," *Theol. Zeits* 27, 1971, 201-222.

[105]Nowhere in the texts of Vatican II can one find the word "collegiality," which explains our expressions "episcopal solidarity" or "collegiality."

204 Church of Churches

is only one unique Church spread throughout the entire world in several members, one unique episcopate represented in a multitude of bishops united among themselves. The unity of the Church is such, in the diversity of its parts linked and adhering together everywhere . . . that, entirely one, the Church is not in several separated pieces but that it forms only one single whole and it is the union of the bishops which is the bond.

Elsewhere the same Cyprian writes:

> The episcopate is one and indivisible. The episcopal dignity is one and each bishop possesses a portion of it in solidarity without division of the whole. And there is only one Church which, by its evergrowing fruitfulness, embraces an always more vast multitude.[106]

The word of Christ to Peter aimed at this unity of the episcopate.

This oneness is expressed by a solidarity making Cyprian himself attentive to the problems of the bishops of the Gauls[107] or urging the bishops to remain united by the exchange of letters thanks to which they control the unanimity of their teaching and in a mutual way enlighten one another.[108] There even were requests made that the letters circulate from Church to Church, as it happens for the recitation of the martyrdom of bishop Polycarp. There also exist letters which the new patriarchs sent to other important Sees, with their profession of faith, to indicate their communion.[109] All are in a position of solidarity in a unique mission. It belongs to them *in a body*. In each one of his major decisions each bishop must be able to say: "we, the bishops."

b. The organization of the Church into provinces, usually following the borders of civil provinces,[110] then the establishment of a hierarchical order in the very midst of the bishops of each province—who very early in Asia Minor will gather together annually in synod—are not without a link with this episcopal solidarity. This does not come down to a purely administrative question. The jurisdiction that canon six of Nicaea recognizes for the "primates" of the major Sees is not any longer a simple matter of prestige. It implies a service to unity and cohesion, with respect to the

---

[106]*Epist.* 66, 8, 3, Hartel III, 2, 733; *De Unit.* 5, see also *Epist.* 36, 4, Hartel 575; *Epist.* 55, 24, Hartel 642.

[107]*Epist.* 68.

[108]That is well emphasized by P. Batiffol, *L'Église naissante et le catholicisme,* Paris, 1911, 203.

[109]See the texts cited in Y. Congar, "La réception comme réalité ecclésiologique," 381, note 30.

[110]Without doubt because evangelization started ordinarily with the capital cities, the other Churches appear then as daughters of this mother Church. It is well known how much the Church of Carthage will respect everything that this "maternity" implies. See Joseph Cuoq, *L'Église d'Afrique du Nord, du IIe au XIIe siècle,* Paris, 1984; P. Monceaux, *Histoire littéraire de l'Afrique chrétienne,* t. IV, Paris, 1912, 8-10.

differences in regions. The bishops, while enjoying the power of initiative which documents testify to, act in the spirit of unity which will inspire (around 400) canon thirty-four of the apostles: "It is necessary for the bishops of each nation to know which one among them is the first and look upon him as their head; even if it belongs to each one to regulate the affairs of his own diocese and places which depend on it, they must do nothing without his assent. But he, on his part, must not do anything without the assent of all the others. In this way harmony will reign and God will be glorified by the Son in the Holy Spirit."[111]

Modulated in this way according to the needs or mental habits of the different places, episcopal solidarity appears at every level as one of the essential laws of ecclesial ministry. In this way, according to the intuition of Irenaeus speaking about the unity of Tradition (which the episcopate must preserve), the unanimity of transmission and the diversity of expressions will be maintained.[112] "Collegiality," when it is formally exercised in the councils, will bring the bishops together already united in this regional solidarity. Besides, it is in this way that it will fully express the catholicity and total unity in diversity, *communion of communions.*

The difficult question of the origin and status of Patriarchates is placed in an equal way on this vast canvas.[113] Beyond the preoccupation with the hierarchical order of Sees[114] and with political imbroglios, it is very well a question of episcopal cohesion, in the context of the great geographical and cultural blocks. Yet it is not useless to recall that the Western Patriarchate will include Sees claiming quite a large measure of freedom such as Milan, Arles, and Carthage. The quarrels of Leo the Great with Hilary the bishop of Arles are evidence of this, just as the troubles which follow the affair of the Three Chapters in Milan and Africa. Episcopal solidarity does not lead, even within a Patriarchate, to a uniformity which erases local particularities. Gregory the Great understood this when answering Augustine, the missionary to the Angles; he advised him to use his own judgment as to the choice of customs to be integrated into the life of this new Church, even if these customs were not those of the Roman Church.[115] He showed the same attitude when faced with the tradition of the Church

[111]See F. X. Funk, *Didascalia et Constitutiones Apostolorum,* t. I, Paderborn, 1905, 572-573.

[112]*Adv. Haer.* I, 10, 1-2.

[113]See E. Lanne, "Églises locales et patriarcats à l'époque des grands conciles," *Irénikon* 34, 1961, 292-321; H. Marot, "Note sur la pentarchie," *ibid.,* 32, 1959, 436-442. On the thorny problem of autocephaly, see the excellent ensemble of volumes IV and V, 1980 and 1981, of the review *Kanon* (review of the Society of law of the eastern Churches).

[114]Canons 6 and 7 of Nicaea (with the Jerusalem problem), canon 3 of Constantinople (with the problem of the place of the "New Rome"), canon 28 of Chalcedon, then the question of the "Third Rome."

[115]*Epist.* 11, 64 (*Ol* 77, 1186-1187).

in Seville to baptize with a single immersion: "A different custom causes no harm."[116] What was at stake, however, was the sacrament of Christian Initiation. Ambrose had opened up the way by affirming that his will to follow the Church of Rome did not forbid him "from using judgment which is proper to man" and to prefer the wisest practice, even for the baptismal rite.[117]

c. Episcopal conferences in the Western Church, born in the last century with the encouragement of Rome,[118] are also a form of episcopal solidarity within the "collegial" responsibility. Although they only partially express this solidarity and although their juridical status in the "college" is still indefinite,[119] they come from the interior of this solidarity. Their voice belongs to it.

In fact, the question then is not to know if the bishops assembled together are "representatives" of the "college," but—what is totally different—to recognize that they are members of it and act *as members*.[120] It is a question of an action *in* the "college," certainly not implying the authority of this college *as such,* but yet not being able to be considered as the simple meeting of individuals, each one of whom, because he is

---

[116]*Epist.* 1, 43 (*PL* 77, 497). Canon 15 of the Apostles forbade single immersion, and gravely.

[117]*De Sacramentis* III, 1, 5. It is a question of the washing of feet after baptism.

[118]For a global vision of episcopal conferences, F. Houtart, "Les formes de la collégialité épiscopale," *L'Épiscopat et l'Église universelle,* coll. "Unam sanctam," 39, Paris, 1962, remains very useful although somewhat old. On their ecclesial status, see the excellent ensemble *Las conferencias episcopales hoy,* Salamanque, 1977 and the book by G. Feliciani, *Le conferenze episcopali,* coll. "Religione e Societa," 3, Bologne, 1974; G. Alberigo, "Istituzioni per la comunione tra l'episcopa universale e il vescovo di Roma," *L'Ecclesiologia del Vaticano II: dinamismi e prospettive,* Bologne, 1981, 235-266. The finest study on the theological plane remains the brief article by J. Hamer, "Les conférences épiscopales, exercice de la collégialité," *NRT,* 85, 1983, 966-969. See also Id., "La responsabilité collégiale de chaque évêque," *NRT,* 105, 1983, 641-654 relying on W. Onclin, "La collégialité épiscopale à l'état direct ou latent," *Concilium,* 8, 1965, 79-87. On their limits and mandate, see the controversial book by H. de Lubac, *Églises particulières et Église universelle,* Paris, 1971; Charles M. Murphy, "Collegiality: an Essay toward Better Understanding," *Theol. Stud.* 46, 1985, 38-49; Y. Congar, "Collège, primauté . . . Conférences épiscopales: quelques notes," *Esprit et vie* 96, 1986, 385-390.

[119]The code of canon law makes laws about it in all fidelity to the decree *Christus Dominus,* 36-42, in canons 447-459, but its language is a witness of the vagueness of present-day theology in this area, still being established. The position of the International Commission of Theology is surprising because of its absolute tone, cf. *DC* 83, 1986, 57-73, (65).

[120]Mgr. Philips, in his intervention in the episcopal Synod of 1969, had made a remark of capital importance which has not been organized enough by the theologians. He asked that they look for something much more precise on "hierarchical communion," "particular Churches," "pluralism," *"affectus collegialis."* He feared that the Western and Latin mentality would succumb once again to the temptation to reduce the body of knowledge on "communion" (*koinonia*) to "juridical categories," and that "at the risk of destroying it," and then the whole advantage of the council would be lost. He added: "That is why I beg you . . . to think more about this communion than about powers, as necessary and as indispensable as they can be" (*DC* 67, 1970, 188-189; cf. *DC* 66, 1969, 1018). Coming from the principal author of *Lumen gentium,* these warnings carry some weight. . . .

a bishop, is inhabited by the collegial feeling (*affectus collegialis*). There is more to it.

Here again the temptation of all or nothing must be resisted and also to avoid thinking about a collegial void wherever there is not any action by the "college" *as such,* in its formal act juridically involving its authority and implying the whole *ordo episcoporum* as a body. The *nota praevia de Lumen gentium* specifies very clearly that "the college still exists but is not acting all that permanently by a *strictly* 'collegial' action . . ., in other words, it is not always *fully at work,* and more than that it is only at intervals that it operates by an act which is *strictly collegial,* and if this *is with the consent of its chief.*"[121]

But this language—in accord with the prudence of Vatican II on this subject—varies slightly. They speak here of a *strictly* collegial action, *fully in action.* No one will uphold that an episcopal conference "represents" (with a delegation of its power) the entire "episcopal college," that in it this college is "fully at work," that by it the authority of the college *as such* is juridically involved. But nothing prevents the thinking that, when treating the affairs of the Church, the bishops of a region do so *in the name of* their belonging to the "college" and for the concern of all the Churches—beginning with the nearest ones—that this belonging calls for.[122] In fact, "the concern of the universal Church would be quite vain if it were done at the expense of providing for the needs of neighboring dioceses, or in these natural regions which condition a great part of our existence."[123] Everything tends towards recognizing that it is a question of "a possible expression and an appropriate manifestation of the solidarity of the episcopal body, a reality of divine right in the Church of Christ,"[124] "a limited exercise of episcopal collegiality."[125]

In such a case two points stand out. One sees better why the conciliar decree on the bishops and, in the same vein, the new code insist so much on the "recognition by the apostolic See" of the decisions made during the conferences so that they can "bind juridically."[126] Would this refer-

---

[121]*Lumen gentium, nota praevia* 4.

[122]And as *Lumen gentium,* 23, emphasizes, going back to the beautiful text of the encyclical *Fidei donum* of Pius XII (February 21, 1957). See also *Christus Dominus,* 3, 4–7, which states it in a very explicit way.

[123]J. Hamer, "Les conférences épiscopales, exercice de la collégialité," 968.

[124]*Ibid.,* 969.

[125]*Ibid.,* 968. Father Hamer gives this definition of it which seems to us the best one: "A universal responsibility going back to the bishop by virtue of his charge as successor of the apostles, in solidarity with the entire episcopal body, under the effective direction of the successor of Peter" (967). He adds: "There are not two episcopal collegialities: the one which was exercised on the universal scale and the one which would be manifested on the scale of any region whatsoever. There is only one of them, but which knows an infinite variety of modalities" (969).

[126]*Christus Dominus,* 38, 4 (cf. 38, 3, 5); canons 455, 456 (cf. canons 448, 2; 449, 1; 451).

ence to the binding together of the "college" also be strongly required if it were only a question of the meeting of bishops "fraternally discussing common affairs of their dioceses"? It is interesting to compare this demand with the one that, in the same terms, the code affirms on the subject of the "plenary council" of a region or of the "provincial council."[127] The episcopal conference is inscribed—proportionately and with its juridical limits[128]—in the area of efficacy of the episcopal solidarity but with its "collegial" responsibility . And it is the latter which wishes an explicit reference to the Bishop of Rome. Does each bishop, in his diocese, acting along the line of personal initiative which we have clarified, need this explicit reference? The acting "together" (*conjunctim*) in the episcopal conferences[129] says more than a concerted action. It does not escape from the insertion of the action of each of the bishops concerned into the solidarity and the collective responsibility whose only subject is the "college." There exists no structured work-up—and none purely fortuitous—of the collective responsibility which is rooted in the responsibility of the "college" and which puts it into operation proportionately.

There is an equally better understanding, in this perspective, of the progress of the constitution on the liturgy, made explicit in 1964 by two Roman documents, confiding to episcopal conferences with very few restrictions the adaptation of the liturgy in their area of jurisdiction.[130] For centuries the realm of sacramental and liturgical life was reserved strictly to Rome. The conciliar assembly, where the "college" exercised *fully* its solidarity and responsibility as a "college" in a *strictly* collegial act, wished to prolong its action beyond its plenary assemblage. Everything urges a recognition that it was thinking about a "collegial" extension, but on a regional level and hence limited, of its fully and strictly collegial activity. And this is true the more that what it confided to the episcopal conferences fit in directly with its conciliar decision. It was like its second momentum deployed, in concrete contexts which, together, create catholicity. Whoever returns to the context of this decision can hardly believe that we are thinking of a purely administrative task for experts or technocrats adapting rites. It was a question of the realization by the episcopal "college"— but, this time, dispersed and, therefore, not acting in a *strictly* "collegial" way and in its *full* action—of what this "college" itself had enacted in council. Certainly, these "conferences" are not of divine institution. But is the ecumenical council itself of divine origin? Clearly it is not. It is a form of historical realization of episcopal solidarity which is *jure divino*. This remark clarifies the judgment to be applied to episcopal conferences.

---

[127]Canons 439, 446.

[128]Clear in canon 455.

[129]*Christus Dominus*, 38, taken up again in canon 447.

[130]*Sacrosanctum concilium*, 22, 2.

d. *Communion* appears, again, as the reality in which, under all its facets, even that of ministry, the Church of God is enclosed. In it nothing—not even, we said, the being of its God—escapes *communion*. And it is so much the more itself when it gives this *communion* its full range. That is because it is full *communion* when its ministry is collegial.

This relationship of episcopal ministry to ecclesial *communion* is so absolute that under certain circumstances it can lead to some radical decisions. A moving example of that can be found in the proposition from the African episcopate, dominated by Augustinian ideas, in a full donatist crisis. On the eve of the conference at Carthage in 411, destined to heal the wound of division, this episcopate (except for two bishops) declared themselves ready to renounce their episcopal position in a grand gesture if the return of the African Churches to *communion* demands it. The terms used to justify this decision are of a rare quality:

> Why should we hesitate to accomplish for our Redeemer this sacrifice of humility? He descended from heaven, going as far as taking on human members so that we could become his members. Would we have been afraid to descend from our seats if that is to prevent his members from being torn apart by a cruel division? For us, all that is necessary is to be faithful and obedient Christians. Let us always be that. We are bishops but it is for the Christian peoples that we have accepted ordination; therefore, let us make of our episcopate what is useful for the Christian peoples, in the sense of Christian peace. . . . If we are useful servants, why prefer our temporal dignity to our eternal benefit? The episcopal dignity will be more advantageous to us if, by putting it aside, we gather together the flock of Christ than if, by keeping it, we disperse it. . . . In fact, with what pretention could we expect the honor which Christ promises for the world to come if our episcopal honor prevents Christian unity in this world?[131]

5. Ministerial solidarity is not limited to this register *of* ministries. It implies the involvement of the totality of baptized persons not only in the liturgical celebration[132] but in the service of each local Church. Because if—in the primary sense of the word priest—it is the local Church *as such* which exercises the *sacerdotium,* it is it also which accomplishes the great steps that its fidelity to the evangelical call demands. It is responsible for itself. Its "representation" in the bishop is in no way equivalent to a pure and simple handing over of its responsibilities to one of its members given the charge to act in his place. The symphony of functions which we revealed in the heart of the liturgical act goes beyond this

---

[131]*Gesta cum Emerito Donatistarum episcopo* 7, *CSEL,* 53, 188–189 to be compared with *Epist.* 33 of Augustine to Procubianus *SC* 194, 42–43; 195, 595–599.

[132]See the beautiful book by J.J. von Allmen, *Célébrer le salut,* Paris, 1984, especially 224–244.

one. No one has perceived this better than Cyprian: "I made a rule for myself, from the beginning of my episcopate, to decide nothing without the counsel [of the presbyters and deacons] and without the vote of the people, according to my personal opinion . . . not only with my colleagues but with all the people."[133]

Since we bring up the testimony of Cyprian, it is good to underline that he agrees with the practice of the other Churches, that of Rome included. Because, deprived of a bishop after the death of Fabian, in January 250, this local Church does not hesitate for that reason to exercise its solidarity with the other Churches, by sending four letters to Cyprian and to his clergy.[134] The *Letter of Clement* to the Church at Corinth already showed that all the members of this Church were united in the consciousness of the same responsibility. And if Denis of Corinth wrote to the Church of Rome, it was "with the Church he governed."[135] What we call today the laity enjoyed thus a role recognized in the "affairs" of the community.[136] The new code of canon law of the Latin Church shows a breakthrough towards a return to a full integration of the laity in the ecclesial life.[137] Its insistence on the fundamental equality of all the faithful, based on baptism and in which the particular functions are inscribed,[138] is certainly more significant than the details of these regulations specifically concerning the laity.[139] In fact, it agrees with traditional theology concerning baptismal grace.[140]

---

[133]*Epist.* 14, 4 and 34, 4. See also *Epist.* 32.

[134]See G. Bardy, "L'autorité du siège romain et les controverses du IIIᵉ siècle," *Rev. de Sc. Rel.*, 14, 1924, 255-272, 385-410 (261-265).

[135]See Eusebius, *Hist. Eccl.* VIII, 9, 6.

[136]On the notion of laity and the evolution of this, see A. Faivre, *Les Laïcs aux origines de l'Église,* Paris, 1984 (to be clarified by Id., *Naissance d'une hiérarchie,* Paris, 1977). On the role of the laity, the classic work remains Y. Congar, *Jalons pour une théologie du laïcat,* coll. "Unam sanctam," 23, Paris, 1953 (for the precise point here in question see especially 327-329); see also P. G. Caron, *I Poteri del Laicato nella chiesa primitiva,* Milan, 1948.

[137]See especially G. Ghirlanda, "De laïcis juxta novum Codicem," *Periodica* 77, 1983, 53-70 (revived by G. Bonnet and G. Ghirlanda, *De Christifidelibus: de eorum juribus, de laïcis, de consociationibus; adnotationes in Codice,* Rome, 1983); G. Thils, *Les Laïcs dans le nouveau code de droit canonique et au IIᵉ concile du Vatican,* coll. "Cahiers de la Revue théologique de Louvain," 10, 1983. See also J. Komonchak, "Le statut des fidèles dans le droit canonique révisé," *Concilium* 167, 1981, 67-78.

[138]Canon 209 (see *Communicationes* I, 2, 1969, 82-83).

[139]These are found especially in canons 207, 224-231, 811. But see, also, canons 129, 275, 285, 296, 298, 317, 327-329, 377, 463, 512, 517, 519, 524, 528, 529, 537, 759, 766, 776, 784, 785, 811, 899, 907, 910, 930, 956, 1112, 1168, 1282, 1287, 1421, 1424, 1428, 1435, 1528. Compared to the Code of 1917, this ensemble is the sign of an unquestionable ecclesiological turning point (only canons 682 and 683 specifically concerned lay people). The attention of the present code is clear. Some commentators do not seem to have perceived that the most important texts on the laity are in canons directed towards the faithful *in genere* (208-273, 836).

[140]See J.-M. R. Tillard, "Le baptême, sacrement de l'incorporation au Christ," *Initiation à*

It seems necessary to us to make this point more explicit, essential for an ecclesiology of *communion*. We will do it by trying to tie up again here with the great Tradition.

F. *The communion of services in the unique baptismal grace*

1. Our communities are, today, divided by a frontier. On one side of it is the clergy, on the other side is the laity. This frontier has a very complex and long history.[141] In fact, although it is acquainted with the term *kleros,* the first Christian literature is not aware of the opposition between clerics and laity. The *kleros* (part inherited, part chosen) designates the totality of Christians and among this totality above all the group destined for martyrdom. In the New Testament, the letter of Peter asks the elders: "Do not be [you who feed the flock of God] Lords in regard to those who are your *kleros*" (i.e. who have fallen to your lot; 1 Pet 3:3). For its part the Letter to the Colossians says to Christians: "You will thank the Father who made it possible for you to enter into the *kleros* [i.e. to share the lot] of the saints in light" (Col 1:12; cf. Acts 1:17, 26; 8:21; 26:18). This is far from clericalism.

The New Testament besides is not aware of the term "laity," just as the Septuagint was not aware of it. And the first appearance of this word in the *Letter of Clement* is an isolated case, even though it later played a key role:

> Since there are some things here for us which are evident, after pouring over the depths of divine knowledge, we must do in an orderly manner everything that the Master ordered accomplished according to an established time. He ordered that liturgical offerings and functions be accomplished not by chance or without order, but at proper times and on favorable occasions. Where and by whom he wills that they be accomplished, he has determined by his sovereign decision, so that all things will become part of holiness according to his favor and be acceptable to his will. Therefore, those who present their offerings at the appointed times are pleasing and happy, because by following the precepts of the Master they are not deceived. Because, specific functions have been given to the high priest, a special place has been designated for the priests,

---

la pratique de la théologie, t. III, Paris, 1983, 408–436 (426). See also *Les Droits fondamentaux du chrétien dans l'Église et la sociéte,* Actes du IVe Congrès international de droit canonique, Fribourg, 1982; H. Legrand has, in diverse articles, presented a "heuristic model" in which this point is integrated and which it reproduces in *Initiation à la pratique de la théologie,* t. III, 194–209. Our vision agrees for the essential things with that of H. Legrand. See in particular "Nature de l'Église particulière et rôle de l'évêque dans l'Église," *La Charge pastorale des éveques,* coll. "Unam sanctam," 74, Paris, 1969, 103–121.

[141]The essentials of it has been retraced by A. Faivre, "Clercs/laïcs, histoire d'une frontière," *RSR* 57, 1983, 195–220; Id., *Les Laïcs aux origines de l'Église.* See above, note 136.

and special services have been imposed on the levites. As for the layman he is linked by proper precepts to the laity.[142]

The context shows that Clement is not describing Christian worship but levitical worship. He does not yet speak about lay Christians or Christian clergy. When the evolution which led to this usage first began (beginning of the third century if we trust the *Apostolic Tradition* of Hippolytus) the one who will be designated as *cleric* is the one who is ordained for the liturgy (bishop, presbyter, deacon), more precisely the one who receives for this purpose, from the bishop, the official designation for worship (*cheirotonia*) which is effected through the imposition of hands (*cheirothesia*).[143]

What is in question here is a diaconia. Through ordination one enters into "the portion of the people of God" destined for its service, "a portion" whose honor consists of being of service for the *leitourgia*. Texts show that it remains evident again that it is the *entire* People gathered together who celebrate it. One is chosen for a role among this entire People, a role integrally contained within the dynamism of the community and inseparable from it. But soon, this "portion of the people of God" will be tempted to absorb or monopolize the functions necessary for the life of the community. There will be the *ordo* of clerics, including the entire clerical hierarchy, and the other group, the laity.[144] This hardening of the frontier between clerics and laity will contribute to our losing sight of the fact that it is the entire people of God whom the Spirit calls to the service of the gospel and to take charge of its being faithful. It will lead to regrettable distortions in the ministerial function itself.

2. At the moment in fact when the apostolic period was finished, Christian communities took on their characteristic look, and it was at this time that we find an organization which is very typically and totally based on communion within the ecclesial ministry. And it is this ministry which is brought about there on two levels which operate by osmosis. The eccle-

---

[142]*1 Clem.* 40, 5. We give the translation of A. Jaubert, *SC* 167, Paris, 1971, 166–167. On this problem, see especially I. de La Potterie, "L'origine et le sens primitif du mot laïc," *La Vie selon l'Esprit,* coll. "Unam sanctam," 55, Paris, 1965, 13–29.

[143]See C. Vogel, "Chirotonie et chirothesis," *Irénikon* 45, 1972, 207–235.

[144]That is already certified in the Church of Cyprian. As canon Bayard indicates in his introduction to the *Correspondance* of Saint Cyprian, t. I, Paris, 1925, XLIX-L: "In the Church itself, as in civil society of the time, one distinguishes a common people, lay people among whom there is no hierarchical distinction, but only diverse categories, like that of confessors of the faith (*confessores*) or witnesses of Christ, who have suffered for their Master (*martyres*), that of penitents (LXVI, 5, etc.), that of virgins (IV, 1), widows (VII, IX), catechumens (*audientes, catechumeni,* VIII, 3), faithful (LXVI, 5). Above the common people is an *ordo,* the order of clerics, the *clerus,* where we find, except for porters (3), all the degrees of the present clerical hierarchy: lectors (XXXVIII); exorcists (XXXXIII, LXIX, 15); acolytes (VII, XXXIV, 4, etc.); subdeacons (*hypodiaconi;* XXIX, XXXIV, 4, etc.); deacons, priests and finally the bishop."

sial community abounds with forms of service of the gospel, all recognized and "received" by it, all of which come from the Spirit, but which are unified, coordinated, preserved in communion thanks to the ministry of those who institutionally guarantee the link with "apostolic succession." To these last ones are attached, in the line indicated by Ignatius of Antioch, our three ordained ministries; the other services of the gospel are perpetuated in the multiple functions which, over the course of time, and according to needs which arise, the Churches (borne by the Spirit) cause to spring up in them. The ordained ministries are, according to their nature, a structure which could hardly evolve in its essential elements, at least as to what concerns the episcopate. On the contrary, the other evangelical services are more changeable, created according to the needs of times or places, not because of their link with the institution inherited from the apostles. They vary in function according to the context, flexible as the situation demands. Also—and this is where their importance comes from—it is especially through them that the Churches adapt themselves to different eras and to the continually new demands of human societies. While the episcopal ministry assures especially, from generation to generation, the link with the apostolic nucleus on which the Lord never ceases to "establish" his Church, the services of the gospel which we are talking about permit it truly to take root in the flesh of humanity, always remaining the same yet always open to the necessities of the moment. The more one studies the dossier of these services of the gospel—we prefer this expression to the term ministry, too filled with clerical overtones—the more one discovers their irreplaceable value.

They rise up, normally in the heart of what we now call the "laity," although not exclusively, at the major turning points in the living Tradition of the Church. During the first Christian generations, we meet, for example, raised up by the Spirit of the Lord, Apollos, "who was able to help the believers considerably by the energetic way he refuted the Jews in public and demonstrated from the Scriptures that Jesus was the Messiah" (Acts 18:27-28), who himself was instructed by Priscilla and Aquila (Acts 18:26). Philip, who explains the Good News of Jesus to the eunuch then "proclaims the Good News in every town" (Acts 8:35, 40), is called Philip the Evangelist (Acts 21:8). His service of the gospel is different from that of pastors, whom he precedes on the list found in the Letter to the Ephesians (Eph 4:11), and different also from the service of the apostles. Philip has some daughters who are prophets (Acts 21:9) who, like all the prophets from early times, play an important role in the community (cf. Acts 11:27; 13:1-2; 15:32; 19:6; 21:10-11; Eph 4:11; Heb 5:12): they assure the *didaskalia* and they are said to be "established by God" (1 Cor 12:28) like the apostles and the prophets. Their task is a service of knowledge of the Word, within fidelity to the apostolic witness. Elsewhere, some members of the community are delegated by their Church for some proceeding of communion with another Church (Acts 11:22, 29-30; 2 Cor 8:23), often by accompanying Paul or one of the apostles (as in Acts 15:2, 22, 25, 27, 30, 33; 2 Cor 8:18, 22), which shows that their service is not simply to be a spokesman of these latter. An infinite number of clues leads equally to a revelation of the existence of a service of mutual aid and help to the poor (as in Acts 4:32-37; 11:29-30; Rom 12:8; 15:26-27; 1 Cor 16:1-4; 2 Cor 8:1-9:15) of which the institution of the Seven for "service at table" underlines the significance for the community (Acts 6:1-6). Also very significant seems to be the service of hospitality offered to the entire community when it gathers together (Rom 16:3-5; Col 4:1).

The Church during the first decades lives by this core of services, which are not all supported by some official apostolic *mandate* but simply demand to be recognized and controlled by the community and its leaders. The Spirit himself, giving the necessary competence and causing the desire to spring up to become a true living member in the Body of Christ, puts a particular baptized person, Christian, or couple so converted at the service of the community and its mission. Those who exercise a directive ministry are not considered then like those on whom would depend every initiative in matters of service to the gospel, still less like those who are in charge of other activities which by right would not fall to them but which they cannot accomplish by themselves. More structured ministries (where our ordained ministries find their roots) and other services to the gospel, temporary or permanent, are in *communion*. The primary ones have as their goal that all activities revolve around the benefit of all, in unity and fidelity to evangelical tradition; the secondary ones have as their goal that every gift of the Spirit be for the community and bears its fruit for it. Every service for the Church and its mission rests then neither by right nor in fact on the same ones; responsibilities are carried out in a *communion* which not only respects personal charisms but gives way to the unexpected which comes from the Spirit.

Going over several centuries we find in the *Apostolic Tradition* of Hippolytus—a witness, around the beginning of the third century, a crystallization of Roman discipline and liturgy in the process of taking place[145]—a sign of the importance granted to "non-ordained" ministries or services (here the expression is used explicitly). Alongside bishops, presbyters, deacons—all of them "ordained" (c. 2, 7, 8)—exist widows fulfilling the service of prayer (c. 10), readers (c. 11) and subdeacons called to functions in the liturgy or to the aid of the sick (c. 10, 34), confessors (c. 9), scholars given the responsibility for catechesis (c. 15, 18, 19, 41),

---

[145]See dom Botte, *La Tradition apostolique de saint Hippolyte,* Münster, 1963, XIV.

virgins (c. 12, 23, 25). Certainly, here, everything is seen as a function of the liturgy. But it is necessary to hold back what is said about confessors:

> If a confessor has been arrested for the name of the Lord, hands are not imposed on him for the diaconate or the presbyterate, because he possesses the honor of the presbyterate by his confession (c. 9).

The service of the "confession of faith" through martyrdom or what leads to it is not judged inferior to that of the ordained ministries, the episcopate being the exception. This is remarkable. In this listing, there are some who will say that ecclesial service assured by the hermit or monk, taking up the relay for martyrdom by blood, communicates with the same dignity.

3. The community is *communion,* lives and acts as *communion.* This is where the synod comes on the scene because the Church as *communion* can live by deploying "services" only by being synodal. One of the regrets that can be expressed after *Lumen gentium* is that this text affirms the collegiality of the bishops, which is a considerable step forward, but without having been able to involve it clearly enough in line with being part of the synod. This is a reproach which Orthodox tradition makes about Catholic ecclesiology of Vatican II. Once it has been established, in fact, the local Church always precedes the bishop, and if it cannot exist without him, by the same token he cannot exist without it. A bishop without a local Church would be, for the great Tradition, as monstrous as a father who would not have a son, a husband who would not have a wife, a professor who would not have any students. Such is the sense of a canon as important as canon six of the Council of Chalcedon. One is ordained *for* a precise community. If there is episcopal *collegiality,* in a college, a united and structured group of bishops, making up only one episcopal body, it is because the Church of God has for its very nature to be a *communion* of local Churches. The crown of bishops appears as the crown of episcopal Sees. Collegiality is a manifestation and a service (we should say a *sacramentum*) of the synodal process of local Churches. This is why the Church of God normally expresses its being and its truth fully only in the "ecumenical [synodal] council." Also, is not episcopal collegiality as much an instrument of powers being exercised over the Church of God as the expression, the channel, the service, the instrument for the *communion* of the local Churches and by that of the very nature of the Church of God. It is the expression of the exchanges of communion, witness, service, suffering, and martyrdom which make up the very life of the only *Ekklesia tou Theou.*[146]

---

[146]The Orthodox Nikos Nissiotis remarked after Vatican II that the Roman Catholic notion of collegiality remained the bearer of an ecclesiological misunderstanding precisely on this point

This constitutive law of the Church of God is verified first of all on the level of the local Church. The universal Church is *communion* because the local Church is *communion*. The bundle of services of the gospel of God which we have uncovered and described can preserve the Churches in fidelity to the gospel only if this bundle is all tied together because of instances of communion and dialog. The local Church *as such* lives the gospel thanks to the flowering of all the charisms which compose it and burst forth in a common witness. But it can do so only if it is gathered together and joined together in unity. Outside of the Eucharistic celebration, the normal way for its gathering together is the synod, in other words, as canon law defines it, the meeting (*coetus*) around the bishop both of ordained ministers and Christians charged with an official title for essential services of the gospel, of all those men and women who play a key role in the internal quality of the life of the local Church and the radiance of its witness. This gathering together is a little like the analogical answer, on the level of the local Church, of what a general chapter represents in a religious congregation. It is only there that the Church of God can reveal in total clarity, in the *conspiratio* of the bishop, of the ordained ministers, of all its members, the means of its witness (*martyria*) and of its life.[147]

Who, therefore, is a minister of the gospel? In a total sense the local Church as, on the one hand, it is composed of baptized persons bearing charisms who have decided to put these charisms to work, and as, on the other hand, it knows how, not only to gather together for the Eucharist of the Lord, but also to gather together as a synod in order to examine together its life, to evaluate its needs, to discern the gifts of the Spirit that it bears, to tie together its *martyria* and to reveal the ways to promote it, all within a full consciousness of its *communion*.

4. Is this an abstract or idealistic version?[148] A romantic throwback to

---

(article published in *Kerygma und Dogma* 10, 1964, under the title "Die Ekklesiologie des Zweiten Vatikanischen Konzils in orthodoxer Sicht und ihre œkumenische Bedeutung"). One should read the important article of E. Lanne, "L'origine des synodes," *Theologische Zeitschrift* 27, 1971, 201-222, to be completed by J. Zizioulas, "The Development of Conciliar Structures to the Time of First Ecumenical Council," *Councils and the Ecumenical Movement*, coll. "World Council of Churches studies," 5, Geneva, 1968, 34-51, quite independent of N. Afanasieff, "Statio Orbis," *Irénikon* 35, 1961, 65-75; Id., "Le concile dans la théologie orthodoxe russe," *ibid.*, 316-339.

[147]The Orthodox theologian Alexander Schmemann (*Church, World, Mission*, New York, 1979) saw correctly when he went on guard against an understanding of the synodal structure (such as we present it) what he envisaged as a conflict of powers. It is known that this notion was presented, spread, warmly accepted in several circles. That, in fact, a game, even a conflict of powers creeps in there, is not astonishing for one knows human nature. But the authentic synodal structure is possible only if it is understood as the meeting in *communion* of all those men and women who bear the charisms of the Church and of those who have precisely for a charism to see to it (*episkopein*) that everything is done for the greatest good of communion.

[148]We have been reproached for it, suspecting us of "romanticism" tainted with "gallicanism."

the Church of the early centuries? We do not think so. A judgment cannot be made about ecclesial truth by depending only on what is immediate. Let us examine history. At the time when orders and congregations, monastic or religious, were multiplying, especially after founders felt themselves called to structure their groups around a particular service of the gospel (the charism of their congregation),[149] the great many non-ordained services will take on a new status. They will continue to find their origin not in some decision of the hierarchy but in a call and inspiration of the Spirit always wishing to be original. Those who exercise the *episkopè* over the Church will only be able to welcome them ("receive" them) and watch that they are fulfilled for the benefit of the evangelical koinonia.[150] It is true that, made up as institutions, these forms of service of the gospel will gradually be just as monopolized by those men and women who will feel themselves destined *to follow Christ* in religious life with what this implies, in particular, poverty, chastity outside of marriage and obedience. It will be difficult to find outside of belonging to a religious family the means to exercise them. But they will grow in number and their characteristics will be specified. The service of the gospel expressed by attention to human poverty and misery, for example, will take on a thousand facets, going from the nursing profession or that of doctor to spiritual assistance to the sick and dying, all of it organized in a way to make of it a lasting work, occupying the entire activity of individuals. Involvement for justice and the promotion of the rights of the human person will become for certain groups the main work. In another domain, service of the Word of God will become more explicit according to a great number of forms: children's catechesis, reevangelization of Christian countries, theological research, permanent formation of adults. Some entire congregations will be consecrated to perpetual intercession for the people of God and the world, others to praise. And the last century saw foundations prosper which were more especially concerned with evangelical service to prostitutes, and to victims of the sins of others. It is useless to lengthen the list. These few examples will sufficiently show that services of the gospel accomplished by persons not ordained for the pastoral ministry, men and women, always remain inscribed in the progression of the life of the Church, whatever tendency there may be to put them apart from the common mission of the baptized.

Situations vary and new services appear. The great missionary adventure of the West has, already, from the time of Francis Xavier (around 1543) and John Baptiste de Pesano (on Macao, around 1580), necessitated

---

[149]See our article, J.-M. R. Tillard, "Le dynamisme des fondations," *Vocation* 295, 1982, 18–33.

[150]See J.-M. R. Tillard, *Devant Dieu et pour le monde, le projet des religieux,* coll. "Cogitatio fidei," Paris, 1974.

the creation of catechists. Natives, and, in our era, most often married people, sometimes itinerants but normally in charge of a place, are Christians who have taken on, without any doubt, one of the most essential ministerial services of the mission. Before our eyes, in Latin America, basic communities, whose birth is closely linked to the necessity to bring forth the people of God among the poor, are giving the types of service of the gospel which suit their situation.[151] There, the poor themselves evangelize, by the rebirth of the ecclesial service par excellence, that of martyrdom, whose impact and ecclesial value the mass media do not underline enough, because they too often look only at the political connotations. They also create a type of direction for the community, even of regulations for the sacramental life when the regular presence of the ordained minister is impossible, which permits the gospel to be the leaven of the Kingdom of God. Thanks to these authentic services of the gospel, the faith becomes a dynamism which strikes fear in the heart of the powers of evil: We are a hundred leagues from the assimilation of Christianity into a drugged religion which would put it to sleep!

And the evolution continues, before our eyes. We are, and this is evidence of it, on the verge of a new period of the history of living Tradition. There has been talk, and not without reason, of a post-Christian period. It is stamped by two strong characteristics. On one side, Christian institutions of the modern era, perpetuated until the beginning of the sixties, are changing profoundly. The case of congregations and religious orders mentioned above furnishes the best proof of that. While they were organized with a specific purpose in mind, dedicated to a special work, many modern foundations feel that they must, *as* a religious group as such, break with too narrow an identification to a well-defined service of the Church or of societies. The needs with which they want to get involved always exist, but it is for the Christian community *as such* to tend to these, not for a specific group linked to a special kind of existence which, without cutting it off from it, sets it nevertheless apart *in* the Church. Besides, the advent of new types of what has been called the apostolate of the laity is not alien to this awakening of consciousness. There is no need today to be a religious (vowed to celibacy) to go to a foreign country to help the poorest of all "in the name of the gospel"; it is no longer necessary to be a monk to lead a life of asceticism and prayer with a handful of friends; every competent lay person can aspire to a chair of theology or exegesis. Religious life is no longer defined by its services. These are returned to the place from which they came forth: the very flesh of the baptismal vocation.

---

[151]The synod of December 1985 recognized them, in a little sentence packed with meaning.

5. Ecclesiology must take very seriously this status of evangelical services. So much more than at other times, especially perhaps in the period which is opening up, it will be necessary to reevangelize. Even in the Churches in Latin America, where requests for justice remain urgent, the fundamental question becomes that of Christian identity and more especially of the faith on which it is founded. It is neither charity nor generosity which is posing the problem, but faith. If a profound need of religion emerges a little bit everywhere in the world, it often coincides with a strange status of the faith, pulled back and forth between a perilous return to a nearsighted fundamentalism and some rereadings which run the risk of taking all the substance out of it. This is where the necessity arises for a presentation which is entirely skillful and faithful to the Word of God. Ordained ministers (bishops, presbyters and deacons) overwhelmed by growing needs of the Christian community and by a surplus which is greatly diminished in its availability cannot be sufficient for it. Besides, they are not called, by their own *munus,* to be sufficient for it. Today as always— but undoubtedly more than before—their ministry can and must be accomplished only in the midst of a symphony of other ministries or services of the gospel. Such is the foundation on which one must always build. It is a question of entering into this dynamism of *communion* of functions. And it is there that the non-ordained evangelical services find again the essential place which is restored to them.

A wholesome ecclesiology urges being even still more incisive in the affirmation of this necessity. It comes from a respect for the right (the *jus*) which the sacrament of baptism implies. Because a baptized member of the Body of Christ, becoming by this fact, through the grace of the Spirit, one taking part in the mission which is for the Body to be built by the clear expression of all the functions and charisms, every Christian bears a fundamental right (*jus*) which must be honored. One of the principal functions of the ordained minister consists precisely in recognizing, often to have uncovered, the line on which this right must be respected, taking into account fidelity to apostolic Tradition and the concrete needs of the community, then to insert it in its proper place in the communion of the services of the gospel. It becomes more and more necessary, in this domain, to break with a one dimensional vision of right in the Church. The respect of right (*jus*) is not limited to submission to the law decreed by the minister who has officially the responsibility of the *episkopè* of the people of God. It consists also for this minister to respect and promote what the Spirit himself has inscribed in each member. And for the Spirit, this baptismal *jus* is not equivalent to a mere decoration.

6. The question will be asked: what are these services of the gospel, authentic ministries accomplished by non-ordained Christians? It is impossible to answer in a precise way. Everything depends on the circum-

stances of time and place, on concrete situations. Besides, this would be to doom them to sterility rather than to present a diagram which would open them up to all avenues: by them, the Church is embodied in the diversity of needs and cultures. One can at least open up several trails.

A first point is capital. Wherever a competent lay person exists, capable of being "recognized" by the Christian community, he can be destined for any ecclesial service which does not require ordination. The scale of possibilities is broad. It covers in fact the great traditional networks in which the service of the gospel is deployed: word, sacrament, mission, social and charitable action, even a certain *leadership* in the community. Several examples taken from today's situation will suffice to illustrate our thinking. In several areas, either because of a lack of pastors, or because of an extremely reduced number of baptized persons making the permanent presence of an ordained minister impossible, or for reasons of a territorial restructuring of the entire local Church, there are a growing number of communities deprived of pastoral help normally required for an authentic Christian *koinonia*. Their contacts with the minister who is responsible for the district are episodic. From this fact arises the urgency to confide to a Christian man or woman—perhaps to a married couple—the responsibility to take care of fraternal mutual help, religious formation of the young, preparation for baptism and marriage, for common prayer (perhaps under the form of a Liturgy of the Word). Elsewhere, especially in de-Christianized areas, threshold communities, which we prefer to call catechumenal, are being formed more and more: they group together persons drawn by the gospel but who cannot yet find their place in an ordinary parish. It is necessary for them, first of all, to examine thoroughly together the gospel message, to discover in a prayer which is not yet the sacramental Eucharist the profound meaning of entrance into the Church of God. Wherever a lay person—especially if he has received the faith late in life—very knowledgeable about the implications and the significance of the Christian mystery, is available, he is designated to take charge of those catechumens or baptized persons renewing relations with a faith which they have never practiced. Such a practice, in frank dialog with ordained ministers, can be very often the only one capable of recreating a conjunctive ecclesial fabric. In certain countries, profoundly eaten away by a slow de-Christianization, the task of didascalia, in the strongest sense of the term, becomes again a real urgency. By its history, it no longer is linked to an ordination but simply to a solid understanding of matters of faith, to communion with those who exercise the *episkopè* for the community, to the pleasure of this one, to a harmony of life with the faith professed.

But these services are not reserved to cases of urgency. They can also enhance with a correct understanding the nature of ecclesial *communion*.

Here again history testifies to this. Even for a Church having a sufficient number of vocations to the priesthood, it is hardly normal that, for example, what affects the ecclesial right be more or less reserved to clerics. Certainly, the exercise of jurisdiction could not find its source elsewhere than in the bishop. However, that does not imply that it belongs to clerics to withhold the privilege of ecclesiastical right and to consider themselves as its primary specialists. A specialized knowledge of ecclesiastical right and authority relating to respect and application of this right are not to be confused; *scientia juris* and *jurisdictio* are not placed on the same level. A breath of fresh air and a fresh breeze of realism, for example, would flow through the matrimonial courts, which are sometimes overloaded, if—always in communion with the bishop and at the service of his jurisdiction—lay jurists, men and women, properly prepared in canon law, fulfilled key functions there. On another level, lay people have been teaching theology for a long time in the Orthodox Church, sometimes in the seminaries, while in the Russian Church the direction of consciences is sometimes confided to lay people filled with the Spirit.[152] In our milieu, theological thought remains essentially clerical thought. Finally, in the area of administration of the local Church—always with a sincere respect for the *munus* proper to the bishop and to his *presbyterium*—the example of certain basic communities could, without being copied, inspire initiatives which are even being put into practice in old Christendom. The fidelity of a pastor to his vocation does not require that he run everything (wear all the hats). The fact of bearing *before God* responsibility for the flock, to have to watch carefully that the benefits of the gospel are passed on to them is one thing, the fact of not having to have confidence, with the whole community, in those men or women who have seriously wished that confidence be placed in them in certain areas is another thing. In this whole question, if one remains attentive to what the tasks are in *communion,* in an interdependent responsibility, in a frank dialog, conferring on some non-ordained faithful certain functions presently concentrated in ordained pastors does not contradict the intention in Scripture which orders the institution of ministry. The essential thing is communion with the bishop and his own communion with the apostolic witness.

The services which we have just mentioned are not, we should point out, subordinate jobs, an exception being made for the responsibility of a Christian community without a pastor, nor even jobs derived from ordained ministerial functions.[153] If, at first glance, they create a similar im-

---

[152]See in *Ministère et laïcat,* Taizé, 1964, the study by Nikos Nissiotis, "Le fondement ecclésiologique du plérôme de l'Église: l'unité du laïcat et du clergé dans la tradition orthodoxe," 158–172. See also the studies of E. Lanne, W. Rordorf, J. J. von Allmen.

[153]Karl Rahner, "L'apostolat des laïcs," *NRT* 78, 1956, 3–32, wrote: "The lay person is the one whose Christian involvement is determined by his temporal involvement itself, while the cleric,

pression, that arises from our distortion, spontaneously Catholics think that it accrues normally to ordained ministers (whom they sometimes call the "official ministers") to do everything, and they see in ecclesial services fulfilled by other Christians as something being assigned or delegated to them. Still less, these non-ordained "ministries" represent—especially when they are confided to women—concessions, destined to compensate for the frustration which the impossibility for certain categories (women, married men) to have access to the "sacred ministry" would represent. The difficult question of the "mandate" for Catholic Action is to place it in the same perspective. The definition of Pius XI "participation of the laity in the hierarchical apostolate of the Church," then takes on a new meaning of being reimmersed in the baptismal vocation and what it implies for every Christian both as far as responsibility and right, *before God*.[154]

The same *communion* of ministries and services, tied together by the bishop of each local Church, is called to play an essential role in the restoration of visible unity. If until this time ecumenical involvement has been the business more of the bishops and theologians than of other Christians, it is undoubtedly because it was necessary to open up the way. And that belongs to the mission of the ordained ministry. But the task as such reverts

---

the priest, the minister as a man in an established ministry, is the man whose Christian service is determined not by the temporal involvement as such but by a Church designation, by a Church mission." What led Rahner to hold that a lay person involved full time in a religious question was no longer a lay person in the strict sense but a cleric. We extol, on the contrary, the restitution to the laity of the "spiritual" and religious mission, properly linked to evangelization and to the gathering together of the Church of God, which comes to it by baptism, at the same time as its entry into the problems of the world in the name of the Gospel of God.

[154]"The sense of Pius XI's thinking will be found in the speech of April 19, 1931, in which everything is explained in this way: on the one hand, "the Church alone received from God the mandate and the mission to intervene in the world" for Salvation and, on the other hand, "the catholic hierarchy alone is authorized to give a mandate and directives" for this purpose of Salvation. Pius XII, bothered by the term participation, which could lead to a belief that lay people took part in the power, preferred the term cooperation. All of these texts will be found in *Pie XI, l'Action catholique*, coll. "Tr. fr. des documents pontificaux, 1922-1932 par la Documentation catholique," Bonne Presse, Paris, 1933. Let us quote this commentary, which seems to reflect very well the common spirit, by P. Pollet, O.P., *L'Action Catholique à la lumiére de la théologie thomiste*, Gembloux, 1937: "The unique and same mandate received by the Apostles has passed by divine right to the hierarchy and has been retained by it as its exclusive property, until the Sovereign Pontiff, inspired by the Spirit, has taken the initiative to transmit it to the laity under form of a communication or delegation of power. By virtue of this mandate . . ., the apostolate of the laity, private as it was, becomes public or official, in other words, endowed and vested with a mandate, an authority and a force, all of which are divine. Henceforth the laity . . . act for the benefit of the hierarchy"; in this way, the mandate is "the formal establishment of the A. C." (31-33). The same view is found in the classic work on the subject by P. Tiberghien, *L'Action catholique*, ed. Fides, Montreal, 1947, 60; see also L. Civardi, *Manuel d'Action catholique*, ed. Lethielleux, Paris, 1934 who writes: "The hierarchy has drawn up the plans, the workers of 'Action catholique' work to execute these plans under the direction and supervision of their technical directors" (221).

to the whole Christian community, taking into account charisms and functions. In the face of the splits and divisions with which Christians live, this difficult question of the reuniting of visible *communion* among communities makes up an essential chapter of an ecclesiology of *communion*. That is why it is necessary to treat it fully. It is a question of something entirely different than a simple digression. The realism of the state of *communion* and the situation of the Church as it exists, considering the command of God, is being described here.

G. *The local Church, a minister of unity*

1. The responsibility of the local Church in regards to the problem of division can be summed up in this way: to act in such a way that what the Spirit gives it and what it proclaims at the Eucharistic celebration become in all truth imbedded in its being and in its action. In other words, it must live in the truth of its Eucharist and for this truth. Let it be what it receives, as Augustine would say. And since what it receives is the Body of reconciliation, of universal *koinonia,* of *catholica,* it has to live with "the concern of all the Churches," let us understand by this "communion of all the baptized" in the grace of the Spirit of the Risen One. This concern should be such that it belongs to its prayer, determines certain of its undertakings and even dwells in its most decisive pastoral options. Because if, by virtue of the division, the "universality" of the Church of God is gravely wounded, it is the Church itself—as local Church and in what makes up its profound being—which is affected, in a grave way. The *ut sint unum* of the Johannine Gospel does not in any way express the desire *ad bene esse.* It expresses a wish of Christ about the nature of his People.

The drama of division affects the status of *catholica,* communion of Churches, even as far as its mission is concerned. All of the baptized, all called by the Spirit of God who has marked them with his seal and whose grace without any doubt is at work in them, do not give the visible witness of reconciliation which the Johannine Gospel puts at the heart of Jesus' prayer. Christians are not as a whole the Church that God wishes, the one which glorifies the Father. The design of God is in this way being scoffed at. The disciples of Christ form *some* communities or *some* Churches, but they do not form *one Church of churches.*

Therefore, it is impossible for a bishop who has charge of a community which is the Church existing in a particular place, culture and time, not to be deeply concerned about unity. This is not something that is an accessory to his mission. It belongs to his responsibility for the Church of God *in this place.* When he celebrates the Eucharist with his people, he cannot forget the other baptized people, members of the Body of Christ by their baptism, unable to shout the *Amen* which seals his anaphora. Through the Spirit he gives his people the mystery of the Body of reconciliation, without being able to make all the members of this Body an integral part of this gift. The scandal is still greater when the neighboring group also celebrates a true Eucharist, when, for example, the catholic *Amen* and the orthodox *Amen* are superimposed without being united. The entire community must bear and live this concern with the bishop.

2. As far as what concerns its proper identity, a local Church is first of all supposed to be seen so that the other local Churches—gathered together for a true Eucharist—can *recognize* themselves in it. And that implies the bishop (and his *presbyterium*) as much as the community.

a. This theme of *re-cognition* seems essential to us. It is one of the principal categories of an ecclesiology of *communion*. By *re-cognition* is understood, in this context, the attitude by which a Church discerns within the differences of expressions or rites and within the plurality of traditions the evangelical faith and practice which are proper to it. In other words, within the difference of words and forms, the multiplicity of responses required by the extreme variability of situations, even the variety of readings and interpretations, it perceives the same fidelity to the one and same Revelation. The story of Cyril of Alexandria and of John of Antioch is well known.[155] In our day, in the midst of the Catholic Churches, it is this process which permits a Parisian to *re-cognize* his won Eucharist in the Sunday celebration of a Maronite community, for a parishioner from Warsaw to *re-cognize* his own evangelical conviction in the preaching in a basic Brazilian community, for an adult to *re-cognize* his own faith in the catechesis of his young child. The search for unity wishes that this same *recognition* might be accomplished equally on both sides of the confessional frontiers.

For that to be possible, it is required that each local Church—in *communion* with the bishop and the faithful people who make it up—be seen as extremely clear about the content of its faith and the sense which its attachment to apostolic Tradition gives to it. It is not the Church of such or such a theology, but the Church of a faith which is able to feel itself more in sympathy with a certain theology or a certain practice than with any other. The ecumenical experience proves that this fine distinction is of capital importance. If the Churches do not show very plainly their true face as far as the faith is concerned, a dialog among Christian communities will never be able to be initiated. It will be written on sand.

---

[155]See E. Lanne, "Pluralisme et unité: possibilité d'une diversité de typologie dans une même adhésion ecclésiale," *Istina* 14, 1969, 171–190; Id., "Le comportement de saint Basile et ses exigences pour le rétablissement de la communion," *Nicolaus* 5, 1982, 303–313.

What enters into play here especially is the margin of freedom and initiative which each local Church has within ecclesial *communion*. In order to avoid any ambiguity, let us remember that we are talking about local Churches in communion with the great apostolic Tradition. We consider them in agreement with Christian groups cut off from this communion whom they are close to. But situations oblige some of these local Churches to make courageous decisions, sometimes leading them to break with ways of doing things which other local Churches preserve, or to set up new types of behavior. It must seem clear then—it belongs to the bishop to be concerned about it—that this evolution is accomplished within traditional faith and for it, in order to correspond better to its needs.

We will give only two examples of this, taken from two situations in the Catholic Church today. Several local Churches are constrained, should we say, because of the severe crisis of priestly vocations in them, to multiply the "Sunday gatherings without a priest," especially in rural areas. But it seems essential to us—it happens that it is neglected—that the bishop clearly indicate what is at stake here and work hard to avoid false interpretations of this pastoral modification, rather delicate for Catholic tradition. It is extremely grave to consider these gatherings as "a Mass without a priest" (*sic*), to describe them as "a Eucharist without the words of consecration and the canon" (*sic*), or to see in it "the first crack in the traditional Catholic vision" (*sic*). It is necessary, therefore, that every other local Catholic Church be able, in spite of the absence of an ordained minister, *to re-cognize* in this Sunday worship—which is not a Eucharist although it is done in a Eucharistic reference—a worship in the Catholic tradition, expressing as it can, according to the circumstances, the intention of the Lord's Day. But it is also necessary that the other Christian communities, which are not Catholic, be able *to re-cognize* in this worship service an authentic catholic celebration, not "the proof that the changing times contest the Catholic intransigence concerning the nature of ministry" (*sic*). That requires, evidently, that, on the one hand, the limit of this worship and its tending towards the celebration of the Memorial of the Lord be shown, and, on the other hand, that there be no question about its link with the bishop and its communion with all the Sunday Eucharists (or "the gatherings without a priest") of the diocese.

The other example, better known, is that of catechesis. It is important to mention it, because the stakes here are grave. No one will deny that the teaching of the faith could not be done in the same way for all ages of life and for all cultures. It calls for a broad variety of methods and pedagogies. It accepts also a progress which is done in stages. To refuse it would be senseless. It is equally evident that in our Western world the proceedings in Antioch, more attentive to the singular humanity of Jesus and to its historical rooting, has at the outset more of an impact than the proceedings in Alexandria.

It is important, nevertheless—and again it is a very serious responsibility of the bishop in regard to unity—that the local Church know that adaptations in the catechism do not question its baptismal faith, in particular its conviction that Jesus is the Son of God and the only Savior. The other forms of teaching and proclaiming the Word, in which the catechism is explained, have to show that this does not, in any way, make the faith relative, and is only looking for the most suitable way to transmit it. This is the business of every local Church. In the osmosis of functions and charisms, it must put the transmission of the faith in concert with the needs and mental habits of its milieu, its culture, and its time. But it is necessary that the neighboring Church always be able *to re-cognize* in it its own faith, in such a way that their Eucharisitc *Amen* have the same content.

These are only two examples. Others could be added, just as significant—such as setting up new ecclesial lay services, establishing new types of religious life—which would support our affirmation. The primary responsibility of the bishop and his Church for unity is *ad intra*: to see that in the necessary evolution of the life of this Church the other local Churches always be able *to re-cognize* their faith and that the other Christian communities are not able to have the impression that it is playing tricks with Catholic communion. What is at stake here is truth.

b. This *re-cognition* must, in the *ad intra* life of the local Church, be allied with a sympathetic look on Christian groups cut off from communion with it and to a welcoming of their criticisms. One of the graces of our century will have been the break, at least official, with an ecclesial self-sufficiency enclosing each Christian confession in its good conscience and preventing it from recognizing its errors and its limitations. What is worthwhile on the universal level is worthwhile also on the local level.

Instinctive types of behavior exist, rooted in centuries filled with aggressiveness, suspicion, rancor, memories, which make reciprocal confidence impossible, without which unity becomes a mere dream. The Christian sister or brother—even belonging to the lowest Protestant congregation—would never be considered by a Catholic as an enemy, even if in the past his religious family persecuted the Catholic Church (which has known undoubtedly, on the spot vigorous reprisals!). Reproaches (often well-founded) by others, the expression of their annoyance in the face of certain attitudes or practices must be seen today more as proceedings of *fraternal correction* than as hateful oppressions.

A local Church which desires the unity of all baptized persons and is prepared to live it must accept correcting in itself, without questioning its fidelity to the great Tradition, what wounds other Christians. Unity will not come about without both sides giving proof of the sincerity of their search for fraternal understanding. But there is a whole network of epidermal behavior, without a profound link to the faith, which often seems in the eyes of others if not as a provocation at least as the proof that a deaf ear is being turned to their wishes, based not on a bitter claim but on a sincere love of the gospel. When fidelity to Catholic communion is not questioned, the search for unity must sometimes lead to magnanimity, even if this turns out to be costly. It is up to the bishop to explain the situation clearly to his people, and up to the people to seek seriously to understand. The local Church has in this case a responsibility that it sometimes forgets but which experience reveals as very important for unity. And when it cannot respond to a desire, which often makes itself insistent, of other Christians in its area, it has the duty to explain its reasons clearly. All we have to do is think of the thorny problem of Eucharistic hospitality and the question of mixed marriages.

c. This need calls for a more fundamental and more radical attitude, compromising every local Church. Unity can be realized and even the most official decisions can take effect concretely only if in each local Church there exists a climate which shows a desire and a hope. And it comes above all from community prayer nourished by preaching.

Still it is important to recall again the ultimate intention of this prayer, the authentic goal of this hope. They are doxological. It is a question of the full realization of the design of God and through it of the glory of the Father. It is necessary, as we said, that all of those who have been baptized become the Church which God wills. The end which ecumenism proposes is not first of all pragmatic. It is not to do everything in order to be able to involve together in a "more efficacious" regrouping energies and means. It is to be faithful to the will of the Father, living in this way in the logic of grace. The ecclesial body, which the Spirit causes to be born from the Body of reconciliation, has to become its reconciled body in communion in the same means of grace, in the same mission, in the same destiny. And since it is the Eucharist which manifests the local gathering being struck by the reality of "universal" communion, all Christian communities present on the same territory have to become one single Eucharistic gathering, capable of singing truly, in a unanimous way, a single *Amen,* to the glory of the Father.

This *Amen* makes demands. It is not equivalent to the pure and simple will to give each other a kiss of peace, at the price of minimal concessions, while retaining one's own identity. A like mosaic, joined by goodwill alone, would contain a subterfuge far from the unity which God wishes. The kiss of Eucharistic peace is true only if it is that of Christians *re-cognizing* each other as brothers or sisters because they find in each other the same essential characteristics. It is not a kiss of cousins or of relatives. The ecumenical task consists to give to each other mutually these fraternal characteristics, without cheating, by listening to Revelation. It passes through the local Church especially for this reason.

It is on the local level, in fact, that confrontation between Christians of different confessions takes place; it is there that unity will be reestablished. But contacts out in the field, so to speak, the experience of a climate of evangelical friendship, sometimes common involvement for common causes are a source of mutual understanding. A local Church working towards unity owes it to itself to be as deeply acquainted as possible with the faith of other Christian communities which are located in its area. It would be disastrous for the ecumenical cause if it were questioned about this topic and it had nothing to say. That would be an unquestionable sign that it is unfaithful to its mission. The truth of its Eucharist obliges it to do everything it can for the "gathering together again in unity the dispersed children of God."

3. We have seen up to this point only the *ad intra* behavior of a local Church which takes the call to unity seriously which the Spirit of Christ continually puts in the hearts and minds of his People. But the same call compels it to an *ad extra* attitude marked by the preoccupation with the full accomplishment of God's design.

a. An element which has been neglected for a long time concerning agreement among Christians is the humble attitude which refuses absolutes and which expresses the need to *re-cognize* in others authentic evangelical values. The levels where that is imposed today are numerous. And the *sensus fidelium* has instinctively broken through them. Let us think, for example, about the growing enthusiasm of numerous fervent Catholics, disappointed by the barrenness of Western communities during the last decades, as far as prayer and the spirit of orthodox spirituality are concerned. These are things in which they find a source of evangelical life which, without any doubt, is offered to them by the Spirit of God. This must be admitted and expressed, without being too afraid that that will question the attachment of some faithful to their own confessional identity. On another level, in Western context, we must not hesitate to confess that several of the important points of liturgical restoration established since Vatican II are in response to certain requests for orthodoxy and Reform.[156] And it is clear that, certainly at the price of a regrettable hardening, this liturgical restoration has maintained a worship for the Word of God and a will for constant contact with Scripture which have taken some

---

[156]See J.-M. R. Tillard, "La réforme liturgique et le rapprochement des Églises," *Liturgia opera divina e umana, studi sulla riforma liturgica offerti a S.E. Mons. Annibale Bugnini*, coll. "BEL," Subsidia 26, Rome, 1982, 215-240.

of the color out of Catholic ways and customs, in favor of biblical renewal. The local Church—bishop and faithful people, each in their own place—serves unity when it admits not only that there are "in others (confessions)" authentic evangelical values but even that thanks to "these others" it renews itself in these values. There is an ecumenism of the Holy Spirit creating spiritual bonds well before Christians happen to accept them mutually. He transcends in this way their sin.

b. It is necessary to recall, as we prolong this vision, a principal often put forward in the counsels of Churches but which has usually annoyed local Catholic Churches. The preparation for unity demands that, while avoiding every ambiguity and especially by not giving false hopes that the goal will be achieved, we do together already all that can be done together.

It is hardly remembered anymore that this is what sanctioned the appointment, as early as 1920, of the ecumenical patriarchate of Constantinople in its famous encyclical letter.[157] The idea is not, therefore, as was wrongly stated, "typically Protestant." The encyclical—which even thinks about a collaboration in the teaching of theology and the formation of ministers—wishes that in everything which bears on the Christian understanding of human life, believers ("the churches") will act together, speak together, argue together, and build together. It is a question of common fidelity to the will of God about the world. If dogmatic or doctrinal differences prevent a common Eucharist, if even they falsify or cause ambiguity in a proclamation in common about the faith, they do not prevent, however, that in the field (in the same city or the same area) the different Christian confessions put up a common front for action and witness. Everything which destoys what is human harms the design of God: injustice, seeds of war, a decay of morals. More radically still, whatever aims at erasing the Name of God and respect for transcendence from the human conscience questions the Salvation of the world. This is what happens when aggressive ideologies reign by force, often bringing back hypocritical faces right into our post-Christian societies. The local Church could not distance itself from all the initiatives which aim at restoring to humanity the sense of God and the sense of its own dignity. And then, by this *praxis,* it contributes to giving unity a firm basis: that of a common and generous love for the God and Father of the Lord Jesus Christ.

4. Such is the breadth of services and ministries in the Church of God. They all spring forth from *communion* and, since *communion* is its nature, the Church is in fact manufactured from the fabric of these ministries, from the time of Christ and the apostles. They constitute the face

[157]This text will be found, as an appendix, in W. A. Visser't Hooft, "The Genesis and Formation of the World Council of Churches," Geneva, 1982, 94–97.

of *Agape* for its *koinonia*. Nothing escapes this universal concern for services and ministries, not even the division of Christians. Each local Church knows that it cannot, *before God,* enclose itself in its own needs: it must be of service to visible unity. But in this way is it not the servant of the design of God, active in Salvation?

II. The Church of God, Minister of Salvation

More and more Christians are in agreement on seeing a sign of Salvation in the Church of God. In return, the understanding of its role in Salvation remains one of the points of friction among Christians of the Reformation and those of Catholic tradition. While the "old Churches" do not hesitate to affirm that the Church is the agent—"sign and instrument," *sacramentum*—of Salvation which it is the beneficiary of, communities which have sprung up from the Reformation prefer to avoid every formula which could conceal the great affirmation of the faith: Salvation comes from God alone.

In the past, controversy has been centered especially on the link between the reality of the Church of God and the question of justification by faith. But today serious and credible studies have shown how much our views on this last subject were closer than we had thought during the heat of quarrels.[158] It is possible to approach the problem from a new angle. The question, therefore, can be asked in this way: Is the Church entirely outside the work of Salvation? Is it only the fruit of it? In the course of our study on the ministry, we can give the question an irenic answer. The true minister of Salvation is the Church, not the ministers.

A. The humanity of the Church in Salvation

1. GRATUITOUSNESS OF SALVATION AND ACCEPTANCE OF FREEDOM

It is evident that the ecclesiological debate concerning the instrumentality of the Church depends on a problem infinitely broader: the relationship between Salvation and human freedom. That the "yes" of faith, which indicates a free acceptance of the design of God and expresses basing one's entire life on the Word of the Covenant, is required, no one has ever doubted it. Even more so, theologies of the Reformation, reacting against a Christianity which was too "social" and insufficiently "per-

---

[158]See Vincenz Pfnür, "Beyond an Old Polemic: Sola fide, opus operatum," *Origins* 8, 1979, 478–480; Id., *Einig in der Rechfertigungslehre der Confessio Augustana (1530) und die Stellungnahme der katholische kontroverstheologie zwischen 1530 und 1535*, Wiesbaden, 1970; O. H. Pesch, *Die Theologie der Rechtfertigung bei Martin Luther und Thomas von Aquin*, Mayence, 1967. See also the Lutheran-Catholic document of the U.S.A.

sonal," have often given this "yes" a capital importance.[159] Therefore, it is admitted by all of the traditions that the absolute gratuitousness of Salvation is in no way equivalent to an aggression on the part of God. It is necessary at least that the human person accept being taken hold of by the power of the *Agape*.

Since the beginning, besides, this is the way Fathers and theologians have interpreted the usual finale of the great kerygmas in the Acts of the Apostles: "You must repent" (Acts 2:38; 3:19, 26; 5:31; 17:30; 26:20). There is a recognition that these speeches are articulated and structured around two affirmations. The first concerns the power of God in the work of Jesus Christ: "It is through him that forgiveness of your sins is proclaimed; through him justification from all sins which the Law of Moses was unable to justify is offered to every believer" (13:38, kerygma of Paul; cf. 15:11); it is to him that all the prophets bear this witness: "that all who believe in Jesus will have their sins forgiven through his name" (10:43, kerygma of Peter). The second is a call for freedom: "I started preaching, first to the people of Damascus, then to those of Jerusalem and all the countryside of Judea, and also to the pagans, urging them to repent and turn to God, proving their change of heart by their deeds" (26:20, speech by Paul); "now you must repent and turn to God, so that your sins may be wiped out" (3:19, kerygma of Peter).[a] Exegetes underline the relationship of these two emphases in Acts with the evangelical tradition of Luke which, if it affirms vigorously—especially in chapter fifteen—the gratuitousness of divine mercy, specifies besides: "I have come . . . to call sinners to repentance" (Luke 5:32), "unless you repent you will all perish" (13:3).

Reading the most central portions of the controversial dossier of the Reformation and the Counter-Reformation causes us to perceive, on this basis, a point which has been specified thanks to the ecumenical dialog. Christian traditions are in agreement concerning the certainty that Salvation comes from the absolute initiative of God. They all admit that in the person of Jesus Christ human freedom as such has been assumed. They all affirm that "my" Salvation comes from this assumption of "my" freedom into that of Jesus. But some see this Salvation *first of all* as a finding of grace: you are liberated. Others, on the contrary, see it *first of all*

---

[159]The discussions which arose with groups who admit only the baptism of *believers* and raised again by the Lima document (BEM) show that for them this "yes" of *personal* faith plays a role on this essential point that without it there is neither baptism properly speaking nor even a Christian act preparing for baptism. See the beautiful book by J. J. von Allmen, *Pastorale du baptême*, Paris, 1978 (written by a Protestant theologian) and the classic work by O. Cullmann, *Le Baptême des enfants et la doctrine biblique du baptême*, Neuchâtel-Paris, 1948. For older sources, see A. Booth, *Pedabaptism Examined*, London, 1829; J. Gill, *Infant Baptism: a Part and Pillar of Popery*, New York, 1851. Documents in James Leo Garrett, "The Theology of Baptism: a Southern Baptist View," *Southwestern Journal of Theology* 18, 1986, 65–72.

as a re-creation of the freedom given back its true dignity and henceforth capable of living in Covenant with God, according to his responsibility as the image of God. The problem is not the gratuitousness of Salvation but its nature.

The oldest traditions emphasize Salvation as new life led by the Spirit *given* at baptism. Depending on the New Testament, where moral teachings hold a prominent place, they believe themselves forced to deduce from that that for the apostolic writings the contemporaneousness of the course of God and the attitude of man, the fitting in of the divine offer and the conversion which characterizes entrance into the New Covenant, must be locked in the totality of existence. There is according to these texts, authentic *Christianity* only if, through the Spirit, the believer *lives "converted,"* in other words in a *state of metanoia,* therefore, spiritually "turned towards God" (1 Thess 1:9; Gal 4:8-10; Rom 6:12-19; etc.). Certainly, radically, Salvation is not the work of personal freedom. It comes only from God by the grace of the Spirit. However, it is not accomplished *without freedom.* The Covenant between God and man, which faith in the gospel opens up sealed by baptism, must be shown off and made explicit throughout one's existence. This existence is not only the action of graces for forgiveness received. It is *also* obedience to the demand of which the Sermon on the Mount (Matt 5:1-7:27), orchestrated by the totality of pareneses of New Testament literature, expresses the essential lines. And this obedience has nothing juridical about it. It accomplishes the actualization of Salvation, in other words, putting to work the recreation of freedom by the power of the Spirit. It is in no way the cause of Salvation, it is, however, demanded as a *consequence and sign* of belonging to the New Covenant (Jer 31:31-34). To be saved is not only to be forgiven.[b]

Besides, in the New Covenant the structure of the Old Covenant is not suppressed. It is "accomplished" in it. The accomplishment does not mean that you put an end to what preceded it. It implies, we have seen, that what prepared the Event of Jesus Christ is arriving at an end. If at his Passover the Promises reach their "accomplishment," it follows that the Covenant, with what it includes not only of mercy and forgiveness on the part of God but also of responsibility on the part of the People, reaches its fullness. In the Covenant, the People, and in that People each believer, is not only a beneficiary of forgiveness. He is *also* the one who lives Salvation by becoming the authentic *servant* of God for the realization of the divine design over humanity. He does it in proportion whereby, by his behavior, he is truly "light of the world" and "salt of the earth" (Matt 5:13-16), a witness of Christ up against the hatred in the world, letting himself be led by the Spirit into the *martyria* of Jesus (John 15:18-27), an imitator of the Lord (Col 1:24; 1 Cor 6:20; 2 Cor 4:10). This behavior implies freedom. Restored—through forgiveness and the gift of the

Spirit—the image of God can be what the Creator wanted it to be, his member. That is his Salvation.ᶜ

This nature of Salvation, completely a work of the power of God transcending human forces and perhaps assuming them, explains the passage from the indicative to the imperative, from the declaration of Salvation to the requirement of the attitude to be adopted, which is stated in most of the moral texts of the New Testament. The ethical demands are not prerequisites for Salvation. However, they are an element of it. They are called by the new quality that the grace of the Spirit confers on the individual. They do not constitute the price (meritorious) to be paid for *having Salvation*. Yet they indicate the attitude to be embraced in order *to live in the logic* of Salvation. The nuance—which our Western mentality has a difficult time translating but which Semitic thought perceives instinctively—is of capital importance.

For want of understanding this distinction, Catholic polemists have often falsified the intuition of the New Testament. They have, for example, forgotten that if the Letter to the Colossians asks that the faithful "lead a life worthy of the Lord and which is pleasing to him in everything, producing all kinds of good works (*en panti ergo agatho karpophorountes*) and growing in the knowledge of God" (Col 1:10), it is because God "has taken us out of the power of darkness and created a place for us in the Kingdom of the Son that he loves, and in him we gain our freedom, the forgiveness of our sins" (1:13-14). The implicit reasoning of this text— and others like Rom 6:20-23; 1 Cor 6:12-20; Eph 4:22-24; 5:8, 11; Col 3:1-15; Jas 2:14, 26; 1 Pet 2:21-25; 1 John 3:17-20; 4:20—could be translated by the following imperative: *since you are* in the Salvation which comes from Christ *do* the works of Christ. And it could be explained in this way: *since you are* re-created by the Spirit of Christ, *do* the acts of a new creature; if not your Salvation will be only theoretical and abstract. Salvation does *not come* from an action of the believer but it *includes* it.

Perhaps it should be remembered that this behavior—which we would qualify as epiphanic (of the work of grace)—is placed in the prolonging of a vision which was outlined in the Old Covenant. When Deuteronomy prescribes freeing the slave, it explains: "Remember that you were a slave in the land of Egypt and that Yahweh your God redeemed you; that is why I lay this charge on you today" (Deut 15:12, 15). The same reason is given for what has reference to the protection of the weak: right of the stranger and the widow, tenderness for the orphan (Deut 24:17, 22). The action of the faithful Israelite becomes a "memorial," a repercussion, an "epiphany" of what the grace of God has accomplished for him.[160] Evi-

---

[160]This is shown very well by Jean L'Hour, *La Morale de l'Alliance,* coll. "Cahiers de la Revue biblique," 5, Paris, 1966, especially 19-20, 42-51. The author emphasizes first of all forcefully

dently worship is enclosed in the same perspective. Salvation is a gift received and for that reason a gift radiated.

Mentioning the acceptance of the kerygma, as with most exegetes, we were talking about an initial "yes." It would be more correct to speak of the first declaration of the "yes" which is going to take hold of the entire Christian life. Because in that first instant it is this totality of Christian life which finds itself integrally involved, as the entire existence is at that moment of the "yes" which the married couple declare to each other on their wedding day. What is at stake here is one word that commits one's life, an acceptance for a whole lifetime, hence, a "yes" whose truth will be put into practice and put to the test daily in the rough struggle of fidelity (1 Cor 9:24-27).

It could happen—and Paul recalls it for the believers in Corinth in a solemn and Eucharistic context (1 Cor 11:29, 34)—that during the course of this struggle human fidelity is overcome. Within the drama of such a defeat, the initial human "yes" would be dissolved. The act of baptism was to be, according to the imagery used in the Letter to the Philippians, the beginning of a race (Phil 3:12-16 cf. 1 Cor 9:26, 27) "trying to capture the prize for which Christ Jesus captured me." In this race where nevertheless the sufficient and faithful grace of God carried him along, the believer has grown weak. The fact is that God cannot force his royal creature to love him and to serve him faithfully. Respect for human responsibility is an element of Salvation. On this mystery of the relationship between the *Agape* of God and freedom human reason stumbles. If freedom was violated, fidelity (of a slave) would have no purpose; if sinful man remained the master of his destiny, God would no longer be *Agape*. It is known that in order to solve this question several will have only one recourse: the theology of predestination.

2. The relationship between Savior and the saved

In union with this biblical understanding of the Covenant of God *Agape* and the "royal creature" (restored and recreated in Christ), it is fitting to examine carefully once again two of the images which Scripture uses to express the reality of the Church and which we have studied. One, proper to the Pauline block, is that of the "Body-of-which-Christ-is-the-Head." The other, more current, takes up an Old Testament theme by bringing

"the absolute precedence of the benefits of Yahweh" and the radical unilateral aspect of the initiative over which Israel has no control" (13–14), because "it is not Israel who discovered Yahweh or procured him for themselves as God; it is Yahweh who was the first to descend towards Israel" (15). Therefore, there is no due whatsoever for Israel and everything is pure grace. But the author then shows how, by the sole fact that he establishes the covenant and requires a response from Israel, Yahweh "promotes Israel as a moral grandeur" (20). He writes: "The chosen people will understand gradually that its present life is more than the static product, acquired once and for all, of a past event, it is this event continued but this time with the cooperation of Israel" (42).

it up-to-date, that of the Spouse of Christ. Among the numerous images in the New Testament, there are those which the great Tradition gives a privileged place to in its liturgical life, without doubt because it finds them the most appropriate ones to express the authentic relationship which the Spirit establishes between the person of the Savior and the multitude of the saved.

a. *The active Body by virtue of the Head.* It is clear that in the Pauline vision of the Body of Christ, the Head—Christ Jesus—is at this transcendent point where everything comes from it and depends on it: Salvation is new life and life has its basis in the Head. This is the source and center, in the way in which (according to Hippocratic medicine to which the letters to the Ephesians and to the Colossians seem to adhere) the human body receives from the head the influx from the nerves, the great sensory indications which are necessary to it. Thinking, will, essential sensible perceptions (sight, hearing, smell, taste) are, for this Greek wisdom, in the head. We have already pointed this out.

To say that Christ is Head of the Church, therefore, goes back to recognizing him, without any shades of meaning, as the one without whom or outside of whom there would be no Church, simply because humanity (with all its richness) could never by itself become Church. Church depends completely on what God and his Spirit have accomplished and given in Jesus Christ. A wholesome reading of the scriptural dossier on the Body of Christ excludes any stale smell of Pelagianism. Believers find Salvation only by being grafted on the Body of Christ. And this Body exists only by the Spirit whose mastery the Lord Jesus received at his Death and Resurrection (Acts 2:32-33; Eph 4:4). Even the most noble human merits which have been accumulated and added up could never set off the spark which gives life to the Church. This life can come only from the Head which God himself has "constituted" in his Son the Lord Jesus Christ, filled with the Spirit.

Nevertheless, if there is a Head there is a Body. A head without a body would be as delusive as a body without a head. Head and body call for one another. Since Pentecost, Christ is unthinkable without his Body. Because if at the Resurrection God makes him Christ and Lord (Acts 2:36), this Lordship must have an object. It is none other than the community of those men and women who freely welcome the gospel, "become partners with" the group of first beneficiaries of the gift of the Spirit (Acts 2:38-41, to be linked to 2:4). But the ecclesial Body is the form which the Spirit gives to this community. It is not simply a building up of disciples who have only a conviction in common. It is *communion of communion* in the real possession of one and the same life, which has come from life by one and the same Spirit. We know that this *koinonia* has two dimensions. What is in the Head passes into the Body, since the "justice" of

payment for the fall until the final glorification (Rom 8:1-4; 3:21-26; Cor 15:50-53). Elsewhere all the members together have a share in this same reality of "justification" and going forward towards "the transfiguration of the body of misery which will take on the form of his glorified Body" (Phil 3:21). Seen in these two dimensions this *communion* is so narrow and interior that, according to the expression of the exegete J.A.T. Robinson, the Church is as much the Body of Christ as the Eucharistic bread, although under a different mode.[161] This identification designates its most profound being.

Joined to the Head in this way, the Body is not passive. Animated by the Spirit of Christ, it produces acts which are *in* him and *through* him acts of the Lord. The Epistle to the Romans knows this truth well since it makes no explicit allusion to the Body of Christ (Rom 8:10-13). This can be read also running through several passages of other Pauline letters: "I have been crucified with Christ, and I live now not with my own life but with the life of Christ who lives in me" (Gal 2:20; cf. 6:14, 17); "always, wherever we may be, we carry with us in our body the death of Jesus, so that the life of Jesus, too, may always be seen in our body" (2 Cor 4:10). But sometimes the link with the theme of Body of Christ becomes explicit. The realism of the following text has been underlined many times: "Your bodies are members of Christ; do you think I can take parts of Christ's body and join them to the body of a prostitute? Never" (1 Cor 6:15). The Letter to the Colossians causes Paul to say: "I find joy in the sufferings I endure for you, for I complete in my flesh what is lacking in the sufferings of Christ for his Body, the Church" (Col 1:24). At the outset it chains to the hardships of the ministry the charge to realize the coming of the Word (1:25-29). Whoever its author may be, this text is clearly of Pauline inspiration.

One does not add anything to the sense of agreement by concluding from the Pauline dossier that acts of ministry—"ambassador for Christ" (2 Cor 5:20), "a responsibility confided" (1 Cor 9:17)—and the totality of ecclesial activities which contribute to the radiating of the gospel constitute the involvement of the Body of Christ for the manifestation, extension, and actualization of Salvation acquired by the Head. The Church is active in Salvation. Alone, it is true, Johannine literature, in another context, will say that the disciples are sent *as* the Son has been sent (John 17:18), and the Greek conjunction *kathôs* which we translate by *like* evokes a link both with independence and similarity.[162] But in his appreciation

---

[161]J. A. T. Robinson, *The Body, a Study of Pauline Theology*, 85–86.

[162]The difference already encountered between *hôs* and *kathôs*, which the French translates by "comme," is important here. Because usually *hôs* signifies a resemblance founded on imitation, an external resemblance, while *kathôs* signifies the resemblance which comes from an affinity of causality or of origin between the two elements in question.

of the apostolic function—his and that of the others (1 Cor 3:5-15)—
Paul himself is convinced of the essential role which the Church plays in
the diffusion of Salvation.

It is especially necessary, in this framework, to take seriously a major
affirmation in the Letter to the Romans whose impact cannot be mini-
mized: "How can they believe without first having heard, and how can
they hear unless they get a preacher? . . . so faith comes from what is
preached, and what is preached comes from the Word of Christ" (Rom
10:14, 17). Because he knows that he is a "fellow-worker with Christ
Jesus" (2 Cor 6:1), "a minister of the Gospel of God" (Rom 15:16), "a
priest of Christ Jesus to the pagans" (Rom 15:16), "responsible for the
ministry of reconciliation" (2 Cor 5:18), Paul acknowledges:

> I think I have some reason to be proud of what I, in union with Christ
> Jesus, have been able to do for God. What I am presuming to speak
> of, of course, is only what Christ himself has done to win the allegiance
> of the pagans, using what I have said and done by the power of signs
> and wonders, by the power of the Holy Spirit . . . *I have procured the
> accomplishment of the Gospel of Christ* (Rom 15:17-19).

What would happen if Paul were unfaithful? And what does his cry
involve: "I should be punished if I did not preach it" (1 Cor 9:16)?

Certainly the power of God infinitely transcends his most wonderful
accomplishments. This power could have even done something else than
what it freely chose to accomplish in Christ Jesus. We know neither how
nor by what means. But one thing is certain: *within the present economy,*
the association of the Head and Body is such that it implies an active role
of the Church in the work of Salvation. The Church does not have the
initiative of Salvation (1 Cor 9:17). It is only a fruit of grace, a gift received.
However, the gift of benevolence is such that it makes of it—the apostolic group, ministers, the totality of the members of the local Churches—
the servant, the fellow worker (1 Cor 3:9), the propagator, the "missionary" of what it has been the beneficiary.

More than this, the diversity and solidarity of charisms (1 Cor 12:4-30)
do not exist solely in view of a "service" of the grace which would be
internal for the community of the saved, in a kind of secondary arrange-
ment of the gift of God. They also exist for the proclamation and expansion of Salvation, in other words that it may be a Salvation proposed to
the multitude. But this proclamation can be done *only* by the Church.
It accomplishes in this way a function which is not a luxury, an addition
which (within the present economy) one could do without. It is not simply
ad bene esse evangelisationis. It enters into the gift of Salvation, all the

while being the first beneficiary of it. We said that it is a *sacramentum* of it.[163]

b. *The faithful Wife and her association with the Husband.* A passage from the Letter to the Ephesians which has been discussed ties the theme of the Body of Christ to that of the Bride of Christ, contested today in several circles:

> The husband is head of his wife as Christ is head (*kephale*) of the Church, and *Savior of the Body*. But the Church submits to Christ. . . . Husbands love your wives as Christ loved the Church. He sacrificed himself for her by washing her in water with a form of words, so that when he took her to himself she would be glorious, with no speck or wrinkle or anything like that, but holy and faultless. In the same way husbands must *love their wives as their own body*. For a man to love his wife is for him to love himself. For no one ever hated his own flesh, but he feeds it and looks after it. *This is just what Christ does for the Church.* Are we not *members of his Body?* For this reason a man must leave his father and mother and be joined to his wife and *the two will become one body*. This mystery has many implications: but I am saying *it applies to Christ and his Church* (Eph 5:23-32).

We should take note that a text which is undoubtedly Pauline to which we have already referred applies the same symbolism to the work of the apostolic ministry: "I feel a divine jealousy for you because I have arranged for you to marry Christ so that I might give you away as a chaste virgin to this one Husband" (2 Cor 11:2). This is not as alien to Pauline theology as some writings have indicated, in the debates about the authenticity of the Letter to the Ephesians.[164] And while understanding the difficulties that it raises for contemporary thinking, as far as the vision of the woman it assumes, it could not, however, be forgotten. By it an important facet of the reality of the Church is expressed.

The symbiosis of themes of the Body and the Spouse, of the Head ("head" in the double sense of the word, part of the body and chief) and of the Husband is, in fact, remarkable. And Paul's verse which we quoted shows that in the spirit of it the relationship between ministry and the Church is easily inscribed there. In the Epistle to the Ephesians, the transcendency of Christ is firmly emphasized, orchestrated at will by Semite anthropology. He is both the Savior of the ecclesial Body and the Hus-

---

[163]We have depended only on the Pauline idea of Body of Christ. But in other perspectives Johannine theology (Gospel and epistles) shows the same affinity between Christ who gives everything and the community which diffuses this gift.

[164]An excellent reflection on our theme will be found in Daniel von Allmen, *La Famille de Dieu*, Fribourg, 1981, 238–256.

band possessing every initiative and total power. The beauty and holiness of the Wife come from him. In spite of this transcendence, he makes of her his own Body and both of them make up "only one single body," concretely his. Christ and Church are in this way in a complete union, a "communion" entirely beholden to the Husband (the Head) *and to him alone,* in which, however, the Bride (Body of the Husband) is not dissolved by losing her personality. It is entirely to the contrary, sanctified, made glorious, she is seen as called to play the role which is restored to her. The documents of the Old Testament which are read as a background (Hos 1:2; 4:11; Isa 1:21; 50:1; 54:1-7; 62:4-5; Jer 2:2; 3:1-12; Ezek 16:1-63; 23:1-48; Ps 45:1-18) go back to a fidelity of the Wife which is in no way a mere passivity. It is a question of Covenant!

In the Old Covenant, in fact, the People owe to Yahweh (their jealous God, according to Deut 4:24) a fidelity which is specifically that of a wife. This requirement is prolonged in the Church. The fidelity asked for is love, worship, but also a call to help the power placed in it bear fruit, to produce for him. In the account from Genesis to which Paul makes an explicit allusion in 2 Cor 11:2-3, the wife is the helpmate formed from the body of Adam (Gen 2:18-22). One deduces from that that in this way Israel is the helpmate of Yahweh, the Church the helpmate of Christ. And this helpmate transmits life.

Although the Letter to the Ephesians does not say so, one can, in fact, specify, by leaning on Pauline tradition, that in this helpmate the Church is mother, *Mater Ecclesia.* The Epistle to the Galatians (4:21-31) underlines, in this respect, that if ancient Jerusalem gives birth for slavery (4:24), the Jerusalem from on high "is our mother" (4:26) who gives birth in freedom, the messianic Jerusalem whose children are the Christians (4:31). Paul's reasoning is explicitly supported by the chapter of Deutero-Isaiah which sings about the fertility of the one whom Yahweh has chosen for a wife (Isa 54:1-10), because the drama that the sterility of the wife represents in the Old Covenant right up until the dawn of the New Testament (Luke 1:7, 25) is well-known (Gen 11:30; 25:21; 29:31; 30:23; Judg 13:2-3; 1 Sam 1:10; Isa 4:1; 2 Sam 6:23). The transition from the theme of Bride of Christ to that of *Mater Ecclesia* is in no way artificial.[165]

---

[165]Mgr. Cerfaux shows how even if in Gal 4:26 Paul does not speak explicitly of Church, the idea is there (*op. cit.,* 292–293). This theme has been studied especially by Karl Delahaye, *Ecclesia Mater chez les Pères des trois premiers siècles,* coll. "Unam sanctam," 46, Paris, 1964. See the suggestive study by E. Lanne, "Église sœur et Église mère dans le vocabulaire de l'Église ancienne," *Communio Sanctorum. Mélanges offerts à Jean-Jacques von Allmen,* Geneva, 1982, 86–97. Cyprian writes: "The spouse of Christ cannot suffer adultery, she is incorruptible and public. She knows only one home, she preserves with a chaste modesty the sanctity of one bed. She preserves us for God, she destines for the kingdom the sons to whom she has given birth. Whoever separates himself from the Church in order to form a union with an adulteress defrauds himself of the promises of the Church; whoever abandons the Church of Christ will not have

The perspective found in Revelation (19:5-10; 21:1-14) is different. What is found there, however, is the Covenant (21:3), the affirmation of the grandeur of the New Jerusalem (21:2, 10, 12), the splendor which comes to it from the glory of God (19:8; 21:11), the union with the Lamb who redeems and saves (cf. 4:9). The allusion to the good actions of the saints, which form the brilliantly white flax from which is woven the Bride's garment (19:7-8), again forbids an interpretation which is not attentive enough to the effort of the Church. In the splendor of the eternal wedding feast shines something which comes from God, from his fidelity. The letters to the seven Churches show that this fidelity counts: the Lord wants those who are victorious (2:7, 11, 17, 26; 3:5, 12, 21). They alone wear the white garment of triumph (3:5, 18; 7:9, 13-14; 22:14), the wedding garment of the Bride; they alone are inscribed in the book of life (3:5).

The theme of the Bride goes back in this way to the statement which Pauline theology in another context imposed about the Body of Christ. The Church is completely alien to the very act which acquires Salvation for humanity and to which it owes Redemption. Everything comes only from the Cross of the Lord, transformed by the Spirit at the Resurrection into the Tree of Life. The Church is not, however, alien to the preparation, manifestation and diffusion of this Salvation. Bride and Mother, she transmits what she receives. She preaches, baptizes, nourishes (by the means of grace which the Spirit deposits in her for this purpose) the children of God born of the faith and the sacrament. She preserves them in fidelity to their being and their mission by the action of the ministers (to whom the Spirit himself gives what this function requires), incites them to good works which are the epiphany in it of the riches of grace. In this way she "serves as a helpmate" to God for the propagation of salvation acquired by the Lord Jesus. The good actions of the "saints" (in other words, the sanctified) are her proper benefit all the while remaining the fruit in her of the gratuitousness of Salvation. She is the *sacramentum* of Salvation and as such integrated into her radiance in history.

---

access to the rewards of Christ. He is a stranger, a black sheep, an enemy. No one can have God for father if he does not have the Church for mother" (*De Unit.* 6f; cf. *Epist.* 74, 7, 2. The nuptial theme is found in *Epist.* 43, 4, 3; 52, 1, 3; 73, 19, 2). See also Augustine (*In Ev. Joan.* 7, 5; 8, 4; 9, 10; *In Ps.* 91, 8; 94, 4-6; *Epist.* 48, 2; *Sermo* 22, 10; 188, 4; *De catechizandis rudibus* 15, 23) where this theme is central. See P. Rinetti, "Sant' Agostino e l'Ecclesia Mater," *Augustinus Magister*, Paris, 1954, 827–834; and especially E. Schmitt, *Le mariage chrétien dans l'œuvre de saint Augustin, une théologie baptismale de la vie conjugale*, coll. "Études augustiniennes," Paris, 1983. In this book which seems to us to be of capital importance, the author shows the profound link that Augustine establishes between baptism and marriage on the basis of the link of these two sacraments with the mystery of the marriage of Christ and the Church. The fertility of the Church comes from what is consummated on "the nuptial bed of the wood of the Cross" (*De Symb. ad cat.* VI, 15; *In Ev. Joan.* 9, 10). And it is especially in baptism that the childbirth of the members of Christ is accomplished. The insistence of Calvin on the maternal aspect of the mystery of the Church is known.

The famous affirmation in the Epistle of James (2:17, 24), which we have avoided quoting until now on purpose, seems, in terms of this analysis, less cumbersome than was thought. Certainly, it aims immediately at the personal state of the believer and has no ecclesiological claim (Jas 2:14-26). It is inscribed, however, on the horizon which we have discovered. When the author writes: "It is by my good deeds that I will show you my faith" (2:18) and, recalling the case of Abraham, specifies: "Faith and deeds were working together; his faith became perfect by what he did" (2:22), he shows that between faith and deeds there is an osmosis, without, however, putting both of them on the same level.[166]

In the mystery of Salvation, therefore, humanity dominates nothing, is the source of nothing. It exists only completely contained in the power of God. At the root of what it accomplishes the Spirit is always recognized. But Scripture shows that, in this way, taken over by God, it is restored to its freedom, becoming capable of producing "deeds" which are those which God awaits from his royal creature. In the mystery of Salvation—perceived as much in its collective light as in its personal light—humanity (even restored) is never at the origin, and yet it is everywhere else. In the sacramental aspect of the Church is understood, awkwardly perhaps, designating this articulation of the "everywhere else" and of the "never at the origin," this taking hold of the omnipresence of humanity—respected because restored to its nature as image—by the transcendent and only "justifying" power of the Spirit of the Lord. Don't we recognize the economy (*oikonomia*) which presides over the incarnation itself?[167]

---

[166]See Peter Davids, *Commentary on James,* Grand Rapids, 1982, 47–51, 120–134, for whom, although he assumes the value and validity of the Law, Saint James "is not a legalist" and does not situate the essential aspect of Christianity in anything else than in giving oneself to God in Christ or by welcoming the grace of God. The dispositions which he inculcates do not cast aside Paul's teaching. The *erga* which Paul rejects are always, according to Davids, the *erga nomou,* not some moral precepts but rather some ritual payments which one would like "to add" to the work of Christ. With Saint James, *erga* always designate moral actions, especially acts of charity, of the kind which Saint Paul recommends. In short, according to James, one becomes Christian by a gratuitous action of God, to which one responds by repentance and faith. This involvement must be expressed by a moral conduct, fruit of a renewed life. The faith of Abraham has been brought to its full maturity by his actions. In a balanced teaching, James excludes neither faith nor works. See also Sophie Laws, *A Commentary on the Epistle of James,* London, 1980, p. 134: "The relation between Abraham's faith and his works is not properly one of consequence, demonstration or confirmation, all of which terms assume a measure of distinction between the two: for James they go together in a necessary unity, faith co-operated with his works, and by works faith was made complete."

[167]One can see how our position is not placed in that line, difficultly acceptable, where the Church would be considered "a prolonged incarnation." See Y. Congar, "Dogme christologique et ecclésiologique: vérités et limites d'un parallèle," *Sainte Église,* coll. "Unam sanctam," 44, Paris, 1963, 69–104.

B. The form of the sacramental aspect of the Church

Tradition, very early, became conscious of the status of the responsibility of the Church in the Covenant, establishing its function as minister or servant of Salvation. It expressed this in terms which showed some tension, because it felt that truth was fully respected only if two affirmations were united into one, which at first sight seem contradictory to each other: "Salvation comes only from God and from him alone" and yet "he restores to human freedom its authentic dignity and, therefore, its function." Thomas Aquinas tried this reconciliation of both affirmations with his idea, which limps somewhat, it is true, of merit *non de condigno sed de congruo,* in other words, having a relationship with Salvation, although it is not a question of a recompense in strict justice as if man "were paying for his Salvation," by becoming "the buyer."[168] The West, always tempted to choose, because of a concern for logic, between two components of the Christian mystery, which, at first glance, are difficult to reconcile (*aut . . . aut*) and because of a desire to relieve this tension (*et . . . et*), has shown that it is not as wise as the East. Several—following Pelagius' line—have opted for human "merits" seriously forgetting the absolute of divine transcendence; others—who will be inspired by important pages by Luther, but will interpret them without making any distinctions, have exalted this transcendence in a way which seems to reduce extremely the dignity of the "image of God."

1. The "evangelized" Church and who "evangelizes"

The Church is evangelized by God, but it is also the one who evangelizes for God. This is the first register, without doubt the most fundamental, where the tension we mentioned is being played out, because it is clear that the mystery of the Church is based on Revelation which God creates of himself. And this is, as the Fathers will say, *jam ab Abel justo.*[169]

Salvation comes from faith, and the distance between the Risen Lord and the *believer* who puts himself, "with his misery," "under the mantle of Christ's justice" is infinite, incommensurable. Man is saved only if he reclothes himself with the Justice gratuitously offered by God. This gratuitousness of Salvation is revealed and proposed by faith. And this process

---

[168]On this merit *de congruo* and *de condigno,* see especially in the *Summa theologica,* I-IIae, q. 114, art. 3. The *de congruo* is already found in a manuscript of the 12th century kept in the British Museum, Harley 957, fol. 179 *("digno non dignitate meriti sed dignitate congrui").* Thomas Aquinas emphasizes that this is not a justice in the usual sense. See Alister McGrath, *Justitia Dei,* t. I, Cambridge, 1986, 109–119.

[169]John Chrysostom, in a text which is too seldom quoted, writes: "What must be understood by the one Body [of Christ]? The faithful spread throughout the universe, those who were and those who will be, even those who lived before Christ and whose life was pure belong to this body" (*In Ephes.,* Hom. X, 1). For other texts, see Y. Congar, "Ecclesia ab Abel."

rests on the Word. Yet it is necessary to avoid a naive, fundamentalist vision of the transmission of the Word. God speaks. But how does he speak? The Word which gives rise to faith is the Word preached by a believing (confessing) community (Rom 10:14-18). And what is the content of this preaching?

The Koran falls from heaven into the intellect of the prophet Mohammed in its precise, literal form, as a "literary miracle," a direct transmission of the Book present in heaven from all eternity.[170] We have seen for a long time that the Bible is composed under the inspiration and direction of the Spirit of God through the holy People. It comes completely from God, whose initiative, lofty deeds and *mirabilia* it transmits. But it is also of the People whom the Spirit enlightens and who by its prophets, chroniclers, psalmists, lawmakers, and compilers perceives and expresses, the sense and the implications of the intervention—entirely gratuitous—of God. It is the Revelation of God through the soul of Israel. Also it is by recalling for us the era of its origins, by deploring its disappointments, by singing its Hope that the holy People will make its God known and the Good News of Salvation which he promises.

The same process is found in the New Covenant. The New Testament does not want to betray the *bruta facta*. It always transmits events as they are interpreted according to the apostolic faith. This faith—inseparable from the Event of the Death and Resurrection of the Lord which has brought it forth precedes and conditions every interpretation. It comes from the Spirit of God, whose gratuitous gift it is. But because of this faith, the apostolic community, when it intends to transmit even the message *of* Jesus, cannot put its proper conviction in an abstract way. It interprets the *acta et dicta* of Jesus in the light of what it believes *about* Jesus. In his lecture in Marburg on "the problem of the historical Jesus," Ernst Käsemann acknowledges that "all history (*Historie*) becomes accessible to us only by tradition and understandable only by interpretation." He proceeds:

> Primitive Christianity was clearly conscious of it. And this alone explains that it did not compose the gospels first of all as reports and that its own kerygma was superimposed on the figure of the historical Jesus and disguised him. . . . It is not because of a lack of attention or foolishness that the community combined its own message with that of the Lord, or even substituted it for his. It could not proceed in any other way if it were a question for it, not of reproduction of a memorable event but of the decision between faith and unbelief which was asked of it. . . . Using a paradoxical point one could say that it maintains the historical continuity with the one which formerly appeared on the earth, in such

---

[170]*Coran* LXXXV, 22; cf. Louis Massignon, *Situation de l'Islam*, Paris, 1939, 9.

a way that it lets the historical events of this earthly life fall by the way-side, for the most part, in order to replace them with its own message.[171]

To preach is to proclaim the Word, just as the apostolic community understood it *in the Holy Spirit.* Those who have put into writing the traditions preserved by their communities could not separate in "what had been transmitted to them" the Word of Jesus from the apostolic word. Only this last description guaranteed the first one. The *preached* Word—the one which stirs up faith—comes in this way *both* from God (who alone has the initiative, since he sent his Son, created the events whose sense is made clear, and gave the Spirit who assures the truth of this progression) *and* from the Church which has been solidly anchored in the apostolic word. The Word of God appears, therefore, as a Word to which the Church is not a stranger. By "reminding" itself (John 14:26) *in the spirit* what God said and accomplished in Jesus Christ, it "creates the Word." And this Word (which comes from God) is the one from which sprouts forth the faith which justifies (Rom 3:22).

Such is the first stratum of the sacramental aspect of the Church. Completely "evangelized" by God—in other words, transformed by the Good News of Salvation (*Euanggelion tou Theou*)—it is, therefore, the one which, on the basis of what favors it gratuitously, causes to sprout forth from its experience, which comes *from* God, a Word which "evangelizes" *for* God, *so that* the saving design reaches all of humanity. Through the Word it becomes servant of the eternal *mysterion* (cf. Rom 16:25-26; 1 Cor 2:7; Eph 1:9; 3:3-9).

Earlier, when we were presenting preaching as it is understood in Paul's Letter to the Romans, we said that the Church of today had the responsibility "to serve" the Word by spreading it. What we have just examined carefully shows, we dare to say, the radicalism of this "service" in the present economy. Faith comes only from God; but the Word of God which incites it wishes to pass through the Covenant. The revelation of a gratuitous Salvation springs forth from God as a "source of living water," but after slow infiltrations through the rock of human history.

2. The reconciled Church and who reconciles

a. The Church is reconciled *by* God, but it is also the one who reconciles *for* God. It is striking that Paul describes at the outset his ministry as centered on reconciliation (2 Cor 5:18; cf. Col 1:20) in a text dominated by the certitude that God alone reconciles:

> Everything comes from God who has reconciled us with him (*katal-laxantos henas heauto*) through Christ and who has confided to us the

---

[171]In Ernst Käsemann, *Essais exégétiques,* Neuchâtel-Paris, 1972, 148, 149–150.

ministry of reconciliation (*ten diakonian tes katallages*). Because at any rate it was God who reconciled the world in Christ (*kosmon katallason*) to himself, not holding the faults of men against them and he has entrusted to us the news that they are reconciled (*ton logon tes Katallages*). It is in the name of Christ that we are ambassadors; and it is through us (*di' hemon*) that God himself, in fact, is appealing to you. In the name of Christ, we beg you, be reconciled with God (*katallagete to Theo*). The one who knew no sin was made sin for us so that in him we might become the justice of God (*dikaiosune Theou*) (2 Cor 5:18-21).

This text has an undeniable density, and its link with chapters five and three of the Epistle to the Romans (Rom 5:9-11; 3:21-27) is evident.[172] It makes reconciliation the goal which God wishes to attain in Christ. If he has "identified" the latter "with sin," it is so that we might be reclothed with "justice" by the initiative of his benevolence, our faults no longer being held against us. He reconciles humanity to himself by justifying it. Chapter three of the Letter to the Romans will speak of free justification (3:24). This preciseness eliminates the least form of self-justification (cf. 4:2-10; 10:3-4; Gal 2:16). It puts all of Salvation on the side of God, whose verdict is completely a verdict of grace. And it is clear that the Church exists only because it is the fruit of this reconciliation received. We owe a debt of gratitude to Protestant traditions for restating it for us with a healthy stubbornness.

b. However, in this total freedom which remains the fundamental cornerstone of its being of *communion,* the Church knows that it is given the responsibility of also becoming the servant by whom this reconciliation is proclaimed and put into practice. By its ministers (who preach and preside at the sacraments) but more broadly by the totality of the life of the local Churches, it acts so that individuals find themselves put under the "justice" of Christ, their freedom being called, invited to say "yes" to the divine offer. In this service it does not remain passive, it is not reduced to the role of a simple channel, a lifeless passageway of a gift totally outside its responsibility and which, at any rate, would be accomplished without it, because making reconciliation real in the world is not foreign to its *obedience* to the ministry which God confides to it (cf. 1 Cor 9:16-18), not so that it might acquire merits—"it is a responsibility"— but solely so that it serve its design, according to what the logic of the Covenant demands. But to speak of obedience is to evoke a decision of freedom, the one of bowing to what is asked.

Besides, it is the Church which preaches. And it does so by involving the quality of its attachment to Christ in it. The difficult sentences of Paul

---

[172]But it will be noted that the idea of reconciliation does not appear in chapter 3. The most explicit parallel is 5:9-11.

to the Galatians show that one can proclaim "another Gospel," "to change the Gospel of Christ" (Gal 1:6-9). And what would happen if the Church kept quiet, crossed its arms? As far as the Letter to the Philippians is concerned, "service" of the Word even becomes a "necessity" which the progress and fidelity of the community call for (Phil 1:22-26). The Church is still the one which through baptism seals the entrance of the believer into reconciliation (Col 2:12-15). In certain cases, it decides to give or to refuse this baptism (cf. Acts 10:47-48). Even more than this, the local Church as such celebrates the Memorial of the Event at which reconciliation is accomplished. *In the Holy Spirit and with him* it is not then merely passive, because the Holy Spirit responds to *its* undertaking, to *its* prayer, to *its* epiclese; liturgically, he never imposes himself. Paul knows how to tell the Corinthians that by certain ways of celebrating the Supper of the Lord, far from immersing the congregation in the mystery of reconciliation, they cast it into condemnation "with the world" (1 Cor 11:27-34).

In the heart of this very vast service of *communion* with God, calling for fraternal reconciliation, a more specific ecclesial activity appears already in communities whose act of witness the New Testament records. It can happen that a member is cut off from the community or that the community is forced to exclude him. The question of excommunication came up very soon, as did its opposite: that of the "reconciliation" of those repentant members who had been excluded.[173] Here, evidently, the term "reconciliation" no longer has the exact and very rich meaning which the texts we mentioned give to it (2 Cor 5:18-21; Rom 5:9-11; cf. Eph 2:16; Col 1:20). It signifies to enter *again* into communion after being separated from it. Already the Old Testament was acquainted with exclusions, sometimes temporary. Several exegetes see the influence of this legislation in Matthew's text on fraternal correction (Matt 18:15-17).[174] Paul himself sometimes complies with the most radical regulations of Jewish legislation: "Drive out the evil-doer from among you" (1 Cor 5:13, quoting Deut 17:7; cf. 1 Cor 5:5; 16:22), although he knows how to intercede for the repentant person who had been banished (2 Cor 2:6-11).[175] When doctrine is at stake, the pastoral letters are seen to be severe. The author of the First Epistle to Timothy says of two disciples who have lost the

---

[173]The dossier of the first centuries will be found in Heinrich Karpp, *La Pénitence. Textes et commentaires des origines de l'ordre pénitentiel dans l'Église ancienne,* French version by A. Schneider, W. Rordorf, P. Barthel, Neuchâtel, 1970. See also J. Palmer, *Sacraments and Forgiveness, History and Doctrinal Development of Penance, Extreme Unction and Indulgences,* coll. "Sources of Christian Theology," 2, London, 1960.

[174]See K. Stendhal, *The School of St. Matthew,* New York, 1954, 138-139. See also Dupont-Sommer, *Les Écrits esséniens découverts près de la mer Morte,* Paris, 1960, 100, 163-164.

[175]The punishment inflicted on this believer by the community ("the numbers" in the sense of Qumran). Many exegetes think that Paul is arguing for a re-integration into the community.

faith: "I have handed them over to Satan" (1 Tim 1:20), which reiterates a counsel given given by Paul to the Corinthians (1 Cor 5:5). Exegetes interpret this formula as meaning exclusion from the community.[176] The second Johannine letter asks that no bond of communion be maintained with the spreader of false doctrine (2 John 1:10). And the Third Letter deplores the fact that Diotrephes is doing the same thing with the disciples of the Old Testament (3 John 1:9-10).[177]

It is clear, therefore, that very soon the Church assumed—in order to be faithful to its Lord and its vocation—a certain margin of authority as to keeping the baptized in the community-of-reconciliation. To excommunicate represents a serious decision, even if one does not prejudge the status of the eternal Salvation of the person and if the measure attempts above all to be medicinal.[178] Because—in the ecclesial rite of baptism—the Spirit himself has integrated the believer in the *communion* of this local Church. In the opposite sense, the fact of being re-integrated in it, signifying in this way the forgiveness of God, is filled with implications. Because—what it did not do at baptism—the local Church judges then about the situation of the guilty one, about the truth of his repentance. Here there is quite a profound intrusion in the field of reconciliation.

The complicated development of laws and rites about penitence in the first centuries shows the theological implication of this role of the ecclesial community and those responsible for it in the reconciliation of the *lapsi* or of sinners in a broad sense. Tradition considered it as a close association with judgment, with healing and forgiveness whose source is the Passover of Christ. The local Church recognizes the responsibility it has to put "outside of its communion," the faithful who according to its own judgment must perform some penance, in other words, go through the mysterious game of demand and triumphant mercy which characterizes the attitude of the God of faith, by depriving them in this way of a whole register of means of grace, then to correct them and reintegrate them in this *communion*—which is that of the Body of Christ.[179]

3. THE ASSEMBLED CHURCH AND WHO ASSEMBLES

The Church is assembled *by* God, but it is also the one who assembles *for* God. Proclamation of the gospel, reconciliation, actualize the goal

---

[176]Thus C. Spicq, *Les Épîtres pastorales,* coll. "Études bibliques," 44, Paris, 1947, 50-51; C. K. Barrett, *A Commentary on the First Epistle to the Corinthians,* London, 1968, 125-127.

[177]On this question, see the explanations by R. E. Brown *The Community of the Beloved Disciple,* complete in Id., *The Epistles of John,* New York, 1982.

[178]See C. Spicq, *loc. cit.;* C. K. Barrett, *loc. cit.*

[179]See our article J.-M. R. Tillard, "La pénitence sacramentelle, une théologie qui se cherche," *Studia Moralia* 21, 1983, 5-30.

which the Johannine Gospel presents as that of the Death of Jesus, "to gather together in unity the dispersed children of God" (John 11:52). Specialists underline the solemn tone which the author attaches to this sentence, by making of it a prophecy of the high priest (11:51).

Fundamentally, the Church is a gathering together by God in this narrow and compact point where he forms a *communion of communions.* Johannine literature and the Epistle to the Ephesians, undoubtedly united in the same milieu—the Church of Ephesus, a place of confrontation of diverse apostolic heritages[180]—permitted us to understand the authentic nature of this *koinonia.* In the Letter to the Ephesians, the famous affirmation: "It is by grace that you have been saved . . . not by anything of your own, but by a gift from God" (2:8) is equal to both the collective and personal form of Salvation, the reverse of division and hatred (2:14-15) which is access of all to the Father in the one Spirit (2:18), to become one single body (2:16), one single Temple, one single dwelling (2:20-22), one single family of God (2:19). There is only God, and him alone, to gather together in Christ Jesus a humanity that is torn apart.

Gathered together by the Spirit of the Lord, and him alone, the Church knows that it is given the responsibility to act as a mediator for the gathering together of humanity *en christo.* In the present economy, there is nothing accidental about this intervention. It is integrated by God in the actualization of the eternal *mysterion.*

We find a clear indication of this in the Letter to the Ephesians which describes in this sense the responsibility of each one of the faithful because of the gift of the Spirit which each one bears. Christ "fits and joins together as is necessary, thanks to the joints" (4:16), but yet it reverts to the faithful to "preserve the unity of the Spirit (*ten henoteta tou Pneumatos*) by the bond of peace" (4:3). If each one must put into practice what he has received, he must do it in such a way that the entire Body of Christ comes "to unity in faith and knowledge of the Son of God, fully mature with the fullness of Christ himself" (Eph 4:11-13).

Because it is always the primary action of God the Father, the Lord and the Spirit (4:4-6), which explains to some extent the existence of ministries (4:7-13), this does not excuse the community from putting forth an incessant effort to avoid falling into the snares of division (4:2) or from being carried along by every wind of doctrine (4:14).

Paul's advice on the subject of charisms (Rom 12:6-8; 1 Cor 12:1-14:25) and his emphasis on fraternal charity (1 Cor 13:1-13) refer back to the same certainty. If love is "the way that is infinitely superior" for exercising all the gifts (1 Cor 12:31), it is because, as a reflection of the love of

---

[180]See R. E. Brown, *The Community of the Beloved Disciple,* 171–182; R. E. Brown and J. P. Meier, *Antioch and Rome,* 214.

God, it constitutes what cements fraternal unity, because God wishes "that there may not be disagreements inside the body but that each part may be equally concerned for all the others." For all are "the Body of Christ and his members, but each one is a different part" (12:25-27). The fidelity of the community to the gift which it has received brings about the realization of *communion* day after day. Without it, this *communion* would remain a gift which has been proposed to believers, but not something accepted *in truth*.

The Johannine Gospel underlines the serious consequences of this acceptance, which go beyond the confines of the community. Twice he puts on the lips of Jesus this request: "That they may be one, so that the world may believe it was you who sent me . . . may they come to perfect unity so that the world will realize that it was you who sent me and that I have loved them as much as you loved me" (17:21, 23). *Communion* which is lived[181] constitutes not only the proclamation of the salvific course of God but the demonstration of its truth. On this plane, it says more than the proclamation of the Word. It is the accomplishment of this Word. It also permits the ecclesial gathering to be expanded. Certainly the faith of those who, thanks to the community, will come to believe in Christ (cf. 17:20) will come from God, and solely from God (cf. 6:37). And it is he who—according to the noteworthy expression from Acts (Acts 2:47) which concludes one of the summaries about the first apostolic *koinonia*— "will join to the community" those who in this way will find Salvation. However, without ecclesial witness, would it not be the Spirit—who calls, unsettles hearts and illumines minds—who would be the material, the human reality adapted to the speakers (because in accord with their expectations) who causes, then supports and finally confirms his intervention?

This dialectic is found, in an eminent way, in the demand for truth which the New Testament already, through Paul, ties to the thriving of the Eucharist. Its principal fruit is the deepening of the community feeling. In the reception of the Eucharistic Body, *communion* is affirmed. But there is nothing automatic or magic about this effect. It happens in a local Church which wants to be faithful and loyal to what it has become through God's initiative, which is living its coming together in charity. The Spirit who causes this gathering together wants to find in the community a response to his action. He will not gather together a community which *is* divided.[182]

---

[181]But the term *koinonia* is not used here. Exegetes emphasize that the unity in question is ecclesial unity incarnated into a community-like life. See R. E. Brown, *The Gospel according to John XIII-XXI*, New York, 1970, 776-779; E. Käsemann, *Jesu letzter Wille nach Johannes 17*, Tübingen, 1967.

[182]It would be interesting to show how the Anglican theories of receptionism, such as those

Ministries represent, for their part, one of the key elements of the status of the New Covenant. We have seen that they are given to the Church so that it might become and remain *communion of communions* gathered together by the Spirit. The New Testament presents very clearly two types of "ministerial" intervention. They must not be confused. The first intervention is that of the apostle or preacher proclaiming the Word which elicits a strong attachment to the faith. From this basic ministry which puts the "believer" face to face with the absolute, Salvation as a free gift, and placing him in *communion* with Christ, we would state that he is pointed towards "the faith which justifies" (cf. Eph 2:8). The second type of ministry is different. Its purpose is to keep the local Church faithful to its basic essence of *communion,* and to make it grow in it. We have called it the ministry which preserves and sustains the fidelity of the local Church, in other words, *episkopè.* Rereading the pastoral epistles we discover that their most important advice is about the *state* of communion to be fed and deepened. They exhibit more of an interest in the *episkopè* than in the kerygmatic proclamation.

This distinction seems to us to be of capital importance. It leads to a preciseness which is capable of clarifying our research on this point, which is very difficult ecumenically. For a long time it has been very evident that apostolic preaching is addressed to all of humanity ("all nations," Matt 28:19; Acts 1:8) aiming at an attachment of the listener to God himself, which signifies obedience to the faith.[183] Human authorities, even ecclesial ones, fade into the background in this case. One does not believe *in the* preacher: his message is accepted and one believes *in the* God whom he is proclaiming. No human authority could order one to believe. Let's be even more radical. The task or function (*munus*) of the Church is to proclaim the Word. It has no power (*potestas*) over the act of faith. It serves the Word by expressing, articulating, reflecting in it the experience *which the Spirit has given it to live* and which is contained in the event of Pentecost whose initiative came from God alone, but the Church has no power over the effect of this Word on the believer.[184] On this level—which is the fundamental one—the Church has only one function: to restrict itself to present to men the means *which God himself has put in its hands.*

<hr />

expressed by Cranmer or Jewel, are, in their way, in line with what we evoke here. In *Sermo* 272, PL 38, 1105, Augustine comments in these terms: "If therefore you are the Body of Christ and his members it is your own mystery which rests on the table of the Lord. You receive your own mystery. You answer Amen to what you are and this response stamps your adhesion. You hear: 'the Body of Christ'; you answer Amen. Be therefore a member of the Body of Christ so that your Amen may be true."

[183]See J.-M. R. Tillard, "Obéissance," *Dictionnaire de spiritualité.*

[184]See Y. Congar, "Sur la trilogie: Prophète-Roi-Prêtre," *RSPT* 67, 1983, 97–115.

However, it has always been evident that on this level, when it is a question of the local Church *as such,* already constituted and provided with services, ministers are seen everywhere endowed with power (*potestas*) and by that fact with a certain distraint, not over faith as such but over life-which-is-conformity-with-faith. If in the sacramental celebration, especially the Eucharistic one, the minister is only an image of Christ, a pure transparency, his intervention in the internal management of the community allows for a wide margin of initiative. We have proved this by examining very carefully the question of excommunication, but other areas of ecclesial life and even of its services are concerned here. From the time of the New Testament, those who are responsible for the community can ask the faithful to obey their orders. The verb "to obey" then no longer has the same connotation as when one speaks of obedience to the faith. It is a question of submitting to an order, to a leader. Besides the Greek language uses another term, no longer *hypakoè* (to be all ears) as in the case of faith but *hypotagè* as when one describes the attitude of a child towards his parents, of a citizen towards the head of the city.[185]

This obedience to the decisions of those who are in positions of responsibility in the community reaches a point where it becomes an integral part of Christian fidelity *as such.* Something of the *potestas* which Christ, Head and Lord, alone possesses (because he is, in the Spirit, both the *auctor* and the source) is diverted to the minister. The minister is in this way qualified to discern and decide—according to his own judgment, enlightened by the Spirit, confronted continually with the Word and intuitions of the *sensus fidelium*—what the community *must* do or avoid to be faithful. And if in several cases it is a question of simple advice (as in 1 Cor 7:6, 12, 40), in others the order is imperative (1 Cor 5:5; 5:11; 10:25-28; 11:10; 14:34-35; 2 Cor 6:14; 2 Thess 3:6; 1 Tim 2:8-12; 2 Tim 4:1-2; Titus 3:1; 3:10; Heb 13:17; 1 Pet 3:1-3; etc). Certain expressions are to be taken special notice of: "We order you in the name of the Lord Jesus Christ" (2 Thess 3:6), "I am not giving permission for a woman to teach or to tell a man what to do" (1 Tim 2:12). We find ourselves here in the area of the power of "binding and loosing" (Matt 16:19; 18:18).

Inhabited by the power of the Risen Lord and his Spirit, the Church *has thus received* (it has not given it to itself) the task—furnished with the power it requires to be properly fulfilled—of collaborating actively in preserving itself in the *gift of God.* By the "articulations" of its ministries (Eph 4:16) and especially the faithfulness of all those who have been baptized, it preserves *itself* in its entirely *free communion* of grace. It does not live in a continual state of waiting for the dictates of God. The Spirit

---

[185]See J.-M. R. Tillard, "Obéissance," where we have studied the distinction between obedience as "listening" to God and "obedience" as "submission."

has given it a mandate and the grace of perceiving by itself what is willed and of devoting *itself* to them. This gift arises from its nature as Spouse and out of respect for its re-created freedom. God wished it to be the minister of its own Salvation as much as of the Salvation of the world. It is *in* this fundamental ministry and *for* it that the ministry *of the* ordained ministers is contained or services which we have described.

If we finish our study of ministry with this long reflection on the Church-as-minister, it is in order to restore to this notion of ministry—which has always been recognized as constituting the ecclesial being—its full dimension. To speak of ministries without speaking of the Church as minister simply amounts to touch upon this subject lightly. Is that not the limitation of certain "ecumenical" theologies concerning ministry?

In this way the depth of *communion* is clarified. The assumption of humanity into the service of grace constitutes an important element in the nature of it and its revelation. We have continually said that the Church of God is an absolute gift, a completely free benefit of the *Agape* of God. At the center of this gift is inserted an act which shows the supreme generosity of God: he saves his "image" by making it capable of being inseparably "justified *by* him" and "joined *to* him." He redeems his image by immersing it in a Covenant where it is respected, loved not as a slave but as a Spouse. It is never she who "justifies" herself. However, by the way in which she is "justified" she can act according to the justice which God grants to her in the Cross and Resurrection of Jesus Christ.

A text which originated in a Brazilian community and which was written during the height of a difficult involvement for the Kingdom, states very simply what we have tried to make explicit in terms which are perhaps too complicated:

> God alone can give faith
> but you can give your witness.
>
> God alone can give hope
> but you can give confidence to your brothers.
>
> God alone can give love
> but you can teach others how to love.
>
> God alone can give peace
> but you can sow unity.
>
> God alone can give strength
> but you can stand by someone who is discouraged.
>
> God alone is the way
> but you can point it out to others.
>
> God alone is the light
> but you can make it shine in the eyes of all.

God alone is the life
but you can give others the will to live.

God alone can do what seems impossible
but you will be able to do what is possible.

God alone is sufficient for himself
but he prefers to count on you. . . .

Prayer of a team of Campinas (Brazil).

Excursus

a. As a typical text, we would like to quote this beautiful passage from the first homily by John Chrysostom on the beginning of Acts, found in the translation by J. Bareille, *Oeuvres complètes de saint Jean Chrysostome,* v. V, Paris, 1866, 101-103: "At this time I want to speak to the newly enlightened. I call newly enlightened both those who were two, three or ten days ago, and those who were more than a year ago and even longer still; because this term fits all of them. Let us look after our souls zealously, and at the end of ten years we will have the right to reclaim this title, when we have maintained the youth with which we were clothed at baptism. It is not time which creates the newly enlightened person, but the purity of life. It is easy, if one is not careful, to lose the right to wear this title after two days. I will give you an example on this topic, and I will tell you how a newly enlightened person lost, after two days, this honor and this grace. I state an example so that with this fall in mind you will work to assure your own salvation. It is not only those who remain faithful and upright but those who have fallen, whose memory must serve to heal you and help you reform your lives. Simon the Magician was converted; after his baptism he became attached to Philip, whose miracles he had witnessed. But a few days later he returned to his original perverseness, and he wanted to buy his salvation with money. How does Peter respond to this newly enlightened person: 'It is plain to me that you are trapped in the bitterness of gall and the chains of sin. Pray to the Lord that he will forgive your malice.' (Acts 8:22-23). He had not yet started his career and there he is immediately falling in the most deplorable way. If it is easy to fall after two days, and lose the name and grace of a newly enlightened person, it is just as easy to preserve for ten years, twenty years, and even until our last breath, this name which is so beautiful, this advantage which is so precious. We have Paul himself as a witness of this, who, in his old age, shone with the greatest brilliance. What we have here is not a youthfulness which depends on nature, for these two things depend on our will; it is in our power either to grow old or to retain our youthfulness. . . . Do you want to understand how after a very long time one can still be a newly enlightened person? Listen to the language Paul uses with some men who had been enlightened such a long time before: 'You will shine in the world like bright stars because you are offering it the word of life,' (Phil 2:15-16). You have been stripped of your old clothing which was in shreds, you have been anointed with spiritual healing, and you have all recovered your freedom: let no one from now on revert to his original slavery. This is a war, it is a fight which you have to keep up. . . . Do you see the kindness of the President of our athletic games? He is not concerned with our former actions but those which followed our baptism; he asks us for an accounting of them. When you were still a slave, you had an infinite number of accusers, your conscience, your sins, all sorts of demons. Yet, the Savior says, none of them has angered me against you; I did not consider you unworthy of my struggles, and I gave you access to the arena, paying no attention to your merits but to my mercy. Therefore, stay there and fight, whether it's a question of a race, a boxing match or a pancratium; do it in full daylight with a fixed plan and goal.''

b. Chrysostom's text quoted above states it happily. See also Augustine, *Sermo* 231, 3, 62-85; 5, 165-169 which we quote in the translation of S. Poque, *Sermons sur la Pâque,* SC 116, Paris, 1966, 249-253, 259: ''Let us listen to the word of the apostle: 'If you are raised with Christ . . .' When will we rise up, we who are not yet dead? What did the apostle mean: 'If you are raised with Christ'? Would he have been able to rise, if he had not been dead before? But the apostle was talking to the living, to people who were not yet dead. And yet already risen? What does that mean? See what he says: 'If you are raised with Christ, taste the things of heaven where Christ is seated at the right hand of the Father. Look for the good things of heaven, not those of the earth, because you are dead.' It is he who says it, not I; but what he says is true, that is why I say it too . . . Why do I say it too? 'I believed, that is why I spoke.' If we live well, we are dead and raised up. Whoever continues to live badly is neither dead nor raised up. But whoever lives badly is not living. Let him die so that he will not die. What does that say: let him die so that he will not die? Let him change so that he will not be condemned. 'If you are raised with Christ—I repeat the words of the apostle—taste the good things of heaven where Christ is seated at the right hand of the Father. Look for the good things of heaven, not those of the earth, because you are dead. And your life is hidden in God with Christ. When Christ your life appears, then you also will appear with him in glory.' These are the words of the apostle. To you who are not yet dead, I tell you to die; to you who continue to live badly, I tell you to change, because whoever was living badly, but now has renounced this way of living, is dead. If he lives well, he is raised. . . . At the present time, while we are living in this perishable flesh, let us die with Christ, by changing our life. Let us live with Christ by loving justice. We will not find happiness if we do not go towards him who has come to us, and if we do not begin to live with him who has died for us.''

c. Chrysostom's text which has been quoted continues in this way: "Listen to an idea of Paul: Hardly had he gone up into the pool and received baptism when he marched into combat, preaching that that one is the Son of God, and in this way confounding the Jews, from the time of his conversion. You say that you cannot preach and dispense the doctrinal word? Well then, teach by your deeds, by your conduct, by the brightness of your actions. 'Let your light shine in the sight of men, Christ said, so that seeing your good works they may glorify your Father in heaven.' (Matth 5:16). You say that you cannot confound the Jews by word of mouth? Then confound them by your ways; move even the Greeks themselves by your change of heart. When they see you, not long ago lewd, wicked, indifferent and corrupt, and suddenly changed, confirming this change whose grace is the principle for the change of your ways, won't they be confounded and won't they say what the Jews said before about the blind man: It's he, it's not he, no, is it he?''

4

The Visible Communion of the Churches

The profound *communion* which the Eucharist—and it alone—accomplishes emerges in a visible way only when those who preside at the Eucharistic celebration today everywhere in the world and who have presided at it since Pentecost as an image of Christ "gathering together in unity" the people of God, are themselves united in one single ministerial body. They form in this way, in the multitude that they are, one single instrument of ecclesial gathering together. Tradition says that they are a college having for their core the ministry of unity of one among them. It sees there a requirement of *communion.*

When the Catholic Church affirms that it is the community in which the Church of God subsists (*subsistit in*) in all its force and with the fullness of the means of Salvation, it puts among the guarantees of this fullness the presence in it of the ministry of unity confided to the Bishop of Rome. More than that, it holds that it alone possesses such a ministry. Whereas for the totality of faith and sacramental life—even in what concerns the apostolic origin and the significance of the episcopal ministry—it is recognized with the Eastern Churches (which it calls for that reason, since Paul VI, its sister Churches)[1] in a basic *communion,*[2] this point forbids it to solidify this unity in a full *communion* of life and structure. In fact, the ecclesiology which we have presented can—at least for what is essential—be accepted by these Churches. But from the time that the

---

[1] See J. Meyendorff, "Églises sœurs, implications ecclésiologiques du Tomos Agapis," *Istina* 20, 1975, 35–46; E. Lanne, "Églises sœurs, implications ecclésiologiques du Tomos Agapis," especially 59–61; M. Fahey, *op. cit.*; Y. Congar, "Le développement de l'évaluation ecclésiologique des Églises non catholiques," *Revue de droit canon* 25, 1975, 168–198 (193–197).

[2] On their side, some of these Churches, placing themselves especially on line with Cyprian and doubting the Roman interpretation on certain points of faith, hesitate to admit this *communion.* See J.-M. R. Tillard, "Œcuménisme et Église catholique," *NRT* 107, 1985, 43–67 (especially 59–63).

chapter on Roman primacy is opened up, everything is spoiled. It is evident that the problem is complicated because of the groups which were born of the Reformation or its spirit.[3]

I. The Servant of the Servants of God

1. In order to get rid of any ambiguities, it is important to begin by clearing all the underbrush from the terrain. When, rereading Vatican I in light of an episcopal theology which ties together with that found in the great Tradition, Vatican II presents the ministry of the Bishop of Rome, it is careful to inscribe it in the ministry which is confided to the entire episcopal body. It does not make him a bishop above this body but on the contrary it makes him one bishop among the bishops. The papacy is not a sacrament, nor even a degree in the fullness of the sacrament of orders. It is a particular way of putting into operation the episcopal, sacramental, common grace. For a tradition which maintains the absolute priority of the sacramental over all the rest and even affirms that the Church has only a sacramental source, this remark is of capital importance. The Church, born of the Spirit and growing through him, gets its life from baptism, which seals the acceptance of the Word of Salvation, and of the Eucharist around which radiate other rites. It celebrates these sacraments in the local Churches whose preservation in the heart of apostolic tradition is guaranteed by the ministry of the bishop conferred in the sacrament of ordination. The papacy would not be in harmony with the economy of God for his Church if it would not insert itself in this sacramental circle.

It is, therefore, in the mission of the episcopate *as such* that it is necessary to understand the function of the Bishop of Rome. And everything depends on what we have said at length about the why of the collegial nature of the episcopal ministry and the link of each bishop with his Church. On one hand, the Church is one in the unity proper to a *communion*. It is neither an addition of parts, nor entirely shared: it is a *communion* of local Churches, *Church of Churches*. On the other hand, in his local Church, each bishop, especially by the teaching of the faith and presiding at the Eucharist, has a mission to preserve the total fidelity of the community to what has been transmitted and lived since the time of the apostles and in total harmony with what is taught and lived *hic et nunc* in the other communities of the same apostolic tradition, guaranteeing in this way its insertion into *communion*. Bishops and communion in the *catholica,* episcopal thrones and ecclesial *koinonia* are on this point united

---

[3]See the last article by W. A. Visser't Hooft, "Le conseil œcuménique et l'Église catholique; ultimes réflexions du pasteur W. A. Visser't Hooft," *DC* 83, 1986, 125–129.

that a break in episcopal unity implies a break in ecclesial communion. The schism of a bishop leads to the schism of his community because he can no longer preside at the Eucharist (where his local Church "manifests" itself) in communion with the other bishops and their Churches. It is necessary, therefore, to have an unbreakable communion of the bishops—in faith, witness and service—if one wishes both to assure and intimate the communion of local Churches. It is the local Church which creates the unity of the Church of God on this earth.

Besides, the local Churches are different in their customs, traditions, problems, soul, often even in their organization. Certainly the word inculturation is recent, and its application to the ecclesial reality only entered recently into the official language of the Churches.[4] In addition, for the new Churches, which have sprung up from the missionary activity of the last centuries, incarnation into the proper cultural values is still only in its infancy.[5] Yet since the beginning the Church has spread by taking on characteristics which have come from the territories where they were born. The response of Pope Gregory the Great to the one who preached the gospel to the English, Augustine, is often quoted.[6] Less known is the *Instruction de la Congregation de la propagande* of 1659 to the missionaries of China, of Cochin China and of Tonkin:

> Do not put forth any enthusiasm, do not advance any argument to convince these peoples to change their rites, their customs and their ways, unless they are clearly contrary to religion and morality. What is more absurd than to bring to the Chinese France, Spain, Italy or any other country in Europe? Do not bring our countries into theirs, except for the faith, this faith which neither rejects nor harms the rites or customs of any people, provided that they are not odious, but on the contrary

---

[4]At first in the discussions of the ecumenical Council of Churches, especially of Faith and Constitution—the meeting of the commission in Bangalore (in 1978) discussed *contextualization,* "indigenization," acculturation, inculturation, of faith and hope—then in the speeches of John-Paul II. See already *DC* 79, 1982, 249. The clearest texts on this are his African speeches, in August 1985 at Lome (*DC* 82, 1985, 903–904), at Yaounde (*ibid.,* 915, 917), in Nairobi (*ibid.,* 935–936). See the message by Paul VI, *Africae terrarum* (*DC* 64, 1967, 1937–1956), John-Paul II delares: "The Christian faith must be able to be assimilated into the language of every people, find its application in the secular traditions which its wisdom has gradually worked out to guarantee social cohesion, the maintenance of physical and moral health . . .; the break between the Gospel and a culture would be a drama. The positive elements, the spiritual values of the African man must be integrated more. There is an effort of acculturation to be pursued so that the faith does not remain superficial" (*DC* 82, 1985, 914). See also the declaration of the African bishops and those of Madagascar, in Rome in 1974 (on the occasion of the third synod), in *DC* 71, 1974, 995.

[5]See Efoé J. Penoukou, *Églises d'Afrique, propositions pour l'avenir,* Paris, 1984 (in particular, 48–52).

[6]See our study J.-M. R. Tillard, "Pluralisme religieux et théologie." Regarding the authenticity of the *Libellus responsionum,* see S. Brechter, *Die Quellen zur Angelsachsenmission Gregors des Grossen,* Münster, 1941. But see the response to Leandre for Spain (*Reg.* I, 41; *M. G. H. EPP,* t. I, 57, 18; see also *PL* 77, 497).

wishes that they be preserved and protected. It is in the nature of all men to esteem, love and put above everything else in the world the traditions of their country, this country itself. Also is there any more powerful cause of estrangement and hatred than to bring about changes in the customs of a nation, principally in those which have been practiced since the time of their ancestors. What will happen, if having done away with them, you look to replace them with the customs of your country, introduced from without? Therefore, never put on a parallel the customs of these peoples with those of Europe; on the contrary, be eager to get accustomed to theirs.[7]

There is a repetition of this two centuries later in the advice given by that great founder P. Libermann to his religious.[8]

However, pluralism ceases to be in harmony with the very nature of the Church of God when it is no longer founded on a unity of faith, sacramental life and mission. It is then transformed into division. Inculturation cannot turn into the process of making differences absolute or the claim that in either one of the communities alone can the valid essence of the Church of God be carried out. It belongs to the identity of the local Church to be a group which does not take refuge behind its special qualities which it would consider absolutes. It is the one which, so inculturated with Christianity, confesses and celebrates the faith which is also lived *hic et nunc* elsewhere, which was lived in the past since the time of Pentecost, and which will be lived in the future until the coming of the Lord. The local Church finds its identity only in this totality: elsewhere, since the apostles, until the Coming.

That is also why every local Church must convey in its very life concern for other local Churches. The intervention by the Church of Rome, still deprived of a bishop, for the Church of Carthage, which was in the midst of a crisis, is well known.[9] Closer to us, especially since the letter *Fidei donum* of Pius XII,[10] the sending of clerics to new Churches by the local Churches of old Christianity continues to make this concern a reality.[11] But in a wider manner, for centuries in the West, this solidarity

---

[7]We give this text in the excellent translation of M. Legrain, "Diversité des cultures et mariage des chrétiens," *Lumen Vitae* 40, 1985, 207-220 (209). See on the whole of this question A. V. Seumois, *La Papauté et les missions au cours des six premiers siècles,* Louvain, 1953.

[8]See J.-M. R. Tillard, "L'intuition missionnaire du P. Libermann," *Les Fondateurs des spiritains,* special edition of *Spiritains aujourd'hui* 4, 1985, 80-98.

[9]In Cyprian, *Epist.* 8, 3. See G. Bardy, "L'autorité du siège romain et les controverses du IIIᵉ siècle," *Rev. de Sc. Rel.* 14, 1924, 255-272, 385-410 (260-265), who quotes A. Harnack, "Die Briefe des römischen klerus, aus der Zeit des Sedisvacans im Jahre 250," *Theologische Abhandlungen Carl von Weissacker gewidmet,* Fribourg, 1892, 36.

[10]*A.A.S.,* 1957, 245-246.

[11]See *DC* 58, 1961, 125; 60, 1963, 953-968; 64, 1967, 861; the decree of Vatican II *Ad gentes,* 19, 38; the *motu proprio Ecclesiae sanctae,* 1, 2, *DC* 63, 1966, 1444; the message of Paul VI,

is accomplished in large part because of religious Orders or Institutes. This was not always understood. When a local Church gives one of its members to the Company of Jesus, to the Fathers of the Holy Spirit, to the Little Sisters of the Assumption, to Franciscan missionaries, to the friar preachers, to the Sisters of Saint-Joseph-of-Cluny, it is not depriving itself of this person. On the contrary, it shows by this gift its concern and its service of all the Churches. By this missionary, this theologian, this pastor baptized in it and born in it, it serves the local Church in Chad, Madagascar, San Salvador or, more prosaically, the neighboring diocese. One of the limitations, among many others, of the decree *Perfectae caritatis* of Vatican II about religious life is to have forgotten this solidarity of the diocese with those men and women who have left it to join an Order or a Congregation. What they have done is act as if their baptism did not involve the local Church *as such*.

Also the bishop of every local Church has among the essential components of his responsibility, by his ordination for the service of this local Church, the responsibility of seeing to the opening up of his local Church to *all* Churches. He accepts the *sollicitudo omnium Ecclesiarum*.[12] He exercises it in communion with the other bishops, in a dialog which create harmony between the one and the multitude.

The function of the Bishop of Rome is none other than a very special form of this *sollicitudo omnium Ecclesiarum* given with the episcopal grace, hence a particular form of exercising the common sacrament of the episcopate. It is a service within the all-encompassing mission of the episcopal college, the function of the "servant of the servants of God"[13] according to the ideal which Gregory the Great put forth and which is expressed in the title of every conciliar document of Vatican II.[14] It does not support this mode of a sacramental hierarchy which would make him a "super-bishop." But, a bishop like all the other members of the episcopal college, it is he, on the *cathedra* of the local Church of Rome, whom his link with Peter and Paul invests with a special responsibility (a *sollicitudo*) for the communion of all the Churches within the faith, witness and service. It is from this primacy of *his* local Church in the midst of *all* the local Churches that the Bishop of Rome has his primacy in the college of bishops. In this college, which possesses *in globo* the full and

Africae terrarum, DC 64, 1967, 1949; the circular on "La vocation et la formation des missionnaires" of September 19, 1970 of the Congregation for Evangelization, *DC* 67, 1970, 968. See also *Presbyterorum ordinis* 6, 10; *Christus Dominus* 36.

[12]See *Christus Dominus* 3.

[13]On the formula, see H. Leclercq, *DACL* 15, 1950, 1360–1363.

[14]"Paul, bishop, servant of the servants of God, in union with the Fathers of the Holy Council, so that the memory may be maintained forever."

supreme responsibility over the whole Church[15] he guarantees a particular and necessary function which affects precisely the cohesion of the bishops and their unity in the faith which Peter and Paul sealed by their martyrdom. The constitution *Pastor aeternus* of Vatican I, and *Lumen gentium* of Vatican II which reiterates the former, do not say anything different:

> The eternal shepherd and *episcope* of our souls (1 Pet 2:26), in order to perpetuate the salutary work of Redemption, wished to build the holy Church in which, like in the dwelling of the living God, *all the faithful would be gathered together by the bond of one single faith and one single charity.* This is why before being glorified he prayed to his Father not only for the apostles but also for those who because of their word would believe in him, *so that all may be one* as the Son and Father are one (John 17:20s). In the same way as he sent the apostles whom he has chosen in the world, as he himself had been sent by the Father (John 20:21), in the same way *he wished that there would be in his Church shepherds and teachers until the end of time* (Matt 28:20). *So that, in fact, (ut vero), this episcopate (episcopatus iste) might be one and undivided and that thanks to the close and mutual union of priests the entire multitude of believers would be preserved in the unity of faith and communion,* by putting the blessed Peter at the head of the other Apostles, he established in this way his person as the durable principal and visible foundation *of this double unity.*[16]

On the plane of unity of faith, the aim of this *sollicitudo* is the ''recognition'' which we have already treated at length. It is necessary that under all of its own characteristics, the fruit of its inculturation, the Church of Tokyo be such that the Church of Milan can recognize in it not only some elements of its faith but its entire faith, and *vice versa.* It is also necessary for it to be able ''to recognize'' in it all that it itself holds of the faith from the generations which preceded it. The Bishop of Rome must—by the position of his Church in the heart of the Churches—see to it that the faith of these Churches is not only involved with today's questions but remains in full *communion* and harmony with what has been transmitted by the apostles and lived since that time. It is incumbent upon him to be, on this point, the permanent ''memory'' of his brother bishops and, with them, of their Churches.

As far as what concerns the opening up of each local Church to the needs of others, the task of the Bishop of Rome is still ''to be on the watch.'' The *sollicitudo omnium Ecclesiarum* could very well be buried, even refused, because of the urgency of local problems. It could also be

---

[15]*Lumen gentium,* 22; *Nota praevia* 3; *Christus Dominus* 4.
[16]*DS* 3050; see *Lumen gentium,* 18, 23.

put into practice by a scattering of things around but ignoring those things which are urgent. By his place in the episcopal college, the Bishop of Rome has the responsibility to promote and harmonize ecclesial solidarity which—as Paul's preoccupation already shows at the time of the collection for the Church of Jerusalem—belongs to the soul of the Church.

One cannot imagine, therefore, this function of the Bishop of Rome as that of the "universal bishop." And if Paul VI adds to his signature on the actions of Vatican II the title of *episcopus Ecclesiae catholicae,* it is in the old sense of "bishop of the local Church of Rome who has remained faithful to the apostolic faith."[17] A person is bishop of a local Church,[18] and it is necessary at any price—with the danger of confusing everything—to respect the link between bishop and local *cathedra.* It is precisely because their mission, in large part intransmissible, precedes every local Church that the apostles cannot be called the "first bishops."[19] It is known that Irenaeus does not make Peter a bishop: it is on the *cathedra* of the Church referring to him and to Paul that the bishops will succeed each other.[20] In this sense of founder and transcendent, he is for this See *initium episcopatus,*[21] and in the bishops of this Church he will have vicars,[22] according to the expression used by Cyprian which will come down through the centuries.[23] The Bishop of Rome is, therefore, "vicar of Peter" on the *cathedra* of the Church which, as Irenaeus says, possesses the *potentior principalitas* to which it was its origin.[24]

Lumen gentium says that every bishop represents Christ.[25] What we have here is the repetition of an episcopal title mentioned especially around the

---

[17]See H. Marot, "La collégialité et le vocabulaire épiscopal du Ve au VIIe siècle," *La Collégialité épiscopale, histoire et théologie,* coll. "Unam sanctam," 52, Paris, 1965, 59–98. On the discussions at Vatican I, see R. Minnerath, *Le Pape évêque universel ou premier des évêques,* coll. "Le point théologique," 30, Paris, 1978.

[18]What wishes to respect the approval of an ancient See for titular bishops.

[19]We found this expression in the very rich work of M. Guerra Gomez, *Les nombres del papa. Estudio filologico-teologico de varios nombres del papa en los primeros siglos del cristianismo,* Burgos, 1982, 45.

[20]*Adv. Haer.* III, 3, 1–3.

[21]See P. Batiffol, *Cathedra Petri, études d'histoire ancienne de l'Église,* coll. "Unam sanctam," 4, Paris, 1938, 95–103.

[22]See G. Corti, *Il papa vicario de Pietro, contributi alla storia dell' idea papale,* Brescia, 1966; V. Monachino, "La perennita del primato di Pietro in uno studio recente," *Archivum Historiae Pontificiae* 5, 1967, 325–339; J.-M. R. Tillard, *L'Évêque de Rome,* 122–134; M. Guerra Gomez, *op. cit.,* 437–471.

[23]See J.-M. R. Tillard, *L'Évêque de Rome,* 129–133.

[24]*Adv. Haer.* III, 3, 1–2. See the position (which is not very convincing) of M. Guerra Gomez, *op. cit.,* 309–351.

[25]*Lumen gentium,* 21, 27, 37.

end of the fifth century,[26] "vicar of Christ." This is a very ticklish usage, open to many interpretations lacking in detail, so that this title can obviously be applied to the Bishop of Rome, Bishop among the bishops. But it becomes ambiguous when it is transformed into an exclusive title, destined to signify what the function of this bishop of the seat of the *potentior principalitatis* has in particular in the heart of the episcopal college. Innocent III, in the era when the papacy triumphed, in the thirteenth century, wants us to recognize in the Bishops of Rome not "the vicars of some apostle or of some man but the vicars of Christ Jesus himself . . ., truly vicar[s] of the true God."[27] Later Robert Bellarmine will call the Church "a gathering of men . . . under the authority of legitimate shepherds and above all (*praecipue*) of the sole vicar of Christ on earth, the roman Pontiff," who "represents him for us as he was when he lived among men."[28] A catechism, written in 1795, makes the following comment:

> The Pope is the successor of S. Peter, consequently the vicar of Jesus Christ; he has the same power over all the faithful as our Savior had during his mortal life and such as he would exercise still, if he were visibly among us. . . . Respect Jesus Christ in his person, and in his power that of this Savior God . . .; whoever is bold enough to utter abusive or contemptuous words against the Pope abuses and shows contempt for Jesus Christ himself.[29]

And the questionnaire states very precisely:

> D—When a sovereign is replaced by another after his death, doesn't this one have the same power as his predecessor?
>
> R—Yes, M., he inherits his power as well as his place.
>
> D—Saint Peter then has the same power as Jesus Christ?
>
> R—Yes, exactly the same.
>
> D—. . . Saint Peter was, therefore, the supreme shepherd, and superior even to the apostles. . . . Do you believe that these successors (after he was really dead) did not have the same power as those whom they succeeded?

[26]See M. Guerra Gomez, *op. cit.*, 465; M. Maccarrone, *Vicarius Christi, storia del titolo papale*, Rome, 1952. One knows the formula of Pierre de Blois: *Pauper est vicarius Christi* (*Epist.* 91; *PL* 207, 286 c).

[27]*PL* 214, 292 A. See J. Rivière, "Le pape est-il un Dieu pour Innocent III?," *Rev. des Sc. Rel.* 2, 1922, 447–451.

[28]*Prima controversia generalis*, lib. III, *De Ecclesia militante*, cap. 2; and *Controversia* V, cap. 4.

[29]*Private talks in the form of a catechism by a country priest with youth, translated from the German by an exiled French priest*, V. II, Constance, 1795, 298–299.

R—By succeeding to their dignity they were invested with all their power.[30]

It is true that, from the first decades of the fourteenth century, Augustine Trionfo (who died in 1328) had exalted the transcendence of the function and the power of the pope in such a way that only hell and limbo escaped his jurisdiction.[31] And the opinion was already circulating that within his responsibility the pope *"quodammodo Deus est, id est Dei vicarius."*[32] But because of this the ecclesiology of the West strayed into a deviation which Vatican II, it must be admitted—despite its onesidedness—channeled and corrected. The Church is founded on *the* apostles, not on a super-apostle. And *Pastor aeternus* refuses to separate the Roman primacy from what he calls the *episcopatus* one and undivided, in other words all of the bishops in their communion. He sees it totally finalized by the radiance of the mission confided to the apostolic body. Even more so, it is to this finality that he attaches his powers. A vision which places the Bishop of Rome so far above the bishops that the rooting of his function in the episcopal grace becomes accidental[33] is, to revive an old formula which marked the discussions of Vatican I, *ad destructionem et non ad aedificationem Ecclesiae.*[34] It contradicts the nature of the Church. In the constitution *Lumen gentium,* Vatican II studied and refined *Pastor aeternus* in this sense.

Bishop among bishops, but Bishop of Rome and for that reason charged with the *singular* power attached to the seat of the *potentior principalitatis;*[35] such is the episcopal status of the Primate in the episcopal college and in regard to the *communion* of the Churches confided to him. Noth-

[30]*Ibid.,* 296, 298.

[31]See J. Rivière, "Une première somme du pouvoir pontifical: le pape chez Augustin d'Ancôme," *Rev. des Sc. Rel.* 18, 1938, 149–183; Id., "Trionfo," *DTC* 15, 1855–1860; M. J. Wilks, "Papa est nomen jurisdictionis, Augustinus Triumphus and the Papal vicariate of Christ," *JTS* 8, 1857, 71–91, 256–271; J.-M. R. Tillard, *L'Évêque de Rome,* 80–81.

[32]See J. Rivière, "Sur l'expression Papa-Deus au Moyen Age," *Miscellanea Francesco Ehrle; Scritti di Storia e Paleographia,* t. II, Rome, 1924, 276–289; and the texts of cardinals Colonna (in 1297), of Jean André (who died in 1348), of Alvarez Pelayo (who died in 1349), of Beldus de Ubaldis, from Panormitanus (who died in 1445) quoted in J.-M. R. Tillard, *L'Évêque de Rome,* 81–82.

[33]This is the vision of Trionfo. See M. J. Wilks, *art. cit.*

[34]See the intervention of Mgr. Zinelli (Mansi 52, 1105 C.D.). This is already found in the writings of the dominican Jean de Paris (see J. Leclercq, *Jean de Paris et l'ecclésiologie du XIIIe siècle,* Paris, 1942, 188, 240). For Thomas Aquinas, see *Summa theologica,* IIa-IIae, 88, 12, ad 2; *opusc.* 20, lib. III, cap. 10.

[35]"We are conscious of being bishop of Rome, a consciousness which justifies and sustains the one which we have of being Pontiff. It is in fact as successor of Saint Peter on the seat of Rome that we are conscious of having the formidable mission of being Vicar of Christ on the earth and therefore supreme Shepherd and visible head of the universal Church," said Paul VI (*DC* 74, 1977, 105, 101).

ing in his function, and the power which corresponds to it, escapes the episcopal grace. But this grace—which in every bishop is always given for *communion*—is proportionate to the place of *his* Church in the heart of this *communion*. His relationship to Christ and to the Church is situated there, inside the relationship of the episcopal college *as such,* a college which bears in itself as a principal of unity the singular "service" of one of its members, charged with going back continually to the witness of Peter and Paul. This *singularity* is episcopal; it remains in the control of the episcopal grace *as such.* However, it is proper to this bishop and makes him not a super-bishop but certainly *the first* in responsibility.

Will such terms as "supreme shepherd of the Church," "shepherd of the universal Church"[36] be used? The best expression seems to us to be "servant of the servants of God," but it has been thought that this expression does not indicate enough the hierarchical place of this "first." Vatican I wanted itself to be in full harmony with "the permanent usage of the Churches," "the actions of the ecumenical councils and the holy canons," especially there "where the East would meet the West in the union of faith and charity," in brief, with "the old and constant faith of the universal Church."[37] Why then not speak simply, with Tradition, of the supreme office of first guardian of Communion?[38]

Hence it is clear that the function of the Bishop of Rome could not be perceived as dimming the authority of each bishop in his local Church. Vatican I, urged on by the Fathers of the minority and some members of what has been called its third party,[39] quotes in *Pastor aeternus,* concerning the express request of the archbishop of Baltimore, some lines taken from one of the most beautiful pages of the document on the papacy.[40] They come from a letter of Gregory the Great to the patriarch Eulogius of Alexandria, who greeted him with the title of universal bishop:

> Your blessedness . . . speaks to me saying "as you have stipulated." I ask you not to use these words when speaking about me, because I know what I am and what you are. By rank you are my brothers, by your ways you are my fathers. I have not ordered, but I have simply forced myself to indicate what seems useful to me. And yet, I do not have the impression that your Blessedness has been careful to preserve perfectly in his memory what I wanted to inscribe there. Because I had said that neither you to me, nor someone else to another could write in this way. And

[36]*Lumen gentium,* 22, and especially *Nota praevia,* 3, 4.

[37]*DS* 3065, 3059, 3062.

[38]It is in the same way that *Pastor aeternus* understands it (*DS* 3050).

[39]R. Aubert, "Documents concernant le tiers parti au concile du Vatican," *Abhandlungen über Theologie und Kirche; Festschrift für Karl Adam,* Düsseldorf, 1952, 241-259.

[40]*DS* 3061.

> here I discover in the heading of your letter this "superb" title of universal
> pope which I have refused. I beg your very beloved holiness not to do
> that any more in the future, because then they would take away from
> you what they would attribute in an exaggerated manner to another. It
> is not in words that I wish to find my grandeur but in my ways. And
> I do not consider as an honor what, I know, would bring harm to the
> honor of my brothers. *My honor is the honor of the universal Church.*
> *My honor is the firm strength of my brothers. What truly honors me*
> *is when each one is not refused the honor which is due him.* But if your
> Holiness treats me as the universal pope, it refuses to itself what it at-
> tributes to me of the universal. Let that not be. Let the words which in-
> flate vanity and wound charity disappear.[41]

The charge confided to the Bishop of Rome is a service of the Church
accomplished not by short-circuiting that of the bishop of each local
Church but, on the contrary, as even the text of Vatican I states, by "affirming it, strengthening it and defending it."[42] This service consists in
preserving with the uneasiness about the universal (of the *catholica*) the
ministry of each bishop and maintaining it at any price within the demands
of the unbreakable solidarity of *communion.* It is the ministry of *this* local
bishop which is at the heart of the life of this local Church. The role of
the Bishop of Rome does not consist in an intervention which is added
over and above, as that of the Prime Minister compared to the mayor
of the city. It is the question of a presence making itself felt inside even
the involvement of this bishop, "evangelizing it" so that it will be what
it is supposed to be. The pastoral authority of the bishop of the place is
not that of a subordinate, of an auxiliary. *Lumen gentium* is explicit on
this point:

> Charged with particular Churches as vicars and legates of Christ, the
> bishops direct them by their advice, their encouragement, their example,
> but also by their authority and by the exercise of the sacred power whose
> use, however, belongs to them only in view of the edification in truth
> and holiness of their flock, remembering that he who is the greatest must
> become the smallest, and he who commands, must become like the ser-
> vant (cf. Luke 22:26-27).
>   This power that they exercise personally in the name of Christ is a power
> which is proper, ordinary and immediate: it is subjected, however, in
> its exercise to the last regulation of the supreme authority of the Church
> and, considering its usefulness for the Church or certain faithful, it can
> be, by this authority, confined to certain limits. By virtue of this power,

---

[41]*Epist.* VIII, 30; *PL* 77, 933c (the lines which are *italicized* are those which *Pastor aeternus*
quotes).

[42]*DS* 3061.

the bishops have the sacred right, and before God the duty, to produce laws for their subjects, to render judgments and to regulate everything which concerns the order of worship and the apostolate.

The pastoral charge, in other words the habitual and daily care of their sheep, is given fully to them: they must not be considered as the vicars of the Roman Pontiffs, because they exercise a power which is proper to them and, in all truth, are, for the peoples whom they direct, the leaders. So, their power is in no way erased by the supreme and universal power; on the contrary, it is strengthened, reinforced and defended by it, the form established by Christ the Lord for the government of his Church which is indefectibly assured by the Holy Spirit.[43]

Besides, Pius IX had already warmly approved the response of the German bishops to a telegram from Bismarck, dated May 14, 1872. This telegram made the authority of the Bishop of Rome a power added over and above that of each bishop and, by this fact, being able to dominate and suppress it:

This telegram claims that the decisions of the Vatican Council bring about the following consequences:

1. The pope can assume in each diocese the episcopal rights and substitute his episcopal power.

2. The episcopal jurisdiction is absorbed by the papal jurisdiction.

3. The pope no longer exercises, as in the past, certain reserved and fixed rights, but he is the trustee of the full and entire episcopal power.

4. The pope replaces, in principal, each bishop individually.

5. It belongs only to the pope to put himself in practice and at any moment in the place of the bishop vis-à-vis governments.

6. The bishops are only instruments of the pope, his servants without proper responsibility.

7. The bishops have become, vis-à-vis governments, servants of a foreign sovereign, and, in truth, of a sovereign who, by virtue of his infallibility, is a completely absolute sovereign, more than any other absolute monarch in the world.

To that the German episcopate responds:

Undoubtedly, the decisions of the council declare that the power of ecclesiastical jurisdiction of the pope is: *potestas suprema, ordinaria et immediata,* a supreme power of government given to the pope by Jesus Christ, Son of God, in the person of Saint Peter, which extends directly over the whole Church, consequently over every diocese and all the faithful, in order to preserve the unity of the faith, the discipline and govern-

---

[43]*Lumen gentium,* 27. Take note of the expression "vicars and legates of Christ" to designate all the bishops.

ment of the Church, and is in no way a simple attribute consisting of several reserved rights.

But this is not a new doctrine, it is a truth recognized in the Catholic faith and a principal known in canon law, a doctrine recently explained and confirmed by the Vatican Council, in accord with the decisions of the former ecumencial councils, against the errors of the French, the Jansenists and the Febronians. According to this doctrine of the Catholic Church, the pope is bishop of Rome, but not bishop of another diocese nor of another city; he is neither bishop of Breslau nor bishop of Cologne, etc. But by his rank as bishop of Rome, he is at the same time pope, in other words, the shepherd and supreme head of the universal Church, head of all the bishops and faithful, and his papal power must be respected and listened to everywhere and always, and not only in special and exceptional cases. In this position, the pope must see to it that each bishop fulfills his duty to the entire extent of his charge. If a bishop is prevented from that, or if some type of need should be felt, the pope has the right and the duty, not by his rank as bishop of the diocese, but by that of pope, to order everything which is necessary for the administration of the diocese. . . .

The decisions of the Vatican Council do not furnish the slightest pretext to claim that the pope has become by them an absolute sovereign.

And Pius IX makes the following comment:

Your collective declaration gains such distinction by its clarity and accuracy that it leaves nothing to be desired, that it has been for us the cause of great joy, and that there is no need for us to add anything to it. But the false assertions by certain periodicals demand from Us a more solemn witness of our approval, because, in order to maintain the assertions refuted by you by the so-called circular, they had the audacity to refuse to give credit to your explanations, alleging that your interpretation of the decrees of the Council was only a watered-down interpretation and answered not in the least the intentions of this apostolic See.

We condemn in the most formal manner this false and slanderous supposition. Your declaration gives the pure catholic doctrine, and consequently that of the Holy Council and of this Holy See, completely established and clearly developed by obvious and irrefutable arguments, in a way that it demonstrates for every man of good faith that, in the accused decrees, there is absolutely nothing which is new or which changes anything in the relationships existing until the present time, or which could furnish a pretext for oppressing the Church again or for thwarting the election of a new pontiff.[44]

[44]One find these texts commented on by dom O. Rousseau, "La vraie valeur de l'épiscopat dans l'Église, d'après d'importants documents de 1875," *Irénikon* 29, 1956, 121–142, 143–150 (reproduced in Y. Congar and B. D. Dupuy, *L'Épiscopat et l'Église universelle,* 709–736). See also J.-M. R. Tillard, "L'horizon de la primauté de l'évêque de Rome," *POC* 25, 1975, 217–244, *L'Évêque de Rome,* 174–177.

He comes back to it again on March 15, 1875 in his consistorial speech: not only, he says, does he accept the interpretation of the German episcopate but he confirms it "by the fullness of his Apostolic Authority (*Apostolicae Auctoritatis plenitudine confirmamus*)."

This is like a *synergism* of the function of the Bishop of Rome, of that of the entire episcopal college and of that of each bishop. And *synergism* is a word belonging to the vocabulary of *communion*. It expresses more the compenetration of the dynamisms in question than their complementarity, more the inseparability of the agents than their plurality, more the unbreakable unity of the effect which results from it than the sum of the influences. In each Church of this *communion* of local Churches which the Church of God is, through the ministry of its bishop, who is the one in whom the solidarity of the episcopal college produces its effect—since the college serves the Church only by serving the Churches—it is this osmosis which is made real. Wherever the local bishop acts in *communion* and in function of it, and wherever the Bishop of Rome is faithful to not going beyond the specifics of his function, then there are not two authorities in the diocese (the local Church). There is that of a bishop in whom are transmitted faith, witness, concerns, objectives, teaching, and mission which are those of the entire episcopal college and that he "receives" in his *communion* with the one who has the responsibility of seeing to the cohesion of this college in fidelity to the apostolic deposit of faith. It happens, obviously, that a bishop may slip out of *communion* or that the Bishop of Rome may act as if he were the only bishop. Reading history is enough to be convinced of it. Then the osmosis is broken; two authorities superimpose themselves. But then also the nature of the Church is falsified.

3. It is true that in what the code of canon law continues to call the Latin Church,[45] relations between the Bishop of Rome and other bishops are complicated by the fact that the limits of the patriarchate of the West (whose patriarch is the Bishop of Rome) and those of the totality of Churches in communion with the Roman See are clouded over. One of the consequences of the break with the East has been this narrowing of the ecclesial space where bishops preside in communion with the Bishop of Rome, and the quasi-identification of this space with the patriarchate of the West.[46] The exercise of primacy and that of the patriarchal authority

[45]The Code opens in this way: *"canones hujus codicis unam Ecclesiam latinam respiciunt."*

[46]See J.-M. R. Tillard, *L'Évêque de Rome*, 70–71 (bibliography). Y. Congar, "Le pape comme patriarche d'Occident; approche d'une réalité trop négligée," *Istina* 28, 1983, 374–390 (388), in addition to recalling a well known passage of Bossuet, quotes a text of Nicolas de Cuse linked to the Council of Bale (1432–1433) taken from the *Concordia catholica*, lib. II, cap. 7 (ed. G. Kallen, Hambourg, 1964, 126) and some texts of Jean Raguse (*De Ecclesia* III, cap. 3, ed. Fr. Sanjek, Zagréb, 1983, 222) showing that there was a consciousness of this reduction and its ecclesiological consequences.

have almost become one and the same. But the patriarchal authority is by nature administrative and centralized. It implies making decisions for the Churches in his jurisdiction and a vast right of inspection. Very attentive to the choice of bishops, it exercises in their regard a particular "surveillance" judging their offenses, exempting certain groups from their authority, sometimes nibbling away at their influence, receiving appeals, intervening in major problems. Since the exercise of the primacy assumes several of these characteristics of the exercise of the patriarchate, it can no longer be seen in all its purity. It appears under a disguise which no longer permits an adequate perception of its identity.[47]

Certainly, it must be recognized that even in what concerns its relations with other patriarchates before the break, the Roman See was tempted to add to prerogatives which came from the primacy of claims which exceeded the nature of it. It will hint, then affirm that the authority of other primates and other patriarchs—like that of the metropolitans and bishops of these Churches—comes from a concession of privileges and powers which come from it.[48] The famous theory of the three chairs of Peter—in Antioch, Alexandria and Rome—will often serve to justify this "patriarchal" meddling of the vicar of Peter beyond the West, provoking in this way a meshing of primatial authority over patriarchal rights.[49] The East, although it saw in Rome a center of doctrinal reference and even under certain circumstances resorted to mediation from the bishop of this seat,[50] obviously resisted a similar infringement. It was not a stranger to a climate ending in schism.[51] Besides, even in the West, important areas vigor-

---

[47]"One thing is the power of real jurisdiction of the pope over the whole Church, another thing is the centralization of the power. The first is of divine right, the second is the effect of human circumstances. The first is a virtue abundant in benefits, the second is objectively an anomaly," Mgr. Benelli, "Les rapports entre le Siège de Pierre et les Églises locales," *DC* 70, 1973, 1072.

[48]The documents are known. Let us recall the Council of Lyon of 1274 (profession of faith of Michel Paléologue), Boniface VIII (1294-1303), the speech of Zinelli at Vatican I (July 5, 1870). On this question, see M. J. Le Guillou, "L'expérience orientale de la collégialité épiscopale et ses requêtes," *Intina* 10, 1964, 111-124; W. de Vries, "Die Entstehung der Patriarchate des Ostens und ihr Verhältnis zur päpstlichen Vollgewalt," *Scholastik* 37, 1962, 341-369; E. Lanne, "Églises locales et patriarcats à l'époque des grands conciles," *Irénikon* 34, 1961, 292-321; C. Vogel, "Unité de l'Église et pluralité des formes historiques d'organisation ecclésiastique du IIIe au Ve siècle," *L'Épiscopat et l'Église universelle,* coll. "Unam sanctam," 39, Paris, 1962, 591-616.

[49]This will be found with Leo the Great and even Gregory the Great.

[50]See canons 3, 4, 5 of the Council of Sardis (343), in P. I. Joannou, *Fonti IX, Discipline générale antique 1/2, Canons des synodes particuliers,* Rome, 1982, 162-165; first canon of the Council of St. Sophia (879-880), *ibid.,* 482-484. For the whole, see H. Marot, "Décentralisation structurelle et primauté dans l'Église ancienne," *Concilium* 7, 1965, 19-28; Id., "Note sur la pentarchie"; for the ecclesiological context, see P. Batiffol, *Cathedra Petri; études d'histoire ancienne de l'Église,* 41-79; Leslie W. Barnard, *The Council of Sardica, 343 A. D.*; Y. Congar, *L'Église, de saint Augustin à la période moderne,* coll. "Histoire des dogmes," III/3, Paris, 1970, 269-277; T. G. Jalland, *The Church and the Papacy,* London, 1944.

[51]See J. Le Guillou, *op. cit.*; W. de Vries, *Orient et Occident; les structures ecclésiales vues dans l'histoire des sept premiers conciles œcuméniques,* Paris, 1974.

ously affirmed their right to a relative autonomy. The case at Carthage is well known.[52]

These reactions must be taken seriously. They show that in the undivided Church, for reasons that it would be thoughtless to identify solely or without fine distinctions in regard to their political aspirations—although desire for power and prestige are not absent from them—the compenetration of various types of authority with which the Bishop of Rome is invested has not gone on by itself. In particular the quasi-confusion of his authority as primate of all the Churches and his function as patriarch of the West, inducing him to act with the bishops of other patriarchates in the way which his title as patriarch authorized him to do so in the West, has caused a problem.[53]

It has been felt that the very nature of *communion*, if it demanded unity, was contrary to the fact that the ministry charged with watching over it in a particular style gradually confuses it with the exercise of a haughty imperialism,[54] because who says *communion* also says respect for plurality and, in particular, for what could be called the "fundamental plurality," that of the members of the apostolic college from which the witness and authority of different "apostolic seats" comes. Tertullian is remembered as the one who saw in the apostolic Churches "the Mother Churches and the sources of the apostolic faith," Irenaeus for making compulsory points of reference, and even Augustine by presenting them as the *arx auctoritatis* by which the entire Church is strengthened.[55] The special place of Peter in the midst of the apostolic group, and that of the Roman See (primatial) which is tied to it,[56] could not question this place and this common authority of all the apostolic seats.

Restudying Vatican I in the light of the great ecclesial Tradition, the constitution *Lumen gentium* did not specify the way in which the primatial authority and that of the local episcopate fit together harmoniously,

[52]See especially W. H. C. Frend, *The Rise of Christianity*, Philadelphia, 1985, 339-357: "the relations were more often proper than friendly, and each generation was stamped with fundamental discords touching on theology and the structure of the Church" (339). See also Ch. Munier, "Un canon inédit du XXe concile de Carthage—ut nullus and Romanam Ecclesiam audeat appellare," *Rev. des Sc. Rel.* 40, 1966, 113-126; on the whole history of the African Church, see J. Cuoq, *L'Église d'Afrique du Nord, du IIe au XIIe siècle*, but we point out *ibid.* 122-134 on the preservation of *communion*.

[53]Let us note that his function as metropolitan of suburban Italy has also influenced his two other types of authority. See H. Marot *art. cit.* and P. Batiffol, "Les trois zones de la potestas papale," *Cathedra Petri*, 41-79.

[54]One is acquainted with the important work of Fr. Heiler, *Altkirchliche Autonomie und päpstlichen Zentralismus*, t. I, Munich, 1941.

[55]Tertullian, *De praescriptione* 21, 3-4; Irenaeus, *Adv. Haer.* III, 4, 1; Augustine, *Epist.* 118, 3 (*PL* 33, 448); cf. *Epistola ad catholicos de secta Donatistarum* (*PL* 43, 415).

[56]See Augustine, *Contra Julianum* I, 4 (*PL* 44, 648). See J.-M. R. Tillard, *L'Evêque de Rome*, 100-114.

although it strongly underlined the authority of each bishop. Therefore, this point remains open to some quiet research, respectful of all elements in the document. But in Catholic conscience a certainty is henceforth acquired. Although all Churches are confided to him under a special title, the authority of the Bishop of Rome is to be understood within the authority of the episcopal college. His authority is at its service and not above it, even when as primate this bishop is the only one to intervene, by virtue of his function. Because this authority is primatial, it is certainly not on the same level as that of the other bishops; it is not a simple title. However, it is an authority of *service in and for* the college of *ministerium*, and not of *dominion over* the college. What is recognized here is the ideal of Gregory the Great. It is a question of confirming and helping, not of absorbing or supplanting.

For reasons which are related to relations with the Orthodox Churches always recognized as sister Churches,[57] the situation of Eastern uniate Churches—in other words, in *communion* with the Church of Rome— poses delicate and serious questions for ecclesiology. However, one can see in discussions about the Eastern Code a will to make an adjustment in this osmosis of the two authorities, that of the Bishop of Rome and that of the bishops of the other seats. In history, not without some foundation, uniate Churches often complained of the Roman attempt to centralize, even of bringing everything back to Western ways. And even the old Maronite Church—which is not uniate—was seen forced by waves of Latinization which modified several of its characteristics. But challenged by the elaboration of the code of canon law which is intended for them, several members of these communities are attentive to this problem.[58] It is more and more clear for many that in what concerns the internal structure of these Eastern Churches, inherited from the most ancient Tradition,[59] their strict liturgical regulation, their present discipline, especially their synodal discussion, the Bishop of Rome should not interfere in such a way that he would act like a super-patriarch. His primacy must be inscribed within the network of episcopal functions and hierarchies proper to these ecclesial bodies, without violating their dignity and the perception they have of being responsible for their own fidelity to a long tradition. They could not live under a protectorship, a guardianship.

---

[57]As the correspondence of Paul VI and Athenagoras testifies, published in the *Tomos Agapis*.

[58]See the excellent works published in the review *Kanon*. For the history, see W. de Vries, "La S. Sede ed i patriarcati cattolici d'Oriente," *Orientalia Christiana Periodica* 27, 1961, 313-361. See also the important study of N. Edelby, *Vatican II; les Églises orientales catholiques,* coll. "Unam sanctam," 76, Paris, 1970, 267-376.

[59]It is no longer a question here of inculturation, as for the young Churches, but of respect for the ancient ecclesial heritage as old as the heritage of the West, which they have preserved.

At Vatican II, this was the privilege especially of the East—by the vote of Eastern bishops such as Maximos IV[60] but also through the research of several Western theologians examining carefully the documents of the great Tradition—making the Fathers of the Council aware of this need. It specifies the contours of primacy. It is not enough to say that this primacy does not stifle the authority and responsibility of the bishop of each local Church. What must be added is that it respects the rights and privileges of those episcopal seats whose history attaches them more directly to the apostolic Churches. In other words, this primacy does not turn up its nose at history.

4. Within these perspectives, it becomes possible to get to the core of the authority which Catholic tradition recognizes in the Roman primate and to measure with greater clarity the "power" that its exercise requires. In a negative way, it is necessary, first of all, to restate that it is not a question formally of a power of *dominium* but of a "power" which is pastoral and oriented towards service. It is regulated by the authority which others (the other bishops) have received and which it must strengthen and guarantee. Besides, *by himself,* it is not up to the primate "to make bishops."[61] We have seen that down through the centuries the Churches have chosen their pastors, according to their own customs, all the while remaining in communion with the Bishop of Rome.[62] And in nothing did he contest this right of each local Church to take one of its own whose faith it knew and whose uprightness it was aware of, in communion with the neighboring Churches, then to have him ordained.[63] Therefore, he does not take control or wield a heavy hand over the episcopate. It is not even, in the political sense, a power of government but a "power" of leadership. The nuance is important. To govern, is to rule (sometimes by giving in to the temptation to dominate or to coerce); to exercise leadership is to win over, to guide, to lead each one towards what the Spirit wants him to become. Gregory the Great wrote:

> Indeed, they govern with violence and harshness, those who are eager not to straighten out their inferiors by peaceful arguments, but to weigh them down by dominating them harshly. . . .

[60]On the role of Maximos IV Saigh, read especially M. Villain, "Un prophète: le patriarche Maximos IV," *L'Église melkite au concile,* Beyrouth, 1967; Emilios Inglessis, *Maximos IV, l'Orient conteste l'Occident,* Paris, 1969; *Voix de l'Église en Orient,* Paris, 1962. See also N. Edelby, "Notre vocation de chrétiens d'Orient," *POC 3,* 1953, 201-217. On the Catholic vision of the patriarchate since Vatican I, see G. Dejaifve, "Patriarches et primauté de Vatican I à Vatican II," *Pluralisme et œcuménisme en recherches théologiques, mélanges S. Dockx,* coll. "Bibl. Ephem. Theol. Lov.," 43, 1976, 193-218.

[61]*L'Évêque de Rome,* 224-225.

[62]Leo the Great intervenes when a serious irregularity is pointed out to him (*Epist.* 4, 1-5; 12, 1; cf. *PL* 54, 611-614, 645-646).

[63]And thus Leo, *Epist.* 14, 5 (*PL* 54, 673).

When Saint Paul said to his disciple Timothy: "This is what you must prescribe and teach with authority," he does not recommend to him a tyrannical domination, but this authority which comes from the way to live.[64]

One is closer here to the choir director who, for the harmony of all parties, "sees to" the accuracy, the tone, the volume of each voice by putting it in its place within the context of the whole choir, like the power of an army general. And the quality of a choir depends on its director, on the experience which he transmits.

Positively, the "power" of the primate is that of intervening, in certain cases, in the life of a local Church, when the good of *communion* demands it. In fact, it happens that through a lack of resources or simply because it does not have the means to make by itself the decisions which are imposed, a Church slips into a situation which compromises its quality, perhaps even its fidelity to the gospel. Certainly, the primate must first of all urge the local bishop to act by himself, to alert the neighboring Churches. But a direct intervention can be imposed: an explicit request for help made to another Church, a convocation of a local synod or of a provincial council, the sending of the necessary men, or an official expression of his disagreement.[65]

The most ancient history shows that the Bishop of Rome can equally, in response to his "appeals," judge an affair. Cyprian addresses himself to Steven, the Bishop of Rome, so that he will react to the position of the Bishop of Arles, Marcianus, attracted by Novatian.[66] He asks him to write to the bishops of Gaul so that they will excommunicate this false brother and choose a successor to him. In the same era, in a very complex affair involving the bishops of Leon and Merida, in Spain, it is towards Steven that Basilides, one among them, turns so that they might recover their See, after their return to the Church.[67] Later, the canons of the Council of Sardinia, in 343, under Pope Jules, ratify the custom of having recourse to Rome.[68] There are numerous cases that could be cited.[69] It reverts

---

[64]*Comment. in Job* 23:23-24 (*PL* 76, 265-266).

[65]Let us think of the attitude of Leo XIII at the heart of the crisis of Filioque (see V. Peri, "Leone III e il Filioque," *Rivista di storia della Chiesa in Italia* 25, 1971, 3-58; B. Capelle, "Le pape Léon III et le Filioque," *1054-1954. L'Église et les Églises, études et travaux offerts à dom L. Beauduin*, t. I, Chevetogne, 1954, 309-322).

[66]See *Epistola* 68. We will come back to the complex thought of Cyprian on this subject.

[67]See Cyprian *Epistola* 67.

[68]It is canons 3, 4, 5 which decree: "If a bishop thinks that the judgment brought on him must be revised, if it pleases your charity, let us honor the memory of the apostle Peter, and let the judges themselves write to Julius, bishop of Rome, so that the tribunal, if such be the case, might be established again by the bishops of the neighboring province and that it send arbitrators; but if such a tribunal cannot be set up—because it is up to him to decide if the affair needs to be

also to the primate to arbitrate conflicts between Churches, and Leo the Great does not hesitate to intervene so that the privileges of certain Sees will be respected.[70] In the tenth century, the clergy and the people of Carthage will present a poignant appeal for help to pope Benedict VII: that he give them a bishop.[71] He is the last recourse they have in their distress.

Here we are on the level of subsidiarity.[72] This implies that in regard to a community over which it has a real power, but which is confided to a special authority, the "superior" entreaty seeks to reduce the interventions as much as possible. It refuses to meddle with the affairs of this group as long as it has not put its own means into operation, and mobilized all of its resources. In other words, it does not seek to take the place of those who are in positions of responsibility, to substitute for them. Its primary attitude is to awaken their attention, to recall to them (vigorously perhaps) the task which is incumbent on them. But, when it ascertains that alone they cannot overcome the crisis, it owes it to itself to intervene. Without that, in fact, this group will let itself deteriorate or vegetate in a way which threatens its identity. In this sense, the Bishop of Rome has the power, and the duty, to act for the good of the whole Church (at stake in each local Church, since this is where it is realized) when a local Church

revised—what was already decided must not be questioned again and the decree will be confirmed. . . . If a bishop is deposed by the judgment of the bishops of the neighboring province and claims to have to add still something else to his defense, a successor to his seat should not be given to him, before the bishop of Rome is acquainted with his affair and has pronounced his sentence. . . . If a bishop is denounced and the bishops of the same province united together depose him from his dignity and if he, lodging an appeal has recourse to the benevolent bishop of Rome, if the latter wishes to hear him and estimates that it is just to re-examine the affair, let him deign to write to the bishops of the neighboring province to examine everything carefully and accurately and to express their vote on the affair in all truthfulness."

"If, however, someone claims that his cause must be heard again and on his request the bishop of Rome judges that it is good to send some priest from his entourage, it will be necessary to add that it will be in the power of this same bishop of Rome in case he judges it good and decides to have to do it, to send persons furnished with the authority of the one who sent them, who will judge the affair with the bishops of that area; and if he estimates that what was done was sufficient to understand and decide the affair of the bishop in question, he will act as it seems good to his very wise judgment. The bishops will respond: What has been said pleases us." (P. I. Joannou, *op. cit.*, 1/2, 162–165). On the Council of Sardis, see the enlightening work of Leslie W. Barnard, *The Council of Sardica, 343 A.D.*, chapters on canons 97–118. These canons come from the "western council," after the departure of the bishops opposed to Athanasius.

[69]See Tr. G. Jalland, *op. cit.*, which assembles and analyzes these cases. See also J. Cuoq, *op. cit.*, (in particular, 122–134).

[70]And thus *Epist.* 106, 5 (*PL* 54, 1007); *Epist.* 119 (*PL* 54, 1042); *Epist.* 129 (*PL* 54, 1075–1077).

[71]See J. Cuoq, *op. cit.*, 124–125.

[72]During the extraordinary episcopal synod of December 1985, this question was discussed, and the final report mentions it. On subsidiarity, see W. Bertrams, *Questiones fondamentales Juris Canonici*, Rome, 1969, 545–562; R. Metz, "La subsidiarié, principe régulateur des tensions dans l'Église," *Revue de droit canon* 22, 1972, 155–176; O. Karrer, "Le principe de subsidiarité dans l'Église," *L'Église de Vatican II*, t. I, coll. "Unam sanctam," 51 b, Paris, 1966, 575–606.

compromises the good of *communion*. The present situation[73] shows that the cogwheels that this type of situation demands are not always well in gear. And it is often the local Churches themselves which, by a certain atavism, address themselves too easily to central authority. But more and more a consciousness of the importance of this subsidiarity is taking hold. It appears as one of the principal expressions of a "primacy of service," reconciling the respect for local authorities and the will to back them up.[74] It permits, besides, to understand better how the immediate power of the Bishop of Rome over the totality of the local Churches and their faithful contributes *ad aedificationem Ecclesiae.*

The primatial "power" of the Bishop of Rome is also, on another level, that of taking the initiative for a statement, addressed to all the local Churches—bishops, clerics and laity[75]—in which he gives his opinion, expresses his judgment on a point which seems important. The encyclical letters are such a statement. The encyclicals of Leo XIII on social questions, continued by those of of Pius XI, John XXIII, Paul VI and John-Paul II, have been without any doubt a service rendered to the bishops and their Churches, permitting them to take a proper position in this crucial area. The encyclical of Pius XII on the biblical question helped to dispel the last doubts about scientific exegesis and in this way prepared the constitution *Dei Verbum* of Vatican II. The encyclical of Paul VI concerning evangelization synthesized and extended the conclusions of an important episcopal synod. Other documents have touched on serious disciplinary questions. Certain ones have made explicit some aspects of the revealed mystery.

These texts—which do not have the guarantee of infallibility—are a "pastoral statement" directed to *communion* of faith and evangelical *praxis* of all the Churches. Confronted with the evolution of ways of thinking and ways of living in their human surroundings, they could, in fact, lack the proper perspective, let themselves become fascinated by strong currents, and accept doctrines which fit in badly with the vision of the human person and the destiny of the world which is specifically Christian. In addition, options which are radically different on serious points would tear apart the ecclesial fabric. Charged with "seeing to" the fidelity of his brother bishops and their Churches in regard to the authentic sense of the revealed Word and its demands, the Bishop of Rome has the

---

[73]Clearly manifested at the time of the synod of 1985.

[74]As the attitude of Gregory VII himself shows on the place of the Church of Africa (cf. J. Cuoq, *op. cit.,* 129-134).

[75]We are surprised that our proposition that this word be addressed *to the bishops alone* and charging them to spread it by explaining it and by contextualizing it was found spiteful and ignorant (*L'Evêque de Rome,* 208-210).

"power" to speak to all of his vision of things. It is his responsibility to alert them as soon as he perceives a danger of division or deviation. It may happen that the primate might not be (according to the ordinary tendency of whoever is exercising a doctrinal responsibility) sensitive enough to the positive aspects of new points which are questionable, that he may remain too riveted on a particular theology, or that his advisors or his surroundings exercise too many pressures on him.[76] His statements, therefore, must be understood, read, with a critical judgment. This judgment alone permits one to measure the objective weight of the matter. However, they should not be scorned or repudiated lightly. They are to be accepted as the "prudent" step of the one who, because of his function, indicates to the Churches that in such and such a situation, such or such behavior, there is a hidden problem and reminds them that they must, therefore, ask themselves questions. And usually he proposes to them an avenue of truth that they should examine carefully and attentively.

In the case of a difficult doctrinal problem, or even simply in view of a mutual enrichment of Churches, there would be nothing against the Bishop of Rome communicating to the other bishops (and through them to the whole of the Christian people) the letter of a bishop or of an episcopal conference, instead of writing an encyclical. He would "receive" it as the adequate expression of the common faith and would make it his own. Such a step would dispel ambiguities about the nature of the doctrinal "power" of the primate. It would be highly desirable for another reason besides, because the proper "power" of the primate is precisely that of putting into operation what, according to his pastoral prudence, seems to him as profitable for the *aedificatio Ecclesiae* in *communion*. But such a communication—tying together with the old custom which we mentioned in another chapter—would contribute to binding tighter the horizontal lines among the Churches just as essential for *communion* as the vertical link of each one with the seat of Rome. Perhaps, in this line, when it is a question of the "power" which he has to refuse doctrinal currents or to judge persons outside of the ecumenical council,[77] the Bishop of Rome would have the benefit of having much broader recourse to local jurisdictions.[78] The "power" of denouncing errors, which he possesses by his

---

[76]Let us think about the encyclical *Mortalium animos* of Pius XI (January 6, 1928) which contrasts so much with the tone of other interventions of this pope in this area. See on the circumstances explaining it O. Rousseau, "Le sens œcuménique des conversations de Malines," *Irénikon* 44, 1971, 331-348 (345-347); Lambert Beauduin, "L'encyclique *Mortalium animos* du 6 janvier 1928," *Irénikon* 1928, 87-89.

[77]During the first centuries, it is the councils which condemn (Arius at Nicaea, Eutyches and Dioskore at Chalcedon, Nestorius at Ephesus).

[78]That was done in certain cases; but recent facts show that some bishops were opposed to the verdict of Rome on certain theologians or certain currents in their Churches.

charge, is not reserved to him. "To see to it" that serious errors are recti-
fied does not demand, of itself, the centralization of complex and delicate steps which lead to a doctrinal judgment. His "power" could be more
that of setting up or even requiring a process than to take this problem
in hand (in the Curia).

The primatial "power" is exercised also on another level. It would be
foolish to pretend that only the Bishop of Rome has the "power" to convoke a council. That would be tantamount to denying history. But it is
impossible to refuse him this "power," even in the hypothesis of an authentic ecumenical council of the Church finally gathered together in unity.
It is clear that then the methods and conditions of exercising this "power"
would be determined carefully. Yet in a world where the Christian notion
of the emperor is no more than a memory, one can hardly see how the
decision to hold a council could be taken without the Bishop of the Roman
See intervening. The idea of such a council can be proposed to him. But
the convoking must at least involve his *placet,* just as the promulgation
of the *acta, "una cum patribus."*[79]

This necessity comes from the very nature of every ecumenical council
and of its crucial importance for *communion.* Authority of the Bishop
of Rome and authority of the council are in a process of osmosis, even
if sometimes there are conflicts or tensions.[80] In the exercise of his func-

---

[79]G. Alberigo, *op. cit.,* presents with care and erudition the position of the canonists at the
time of Constance and Bale, and the waverings of theology on this subject, at the same time.
"Conciliarity" is an essential value of the Church. Therefore, we ask ourselves, how do we assign
a place to the authority of the pope and that of the college of cardinals in the face of the entire
holy, catholic and universal Church, which is *congregatio fidelium* and which the council represents?
Can the college of cardinals, without the pope, convoke the council, wherever the emperor ab-
stains from it? The position of the canonist Zabarella is known. At the council of Constance,
the running out of John XXIII will pose the problem of a council which is deprived of its "head,"
the one even who "authorized" it (although under pressure from emperor Sigismond). Can one,
without all of that, approve dogmatically the superiority of the council over the pope, to admit,
in a situation as complex, that only the council will be able to give the Church a pope capable
of reforming it (*ibid.,* 201-203)? For the link between pope and ecumenical council, the history
of the second Council of Constantinople (553) is without doubt the most typical. The council
argues with Vigile about the right of acting without him over the question of the Three Chapters.
However, both the emperor and the council support the *confirmation* of the council by the See
of Rome (see W. de Vries, *op. cit.,*). On this very difficult problem, a total vision will be found
in W. de Vries, "Ecumenical Councils and the Ministry of Peter," *Wort und Wahrheit Supplemen-
tary Issue* 2, December 1974, 146-161 (very numerous references); see also Amba Gregorius, "The
Ecumenical Council and the Ministry of Peter," *ibid.,* 130-146 (which does not touch the problem
which is from a dogmatic angle, that of the "greatest bishop"). On this *confirmation* by Rome,
the East does not have the same view as the West: it is not a question of a decision added to
the council, but taken in its dynamism. Earlier we studied the question of promulgation *una cum
patribus.*

[80]Even in the full council, as at Vatican II at the time of the malaise caused by changes in
the decree on ecumenism, requested at the last minute. On November 19, 1964, the eve of the
final vote, Mgr. Felici, secretary general of the council, announced to the Fathers that on the

tion, the primate should not forget the principal *"quod omnes tangit ab omnibus tractari et approbari debet."*[81] On their part, however, the bishops of the other Churches cannot forget that the unity of the Church demands a common point of view and a unanimous doctrinal vision on the serious questions which are asked about the faith. But the council is precisely the moment in which all the Churches—by those who represent them—treat together what concerns all of them. And the experience of Vatican II shows that even if the dispersed bishops remain in communion and can be consulted by the Bishop of Rome, there is nevertheless in the conciliar event a "plus-être communionnel." Unanimity is not lived there and expressed there in the same way as in the dispersion. The balance of the diverse authorities is realized there with more realism and truth, in openness and candor.[82] In addition, no one is a good judge of his own cause. Questions concerning the exercise of primacy can be asked, and they certainly will be asked if the Churches which are separated today are reunited. Responsible with a "special" title of *communion,* the Bishop of Rome can feel himself pushed to call forth this conciliar meeting. That belongs to his function. He has "power" to convoke a council. And it is in the same spirit that it is necessary to understand the convocation in Rome of episcopal synods.[83]

request about "superior authority" the Secretariat for unity had introduced nineteen corrections, *ad majorem claritatem textus* in the document already discussed and accepted paragraph by paragraph. From the fact that about forty changes had been proposed. See *Irénikon* 37, 1964, 50-53. On the totality of the pope-council problem, see the basic work of G. Alberigo, *Chiesa conciliare, Identità e significato del conciliarismo,* coll. "Testi e ricerche di Scienze religiose," 19, Brescia, 1981, and M. Wojtowytsch, *Pappstum und konzile,* Stuttgart, 1981. Let us recall the tension created at Chalcedon (where the legates of the pope are present) by the famous canon 28 whose history we know. On the tensions at Vatican II, see J. Grootaers, *Primauté et collégialité. Le dossier de Gerard Philips. Sur la Nota explicativa praevia (Lumen gentium, 3),* coll. "Bibl. Ephem. Theol. Lov.," 73, Louvain, 1986, and the *Acta* (forthcoming) of the symposium *Paolo VI e i problemi ecclesiologici al Concilio, 19-21 settembre 1986.* On the *Nota praevia* as such, see E. Olivares, "Analisis e interpretaciones de la 'Nota praevia explicativa'," *Est. Ecclesiast.* 42, 1967, 183-205; see also U. Betti, *La dottrina sull' episcopato del concilio Vaticano II, il capitolo III della costituzione dommatica Lumen gentium,* Rome, 1984.

[81]On which the classic study is the one by Y. Congar, "Quod omnes tangit ab omnibus tractari et approbari debet," *Rev. hist. droit franç. et étr.* 36, 1958, 210-259.

[82]Let us think about the refusal of the amendment proposed by Paul VI, asking (in July 1964) that in no. 22 of *Lumen gentium* it be said that the Roman pontiff must take into account the collegial power of the bishops but must render account to God alone (*uni Domino divinctus*). See G. Alberigo and F. Magistretti, *Constitutionis Dogmaticae Synopsis Historica,* Bologne, 1975, X, 22, 192-195, 456. On the origin of *uni Domino divinctus* see Cyprian, *Epist.* 55, 21, 2; 59, 14, 2; 72, 3, 2; *Didascalia* II, 35, 4 (Connolly IX, 98-100). Paul VI will come back to it but in a way that shows fine distinctions at the time of the consistory of February 1965, 490. But see *DC* 62, 1965, 1352 (more abrupt) and *DC* 66, 1969, 1054 (in opposition to a vision stating that the power comes from the base).

[83]It is clear that, these synods being new, their operation is still grinding away. For the permanent Eastern synod, see J. J. Hajjar, "Synode permanent," *La Collégialité épiscopale,* coll. "Unam sanctam," 52, Paris, 1965, 151-166.

The Bishop of Rome possesses besides, by his function, the "power" to speak in the name of his brother bishops and their Churches. This is verified in several different areas. The first is the very simple one of the forceful expression, in the face of the world, of a fundamental Christian conviction. We remember Camus, acknowledging to the Dominicans of Latour-Maubourg in 1948:

> And why shouldn't I say here what I have written elsewhere? For a long time during those frightful years I waited for a great voice to speak up in Rome. I, an unbeliever? Precisely. For I knew that the spirit would be lost if it did not utter a cry of condemnation when faced with force. It seems that that voice did speak up. But I assure you that millions of men like me did not hear it and that at that time believers and unbelievers alike shared a solitude that continued to spread as the days went by and the executioners multiplied.
>
> It has been explained to me since that the condemnation was indeed voiced. But that it was in the style of the encyclicals, which is not at all clear. The condemnation was voiced and it was not understood! Who could fail to feel where the true condemnation lies in this case and to see that this example by itself gives part of the reply, perhaps the whole reply, that you ask of me. What the world expects of Christians is that Christians should speak out, loud and clear, and that they should voice their condemnation in such a way that never a doubt, never the slightest doubt, could rise in the heart of the simplest man. That they should get away from abstraction and confront the blood-stained face history has taken on today. The grouping we need is a grouping of men resolved to speak out clearly and to pay up personally.[84]

This document, perceived as an official document of the Church, agrees with the declaration of the leader of the community in whom the personality of the community is concentrated in some way. Its originality, therefore, must not be exaggerated.

Yet it must not be forgotten that in a world where the mass media play a role which is more and more fundamental these "official" interventions have a very great bearing. It is by them that the Church is affirmed, that its notion of the human person and history is made known.[85] So much the more that the Bishop of Rome seems at the outset—by reference to the evangelical message inscribed in his very function—as a symbol of harmony and peace, contrasting with the usual images of war and violence which invade our screens and the news in our newspapers every day. This

[84]Text found in Jean-Claude Brisville, *Camus,* coll. "La bibliothèque idéale," Paris, 1968, 198-199.

[85]We come back to the analysis by Jean-Marc Chappuis, "Pasteur universel, le pape? Essai sur la métamorphose des conditions d'exercice des fonctions de l'évêque de Rome à l'ère électronique," *Les Causeries-débats du Petit-Saconnex,* 24 May 1984.

"power" of presenting itself in this way, *legitimately,* in the name of all and giving a message which wishes to be the faithful reflection of ecclesial thought is heavier with implications than is spontaneously believed. It has become one of the supports and major attributes of the mission of the Roman primate.[86] Ecclesiology must include it in its reflection, just as much must be said about gestures or proceedings, of great loftiness, set up during the pontificate of Paul VI. Some non-Catholics have seen there a new form of the pontifical magisterium: the "word" is not limited to words, it passes also through types of behavior which create communion and radiate the gospel.

Declaring *ex cathedra,* as the primary one responsible for the *communion* of faith, a solemn infallible *judgment* on a point touching at the heart of the Christian content of faith and under very precise conditions is more complex.[87] Let us note very well that it is a question of an infallibility of *judgment.*[88] This signifies formally that *such an* affirmation, declaring "what is," in the area of what is necessary to believe or reject for salvation, is guaranteed by the judgment of the one who made it. He has spoken infallibly. It is neither a revealed word nor an inspired word but a word spoken with the help of the Spirit preventing *at that time* the one who speaks from falling into error. His declaration, or proposition, is undoubtedly true.

In this proposition is found in this way, states Vatican I, a *truth* of the apostolic faith confessed since the beginning by the bishops and their Churches. It may be that its formulation is not the best, that it does not express the entire content of the truth in question, that it may be closely linked to the categories of an era or culture. It is, in fact, a declaration espousing the laws of the human language, therefore limited, and by that fact subject to corrections. But it expresses a truth which will always be true, even if one day the need of formulating it otherwise is felt. It even may be that in other circumstances, while he did not intend to declare himself *ex cathedra,* the same Bishop of Rome has stated debatable words. But infallibility is guaranteed only in certain judgments, declared under very precise conditions, surrounded with numerous precautions,[89] because

[86]Pius IX was without doubt the first to be able to depend on the media.

[87]See *DS* 3074.

[88]The sentence "the Roman Pontiff is infallible" is incomplete, said Mgr. Gasser at Vatican I before the vote, and in the name of the Deputation of the faith, "since the pope is infallible only when he defines, in a solemn judgment, for the universal Church, a question of faith or of morals" (Mansi 52, 1213).

[89]See, after the stirrings provoked by H. Küng, *Infaillible? Une interpellation,* Paris, 1971, the study by Y. Congar, "Après 'Infaillible'? de Hans Küng, bilans et discussions," *RSPT* 58, 1974, 243–252; E. Schillebeeckx, "Le problème de l'infaillibilité ministérielle," *Concilium* 83, 1973, 83–102; G. Thils, *Église infaillible ou intemporelle,* Paris, 1973; F. A. Sullivan, *Magisterium,* New York, 1983 (62–82). For the a history, see Brian Tierney, *Origins of Papal Infallibility,*

it is a question of rare and easily discernible cases where the Bishop of Rome decides to convey by himself the judgment which an ecumenical council normally would have conveyed. And this judgment does not have to be submitted to the verdict of a higher tribunal.[90] The "power" in question is, therefore, plain and clear-cut.

One could think that such an infallible judgment is declared in solitude, that the Bishop of Rome is detached in that respect from his brother bishops. In addition to recalling the extreme rarity of such definitions *ex cathedra,* it is important to emphasize several points which urge that this impression be varied slightly.

First of all, it is evident that the great councils of the first centuries have "defined" once and for all, in *communion,* the truths which constitute the main axes of the faith. They are, for centuries, articulated in the Credo. One could not add anything essential to it, because then one would act *ad destructionem et non ad aedificationem Ecclesiae.* Solemn interventions of the Roman primate must always be found under the control of the decisions of his brothers, the bishops of the undivided Church, and of their Churches. The dogmas defined by Pius IX and Pius XII are only the echo of the declaration of Mary *Theotokos.*

In addition, just as the decisions of the councils, the solemn definitions of the Bishop of Rome have to be "received." At Chalcedon the *Volume to Flavian* of Pope Leo truly stated the faith. Would he have saved it if the Fathers of the council had not "received" it, recognizing in it "the faith of the Fathers. . .," the teaching of the apostles?[91] We have seen at length how the "reception," if it does not create the truth and does not legitimize after the fact the proceeding of the one who "defined" it, causes it, therefore, to pass into the life of the Church and by that fact causes it to be what it must be. By "receiving" it the people of God recognize in it its benefit and make it theirs. A "definition" not "received" is not a truth belonging to life but a truth belonging to archives. But the dispersed episcopate is the compelling instrument of "reception." Even if—a hypothesis that is difficult to imagine[92]—it had not been consulted previously, it is not entirely outside the process by which the Church is

---

1150-1350, Leyde, 1972. But cf. J. Heft, *John XXII and Papal Teaching Authority,* New York, 1986.

[90] It is in this way that *Lumen gentium* 25 renders an account of the *ex sese non autem ex consensu Ecclesiae informabiles* of Vatican I (*DS* 3074), aiming first at an error of the Church of France (see *DTC* 4, 197). *Lumen gentium* states some definitions: "They do not need any other approval and do not tolerate any appeal to another judgment." See H. Fries, "Ex sese non ex consensu Ecclesiae," *Volk Gottes, Festgabe J. Höfer,* Munich, 1967, 480–500.

[91] See W. de Vries, *op. cit.,* 118–119.

[92] At Vatican I, Mgr. Gasser admitted the relative necessity (*aliqua relative necessitas*) of the help of the bishops and of recourse to their advice (Mansi 52, 1215), but refused a *necessitas stricta et absoluta (ibid.).*

told where its faith truly lies. Besides—and it is important to note this—the definitions *ex cathedra* which we are acquainted with have all had as their subject matter truths already "received" in popular devotion and piety.[93] They have sealed a truth on which the totality of shepherds already "had an eye out for."

It must not be forgotten either that the Catholic Church (Roman) has been engaged in these definitions only since the break with the East, therefore, with an important part of the Churches, in the strict apostolic Tradition, guided by an authentic episcopate. These Churches—sister Churches—cast a look on points "defined" by the Bishop of Rome which is different from that of the West. It is clear that at that time the defined truth, without any of it being denied, appears under a different light. In particular, the ecclesiological dimension of Marian dogmas will probably stand out more and the link between Marian privileges and baptismal life will be more clearly perceived.

In brief, the proper "power" of the Roman primate, perceived as we have just done so in his specific acts, is from all its angles united with that of the other bishops, in *synergy* with it. And this is true all the way to the proceedings which at first glance seem to be the most solitary ones, that of definitions *ex cathedra*. It is a service "power" of the episcopate, not the power to supplant the authority of the episcopal college over the totality of the Churches and that of each bishop over his local Church. It is, according to the intuition of Gregory the Great, a "power" of confirmation of the other bishops in their own service of the ecclesial *communion* of faith, of witness and of mission, not the power to absorb their ministry in a "sovereign" way. It is a "power" of promotion and support of the ministry of his brother bishops, not the power of holding everything in his hands. In one word, it is a power *in* the episcopal college and *for* the episcopal college. It is this episcopal college which is the first beneficiary of it.

And if, for the good of peace and justice among the people of God, it reverts to it to receive the appeals of those men and women who feel themselves wronged, it can decide only in reference to the responsibility of the other bishops, refusing to encroach upon their responsibility. One of the dramas of the Catholic Church of the last centuries has been the flood of requests, denunciations, going to Rome as if the local Church did not already have its arbitrator and judge in its bishop. There will be an objection perhaps that the bishops are limited or (as one examiner of our book wrote) "they do not have the breadth of intelligence of a Sovereign Pontiff." That is forgetting that he must refer it to his curia.

---

[93]See J.-M. R. Tillard, "Le sensus fidelium, réflexion théologique," *Foi populaire et foi savante.*

II. The Bishop of the Church of Rome

1. The position of the Bishop of Rome in the heart of the college of bishops and even, before the break with the East, among the patriarchs of the pentarch,[94] depends on the place of his local Church in the heart of the Churches and in the crown of apostolic seats (the *Apostolikoi Thronoi*).[95] That is equal also to the weight of the voice of its legates[96] or of the impact of the documents which expose its point of view[97] at the time of the great councils. The primacy and the authority which are attached to it are linked essentially to the place of the local Church of Rome and its episcopal seat (the *sedes*). They are the primacy and the authority of this Church and of this seat which explain those of the bishop, not the reverse.[98]

In fact, what we have already stated for every local Church is equal to that of Rome: once established, the local Church precedes its bishop (without whom however it would not exist). During the first centuries, it is this local Church which—under forms which will evolve and vary according to areas[99]—will choose the bishop and, he being the guarantor of its faith and its qualities, will have him ordained by the bishops of the neighboring seats.[100] Paul VI will reaffirm it, October 1, 1975, in the apostolic constitution *Romano Pontifici eligendo*. The link between the Church of Rome and Bishop of Rome is such that

[94]Accepted in fact, if not always in law, by the Church of Rome. See H. Marot, *art. cit.*

[95]See for the relationships in the apostolic seats, V. Peri, "Pro amore et cautela orthodoxae fidei: note sul ministero ecclesiale del Vescovo di Roma nella dottrina comune tra l'VIII e il IX secolo," *Rivista di storia e letteratura religiosa* 12, 1976, 341-363 (taking up again the intervention made at the time of the conference of Gazzada, on *Le Sens de la primauté romaine pour les Églises d'Orient entre Chalcédoine et Photius*); M. Maccarrone, "Fundamentum apostolicarum sedium," *La Chiesa Greca in Italia dal VIII al XVI secolo*, Padoue, 1973, 591-662; P. O'Connel, *The Ecclesiology of St. Nicephorus I, 758-828. Patriarch of Constantinople, Pentarchy and Primacy*, coll. "Orientalia Christiana Analecta," 194, Rome, 1972; V. Grumel, "Quelques témoignages byzantins sur la primauté romaine," *Échos d'Orient* 34, 1931, 427-430 (423-427); E. Lanne, "Églises locales et patriarcats à l'époque des grands conciles."

[96]The Bishop of Rome was not personally present at any of the great councils of the first centuries, convoked by the emperor.

[97]And thus the *Volume to Flavian*, of Leo the Great.

[98]See P. Batiffol, *Cathedra Petri*; Id., *Le Siège apostolique*, Paris, 1924; M. Maccarrone, "La Cathedra Petri e lo sviluppo dell' idea del primato papale dal II al III secolo," *Miscellanea Piolanti*, Rome, 1964, 37-56; Id., *Apostolicità, episcopato e primato di Pietro*, Rome, 1976, 64-213.

[99]See R. Gryson, "Les élections ecclésiastiques au IIIe siècle"; Id., "Les élections épiscopales en Orient au IVe siècle"; J. Gaudemet, *Les Élections dans l'Église latine des origines au XVIe siècle*. In Rome the college of cardinals will become the instrument by which the local Church chooses its bishop.

[100]The texts are known. See especially *Apostolic Tradition*, cap 2 and letter 14 of Leo the Great (*PL* 54, 673). Let us take note that the bishop of Rome will be consecrated solely by the one of Ostia. But the most ancient testimonials are perhaps to be understood in the context of a presence of other bishops, of a con-celebration.

the election of the bishop of the Church of Rome has been of the exclusive right of the Church of Rome. It is an historical reality that the other patriarchs have never claimed to interfere upon in this election during the whole period which preceded the schism definitively accomplished in 1054. The electoral college of the roman pontiff, because it is destined to elect the bishop of Rome, must be composed of members who are linked in a substantial way to the Church of Rome.[101]

In order to understand the proper attributes of the Bishop of Rome it is necessary first of all to examine carefully the special quality of his Church.

The primacy which makes the local Church of Rome the first of the Churches—and not the Mother of the Churches, a title due the community of Jerusalem—has certainly been historically conditioned by the fact that at the beginning of evangelization the city of Rome was the capital of the Empire. But—and its famous opposition to canon twenty-eight of Chalcedon has underlined it for a long time[102]—the Roman Church has always refused to see in this political situation the decisive explanation of its special rank. "Felt," perhaps, more than "defined" during the first centuries,[103] its presence is above all of an apostolic order. It comes from the fact that by the martyrdom, in Rome even, of Peter and Paul, the princes of the apostles whose tombs it maintains, it has become the place, par excellence, of apostolic witness.

No one, certainly, will uphold today that Peter—still less Paul (cf. Rom 1:7; 15:28; Acts 28:14-15)—were included among the first evangelizers of the city. And nothing serious proves that he would have been, chronologically, the first "bishop." It is better to follow Irenaeus here and put the names of Peter and Paul before the list of bishops.[104] Because the role of the two apostles in "the foundation and the building" of the Church of Rome—in other words in what gives it its identity and its prestige—is situated on a more profound plane. This Church is founded *on* their witness, sealed by the supreme act of their death for faith in Christ Jesus,

---

[101]Trans. in *DC* 72, 1975, 1001–1011, with the commentary by R. Tucci, *ibid.*, 1011–1012, cited. The pope is elected not as a universal bishop but "as bishop of a particular Church, that of Rome."

[102]We have mentioned it above, while treating "reception." See the revival of this idea in E. Renan, *Conférences d'Angleterre*, Paris, 1882; A. Sabatier, *Les Religions d'autorité et la religion de l'Esprit*. But see A. Loisy, *L'Évangile et l'Église*, Paris, 1902.

[103]According to the remark by Mgr. Duchesne, *Histoire ancienne de l'Église*, Paris, 1911, 535.

[104]*Adv. Haer.* III, 3, 1-2. For him, in a general way, "the Apostles appointed the bishops." Was there in Rome, in the beginning, a collegial ministry? On the origins of the Roman Church, see Ch. Pietri, *Roma Christiana, recherches sur l'Église de Rome, son organisation, sa politique, son idéologie, de Miltiade à Sixte III (311-340)*, t. I, Rome, 1976, 301–401. On Peter in Rome, see D. W. O'Connor, *Peter in Rome*, New York, 1969; on the late conferring on the Twelve the title of bishop of a local church, see R. E. Brown, "Episkoè and episkopos," *Theol. Stud.* 41, 1980, 322–338 (325).

286 Church of Churches

in whom their two apostolates, which are so different in their significance and their implication, unite. Their martyrdom in it makes the Church of Rome the one which God has marked with the seal of the most powerful and greatest apostolic authenticity. It gives it priority over other Churches—like that of Antioch, Corinth[105] and even of Jerusalem—where these two apostles preached and suffered. It is this supreme confession, in it, of the leader or spokesman of the Twelve and of the Apostle of the Nations which confers on it the quality and the title of first in the apostolic witness. It holds in this way the primacy of the first seat, being able to pride itself in what Irenaeus will call, around 180, the most powerful origin among the Churches, the *potentior principalitas:*

> Since it would be very lengthy in such a volume to enumerate the successions of all the churches, *we will speak of the largest church, the best known and the oldest of all, founded and constituted by the two very glorious apostles Peter and Paul in Rome,* the one which has the Tradition of the apostles and the faith proclaimed to men, which has come to us by successions of bishops, and we will confound all those who, by whatever means, either by presumption, by vain glory, by blindness and false judgment gather together inopportunely elsewhere.
>
> It is with this Church, because of its most powerful origin (*propter potentiorem principalitatem*), that it is necessary for every Church to concur, be reconciled, in other words those who are the faithful from everywhere, the church in which this Tradition held by the apostles has always been preserved, by those who come from everywhere.
>
> Having thus established and built the Church, the blessed apostles transmitted the episcopal administration of it to Linus; this Linus whom Paul mentions in his epistles to Timothy. It was Anacletus who succeeded him. After him, in third place since the apostles, the episcopate goes back to Clement, who saw the apostles themselves and spoke to them: he had their preaching in his ears and the Tradition before his eyes—he was not the only one because many others survived, who had been instructed by the apostles. Under this Clement, on the occasion of a quite lively discussion among the brothers who were in Corinth, important letters were written by the Church of Rome to the Corinthians to bring them back peace, to restore their faith and to state the Tradition recently received from the apostles, confessing one single all-powerful God, Creator of heaven and earth, molder of man, who sent the flood and called Abraham, who led his people out of the land of Egypt, who spoke to Moses, who laid out the Law and sent the prophets, who prepared the fire for the devil and his angels.[106]

---

[105]See the letter of Denis to the Romans, in Eusebius, *Hist. Eccles.* II, 25, 6–8 (*SC* 31, 93).

[106]*Adv. Haer.* III, 3, 1–2. See E. Lanne, "L'Église de Rome, a gloriosissimis duobus apostolis Petro et Paulo Romae fundatae et constitutae Ecclesia," *Irénikon* 49, 1976, 275–322. On the sense of *fundata et constituta* see J.-M. R. Tillard, *L'Évêque de Rome,* 110–111. On the sense of *potentior*

At Carthage, around 200, Tertullian also links to the martydom of the apostles the authority of the chair of Rome where they continue to preside. He adds there, it is true, the witness of John:

> Go through the apostolic Churches where the very chairs of the apostles still preside in their place, where their authentic letters are read which echo their voices and put before our eyes the face of each of them. Are you very near to Achaia: you have Corinth. Are you not far from Macedonia: you have Philippi, you have Thessalonica; if you can go from the coast of Asia, you have Ephesus; if you are in the confines of Italy, you have Rome whose authority also brings us its support. Happy Church! The apostles poured out on it all their doctrine with their blood. Peter underwent for it a punishment similar to that of the Lord. Paul was crowned for it with a death like that of John [Baptist]. The apostle John was thrown into boiling oil: he comes out of it unhurt and is relegated to an island.[107]

A century later, in 314, at the time of the Council of Arles, Sylvester is excused for having sent a representative and for not having come in person: "You have not been able to leave these places where the apostles also sit daily and where their blood which was poured out continually gives homage to the glory of God."[108]

There is no break, therefore, with the old tradition which Eusebius mentions from Caesarea by basing it on a letter from Denis of Corinth to Soter, Bishop of Rome:

> [Under Nero] Paul had his head cut off in Rome itself and likewise Peter was crucified there and this account is confirmed by the names of Peter and Paul which until the present time are indicated in cemeteries in this city. This is what affirms quite as much a clerical man by the name of Gaius, who lived under Zephyrin, bishop of the Romans. Carrying on a discussion in writing against Procus, the chief of the Cataphrygian sect, he stated in regard to places where the sacred remains of the above named apostles were deposited these proper words:

---

principalitas, see the suggestion of M. Guerra Gomez, *op. cit.,* 309–351, but we rally to the vision of T. G. Jalland, *op. cit.,* 112–113 (see 112, note 2): it is a question especially of *authenticity* of excellence of the apostolic origin. See also R. P. C. Hanson, "Potentiorem principalitatem, in Irenaeus 'Adversus Haereses' III, 3, 1," *Studia Patristica* 3, Berlin, 1961, 366–369; Ch. Pietri, *op. cit.,* t. I, 300–301; P. Batiffol, "Les principales cathedrae du concile de Carthage de 397," *rev. des Sc. Rel.* 14, 1924, 287–292; Id., *Cathedra Petri,* 83–84. On Linus, see also the canon of the *const. Apost.* VII, 46.

[107]*De Praescriptione* 36, trans. P. de Labriolle, *SC* 46, 137; coll. "Hemmer-Lejay," t. IV, Paris, 1907, 79. A half century later, Firmillien of Caesarea writing to Cyprian, against Stephen, will also dwell on the relationship between Rome and the two Apostles (*Epist.* 75, 2; Bayard, t. II, 293).

[108]Mansi, 2, 469.

"For myself, I can show the trophies of the apostles. If you wish to go to the Vatican or along the way to Ostia, you will find the trophies of those who have established this Church."

That both of them gave witness at the same time, is what Denis, bishop of Corinth, established when he wrote to the Romans: "In such a notification you have also united the plantings made by Peter and Paul, those of the Romans and of the Corinthians. Because both of them planted in our Corinth and likewise instructed us; and also, after teaching together in Italy, they gave homage at the same time."[109]

It is this tradition which Clement of Rome already certifies, around 95, before mentioning the "immense crowd of elect who, because of jealousy, suffered many tortures and who were . . . a magnificant example"[110]:

Peter, who, because of an unjust jealousy put up with so many sufferings—not just one or two!—and who after giving witness in this way went to his dwelling of glory which was his due. Because of jealousy and discord, Paul showed the price reserved for constancy. Laden with chains seven times, exiled, stoned, having become a herald in the East and the West, he received the splendid renown which his faith merited. After teaching justice to the entire world and reaching the boundaries of the West, he gave homage before governors; it is in this way that he left the world and went to his saintly abode—an illustrious model of constancy.[111]

And Ignatius of Antioch reiterated this several years later, linking the Church together with Peter and Paul "which presides in charity" in the region of the Romans: "They were apostles."[112]

The special importance accorded the martyrdom of Peter and Paul which gives the city where they have undergone it (and which preserves "their trophies") a unique place among the apostolic seats comes from the very special quality of these two apostles. This is certified in the composition of the book, the Acts of the Apostles, whose two parts are structured around the ministry of Peter, then that of Paul. By his place in the midst of the Twelve Peter recalls to the faith the fulfillment of the Old Covenant in Jesus Christ—the twelve thrones for the twelve tribes[113]—whereas by his own mission Paul teaches it the absolute newness of the gospel event, which causes the Covenant to open up on the catholicity of the new People.

[109]*Hist. Eccles.* II, 25, 6-8; translated by G. Bardy, *SC* 31, 91-93.

[110]*1 Clem.* 6, 1, translated A. Jaubert, *SC* 167, 109.

[111]*1 Clem.* 5, 4-7, *ibid.*

[112]Rom 4:1-3, *SC* 10, 131: "I do not give you orders like Peter and Paul: they were apostles, I a condemned man; they were free, and I am until now a slave."

[113]We return again to the important study of dom J. Dupont, "Le logion des douzes trones."

Peter attests to the profound continuity which wishes that the New Covenant germinate in the Old Covenant, both of them led by the one whom the Christian faith itself will call "the God of the Fathers," "the God of Abraham, Isaac and Jacob." He is thus the witness of the fidelity of God to his Word. Paul is the witness of the vastness of the design of God, in a Salvation which "comes from the Jews" but is not only for them. And by this title his letters will be known, alongside the gospel accounts, as an authentic explicit expression of the gospel of God. Peter is the one who confesses Jesus as Messiah, Paul is the one by whom probably one of the disciples will express the faith by associating Christ Jesus to the very act of Creation (Col 1:12-20).

The way of the two apostles leads them to Rome, then capital of the world. Their differences (Gal 2:11, 14; 5:11), their personal interpretation of the content of faith, their belonging to two currents sometimes in conflict,[114] had been able to place them opposite each other. But in the blood of martyrdom their *communion* in the one faith, in one single Lord will be sealed. Brothers in the proclamation of the Word and having exercised, each in his own sphere, an authentic magisterium[115] aiming at the purity of the content of faith at the very moment when the gospel passed both to the Jews and to the pagans, by the liturgy of their death (cf. Phil 2:17; 2 Tim 4:6) they make the city which will preserve their tomb a place of witness. There is found, forever, with their trophies, the evidence par excellence of the catholicity of the Christian faith. This catholicity—we have emphasized this at length—does not signify only the universality of the faith. It is a question of a very special universality: it is the one which includes in a single totality both the People of the Old Covenant and the pagan nations. No one has pointed this out better than the author of the Letter to the Ephesians. On this plane Peter and Paul are inseparable. As Augustine will express it, on the feast day of their martyrdom:

> On the same day the Passion of the two apostles is celebrated. But these two were only one, although they suffered on different days they were only one. Peter went before, Paul followed.[116]

In their complementarity they tie together the whole of humanity according to God, the *kath'olon* formed from the Jews who were the chosen people and pagans entering into the *communion* of this choice.

It is very important to emphasize that, since its origins, the Christian community of Rome seems to have been strongly marked by the relation-

---

[114]See R. E. Brown and J. Meier, *Antioch and Rome.*

[115]See *Saint Pierre dans le Nouveau Testament,* coll. "Lectio divina," 79, Paris, 1974, 191-192.

[116]*Sermo* 295, 7-8 (*PL* 38, 1351-1352). Read in this optic the speech of Paul VI to the audience on June 28, 1966 (*DC* 63, 1966, 1282-1294). See also Leo the Great, *Sermo* 82, 7 (*PL* 54, 428).

ship of the Church with the Old Covenant, its traditions, its institutions. It gives witness to the certainty that—through God—a *communion* exists between the two Covenants. The works of Novatian express Jewish themes. It is the same thing for those works attributed to Hippolytus.[117] And the famous paschal quarrel has its link with Jewish heritage. One will even be able to detect some Roman feelings for adopting and modeling their institutions and practices on those imported from Asia,[118] a kind of a smell of solidarity with the faith of the Old Testament. It seems significant to us that the Church planted in the capital of the Empire, and by that fact right in the center of the Gentile world, would remain linked with its Jewish roots. One can see in that, although there may be regrettable misunderstandings and blunders, the mark of catholicity, in the true theological sense of the term, the totality of Israel and the nations in one single Covenant.

It is evident that Peter and Paul could not have successors in those things which touch on their witness, such as we have described it. It can only be preserved, constantly re-proclaimed, transmitted in all truth. It constitutes an *ephapax*, to which it is necessary to come back continually and which serves as a norm for ecclesial life, because no *communion* is possible if there is any deviation from the faith confessed by Peter in the name of the apostolic community and proclaimed by Paul. Because he has written its name in its soil and in the chair of its history, and because it possesses with the tombs of the apostles the somewhat tangible "memory" of their "confession"—and for the first centuries that counts enormously—the Church of Rome has a special responsibility to the place of this witness. It is its place and its guardian. It reverts to it—as an honor and a charge—to preserve it by "watching" that it does not lose its way, that it does not become vain, and, therefore remain throughout the course of history the norm and source of authentic *communion*. That implies that the Church defend it from all deviation but also that it apply itself to preserving in it its essential quality of power of Salvation for the life of the world. And since fidelity to this *depositum fidei* constitutes the essential axis of *communion* which is the very form of Salvation, it is by this fact the first servant of ecclesial *communion*. Its primacy in witness is prolonged in this way into a primacy of service of *communion*.

Such are the place and mission of the "Roman Church."[119] Around 250, writing to the Church of Carthage under circumstances which we al-

[117]That is studied by W. H. C. Frend, *The Rise of Christianity*, 339-347, who thinks that the legalism of Roman Christianity owes more to rabbincal heritage than to Roman law (341). On the situation at the time of the New Testament, see R. Brown and J. Meier, *op. cit.*

[118]"The successors of Victor, Zephyrin (199-217) and Callistus (217-222) were not, it seems, unfavorable to this type of thinking" (W. H. C. Frend, *ibid.*, 344).

[119]On the different meanings that this expression will take, see Y. Congar, "Ecclesia romana,"

ready know, the clerics of the Church of Rome at that time deprived of a bishop, will describe this Church as the one "which watches by itself (*excubat*) with the greatest care (*summa sollicitudine*) over all those who invoke the name of the Lord."[120] Soon the title of *Sedes Apostolica* will be able to be reserved to it.

We have seen that between every bishop and his Church there exists a profound bond, expressed by the nuptial image. The bishop is not without his Church, which precedes him; the Church is not without the bishop, who sits on his *cathedra*. From the second half of the second century, this complementarity is also explicitly affirmed for the Roman Church.[121] It wishes that the bishop of the Church, "watching" over the witness by which all the Churches live, receive as his proper responsibility to be among the bishops the "sentinel" who is on the watch for anything which might affect the essentials of the faith and by that fact also affect *communion*. It is in this respect that Leo the Great will speak of his charge (responsibility).[122] So this charge is in no way solely symbolic. In some grave cases, this charge will be able to compel him to assert himself vigorously. Because it implies the duty of challenging in an authoritative way the other Churches when the faith is in question. In the heart of the episcopal college which possesses as such the *episkopè* of the universal Church, the Bishop of Rome has this proper mission: "to watch" over the fundamental apostolic witness, that of Peter and Paul sealed in his Church.

The Bishop of Rome becomes in this way the "vicar" of the apostles, in relationship with the "once-and-for-all" of their confession. The continuity with them is put into operation by his constant reference to the contents and implications of their witness, concerning the *cathedra* of the Church, founded on this witness, in their death. He is like their voice. At Chalcedon, the Fathers "receive" the *Volume to Flavian* because "Peter has spoken through Leo," at the Third Council of Constantinople (in 680-681) they "receive" the letter of Agathon because "Peter has spoken through Agathon," at the Council of Ephesus (from 431) Celestine was acclaimed as guardian of the faith because in his letter was found Paul's faith.[123] Leo the Great can, therefore, testify that "the very blessed apostle

Christianesimo nella storia 5, 1984, 225-244. Gradually there will be seen in the Roman Church "the totalization of the whole Church," which *"sub se continet ecclesias universas."* But for all of that the primary meaning, that of local church of the city of Rome will not be forgotten.

[120]In Cyprian, *Epist.* 8, 3. See G. Bardy, "L'autorité du siège romain et les controverses du III*e* siècle," *Rev de Sc. Rel.* 14, 260.

[121]See M. Maccarrone, "La Cathedra Petri e lo sviluppo dell' idea del primato papale dal II al III secolo," *Miscellanea Piolanti,* Rome, 1964.

[122]*Epist.* 4, 1; *Epist.* 167, pref. (*PL* 54, 610 B, 1201 A-B). On the idea of "sentinel," see *Didascalia* II, 6, 7-11.

[123]For Leo, Mansi 6, 972; for Agathon, Mansi 11, 683-684, 711-712 B; for Celestine, Mansi 4, 1288 B. See Ch. Pietri, *op. cit.,* t. II, 1382; W. de Vries, *Orient et Occident; les structures ecclésiales vues dans l'histoire des sept premiers conciles cecuméniques,* Paris, 1974, 74.

Peter never ceases to be in his seat,"[124] without all that being taken for a *redivivus* Peter. He is his "vicar," the servant of the primacy of his Church, born out of the *communion* of his witness and that of Paul.

The parallel with the authority of the emperor is illuminating. He plays a decisive role in the convocation of councils and even the signature of their decrees,[125] in the choosing of bishops, in the administration of the Churches.[126] In his palace, with his ceremonial liturgy, he is the object of a religious veneration. But his authority is exercised on the level of government. It does not formally express the apostolic witness *as such*. It is concerned with what orchestrates this witness and in this way permits the Churches to live in unity. It does not belong to him to determine the fidelity of the contents of this witness. This privilege rests with the bishops and among them, with his special title, with the Bishop of the seat of Rome.

2. The role that the reference to Peter plays in this understanding of the apostolic preeminence of the Roman Church in the midst of the totality of Churches, even the apostolic ones, requires besides, that we associate primacy and *communion* with it. It is true that the one who has most vigorously expressed this association, Cyprian, did so by insisting that the power given to Peter passes to all the bishops. And at the time of his quarrels with the Bishop of Rome, Steven, he will know how to call upon the solidarity of the other bishops against everything which seems to him to be an improper exercise of power. Yet it is necessary to recognize the depth of his intuition. In one person alone, who is Simon Peter, the Lord gives

---

[124]*Sermo* 5, 4 (*PL* 54, 153-155); 3, 2-3 (*ibid.*, 145-146); the letter of Peter Chrysologus (*ibid.*, 743). See E. Giles, *Documents illustrating Papal Authority AD 96-654*, London, 1952, 282 (and the note).

[125]The third Council of Constantinople (680-681) asks the emperor to sign the decrees and to send them to the five patriarchs, Leo II gives his consent to him (Mansi 11, 681 CD; 553 DE). See in Leslie W. Barnard, *The Council of Sardica 343 A.D.* the implications of this role.

[126]The *Laus Constantini* of Eusebius of Cesaerea is known which (especially in cap. 2) sees in the emperor the image of the *Logos,* charged with the subjects of the Kingdom of God, recalling to them the laws of this Kingdom, purifying the earth, pilot of the majestic vessel which is the Church. But see J. M. Sansterre, "Eusèbe de Césarée et la naissance de la théorie césaro-papiste," *Byzantion* 42, 1972, 131-195, 532-594; H. Chadwick, "Conversion in Constantine the Great," *Studies in Church History* 15, Oxford, 1978, 1-13; Leslie W. Barnard, *op. cit.,* 11-25; S. Runciman, *The Byzantine Theocracy,* London, 1977; Id., *Byzantine Style and Civilization,* London, 1981. On the way in which Constantius understands his role, see W. Barnard, *op. cit.,* 38-39 (relying on Ammianus Marcellinus, *Rerum gest.,* lib. 16-21). On the vision of Photius (between 856 and 886), see J. Bompaire, "Réflexions d'un humaniste sur la politique, le patriarche Photius," *La Notion d'autorité au Moyen Age, Islam, Byzance, Occident,* (colloques internationaux de La Napoule), Paris, 1982, 45-55. On the more reserved attitude of the West in this area, see Barnard, 20-21, 38, 42, 49. On the vision of Pope Gelasius (in 494), read the enlightening study of Robert L. Benson, "The Gelasian Doctrine: Uses and Transformations," *La Notion d'autorité au Moyen Age,* 13-44. In another context, see J. P. Sommerville, "The Royal Supremacy and Episcopacy jure divino," *Journal of Eccles. History,* 34, 1983, 548-558.

to all the apostles "honor and power"; "he bestows on all the apostles an equal power"; "all of them will be what Peter is." But this will flow from one alone, the beginning having in this way its point of departure in unity.[127] There is primacy, but in *communion* and in view of this *communion*. Augustine, in the homily from which we quoted an excerpt, certifying that Peter and Paul are only one, takes up the same idea: in Peter all are alluded to. In fact, when we read in Matthew: "I will give you the keys of the Kingdom" or in John: "Feed my lambs, feed my sheep," it must be understood that

> This is not one man alone, but the Church in its unity which has received these keys. This enhances the *excellencia* of Peter because he represented the universality and unity of the Church when it was said to him "I confide to you" while it was confided to *all*. For, in order for you to know that it is the Church which has received the keys of the Kingdom of heaven listen to what the Lord says in another place to *all his Apostles:* "receive the Holy Spirit." And immediately: "every man whose sins you shall remit they are remitted. . . ." And it is again deservedly that after the Resurrection the Lord confides to Peter in person the responsibility of feeding his sheep. Because he is not the only one among the disciples to have to feed the Lord's sheep. *But if Christ speaks to one alone it is to show the value of unity. And he addresses himself first to Peter because Peter is the first among the apostles.*[128]

The primacy of the Church of Rome, because it is apostolic and "founded" at the same time as on Paul, on the exceptional position of Peter in the midst of the Twelve, is a primacy which is inseparable from the gift of the attributes which belong to it but are given to the other Churches: these are in the Church of Rome only to be in all of them. In it, is seen what must be seen in *all of them,* is heard what must be heard in *all of them,* is celebrated what must be celebrated in *all of them,* is received from the Spirit what must be received in *all of them,* must defend what must be defended in *all of them.* There is one point which is an exception: precisely this function of being "first," the place where the object of *communion* is established with all these attributes, a permanent "memorial" of the will of the Lord which is that everything begin with

[127]See especially *De catholicae Ecclesiae Unitate*. We have two versions of this text and it is difficult to know if both come from Cyprian. See J. Chapman, *Studies on the Early Papacy,* London, 1928, 33-50; M. Bevenot, *St Cyprian's de Unitate, chapter 4, in the light of the Manuscripts,* coll. "Analecta Gregoriana," 11, Rome, 1937; T. G. Jalland, *op. cit.,* 161-169; P. de Labriolle, *Saint Cyprien. De l'unité de l'Église catholique,* coll. "Unam sanctam," 9, Paris, 1942, XVIII-XXX; M. Maccarone, "Lo sviluppo dell' idea dell' episcopato nel II secolo," *Problemi di storia della Chiesa; la Chiesa antica secc. II-IV,* Milan, 1970, 196-203. See also *Epist.* 68, 4.

[128]*Sermo* 295, 2-8 (*PL* 38, 1349-1352). See also *Epist.* 53, 2 (*PL* 33, 196). See A. Trapé, "La sedes Petri in S. Agostino," *Miscellanea Piolanti,* t. II, Rome, 1964, 57-75.

unity and be completed in *communion*. It has this from Peter, whereas from Paul it has especially its opening up of the Salvation of the entire world and the permanent newness of grace.

The Bishop of Rome owes it to himself, therefore, to be among the bishops the "vicar" of this totally special relationship of Peter of the type of unity which God wishes, the "catholic" unity, the one which is rooted in "one for all." The complex history of the recognition of the position of the Bishop of Rome in the midst of the councils—understood differently in the East and in the West—and in the "crown" of the apostolic thrones[129] comes from the difficulty of living concretely this balance between "preeminence of a seat" and "equality" of all the seats—especially the apostolic seats—and of their bishop. This is why the East will refuse every serious decision affecting the faith, made outside of an ecumenical council. And it wishes that in such an ecumenical council at least those who are responsible for the pentarch be involved in some way.

The special place of Peter in the heart of the apostolic group is better understood if it is studied in this light of "one, with and for all," of "one, with and for the community," of "first in the *communion* of all." There is perceived then throughout the New Testament the conviction that the concrete role played by Peter in the Christian community after Pentecost responds to a precise design of God, united with a will of the Lord Jesus himself ; in brief, that it has a horizon, that of *communion*.

In fact, the first section of the Acts of the Apostles is, according to all evidence, centered on an explicit leadership of Peter. He is the "first" not only because the texts present the apostolic group by the formula "Peter and the Twelve" (Acts 2:14), "Peter and the other apostles" (2:37; 5:29) and by always putting him at the head (1:13; 3:1; 4:1, 19, 23), but especially because they make him the "first great person" of the newborn Church.

It is Peter who pronounces the great speeches in which for the first time is expressed the faith of the apostolic community and its certainty that God made Jesus the authentic Messiah announced and waited for by the People of the Covenant (2:14-36; 3:11-26; 4:8-22; 10:34-43). He is also the first one who receives the great revelation of the offer of Salvation to the pagans themselves (10:44-48; 11:15-18). And it is up to him to convince the "brothers established in Judea" (the Judeo-Christians) of the importance and the seriousness of this "overwhelming" transformation, of the traditional hope, opening up on the "catholicity" of the people of God (11:2-18). At the moment of the gathering in Jerusalem, after the

---

[129]See V. Peri, "Pro amore et cautela orthodoxae fidei: note sul ministaro ecclesiale del Vescovo di Roma nella dottrina comune tra l'VIII e il IX secolo," *Rivista di storia e letteratura religiosa* 12, 1976, 342-343, going back to John of Jerusalem, *PG* 95, 352.

conflict at Antioch, he intervenes in a decisive way (15:7-11, 14-18), in a sense which is probably broader than James attached to certain ritual prohibitions.[130] In the early community it is already Peter who decides on the choice of a successor to Judas (1:15-22), who accepts the first converts for baptism (2:37-41), who judges the case of Ananias (5:1-11), performs signs (3:1-11; 5:15). The Letter to the Galatians testifies to his role in Jerusalem, in regard to his mission to the "circumcised" (Gal 2:7-8). But it is clear that this rank of "first person" does not isolate Peter from the group "of the others." He is there "with the eleven" (Acts 2:14), and it is the witness of *all* that he expresses (2:32; 3:15). For, in the power of the Spirit, it is *all* the apostles who are charged to be witnesses "in Jerusalem, in all Judea, Samaria, to the ends of the earth" (Acts 1:8). He is "first" but in solidarity and *communion* with all the Apostles. He is "first" in what all the others have and are.

The "primacy" of Peter certified thus in the first community is inseparable from the witness which Peter gives at the Resurrection.[131] Here again the same dynamism of the *first* and of *all* is found. It is indeed remarkable that the First Letter to the Corinthians citing probably an old confession of faith states: "he appeared first to Cephas and *then* to the Twelve" (1 Cor 15:5), in a passage of great solemnity . Luke echoes this thought at the end of the episode of Emmaus: the cry of joy of the Eleven is that "the Lord has risen and has appeared to Simon" (Luke 24:33-34). Therefore, it is he, before the witness of the pilgrims of Emmaus, who brought the paschal faith to the Eleven, yet which *all* will be witnesses of.

This priority of the encounter with the Risen One is equally brought up in the Johannine episode of the race to the tomb by Peter and the beloved disciple. The latter arrives first but stays in the background so that Peter may enter first and become the first witness (John 20:3-10), even if he is not the first to have believed. In the same way, on the boat on the lake, this same disciple—the "hero" of the Johannine tradition[132]—will recognize the Lord but will let Peter jump into the sea (21:1-7) and Peter will be in the center of this entire scene.

In this Johannine tradition, certainly, Peter is not the "first entirely," the "first in everything." Chronologically he is not the first to follow Jesus, contrary to what is written in the Synoptics (John 1:40-44; Mark 1:15-20;

---

[130]On Peter's position between James and Paul, see R. Brown, in R. Brown and J. Meier, *Antioch and Rome.*

[131]That has been studied very well by Gerard O'Collins, "Peter as Easter Witness," *Heytrop Journal* 22, 1981, 1–18. On the whole problem of Peter, see *Saint Pierre dans le Nouveau Testament,* where the perspective is ecumenical (a vast bibliography).

[132]See R. E. Brown, *The Gospel according to John XIII-XXI,* 1006–1007; *The Community of the Beloved Disciple.* Johannine tradition is attentive to emphasizing the "primacy of love" which it recognized in the beloved disciple.

Matt 4:18-22). He is not the first to confess the messianic role of Jesus (John 1:41)[133] and his own confession of faith before the Resurrection (6:67-69) does not have the impact which the Synoptic traditions suggest, in particular it is no longer associated as it is in Matthew to a declaration of power. He is not the first qualitatively in the order of love, and the triple interrogation by the Lord seems very much to go back to his triple denial (13:38; 18:17, 25, 27). He retains, however, a primacy which is proper to him. He is the one who speaks here in the name of all[134] and declares the faith of all (6:68), the one whom the author of the last chapter shows as the bearer of a special responsibility for the flock (21:15-19),[135] that which the amazing authority of the beloved disciple cannot supplant in his specific role: first shepherd,[136] in other words (according to the Johannine vision) the person with primary responsibility to preserve the community in the benefits of Salvation and unity (cf. 10:11-18). He and the beloved disciple are the two major figures who dominate this Johannine tradition, at the same time partners (13:23-25; 20:2-10; 21:7, 20-24) and yet different, both of them at the heart of the principal episodes of the life of Jesus and representing two faces of the relationship of the community with Christ: the beloved disciple/the indefectible fidelity of love (all the way to the foot of the cross), Peter/the victory of faith (even in weakness).

The Johannine scene on the shore of lake Tiberias finishes with the recollection of martyrdom: "you will stretch out your hands, and somebody else will put a belt around you and take you where you would rather not go. By these words Jesus indicated the kind of death by which Peter would give glory to God. After this he added: follow me" (21:18-19). Such is the final victory of faith, which is that of a close association with the ordeal of Jesus and with his glorious witness. Between the confession in the name of the Twelve made earlier on the shore of this same lake of Tiberias after the speech about the bread of life (6:66-71) and the encounter with the Risen One after the Resurrection there certainly was the contrast between the enthusiasm of the disciple (13:37) and his weakness which led him to the denial (13:38; 18:15-27), between his spontaneity and his lack of deep perception about the fidelity of Jesus to his vocation (18:11). Yet it is a question of the same faith, the one which in spite of everything

---

[133]That is emphasized by Arthur H. Maynard, "The Role of Peter in the Fourth Gospel," *NTS* 30, 1984, 531-548. But this article does not seem to us to be convincing in every respect.

[134]As Arthur H. Maynard, *ibid.*, emphasizes it.

[135]And that even if the author of this chapter seeks to restore the authority of Peter, uncertain or contested in the Johannine community. See Arthur H. Maynard, *ibid.*, and R. E. Brown, *The Community of the Beloved Disciple*.

[136]What the authors of *Saint Pierre dans le Nouveau Testament* emphasize.

attaches itself to Jesus. It is important to notice how, whereas the other apostles have left (18:8-9), Peter—with another disciple, perhaps the beloved disciple[137]—follows Jesus all the way to the high priest. He will deny Jesus, but his weakness is not an abandonment. Faith in the Resurrection will give him—as to all his brother apostles and to the entire Church—the strength to *be in communion* with his Lord until the moment of supreme witness, martyrdom. He is the witness of the specifically Christian faith, the one which could not economize on the Resurrection and which, on the contrary, is anchored in it.

Without getting bogged down in an agreement syndrome, we can then compare the text which has, in this area, affected Tradition the most,[138] the one which Luke inscribes in the context of the farewell meal of Jesus with the Johannine document:

> "*You* are the men who have stood by me in my trials (*tois peirasmois mou*), and now I confer a Kingdom *on you,* just as my Father conferred one on me. *You* will eat and drink at my table in my Kingdom and *you* will sit on thrones to judge the twelve tribes of Israel." The Lord says: "Simon, Simon, Satan has claimed *you* to sift *you* all like wheat. *But I have prayed for you that your faith may not fail, and once you have recovered you must strengthen your brothers.*" Peter says: "Lord, I would be ready to go to prison with you, and even to death." Jesus says: "I tell you, Peter, by the time the cock crows today, *you* will have denied me three times" (Luke 22:28-34).[139]

This ensemble of verses is impressive. What is noticed in them, highlighted by the Eucharistic climate of the pericope, is the explicit link between communion with the trials of Jesus and communion with his strength, in judgment. It is also necessary to note the passage from the formal *you* to the familiar *you,* from a valid consideration for all to a declaration which only concerns Peter alone but which is still valid only as a function in a general case. In a common situation for all the apostles

---

[137]Nothing is said about the attitude of this disciple during this scene. Where does Maynard (*op. cit.,* 539) find the affirmation that this disciple *"is presented as not having failed"*?

[138]One becomes aware of it by reading A. Rimoldi, *L'Apostolo San Pietro,* coll. "Analecta Gregoriana," 96, Rome, 1958.

[139]This text was studied, in its Eucharistic context, by H. Schürmann, *Le Récit de la dernière Cène.* The only study specifically treating it that we know is B. Prete, "Il primato e la missione di Pietro; Studio esegetico e critico del testo de *Lc* 22, 31-32," *Suppl. Riv. Bibl. Ital.* 3, Brescia, 1969. Some notes in P. Bossuyt and J. Radermakers, *Jésus Parole de la grâce selon S. Luc,* Brussels, 1984, 473-480 ("to assure the bonds of brotherhood there even where rivalry has broken them," such would be Peter's mission); I. Howard Marshall, *The Gospel of Luke,* Exeter, 1978, 818-823; L. Sabourin, *L'Évangile de Luc; introduction et commentaire,* Rome, 1985, 347-348; A. Stoger, *L'évangile selon Luc,* t. III, Tournai, 1969, 100-102 ("the privilege which distinguishes Peter from the other apostles and disciples is given to him for the others . . . for brotherhood").

(cf. Matt 26:30-35), we find, in fact, both "words said to Peter *and* to the others" and words "said to Peter *rather* than to the others."[140] But these last words deal with a proper charge, their object being to strengthen the faith of all his brothers, whereas his faith will also be put to a difficult trial. We again find in this way what is the essence of the "primacy" of Peter: a special responsibility, affecting the faith, emerging from his realistic and dramatic *communion* with the trials and weaknesses of the apostolic group (Matt 26:30-35), and directing himself to the fidelity of this group.

Does Peter have this position after the Resurrection because already before the Cross, by his personality or—although certain strata of Johannine tradition seem to have that opinion—because of a choice by Jesus himself, he would have stood out in the apostolic group? The gospel accounts, in addition to putting him at the head of the list of the apostles—Matthew specifies "the first *protos,* Simon called Peter" (Matt 10:2)—and to emphasize his change of name (Matt 16:18; Mark 3:16; Luke 6:14; John 1:42) and by that fact the new destiny that Jesus imposes on him, often put him out in front. He belongs to the group of three—"Peter, James and John"—who accompany Jesus on certain more important occasions (such as the Transfiguration, the agony in the garden of Gethsemane) or at the time of "signs" like the miraculous catch of fish or the raising of the daughter of Jairus (Matt 17:1; 26:37; Mark 5:37; 9:2-8; 14:33; Luke 5:10; 8:51; 9:28). He is the spokesman for the apostles when Jesus questions them about what they think of him (Matt 16:13-20; Mark 8:27-30; Luke 9:18-21), the one who is against the declarations announcing the Passion (Matt 16:21-23; Mark 8:31-33). After the encounter with the rich young man, it is he who expresses the point of view of the apostolic group (Matt 19:27; Mark 10:28; Luke 18:28). When it is a question of the tax which Jesus must pay Jesus speaks to Peter and it is he who is charged with finding the didrachmas in question (Matt 17:24-27). At the time of the arrest and trial of Jesus, it is his attitude which is emphasized everywhere. While it is indicated how much the other apostles are hardly any better (Matt 26:31-35), it is not without reason that he alone is named. The message that the women receive from the young man at the tomb is for "the disciples of Peter" (Mark 16:7). And it is he who, according to Luke, after the report by Mary of Magdala, Joanna and the mother of James, "left and went running to the tomb" whereas the other apostles think this is pure nonsense (Luke 24:12). Johannine tradition itself, according to all evidence which has been preserved, continues however, we have seen, to make him the spokesman of the apostolic group and shows

---

[140]According to the fine remark of J. J. von Allmen, *La Primauté de l'Église de Pierre et de Paul,* Paris, 1977, 69 (see also 73, 96).

that he holds, alongside the beloved disciple, a place apart. In brief, before the Resurrection, it is impossible to mention the history of the ministry of Jesus without encountering Peter at key moments, even though his faults and his cowardice are emphasized. It is even impossible to "make the gospel known without speaking of Peter too."[141] For the evangelists, during Jesus' time Peter already counted.

Certainly no one can distinguish clearly what, in these gospel accounts, comes from a theological reading conditioned by the post-paschal situation. The importance that was later understood concerning the person of Peter was able to be projected in a retrospective way on the earlier period.[142] Yet it was certain that, several decades after the death of Jesus, the Christian community has, in the Spirit, the firm conviction that the role played by Peter after Pentecost is not explained by accidental circumstances, since he followed the Cross. For the Christian community it comes from a design of Jesus himself, the one who had called Peter, lived with him during his ministry, this Jesus whose apostles (grouped around Peter) were proclaiming that he was the Risen One whose teaching they were spreading.

The way in which Matthew presents the confession of Caesarea, by inserting in it his long incidental remarks on Peter's role, which is followed immediately by a violent reproach—"Get behind me, Satan, you are an obstacle in my path, because the way you think is not God's way but man's!" (Matt 16:23)—becomes clear at that time. Everything leads one to believe that to the precise recollection, engraved in the memory of the apostolic group, of a confession by Peter going back to the time of Jesus' ministry—the one reported also by Mark, Luke and, in another context, the Johannine Gospel (Mark 8:29-30; Luke 9:20-21; John 6:68-69)—Matthew links that of a post-paschal confession. In the words that the evangelist puts at that time in the mouth of Jesus we can see the proof or at least the influence of Peter's role after the Resurrection.[143] What this did was to permit the weak faith, which was shocked by the announcement of the Passion, (Matt 16:22-23; Mark 8:31-33), to be transformed into a faith which will be at the heart of the kerygma of Pentecost, because as the Johannine Gospel indicates: "They had not yet understood the teaching of Scripture according to which Jesus had to rise from the dead" (John 20:9). The apostle who intervenes in Caesarea, in the name of the others, and the one who preaches in Jerusalem are speaking of the same Jesus. But the image he has of him is not the same: through the

---

[141]*Saint Pierre dans le Nouveau Testament,* 195-196.

[142]See *ibid.,* 195.

[143]With R. H. Fuller, *The Formation of the Resurrection Narratives,* London, 1972, 166; *Saint Pierre dans le Nouveau Testament,* 108-110, 116.

crucible of the trial (with the denial and tears) faith has matured. It is no longer just pure enthusiasm; it is communion, an indefectible welcome of Christ the Lord, in spite of everything . . . even the Cross. It is the faith of the Church.

But this faith which Peter proclaims is his only when it is that of all his brother apostles. And, with a strong current of patristics, it seems to us that it is from this faith *of all,* but *as Peter (Petros) confesses it,* that Matthew creates the stone *(petra)* on which the Church is built.[144] Therefore, we find again the same law. Peter alone says—"rather than another"—what all believe; he alone receives—"rather than the others"—a declaration which is valid for all, since several lines farther on it is stated in the plural (Matt 18:18). The foundation stone of the Church is, in this context, not as much Christ confessed by Peter (cf. 1 Cor 10:4; Acts 4:11; 1 Pet 2:4-7) as faith in Christ *as confessed by Peter* and which is that of all the apostles. Historically, just as much in the scene at Caesarea as Mark and Luke see it as in the encounter with the Risen One and the preaching on the day of Pentecost, Peter is identified with this faith as it proceeds gradually from the beginning of Jesus' ministry. He is like the incarnation of it. It can even be said, by using the term in the sense that contemporary philosophy gives it, that he becomes the symbol of it: by expressing it in the Holy Spirit, he makes it a reality, causing it to emerge in the conscience of the Church. From this time on it will no longer be possible to confess Jesus Christ without making Peter's words one's own. And since without faith there is no Church, it has, therefore, as its foundation the confession by Peter. By inspiring this confession in him (Matt 16:17), "the Father who is in heaven" made him the first in the faith on which the Church is built. He is the first one to have fully expressed this faith, and forever. Faith is equivalent to his words.

---

[144]A whole patristic current, marked by Origen in the East and Augustine in the West, thinks that the rock on which the Church is built is Christ proclaimed. Augustine writes: "And if the Lord says: *On this rock I will build my Church,* it is because Peter had said: *You are the Christ, the Son of the living God.* On this rock which you have just proclaimed, says Jesus, I will build my Church. *In fact, the rock was Christ.* And on this foundation, Peter in his turn has been built. *The foundations, no one can lay down others than those which already exist: these foundations are Jesus Christ"* (In John 124:5; CCL 36, 685). Another current, especially western, to which Augustine belonged at first (cf. *Retractationum Liber I* XXI, 1, coll. "Bibliothèque augustinienne," 12, 401) and which has for its principal representatives Hilary, Jerome, Leo, says that Peter is this rock. Leo comments: "Although I am the inviolable rock, the corner stone, . . . the foundation of such kind that no one can lay down another, yet you also are rock" (*Sermo* IV, 2, *PL* 54, 150; *Sermo* III, 2-3, *PL* 54, 145-146). A third group, which seems to us to be the best to interpret the text, says that the rock is faith in Christ as proclaimed by Peter. John Chrysostom comments: "On this rock I will build my Church, to be known on the faith of your confession" (*In Mt.* 54:2 and 82:4, *PG* 58, 534, 741). On this question, see A. Rimoldi, *op. cit.,* J. Ludwig, *Die Primatworte Mt XVI, 18-19, in der Altkirchlichen Exegese,* coll. "Neutestamentliche Abhandlungen," XIX/4, Münster, 1952; J.-M. R. Tillard, *L'Évêque de Rome,* 142-150.

As Augustine has so well perceived, it is the Church which, in the person of Peter, receives then the keys of the Kingdom, on the basis of this confession.

The Church which is founded on Christ has received from him, in the person of Peter, the keys of the Kingdom of heaven, in other words the power to retain and forgive sins. This Church, by loving and following Christ is, therefore, freed from every evil. But it follows him more in those people who fight for truth until death.[145]

For Judaism, the power of retaining and forgiving is that of excluding or of reintroducing into the community. The apostolic faith confessed by Peter, in a unique way but which involves the whole apostolic group, opens the entrance into the Kingdom. Through baptism, which seals it, sins are forgiven—just as Peter will proclaim it on Pentecost (Acts 2:38)—which "loosens" from the previous situation. In addition, one enters at that time into the ecclesial community, proclaims and engages the eschatological Kingdom.[146] From the excellence of the confession comes the grandeur of the "power" which is linked to it. The first witness of the faith which saves, Peter is, therefore, inseparable from the "power" of this faith, which involves entrance into the Kingdom. His confession of faith puts in his hands the keys of the Kingdom with the authority to declare (in harmony with it) what must be believed and done in order to enter it. All of the apostles have this "power." He receives what the others receive from the Spirit, as he is (as a witness) what the others are. But he receives it with a special title: first in confession, he is first in the authority which is derived from it.

3. Nothing is said in the New Testament that any special person must succeed Peter, if not in his historical role—which is impossible, and we know why—at least in one or another of the functions attached to his primacy. Not even the least allusion is found there to a succession in the places where he has gone to evangelize. This is an indication that nowhere in the New Testament is there any trace of an institution of the papacy *as such* by Christ, no trace of an intuition that the early community would have had and according to which the role played by Peter in this community would have had to have been confided after his death to a minister (priest or bishop) charged with perpetuating it. And yet certain texts in the New Testament are subsequent to the death of Peter. The refusal by certain Anglicans of the dominical institution (in other words, direct, immediate and by Christ himself) of the papacy rests on these findings.

---

[145]In *Jo.* 124, 5; *CCL* 36, 685. But for Augustine the rock is Christ proclaimed (confessed), not the confession of Christ.

[146]See O. Cullmann, *Saint Pierre, apôtre, martyr,* Neuchâtel-Paris, 1952, 183–184.

But, on one hand, the recognition, very early, of the primacy of the Roman Church *as such* and, on the other hand, the knowledge of the role which the special qualification of Peter plays in this primacy (with that of Paul) and especially his own primacy in the midst of the apostolic group have fully justified this silence. From this fact, *mutatis mutandis* has come to be applied to the Bishop of Rome, charged by his special title with watching over Peter's witness, and the scriptural texts concerning this. Is he not his vicar? Minister and instrument of the primacy of the local Church of Rome, and by that fact, minister of the apostolic witness which is of prime importance, isn't there a striking analogy between his place in the midst of the other bishops and that of Peter in the midst of the apostolic group? Is he simply the vicar of Peter's witness or equally of his place?

The role—important and undeniable—played by the local Church of Rome urges, first of all, a recognition that the place of this Church is "providential," in the flow of the divine design, hence willed by God. Because it will be understood that in the rapid multiplication of communities, in the face of divisions provoked by different understandings of the body of faith which contradict the apostolic witness, it is a real benefit to be able to turn towards the community which has received the final message of the two leaders of the gospel. This good or benefit rises out of the providence of God for his own. At the moment when the nature of the episcopate will be determined, it will become clear that the Bishop of the Church of Rome plays a capital role in the fidelity of his Church to this function. This role will be situated in the economy of the Spirit. In this key period—the one also during which the canon of the Scriptures was determined—the Churches will perceive that according to the design of God a part of what was at work, in a unique way, in Peter's function was to endure *aliquomodo*. They will see in some way that the primacy of Peter will reverberate and become real, in fact, in a primacy of the bishop who is his vicar in and for the Church founded on his glorious confession. They will declare, therefore, that the primacy of the Bishop of Rome, linked in this way to a will of God manifested in the very history of the Churches, has a divine source, is a divine institution. In other words, only the primacy of Peter is of "dominical" institution, in other words, that it alone rests on a declaration made explicitly by Christ Jesus before the ascension and certified in the Scriptures. But, in the Holy Spirit, the Church will perceive that the Roman primacy belongs also to the design of God for his People, that it was not only permitted but positively willed by God. But Christ was in communion with the will of the Father, even in those things which he said nothing about during his ministry. The primacy of Peter and Roman primacy are on the same providential line, with, nevertheless, an important difference. The primacy of Peter is the "once-and-for-all" at whose service the other primacy is placed. Scholastic

Thomism (with its correct vision of this analogy) would state that they are two analogous primacies of Peter. But, in the analogy, both the differences and the resemblance must be taken into account. It is in this sense that the texts concerning Peter will be used to characterize the position of the Bishop of Rome.

It can be said that, while interpreting it differently in the East and in the West, and by widening more or less the margin of the differences between Peter and his "vicar," the Churches have, at least since the middle of the third century,[147] accepted this analogy. It is still this analogy which explains the reaction of the Fathers of Chalcedon or of the Third Council of Constantinople: "Peter has spoken through Leo," "through Agathon." The frictions between East and West will come not from this link Peter-Bishop of Rome but from the type of authority which results from it for this last one. In his famous great *Apology,* speaking of Nicaea II, the patriarch of Constantinople Nicephorus will declare, thinking of the Bishop of Rome:

> The Romans have acquired by dividing up performance of duties a function of guide in the priesthood and they have given them the authority of those who are the leaders in the midst of the apostles.[148]

Yet, as Cyprian already stated, everything depends on the way in which one understands the behavior of the "first"—Peter, as also of Steven—in the place of his "equals" in the episcopate. Under the formula "primacy of honor" are hidden a thousand ambiguities.[149]

The council of Vatican II expresses, therefore, the (Roman) Catholic conviction when it affirms that the Roman primacy is of divine institution.[150] By doing this it wisely avoids using the Vatican I expression, declaring in *Pastor aeternus* that by divine right, *jure divino,* Peter has successors,[151] because the notion of divine right is difficult to discern completely. It is, besides, in the ecumenical context, one of the most frequent sources of ambiguity.[152]

---

[147]That penetrates with Cyprian into the climate we know.

[148]*PG* 100, 597 AB. See V. Peri, "Pro amore. . . ." (see footnote 129 for full citation), 349. Recently, J. Meyendorff has noted several times that the radical refusal of the primatial authority since the schism has been able to lead the Orthodox Churches to a lack of cohesion which is *abnormal* and goes counter to the nature of the Church. Thus *Ecumenical Trends* 13, 1984, 120.

[149]For the *full* sense of the expression, see P. Duprey, "Brief Reflection on the Title Primus inter pares," *One in Christ* 10, 1974, 7-12. But today the usual sense given is not as rich.

[150]*Christus Dominus, 2a.* See *Lumen gentium,* 20, for the episcopate.

[151]*DS* 3058 ("it is . . . by divine right that Peter has and will always have successors in his primacy over the whole Church, and that the Roman Pontiff has this succession").

[152]We go back especially to two studies which are very enlightening, Y. Congar, "Jus divinum," *Revue de droit canonique* 28, 1978 (Studies offered to Jean Gaudemet) 108-112; Theodore Ignatz

In fact, basing themselves on Augustine for whom the Scriptures preserve divine right, Luther, then the great currents of the Reformation, will give the name of divine right to what is clearly legitimized by the holy Books[153] and remains in explicit agreement with the *mandatum Dei* such as was received and transmitted by them. What is acquired through history belongs to the vast domain of the *adiaphora*. Catholic ecclesiology, laying stress on faith in the permanent presence of Christ through his Spirit—and this faith is expressly based on the Scriptures (John 14:16, 25-66; Matt 28:20)—affirms that all throughout its history the Church is under the guidance and inspiration of its Lord. The Spirit of the Lord, always at work, is involved in what the necessities of history cause to rise up in ecclesial life so that the people of God remain faithful to their nature and their mission. The Spirit works *ad intra,* in the windings of human history. He does not create the economy of secondary causes, even in what has reference to the Churches. That raises again the idea of divine providence. Wasn't that already the case in biblical times? We have examined this carefully in another chapter.

No clear boundary exists which permits us to say: "What is on this side has been positively willed by God, what is on that side is entirely dependent on human freedom." In light of the "once-and-for-all" of the apostolic witness, it is not a question of searching to see if such or such a structure is or is not explicitly certified, mandated or established in the Scriptures (and then only would it be *jure divino*). It is a question of disclosing if it is not only useful but *necessary* for the Churches, based on what Revelation specifies as the nature of them, and because of that willed by God—even if it is not mentioned in the inspired books—and destined to *last*.[154] In their search carried out, sometimes somewhat fundamentalist, of what is *prescribed* by God (and only Scripture preserves divine regula-

Jimenez Uresti, "The Theologian in Interface with Canonical Reality," in Piet Fransen, *Authority in the Church,* coll. "Annua Nuntia Lovaniensia," 26, Louvain, 1983, 146–175. See also K. Rahner, "Sur le concept du jus divinum dans la conception catholique," *Ecrits théologiques* 6, Desclée de Brouwer, 1966, 9–38. Some enlightening notes, in regards to a particular case, in M. Nicolau, "Jus divinum, acerca de la confesion en el Concilio de Trento," *Rev. Esp. deTeol.* 32, 1972, 419–440; A. Dulles, "Jus divinum as an Ecumenical Problem," *Theol. Stud.* 38, 1977, 688–697; C. J. Peter, "Dimensions of Jus divinum in Roman Catholic Theology," *Theol. Stud.* 34, 1973, 227–250.

[153]On the non-Catholic visions of the *jus divinum,* see in particular in P. C. Empie and T. A. Murphy, *Papal Primacy and the Universal Church,* coll. "Lutherans and Catholics in Dialogue," 5, Minneapolis, 1974, the studies of A. C. Piepkorn, "Jus divinum and Adiaphoron in Relation to Structural Problems in the Church, the Position of the Lutheran Symbolic Books," 119–127; G. A. Lindbeck, "Papacy and jus divinum, a Lutheran View," 193–208. See also E. Wolf, *Ordnung in der Kirche,* Francfort, 1961, 458–469.

[154]See in M. Nicolau, *art. cit.,* the degrees of the *jus divinum* according to a theological note of 1547: what is formally in Scripture, what is deduced from Scripture *bona et formali consequentia,* what is not directly formulated in Scripture but is recognized however, as coming from the apostolic community, what comes from general councils (437-438). The range of meanings is, consequently, very broad.

tions) Catholic traditions prefer researching what is *willed* by God (and this will is discovered in the history of the People of the New Covenant understood in the light of Scripture). The action of God in the Covenant is itself something which carries meaning. The Spirit guides the Church in what its nature demands. The Church discovers in this way "laws" for its life.

In this sense the primacy of the Bishop of Rome appeared as a principle of unity laid down by God (in his Providence) in the very constitution of the Church, in order to preserve the *communion* of faith, of witness and of mission of all the Churches spread over the whole earth and different in their expression, their cultural and historical soil, their mentality, their proper tradition and their specific needs.[155] This primacy emerged in history. Nothing is said explicitly about it in Scripture. Yet what Scripture affirms explicitly about the primacy of Peter in the midst of the apostolic group permits us to understand that this position of Bishop of Rome is in profound harmony with the divine economy and with what was revealed about it in apostolic times. Certainly, it is a question of a ministry, a service endowed with special prerogatives whose aim is to give him the efficacy and the impact which permit him to guarantee *communion*. However, the (Roman) Catholic Church affirms that this ministry belongs to the very constitution of the Church, as a point of unity in the episcopal college in which he is assigned a place. The Church holds that it is willed by God, and not simply permitted. It states that its origin is of divine institution, in other words that it has risen up *because of* the divine will.

Paul, called to the apostolate after the ascension of the Lord, evidently could not have in his role the same link as Peter with the manifest intentions of Jesus during his ministry. He is apart. His importance, equal to that of Peter, in the primacy of the Roman Church[156] does not reverberate in the same way in the ministry of the bishop charged with preserving his witness. Besides, his relation to the *communion* is different from that of Peter. He is the one who puts into relief the subordination of all ecclesial reality to the absolute transcendence of grace.[157] The fact that his wit-

[155]At Vatican I, in the name of the Deputation of the Faith, Mgr. Leahy, an Irishman, used these expressions (Mansi 52, 638–639) in an intervention in a tone which was sometimes not very ecumenical.

[156]Some texts, using falsehoods, circulated denouncing whoever would deny that Paul himself was under the orders of Peter, and that was the case (sometimes) throughout his ministry. So there was a decree from the Holy Office on January 24, 1647 (taking up some former documents). See for the context J. Madoz, "Una nueva redaccion de los textos pseudopatristicos sobre el Primado en Jacobo de Viterbo" in *Greg.* 17, 1936, 563–583; texts of John XXII and Clement VI, 1327 and 1351 in Charles du Plessis d'Argentré, I, 365 and III, 248.

[157]See Y. Congar, "Saint Paul et l'autorité de l'Église romaine d'après la Tradition," *Studiorum Paulinorum Congressus Internationalis Catholicus 1961*, coll. "Analecta Biblica," 17–18, Rome, 1963, 491–516.

ness has been intermingled with Peter's brings to the primacy an essential harmony: it goes back to the absolute initiative of the Risen Lord who makes Paul the one who must become the bearer of his power to lead nations and kings, with the People of Israel, to the knowledge of his Name (Acts 9:15-16). It is revealed in this way totally subjected to the initiatives of the Spirit of God, guiding history towards a mysterious goal, which he alone has the power to bring about. Ecclesial authority could not be content with preserving the community in fidelity to the letter of the deposit of faith. It must also guide itself towards its goal, the justification of Revelation.[158] And that demands that it "preserve" it continually for an opening up that involves the transcendence of grace and its orientation towards the realities "to come." In other words, Paul's case shows that absolute fidelity to "what *has been* said and done" is called upon to remain in symbiosis with a total availability in regard to "what *must be* said and done" so that the "mystery" (in the sense in which we have described it) is realized. Because the confession of Jesus as Christ and Lord is itself enclosed in the totality of this "mystery."

Paul transmits in this way to the primatial power both an intrinsic limitation (its submission to the permanent newness of the Spirit which his reproaches to Peter himself will recall) and a freedom (the refusal of every myopic fundamentalism). If earlier, speaking of Peter, we insisted on the essential relationship of catholicity to the Covenant—what was for Israel is henceforth for all—speaking of Paul it is necessary now to emphasize the essential relationship of catholicity to "all the nations." In Rome, the contribution of each of the two great leaders is united. If Peter brings to the primacy especially the function and its mandate, Paul brings to it especially its perspective. One attaches it to the "once-and-for-all" of the apostolic witness, the other to the meaning of this witness. One welds it to the historical witness of a Covenant which is mercy-and-fidelity, the other sends it back again continually to the superabundance of this mercy. One says that the free gift of God does not create, however, the economy of the involvement of a people and its *martyria,* the other adds that this involvement, whatever there may be in its grandeur and value, is, nevertheless, for all peoples. Both of them show in this way that ecclesial authority is "catholic" (*kath'olon*) only to the extent to which it aims at maintaining, inseparable and in constant tension, invincible fidelity to the "once-and-for-all" of Revelation and the universal destination of this latter, and of faith and mission.[159] Primacy bears the marks of their *communion.*

[158]Several perspectives will be found in this sense in John Howard Schutz, *Paul and the Anatomy of Apostolic Authority,* coll. "Society for New Testament Studies, Monograph Series," 26, Cambridge, 1975.

[159]On this link between faith and mission, some important perspectives will be found in *Go*

Perhaps it is even necessary to add that in their coming together Peter and Paul reveal to the Churches what they are in the depth of their grace-filled being. Because Peter, witness par excellence of the passionate attachment to Christ, is also the one who protests before the Passion and the Cross, and disappears from the courtyard of the high priest; his "views are not those of God but those of men" (Matt 16:23). This is also the situation of the Church, suspended tensely between its basic holiness as spouse of Christ (Eph 5:27) and the constant temptation of not "following" its Lord on his own way (cf. John 21:18-19). Paul, who passes from the denial of Christ to a certain intransigeance, the quarrel with Peter being an indication of it—orchestrated by other attitudes[160]—testifies in return that evangelical truth has an absolute and transcendent power, that the Church itself has no power over this truth, although it is known as the authentic servant of it. It is neither the owner nor the proprietor of it. God asks it to live under the control of this truth which surpasses it and which, in spite of its weaknesses, it can do nothing but obey. Peter and Paul are for each other witnesses not of an abstract Church but of the Church of God in the realism of its call and its circumstances.

Reading the history of Christian communities in light of their faith in the permanent presence of the Lord and Spirit in them, the Churches in communion with Rome affirm that primacy with its essential characteristics is positively willed by God. They declare it destined, providentially, to make the Church of God shine in each local Church. A title of glory? No, rather a title of service.

III. Outside of Visible Communion

1. What we have just presented is the faith of the Churches in communion with Rome. For them, ecclesial *communion* has its full visibility, and in that way its fullness, only when the local Churches "recognize" themselves explicitly united to the apostolic witness of Peter and Paul just as the Church of Rome preserves it and as the bishop of this Church protects it, defends it and promotes it. Consequently, *communion* with this Church and this bishop constitutes, they affirm, an essential element in the realization of full ecclesial *communion* which responds to the design of God. They know, certainly, that everywhere where there is baptism with water and an authentic faith, there is true integration in the commu-

---

Forth in Peace, Orthodox Perspectives on Mission, Ton Bria ed., coll. "WCC Series," 7, Geneva, 1986. See in particular 31-32 where this link is described as an integral element of the fulfillment of the Christian being, image and resemblance of God, and by that of the *theosis.*

[160]Well brought out by R. E. Brown, in *Antioch and Rome.* See also some strong affirmation in J.-M. Lustiger, *Oser croire; oser dire,* coll. "Folio," Paris, 1986, 125-128, 207-211.

nity of Salvation. They also proclaim that wherever a "true" Eucharist is celebrated the Church is "truly" present and manifested. But they specify that this ecclesial community is fully manifested as a cell of *visible communion* willed by the Lord only if the one who presides at its Eucharist—where the reality which constitutes the very heart of the apostolic witness is proclaimed and celebrated—is explicitly linked to the episcopal college in whose center the Bishop of Rome exercises the function which we have described. And according to them the *visibility* of *communion* is not a secondary element or an accessory of the ecclesial being. The apostolic community makes of it an express will of the Lord. According to these Churches, however, the absence of full visibility does not necessarily mean the absence of any *communion*. It means at least the absence of one of the important elements willed by God. In the first chapter, we described the different levels of *communion* which persist despite the breaks. We have even admitted that between the Church of Rome and certain Eastern Churches communion was so profound that the only thing lacking in it was the visible expression.

Neither are we saying that the Church of God exists only in communities in *communion* with the Roman Church. What we are saying is that only there is it in its fullness. Besides, the history of relations between them and Eastern communities, after the break, proves that the West has preserved the conviction that the Church continued to exist in the East. And well before the remarkable affirmations of Paul VI, the texts of Leo XIII and of Pius XI contained in outline form this certitude that the line of demarcation was hardly stressed. Even in moments when obstacles were emphasized more than points of similarity, right in its official documents the Roman Church continued to call Churches these Eastern communities separated from them, whereas it avoided doing it for those which rose out of the Reformation.[161] Gregory VII himself is a witness of that.[162] That situation will last until John XXIII, in documents which treat explicitly questions about the East and in which, consequently, all words are weighed.[163] In a well-known passage, which will be taken up again in the decree of Vatican II on ecumenism, the definition *Laetentur caeli* of the Council of Florence, in 1439, supposed to join together again the

---

[161]See Y. Congar, "Note sur les mots confession, Église et communion," *Irénikon* 23, 1950, 3-36 (30-50), also Id., *Chrétiens désunis*, coll. "Unam sanctam," 1, Paris, 1937, appendix VI, reprinted in *Chrétiens en dialogue*, coll. "Unam sanctam," 50, Paris, 1964, 211-242.

[162]See G. Hofmann, "Notae historicae de terminologia theologica Concilii Florentini," *Greg.* 20, 1939, 257-263 (261) which takes up the following affirmations of Gregory VII, in 1074 and 1075: *"Constantinopolitana Ecclesia de Sancto Spiritu a nobis dissidens," "orientalis Ecclesia instinctu Diaboli a catholica fide deficit"* (PL 148, 385-387, 399-400).

[163]Thus Pius XII, encyclical *Orientales omnes*, of December 23, 1945, text found in *Actes de S.S. Pie XII*, t. VII, 314-368.

communion between Greeks and Latins, uses the image which we are acquainted with, that of a wall separating the Church into two parts, East and West.[164] On both sides of the wall the Church of God exists, *Ecclesia graeca* on one side, and *Ecclesia latina* on the other, the Church of Constantinople and the Church of Rome, the Church in separation and the Roman Church as Pius XII will repeat in the encyclical *Orientales omnes* of December 23, 1945.[165]

These affirmations of the hierarchy are in harmony with the *praxis* of several milieux:

> The facts of communion are so numerous between 1054 and the Council of Florence, that one can no longer speak of a total break simply dotted with several fortunate inconsistencies or exceptions. Even after the rejection of the Council of Florence by the Eastern Churches—a rejection which would furnish again, if it were necessary to indicate one of them, the best point of chronological reference to reckon the true beginning of the schism—many acts of communion have still existed; in addition, union was not rejected with one single event or action and immediately everywhere.[166]

What must be taken into consideration above all is the fact that, in spite of polemics over the epiclesis or leavened bread, on the Roman side, in a general way, there was never any doubt about the truthfulness of the Eucharist celebrated in the Eastern Churches. When, relying on the rediscovery of the essential link between Eucharist and Church, Vatican II will affirm[167] that in every community which *truly* celebrates the Eucharist of the Lord, whether they are small, poor or living in dispersion, "Christ is present by virtue of which the Church, one, holy, catholic and apostolic is gathered together," it will put the final seal on this intuition. The Church of God is present *also* in communities of the East separated from the See

---

[164]See *Conciliorum Œcumenicorum Decreta*, 500; Mansi 31, 1026 E, quoted in *Unitatis redintegratio*, 18.

[165]Thus *ed. cit.*, 318, 320, 329.

[166]Y. Congar, "Neuf cents ans après; notes sur le schisme oriental," *1054-1954, l'Église et les Églises, études et travaux sur l'unité chrétienne offerts à dom Lambert Beauduin*, Chevetogne, 1954, 3-95 (5). See also G. Every, *The Byzantine Patriarchate*, London, 1947, 153-192; N. Jugie, *Le Schisme byzantin*, Paris, 1941, 234-235, and especially H. Rees, *The Catholic Church and Corporate Reunion, a Study of the Relations between East and West from the Schism of 1054 to the Council of Florence*, Westminster, 1940. See also Joan E. Anastasiou, "Some Favourable Aspects in XIII Century on the Communion between Orthodox and Catholics," to appear in the review *Kanon* (it is possible that some Catholic presbyters were ordained by Orthodox bishops). Let us recall some other types of communion: in 1083, the name of Urban II was reinscribed in the dyptics of Constantinople (that lasting nearly two years), the question of marriages between faithful of the two Churches does not seem to have raised canonical difficulties.

[167]*Lumen gentium*, 26.

of Rome. And since they live the Eucharist, what exists in them is something else than a collection of *remains,* of fleeting or fragile traces of the grace of God, of ways of Salvation which have been badly tied together. To live by the Eucharist is to live by the divine gift of ecclesial *communion.* What is lacking in these Eastern Churches in regard to catholic fullness is not, therefore, the very essence of this *communion* but one of its important modalities.

In the enthusiasm of Vatican II, a rather keen realization will take place concerning these fraternal links which have always existed, to the point that, in an official way, Paul VI will be able to apply to relations between the Church of Rome and the Eastern Church the expression which the decree of Vatican II on ecumenism had yet dared to use only for bonds that the East puts between local Churches.[168] It will affirm that the two Churches are sister Churches.[169] It will even go as far as saying to the Patriarch Athenagoras that both must be recognized and respected "as shepherd of part of the flock of Christ which has been confided to them, by taking care of the cohesion and growth of the People of God and by avoiding everything which could separate them or cause confusion in their ranks."[170] The Church of God, therefore, goes beyond the borders of communities which, since they are in communion with it, constitute part of the flock confided to the Bishop of Rome.[171]

Western Tradition has besides a vision of baptism and its effect which, for its part, clashes with affirmations as decisive as one by Pius XII. He wrote in *Mystici corporis* that "schism, heresy, and apostasy separate man from the body of the Church," that "only those are counted among the members of the Church (*il soli annumerandi sunt*) who have received the bath of regeneration, by confessing the true faith" and besides are not, to their misfortune, "cut off from the whole of the Body or have not been cut off from it for a serious reason by legitimate authority."[172] Later, in

---

[168]*Anitatis redintegratio,* 14–15.

[169]See the studies mentioned *supra.*

[170]The brief *Anno ineunte* of Paul VI, July 25, 1967, is easily accessible in *Le Livre de la charité,* 120–121; his allocution *ibid.,* 115–117 (116).

[171]Let us note that the project of an ecumenical council for union between East and West, proposed by emperor Jean Cantacuzène in 1367 and accepted by the legate Paul, implied the recognition of the presence of the Church on both sides of the dividing line. Rejected by Urban VI, this project served as a model at the Council of Florence. This Council was—in spite of the debates on this subject (4th and 5th sessions)—proclaimed in the East as truly an ecumenical council and this title will figure in the first editions of the *Acta.* See J. Gill, *The Council of Florence,* Cambridge, 1959, 150–151; J. Meyendorff, "Byzance et Rome: les tentatives d'union," *Découvertes de l'œcuménisme,* coll. "Cahiers de La-Pierre-qui-Vire," Desclée, 1961, 324–334.

[172]*"In Ecclesiae autem membris reapse* ii soli annumerandi sunt *qui regenerationis lavacrum receperunt, veramque fidem profitentur neque a Corporis compage semetipsos misere separarunt, vel ob gravissima admissa a legitima auctoritate sejuncti sunt."* Also "those who are divided for reasons of faith or government, can't they live in this same Body according to this same divine Spirit" (*DS* 2286).

Humani generis, he went as far as identifying Mystical Body of Christ and Roman Catholic Church.[173] Yet he also declared that baptism brings about incorporation into Christ himself. Therefore, he made a distinction between incorporation into Christ and incorporation into the Church. In his eyes, the latter was an affair of all or nothing.[174] Outside of communion with Rome one could in certain cases be in Christ and his grace,[175] but one was not for all of that *in the Church*. One was in a dependent state on the Church. But doesn't this strict distinction between incorporation into Christ himself as *every true baptism* brings about—what the Western Churches have recognized since the quarrels by Cyprian and the doctrinal restatement by Augustine[176]—and incorporation into the Church as Body of Christ, respond to the Pauline vision of the link between baptism and Body of Christ (1 Cor 12:13)?

The great Tradition itself, in fact, urges a refusal of a complete break between belonging to Christ, the source of Salvation, and belonging to the Church. Because how can one be in Christ without being incorporated in him in some way? And besides, what is the Body of Christ (in the Pauline sense) if not the Church? Can one, then, belong to Christ without, in some way, belonging to the Church? Christ is henceforth inseparable from his ecclesial Body. The boundaries of it coincide, therefore, with those of being-in-Christ. Besides, this is what the nature of grace wishes: one is saved by being made a member of the Body of Salvation which is the Body of Christ. At the time of Vatican II, while theories on the "Church of pure love" which conditioned the rigid position of Pius XII no longer had an impact, scriptural and patristic studies recalled this situation. The limits of the Church are not clear. Therefore, it could not be, from the Catholic point of view, a question of all or nothing, in other words, of being in communion with Rome or of being in no way "in the

---

[173]"The mystical Body of Christ and the Roman Catholic Church are one and the same thing" (towards the middle of the encyclical, in *DC* 47, 1950, 1161).

[174]But Cardinal Bea, *Pour l'unité des chrétiens,* Paris, 1963, 23–29, will testify that the encyclical does not exclude belonging to the Church for Christians who are non-Catholic. See the interesting study by E. Lanne, "La contribution du cardinal Bea à la question du baptême et l'unité des chrétiens," *Simposio card. Agostino Bea* (December 16-19, 1981), Rome, 1983 (also *Cummunio,* n.s. 14, 1983), 159–185, with our response J.-M. R. Tillard, "A propos du baptême: deux regards différents du cardinal Bea," *ibid.,* 186–194. We hesitate to follow the interpretation that the cardinal gives to the passage of the encyclical which occupies us here. But it is clear that he played a large role in opening up Catholic vision on this point. He has been without doubt the main author of it.

[175]*"Inscio quodam desiderio ac voto ad Mysticum Redemptoris Corpus ordinentur,"* says *Mystici corporis.*

[176]It is affirmed in the Council of Florence, in a text which will be taken up again at Vatican II by *Unitatis redintegratio* 3 (cf. also 22). It is a question of a text of the 7th session, in the decree *Exultate Deo.* See *Conciliorum œcumenicorum decreta,* 518; Mansi 31, 1055 A. It is implicitly assumed in canon 87 of the 1917 code; by every valid baptism one becomes a person in the Church.

Church of God." And the deep understanding of certain non-Catholic milieux confirmed this conviction.

Proposed by several episcopates,[177] and made explicit during the discussions,[178] this vision was entered, by Vatican II, into the official teaching of the Roman Catholic Church. The decree on ecumenism, with many fine distinctions, speaks of the establishment on the earth "of one single Body of Christ to which it is necessary that all those be *fully* incorporated who, in a certain way, already belong to the People of God."[179] By using the expressions "complete (*integra*) incorporation," "full (*plena*) unity coming from baptism," it permits in this way an understanding that there also exists an incorporation which is not quite as full and complete, therefore, what is at stake here is not a question of all or nothing. There is a spilling over of the Church outside of its Catholic boundaries. Besides, it specifies the nature of this spilling over in this long paragraph where all the words count: "among the elements or the goods through whose totality the Church is built and given life, several and even many which are of great value can exist outside of the visible limits of the Catholic Church," "it must be recognized that they open up entrance into the communion of Salvation," "the Spirit of Christ does not refuse to be served (by these separated Churches or communities) although we believed them to be victims of deficiencies . . . as means of Salvation."[180] Also, even though "the only Catholic Church of Christ is a general means of Salvation by which the entire fullness of the means of Salvation can be obtained," that it is the place of "full incorporation," what is found outside the boundaries is still a people of God where the Holy Spirit "operates with his sanctifying virtue, his gifts and his graces."[181] He uses these Churches or separated communities as authentic "means of Salvation." He "incorporates their faithful in Christ in such a way that they bear deservedly the name of Christians and that the sons of the Catholic Church recognize them with good reason as brothers in the Lord." They are, therefore, "in a certain communion, even though imperfect, with the Catholic Church." This is why "the Spirit acts in these disciples so that this communion might reach its fullness."[182] And this *communion* implies very much a belonging to the Church.

[177]These texts are found in G. Alberigo, F. Magistretti, *Constitutionis Dogmaticae Synopsis Historica*, Bologne, 1975, 384, 397, 419, 426.

[178]Especially by Cardinal Lienart, December 1, 1962. The complete text is found in *Acta synodalia sacrosancti concilii œcumenici Vaticani II*, vol. I/4, 126, 127, summed up in *DC* 60, 1963, note.

[179]*Unitatis redintegratio*, 3, cf. 22.

[180]*Ibid.*, 3.

[181]*Lumen gentium*, 15.

[182]*Ibid.*

With less density, the constitution *Lumen gentium* had made explicit some of these links for communion:

> With those who, having been baptized, bear the name of Christians, but do not profess the fullness of the faith or do not preserve the unity of communion under the successor of Peter, the Church is itself linked by more than a motive or incentive. Indeed, numerous are those who, by venerating holy Scripture as a rule of belief and life, prove themselves of sincere religious zeal; they believe, with love, in God, the all-powerful Father, in Christ, the Son of God, the Savior; they are signed by baptism which unites them to Christ; in addition, they recognize and receive other sacraments in their particular Churches or their ecclesial communities. Several among them even have an episcopate, celebrate the Holy Eucharist and encourage devotion to the Virgin, Mother of God. To that is added communion in prayer and other spiritual benefits, and besides a kind of real union in the Holy Spirit, since it is he who, in them also, works by his sanctifying virtue, by his gifts and graces, having strengthened some among them even to shedding their blood. In this way the Spirit stirs up in all the disciples of Christ a desire and an action which reaches out to a peaceful union of all, according to the mode established by Christ, in one single flock, under one single Shepherd.[183]

This constitution illustrated in this manner its conviction that there exist, "outside of the visible organization [of the Catholic Church], numerous elements of sanctification and of truth which, being gifts proper to the Church of Christ, carry by themselves an inclination towards Christian unity."[184]

Non-Catholics, cut off from *communion* with the Church of Rome, no longer appear, therefore, as strangers to the work of Salvation, but at the very most on the doorstep of the Church. They may be in it. Catholic Churches think that they lack the fullness of incorporation into the full richness which has been revealed and transmitted by the apostolic Tradition. But their communities—even if they are not called Churches, as when they celebrate an episcopal Eucharist—are ecclesial communities.[185] The Spirit lives in them and causes Salvation to pass through them. But, according to the beautiful formula by Irenaeus, "where the Church is, there is also the Spirit of God; where the Spirit of God is, there is the Spirit of all grace."[186] To declare that the Spirit of baptism acts *equally* outside

[183]*Ibid.*

[184]*Lumen gentium*, 8.

[185]This appellation seems to come from an intervention of Cardinal Koenig, in the conciliar discussion of 1963. See *DC* 61, 1964, 40; J. Hamer, "La terminologie ecclésiologique de Vatican II et les ministères protestants," *DC* 68, 1971, 625–628; Y. Congar, "Note sur les mots confession, Église et communion."

[186]In *Adv. Haer.* III, 24, 1.

of the limits of the Churches in communion with Rome, is to declare that the Church is *equally* present there, even if one does not think that it has in it all its *splendor*. The baptized in these communities are *in Christ* only by being *in Church*.

These Christians are thus incorporated, more or less fully, in the one Church of God, by the fact that their community belongs to this Church. They are, to a more or less profound degree, in ecclesial communion not because the Spirit would sanctify them *in spite* of their community—on the basis of *vestigia Ecclesiae*[187] or *elementa seu bona Ecclesiae*[188] that it would have in spite of everything which had been preserved—but because it unites them to Christ *in* and *by* it. It is in it that they receive the evangelical Word, are baptized "with a baptism which unites them to Christ," draw on "a strength enabling them to go to the shedding of blood," communicate "in prayer and other spiritual benefits" with all believers, hear the call for unity, and celebrate the sacraments or the liturgical rites of their tradition.[189] Christian grace in them takes the path of their confessional identity. And the Holy Spirit himself can often tie together in a very living *communion* of charity the life of one or the other of these communities.

2. The status which the other Churches and ecclesial communities have, in the eyes of the Churches in communion with Rome, begins, therefore, to be stated precisely. They are not empty spiritual spaces in which vestiges rise up, more or less numerous, from what existed in the group from which they were separated. By the *elementa Ecclesiae* which they contain, the Spirit enlivens them and—the ecumenical movement, born from them, is proof of it—induces them to find the fullness of being ecclesial. In the measure to which their teaching remains on line with apostolic tradition and to which their practice remains coherent with the essentials of the gospel, they lead their faithful to Salvation, even if they do not offer them

---

[187]On this complex question of *vestigia* or *elementa Ecclesiae*, one should read especially Y. Congar, "A propos des vestigia Ecclesiae," *Vers l'unité chrétienne* 39, 1952, 4–5, which clears up Id., *Chrétiens desunis*, 300–307 and which examines thoroughly Id., "Le développement de l'évaluation ecclésiologique des Églises non catholiques," *Rev. de droit canon* 25, 1975, 168–198. Read also the imposing document studied by J. Hamer, "Le baptême et l'Église, à propos des Vestigia Ecclesiae," *Irénikon* 25, 1952, 142–164, 263–275. See the quick study of G. Baum, "La réalité ecclésiale des autres Églises," *Concilium* 4, 1965, 61–80. An indispensable working tool for all research in this area will be found in E. Lamirande, "La signification ecclésiologique des communautés dissidentes et la doctrine des vestigia Ecclesiae, panorama théologique des vingt-cinq dernières années," *Istina* 10, 1964, 25–58. Add G. Lafont, "L'appartenance à l'Église," in M. J. Guillou and G. Lafont, *L'Église en marche*, coll. "Cahiers de La-Pierre-qui-Vire," 1964, 25–89; H. Fries, *L'Église—Questions actuelles*, Paris, 1966, 131–162; J. McGovern, *The Church in the Churches*, Washington, 1968.

[188]These are the terms used by *Lumen gentium*, 8 and *Unitatis redintegratio*, 3.

[189]*Lumen gentium*, 15.

all the means of grace confided by God to the ecclesial institution. They cannot be seen as blocks taken out of the Roman Catholic Church and whose specific characteristics would be created solely from what they brought from it. On one hand, that is not valid for the Eastern Churches. On the other hand, many reformed communities have evolved in a very particular sense, creating a proper tradition whose links with the gospel witness could not be questioned. In addition, since the Church of God is on this earth, in an inseparable way, both a means of Salvation and communion of charity, it is hard to see how the fervor of some of these groups would be "a diversion from Catholic fervor." They are cells, sometimes vigorous ones, sometimes rather pitiful ones, of the Body of Christ, the only place of the reality of Salvation.

Certainly, in these cells of the Body of Christ the Church does not exist in its entire fullness, especially if they do not celebrate the Memorial of the Lord in conformity with the great Tradition. Yet they belong, *as ecclesial cells,* to the Body of Christ which is the Church. Certain ones even are Churches, in the strict sense, which lack only the *visible* link with the seat which has as its function to unite in a *visible* communion all the believing communities. The spreading of the Church of God outside of the limits of the Churches in *communion* with the Church of Rome, is not a spreading of justified individuals but of communities, of "communions." In everything that it is, the Church is a *communion* of communions, even in the abnormal situation where these communions have, among themselves, only an imperfect or partial *communion.* Cardinal Journet spoke of broken pieces.[190] This image does not indicate that the qualitative fullness of the Church would no longer exist anywhere and would depend on the reassembling of the pieces. What is wanted here is to emphasize that in the Christian world separated from it, the Catholic Church (Roman) sees not a sprinkling of individuals of good faith, endowed with grace, but an ensemble of communities which, *as such,* are ecclesial—with what that involves—and yet which are not yet visibly united with it or even have only an imperfect *communion* with it, perhaps even a minimal one.

The great declaration of *Lumen gentium,* according to which the one Church "*exists in* the Catholic Church governed by the successor of Peter and the bishops in communion with him,"[191] can be authentically understood only in light of what we have expressed in an explicit way. Besides, the sentence which we have just quoted specifies that the Church *exists* in this way, "although outside of its visible structure there are numerous

---

[190]C. Journet, *Théologie de l'Église,* Paris, 1958, 348, Id., *L'Église du Verbe incarné,* t. II, Paris, 1962, 724. An irony of sorts, it is one of the most faithful disciples of Mgr. Journet who opposed most violently the use of this image at the time of a meeting in Rome!

[191]*Lumen gentium,* 8.

elements of sanctification and truth which, being the proper gifts of the Church of Christ, push for Catholic unity." If the Fathers of the council passed from the declaration, still present in the projects of 1962 and 1963: "The one Church of Christ . . . *is* the Catholic Church" to the formula: "The one Church of Christ . . . *exists in (subsistit in)* the Catholic Church,"[192] it is without any doubt because of the recognition of this situation of the Catholic Church in the heart of an ecclesial reality which goes beyond its borders. In the spirit of editors then of conciliar bishops who declare themselves in its favor, this modification says a lot more than a simple verbal nuance. The whole of the document shows it. Besides, this is why, in the face of requests for modification, going either to a more liberal sense or to a more restrictive one, the commission refused to change the formula.[193] Because—it explained itself on this matter by presenting it to the Fathers of the council, with its *relatio*—"instead of *is* we say *subsistit in* so that the expression will be in better agreement with the declaration of ecclesial elements which exist elsewhere."[194] The intention could not be any clearer than that.

The sense of *subsistit in* was indicated to us by the one who was the secretary of the theological commission which definitively revised the document:

> This Church, [the Church of Christ] where are we going to encounter it? It is concretely incarnated in the society directed by the successor of Peter and the bishops in communion with him. The text does not persuade: the Church of Christ *is* the Catholic community; likewise, it omits the adjective *"Roman"* which appears in the Tridentine profession of faith, because it intends to extricate what is of prime importance, notably succession after Peter and the apostles. It is to be presumed that the latin expression (*subsistit in,* the Church of Christ *is found in* the Catholica) will cause a lot of ink to flow. We would be inclined to translate: it is there that we find the Church of Christ in all its fullness and strength.[195]

In the sentence "it is there [in the Catholic Church] that we find the Church of Christ in all its fullness and strength," the emphasis is put on "all its fullness and strength." There is a qualification about the *state* of the Church in the community one is speaking about. The statement

[192]The texts of all the preparatory diagrams are presented in a parallel fashion with the final text in the indispensable working tool which is G. Alberigo, F. Magistretti, *Constitutionis Dogmaticae Synopsis Historica,* Bologne, 1975.

[193]*Ibid.,* 506–507.

[194]*Ibid.,* 440, lin. 261–262. See also *Acta synodalia sacrosancti concilii œcumenici Vaticani II,* vol. III/1, 177.

[195]Mgr. Philips, *L'Église et son mystère au IIe concile du Vatican,* t. I, Paris, 1967, 119.

is made: "If you wish to see the Church of God *in all its fullness and strength,* turn towards the Catholic Church." It is not stated: "The Church of God is only in the Catholic Church," but: "The Church of God is *in all its fullness and strength* only in the Catholic Church." Everything which, according to the divine economy, the Church requires in order to be in history what God wills it to be, *visibly and invisibly,* is preserved in the Catholic Church despite the divisions which happened in the life of the People of the New Covenant. It can also be added: "If you wish to know the Church as it ought to exist everywhere in the world as a sign and instrument of the grace of God, it is there that you must look."[196]

3. But this Church of the *subsistit in* remains short of the ideal. In the same context as this declaration with the *subsistit in* and in the same paragraph, *Lumen gentium* takes up the great theme of the permanent necessity for it to cleanse itself. The decree on ecumenism uses the expression "permanent reform." It goes as far as specifying that this "reform" is a permanent need (*perpetuo indiget*) coming from the fact that the Church is also a human and terrestrial institution.[197] Elsewhere, in a long paragraph where it presents the purpose of the "ecumenical movement," it declares:

> Although the Catholic Church has been enriched by the truth revealed by God in the same way as by all the means of grace, nevertheless, its members do not live by them with all the fervor which would be fitting

---

[196]It is interesting to note that when in 1973 (June 24) the Congregation for the Doctrine of the Faith publishes the declaration *Mysterium Ecclesiae* it accompanies it with a note where we read the following paragraph:

"The points which the declaration intended to protect and bring to light later touch on the mystery of the Church. In particular:

1. The oneness of the Church of Christ and the marks which, as such, make it recognized in the Catholic Church.

In other words:

a) The fact that the Catholic Church is governed by the Roman Pontiff and by the other bishops in communion with him, respective successors of Peter and the other apostles, to whom Christ himself confided the government of his institution and of his community of salvation.

b) The fact, tied to the preceding one, that only the Catholic Church possesses in its entirety the divinely revealed truth and all the means which God established for the salvation of men.

The two facts recalled above concur together to give the Catholic Church its fullness and, precisely because of that, makes it the sole Church of Christ. This fullness is autonomous in regard to the numerous elements which are truly Christian which are encountered in the separated brothers in the diverse Christian denominations.

This results in the necessary consequence: the Church of Christ exists one and undivided in the Catholic Church. It cannot be imagined, therefore, as being the sum of all the Christian Churches or communities existing at the present time; neither can one admit in any way that it does not exist truly at the present time and that, for this reason, its existence must be referred to an unforeseeable future, as the fruit of research undertaken by all the Christian confessions." Text found in *DC* 70, 1973, 670-671 (670).

[197]*Unitatis redintegratio*, 6.

and proper. The result of it is that the face of the Church shines less in the eyes of our separated brothers, as well as throughout the entire world, and the growth of the Kingdom of God is thwarted. This is why all Catholics must strive for Christian perfection; they must, each one in his own sphere, strive to act so that the Church, bearing in its body the humility and the mortification of Jesus, is cleansed and renewed day by day, until Christ presents it to himself, glorious, without stain or wrinkle.[198]

* * *

It often happens that turning towards communities which are not in communion with them, Catholic Churches find in them evidence of holiness, apostolic zeal, and charity, which challenge them and urge them to conversion. They understand then that if they have to offer to others, by the ministry of unity, the way to a much greater fidelity to the will of Christ, they also have to "receive" a call to authenticity, which has come to these others in whom the Spirit dwells and who are faithful to him.

The Catholic conviction was able to appear pretentious, and exorbitant to other Christians. They saw in it "an insufferable conceit" (sic), "an implicit refusal for any unity with whoever does not pass under its Caudine forks" (sic). As it is well understood, is it not rather the reverse of a very great suffering? It is the suffering of the group who knows that it is invested with an enormous responsibility in the face of which it takes measure of its insignificance and what Augustine did not hesitate to call its distress: "What have you done with the gift which was confided to you?"

Such is, for the Catholic faith, the reality of the Church of God on this earth. Here the drama of division shows its hideousness. It is also the suffering of this Church. Is it not called to be *communion of communions, Church of Churches?*

This domain of Christ, this heritage of Christ, this Body of Christ, this unique Church of Christ, this unity which we are, is what cries out from the ends of the earth. But what does it cry out? What I said just a moment ago: Hear my groaning Lord, listen to my prayer, from the ends of the earth I cry out to you . . . in other words, from everywhere. But why have I cried out? Because my heart is in anguish. The Body of Christ shows that it is, throughout all the nations, over all the earth, not in a great glory but in a great trial.[199]

---

[198]*Ibid.,* 4.

[199]Augustine, *Sur le psaume 60,* CCL 39, 766.

Conclusion

1. At the beginning of this book, we stated that we would speak throughout it as a Catholic theologian. We have been faithful to this resolution. Everything which we have developed seems to us to answer, in depth, what Catholic tradition professes on the subject of the nature and mission of the Church. But we have studied it in light of one of the hidden notions in this tradition and which appeared to us as the one around which everything is tied together and by which everything is clarified, *communion* (koinonia). *Communion* with God (himself Trinitarian *communion*) in the benefits of Salvation acquired by Christ (whose incarnation was a realistic *communion* between God and humanity) and given by his Spirit, fraternal *communion* of the baptized (recreating the connective tissue of torn apart humanity), all of it made possible by *communion* in the once-and-for-all (irreversible) Event Jesus Christ which *communion* in the apostolic witness guarantees throughout the centuries and which the Eucharist celebrates (sacrament of *communion*). There is the Church in its substance. And from that, Catholic tradition has always lived.

Are we in error when we think that at this depth, after a serious discussion, we could arrive at an understanding of each other among separated Christians? We could then—but only then—regulate the disputed points in our confessional differences. We are surprised that this method—which, either in bilateral dialogs in which we participate, or in Faith and Constitution, we have not hesitated to extol—should be judged "too unreasonable." We think on the contrary that it would allow us to resist the temptation of piecing and patching to which we succumb and which presents the terrible risk of ending up with no lasting result at all. We discuss ministries, for example, without knowing if we are in agreement on the nature of the community which they must serve. We discuss the papacy without having previously examined the ecclesial reality (*communion of communions, Church of Churches*) which corresponds to this function. It may be

319

that our divisions in this area—and they must not be made relative but definitve—show myopic readings of the mystery of the Church of God.

2. The Church of God is *Church of Churches*. We have seen that that does not mean a parcelling out. On the contrary it is a question of the reassembling of the differences into one *communion* where all are mutually enriched in the recognition of the radical link which ties the whole together in one sole and indivisible community of Salvation. Here it is necessary to be realistic. It is evident that if unity is accomplished—at least among some important blocks of Christianity—the situation will no longer be a return to the one which reigned before the major breaks. One could not ask confessional traditions to renounce those specific characteristics of theirs which are in harmony with Revelation and around which they have structured themselves.

The vision of the Church of God as *Church of Churches* is shown here to be valuable. It is more precise than that of reconciled differences. It considers, in fact, this reconciliation only on the basis of a common sharing and experienced in essential values which *communion* requires in order for it to be something else than a negotiated agreement, leaving each group to continue to live *grosso modo* as it formerly did. It demands that there be a change, on both sides, that each partner bring into its concrete life ecclesial values which have been clouded up until this time in its tradition and which are required for complete and visible *communion,* or that it break with imbalances affecting this *communion.* But once that is acquired, each tradition, far from being absorbed by the other one or even copying it can modulate its own community life in terms of its lines of confessional strength, except, of course, if these are in contradiction with one or the other of the essential values of *communion.* It becomes *communion* in *communion,* a Church of Churches.

Therefore, we throw this book into the ecumenical debate. We think that in spite of its limitations it will be able to help Christian communities state the true position on their idea of unity. They often swing between two visions, neither of which answers the authentic nature of the Church as we have discovered it. The reactions at the convention in Lima (of Faith and Constitution) on Baptism-Eucharist-Ministry show in fact that several either dream of a unity very near to uniformity or else cling to the defense of a pluralism which is almost without limitations. But uniformity suffocates *communion,* whereas certain differences on fundamental points make it nonviable. Unity without diversity makes the Church a dead body: pluralism without unity makes it a body which is dismembered. Will we know, with the Spirit of God, how to understand each other with a healthy balance which involves *communion of communions?*

* * *

One single Head, one single Body, one single Christ, there is the Shepherd of shepherds, the shepherds of the Shepherd, the sheep and the shepherds under the crook of the Shepherd. . . . It is I who am the only one, with me all those who remain in Unity create only one. . . . He was speaking of the first sheepfold which was the nation of Israel according to the flesh. There were others who were to share the faith of Israel who were still outside, scattered among the Gentiles, predestined, not yet gathered together . . . they are not of Israel according to the flesh. But they will no longer be outside of the sheepfold. They must be brought to me, he says, because there must be only one flock and one Shepherd . . ., the Shepherd of shepherds.

We have only commented on this page by Augustine (*Sermon* 138). Throughout the course of this study we have had one scruple: not having examined the whole problem completely. We take comfort by making Jerome's confidence our own at the beginning of his commentary on Ezekiel: "I told you, Eustochium, that it was better to say nothing than to say too little; you answered me that it was better to say something than to say nothing at all. . . ."

Index